AF553971

About the Author

Shantha N. Nair, MA, Ph.D, retired as Reader and Head, Department of Economics, SPW College, Tirupathi, Andhra Pradesh and settled in Tirupathi. A woman of many languages, she knows Malayalam, Telugu, Tamil, English & Hindi. She completed her Ph.D in 1985 on "A Study in Urbanization of Tirupathi" (A Socio-economic Study) from SV University, Tirupathi. She did M.A. in Economics in 1961 from SV University College, Tirupathi. She completed a course on Creative Intelligence from Maharishi College of Natural Law, Tirupathi from 1984-85. She also went through a Computer Awareness Programme conducted by SV University (sponsored by U.G.C.), Tirupathi in 1997.

She has risen through many designations to become the Chair Person, Board of Studies in Economics of SV University from March, 1996 to November, 1998. She started with being a Lecturer in Economics from 1965 to 1993, and then becoming the Head of Department of Economics from 1975 onwards at the SPW College, Tirupathi. From 1993 onwards, she was became a Reader as well.

She also has experience teaching English at St. Mary's College, Trichur, Kerala between 1961-63 and at SPW College, Tirupathi from 1963-65.

During different periods between 1979 and 1987, she gained experience being Deputy Warden, Warden-in-Charge, besides tutoring English.

She also did work as a Course Writer for the SV University Correspondence Course for B.A. Economics. She has acted as Chief Superintendent for the SV University Degree Examinations, A.P. Intermediate Board Examinations, A.P. Service Commission Examinations and others at SPW College.

She also has experience as Subject Coordinator for the Refresher Course for Degree College Lectures in Economics, conducted by A.P. State Council of Higher Education and University Grants Commission at SPW College.

Publications *(in Seminar Papers, Newspapers, on Economics, Children-Books, Religion and Spirituality)*

- Paper on 'Agriculture and Prices', presented at a Seminar conducted by SV University, Tirupathi, 1964
- "An approach to reduce Urban–Rural Income Disparity", The Economic Studies, August, 1976
- "Impact of Urbanization on Economic Development", Southern Economist, June, 1981
- "India's Over Urbanization Problem–Some Suggestions", Southern Economist, May, 1982
- Co-author for a chapter on 'Women's Education for Family Health and Planning' in "Health Education for Quality of Life", Delhi, 1992
- "Learner's Dictionary of Economics", New Delhi, 2004
- "2008-2009: Global Recession and Its Impact on India", Chennai
- Reviewing recently published books on Economics as Member, Panel of Experts in the 'Review Projector of India'.
- Translated Children's books on 'Bhishma' and 'Thyagaraja' from Tamil to English for Tirupathi Tirumala Devasthanams, Tirupathi in 2001
- Co-authored 'A Garland of Gems of Wisdom for a Happy and Successful Life', Delhi, 2005
- 'A Synopsis of Srimad Bhagavatham Stories', Trichur, Kerala, 2007
- 'Sree Rama–The Lord Incarnate and Sree Krishna–The Poornavatar', Trichur, Kerala, 2007
- 'The Holy Himalayas', Delhi, 2007
- 'Echoes of Ancient Indian Wisdom', Delhi, 2008
- 'The Lord Shiva – His 12 Jyotir Lingams and 5 Bhoota Lingams', Delhi, 2009
- 'Adi Shankara–The Jagad Guru', 2010
- 'Lord Venkateshwara (Balaji) of Tirupathi–His Sacred Abode Down the Ages', under publication
- Translated a Telugu Script into Tamil for the SV Bhakthi Channel to be started by the TTD shortly
- Completed writing a book for children on Arjuna, the hero of Mahabharatha

E-mail: shanthannair@yahoo.com

COSMOS

Revelations of Ancient Indian Rishis

(AS FOUND IN THE INDIAN SCRIPTURES)

by

Dr. (Mrs.) Shantha N. Nair

Originals

Delhi

First Published 2015

ISBN 10 : 81-88629-14-6
ISBN 13 : 978-81-88629-14-5

Published by
Originals
A-6, 2nd Floor, Nimri Commercial Centre,
Ashok Vihar Phase 4, Delhi 110052 (INDIA)
tel.: +91-11-27302453 fax.: +91-11-47061936
e-mail: info@LPPindia.com web: LPPindia.com

PRINTED IN INDIA

Dedicated to my son

Uday Gowri Shankar (Ponnu Mon)

And my daughter- in- law

Roopa Shankar

Contents

Preface

This book deals with the Science of the Cosmos or Universe as perceived by the ancient seers of India. A study of the Universe is so vast that it includes almost all aspects under the Sun that are both material as well as spiritual. This book mainly deals with certain aspects of the Cosmos namely, the evolution and dissolution of the universe, its astronomy, and the geography of the earth and so on as revealed by the ancient *Rishis* or seers of India that are found in their ancient Indian scriptures. Although there are innumerable Indian scriptures that reveal the ancient wisdom of the *Rishis* about the Cosmos only a few most ancient scriptures are included in this book –namely the four *Vedas* (the *Samhitas* of the four *Vedas)* and their *Upanishads, Ramayana* and *Mahabharatha* that are the *Ithihasas* or Epics, and the eighteen major *Puranas.*

There are seven chapters in this book. The first chapter introduces the readers to the contents of this book. The second chapter gives a glimpse of the four *Vedas* namely the *Rig, Yajur, Sama* and *Atharva Vedas* and their *Upanishads* that are considered as '*Sruthi*' that means what is heard or revealed and more importantly what they reveal about the Universe. The Vedic view of the Universe is dealt here by taking into account the hymns of the *Samhitas* that form the main text of the *Vedas.* As the Vedic hymns are very subtle and hence very difficult to interpret only a few hymns that could be understood are given here. The third chapter similarly deals with *Ithihasas* or Epics that are termed as '*Smrithi*', that means the recollections of the mystic experiences of the ancient Vedic *Rishis.* This chapter gives the views about the Universe as found in the *Adi Kavya* namely *Ramayana* and the biggest Epic of the world namely *Mahabharata.* The fourth chapter describes the views on Universe as presented in the *Smrithis*, the *Maha Puranas.* The *Ithihasas* and *Puranas* interpret the knowledge contained in the *Vedas* through stories highlighting devotion or *Bhakthi* towards *Saguna Brahman that is*, the Absolute with form that is suitable to those who cannot understand the lofty abstract truths that are contained in the hymns of the *Vedas* and *Upanishads.* So the knowledge about Universe also that is there in the *Vedas* is found both in the *Ithihasas* as well as in the *Puranas* in simple language. It is to be noted here that almost all Puranas explain the process of creation, the Yugas, the nature of Yugas, the measurement of time and about the geography of Earth and so on. However the repetitions found in the Puranas are avoided as far as possible. The fifth chapter is about the contribution of *Bhagavatha Purana* in understanding the Universe and its creation. This chapter is an extension of the previous chapter that deals with *Puranas* because *Srimad Bhagavatham* is also one among the major *Puranas.* As this *Purana* gives a very detailed description about everything that is related to the Universe, particularly about Astronomy, it is dealt with in a separate chapter. The sixth chapter gives a very brief outline (Since this book is about the ancient Indian views on Universe and not about the scientific discoveries of the Universe) of what science has to say about Cosmology that is about the origin, evolution and future of the Universe and its structure and Astronomy. The final chapter is all about the greatness of the ancient Indian wisdom, mainly regarding the Universe, that the people of India had inherited since time immemorial and that has made India the stronghold of spiritual wisdom. This chapter includes some astronomical knowledge contained in the writings that emerged after the *Vedas, Ithihasas* and *Puranas* that are based upon the knowledge contained in the *Vedas.*

As Indians it is high time that we know the great ancient wisdom of India, for our own benefit so that we can be proud of the fact that we are Indians. It is also to tell the world, how the ancient advanced material as well as spiritual knowledge that was based upon the strong and remarkable spiritual foundation have made the people of this land even from time immemorial, broad minded and peace loving and how she still retains her past temperament and culture in spite of the ravages of time and in spite of the fact that the India we see today is not the real India. *Ram Swarup*, spokesperson of Hindu religion commented that India has preserved its past but in a form badly damaged. As Dr Suzuki rightly pointed out "lacking profound cultural knowledge and intense cultural pride, India's intellectuals regard the fashionable ideas and ideologies from Europe and America as unquestionably superior to Bharat's thousands of years old *Hindu* culture and wisdom".

The ancient sages of India gave much knowledge about the Universe. They covered subjects like, Cosmogony, Astronomy, Astrology, the long term and short term time span, the different *Yugas* and their nature, the Geography of the earth particularly that of *Jambudvipa* and *Bharata Varsha* that was the ancient India, the worlds that are above and below the earth including those that are invisible to the naked eye like the different upper *Lokas* above and underworlds below the earth and so on and, knowledge about oneself, the being, the false 'I' that is the individual soul or the *Jivatma* that is deluded by *Maya* or ignorance or delusion and its relationship with the supreme creator, the *Paramatma* that is the *Parabrahman,* and about the merger of the *Jivatma* with *Paramatma* or *Parabrahman* that frees one from all miseries and entanglements of life. The *Samhithas* of the *Vedas* however stressed mostly on the creation of the Universe that included the process of creation, its sustenance and destruction, about the Absolute inherent potential internal energy and *Prakruthi,* the cosmic consciousness, the external energy of the Absolute principle (*Prakruthi)* that created the Universe as a result of the will or *Icchha* of the Universal consciousness, the *Purusha*, that is the Absolute energy, Astronomy and Astrology and so on. The relationship of the created beings with that of the universal principle forms the main subject matter of the *Upanishads* that is the end portion of the *Vedas.* Knowledge about the geography of Earth, the cyclical nature of time, the *Yugas* and their nature, the measurement of units of time and Astronomy and so on are all mostly found in *Ithihasas* and *Puranas.*

Although writing a book on such a vast and complex subject like Universe that is shrouded in mystery is highly risky and is a daring task, the author has taken it up as this is one of her cherished subjects and what little knowledge she gained she wanted to share and pass it on to others who are likeminded and who are of her level of understanding and intelligence. It is a fact that the Vedas, particularly Rig Veda that forms the basis of all ancient Indian thinking, contain an ocean of knowledge about everything of this Universe and it is impossible to understand and express all the knowledge revealed by the ancient Indian seers. The knowledge contained in the Vedas is so immense that it can be compared to the Cosmic Ocean that is limitless and expansive and therefore is unimaginable. In Physical terms that can be imagined, this knowledge can be compared to a huge iceberg. The author of this book at the most could only merely touch and feel its tip. Whether even this is so or not only the great men of wisdom can say.

This book is written with two objectives in mind. Firstly it tries to satisfy the interest of the common man in knowing something about the mysterious Universe. This book may seem to be very elementary for the learned ones who are well versed both in the Scriptures as well as in scientific studies. However only an elementary and an overall picture of the scriptures, the revelations of the ancient sages who gave the scriptures for the benefit of mankind as a whole and some of the general scientific findings about the Universe are given here to suit the level of understanding of the common man, who is curious to know something about the Universe but is not proficient enough to understand the deeper inner meanings found in the scriptures and that of the latest findings of modern science . It is also a fact that what all are revealed by the ancient seers about Universe are not available to mankind today as most of them are lost with the passage of a long duration of time or are being taken away from us or destroyed when our country was subjected to alien rule. But at the same time it must be admitted that the translations of the four *Vedas* that are most difficult to be translated, particularly into English by the great scholars even during the time of British rule in India has helped in spreading the Vedic knowledge all over the globe and they have also helped those people in India who do not know Sanskrit *t*o know more about the *Vedas.* The contents of this book particularly of the second, third, fourth and fifth chapters are based upon the English translation of the ancient Sanskrit scriptures although the author of this book knows fully well that translations can never be a substitute for the original versions. However dependence on the translated works in English of the original Sanskrit versions became inevitable as the ancient hymns particularly those of the *Vedas* and *Upanishads* are not only in Vedic Sanskrit but also offer multiple, subtle, hidden and mystic meanings that cannot be interpreted easily, precisely, correctly even by scholars. The second objective is to show the rich heritage of India that reveals that when the whole world was in ignorance and in deep slumber it was India alone that was fully awake with the splendour of both material as well as spiritual knowledge. It is also to prove it to the world what India was once upon a time, so that the whole world can understand the glorious past of India. *Nani A Palkhiwala*, the philanthropist and lawyer stated, "Modern India will find her identity and the modern Indian will regain his soul when our people begin to have some understanding of our priceless heritage. A nation which has had a great past can look forward with confidence to a great future. It would be restorative to national self-confidence to know that many discoveries of today are really rediscoveries and represent knowledge which ancient India had at her command. World thinkers have stood in marvel at the sublimity of our scriptures". Although we have forgotten to remember the rich spiritual and cultural heritage of India it is heartening to note that outsiders do admit that fact. Tolstoy, the Russian mystic writer urged Indians "not to give up their ancient religious culture for the materialism of the west". Stanley Wolpert once said that "India is the world's most ancient civilization. Nowhere on earth can you find such a rich and multi-layered tradition that has remained unbroken and largely unchanged for at least five thousand years". Lord Macaulay in his address to the British Parliament (who ruled India at that time) even as late as in 1835 said "Such wealth I have seen in this country, such high moral values, people of such calibre that I do not think we would ever conquer this country unless we break the very backbone of this nation which is her spiritual and cultural heritage". Mark Twain the famous American writer wrote, "India has the start of the whole world in the beginning of things. She had the first civilization; she had the first accumulation of material wealth; she was populous with deep thinkers and subtle intellect; she had mines, and woods and a fruitful soul". It is the duty of every Indian to understand our rich heritage and then bring back the lost glory of our nation so that India will, as before be on top of the world both materially as well as spiritually. Swami Vivekanda declared that if India of today does not rank the highest in the world as was the case in the past then, we, the children of this nation should undo the damage with our own hearts blood. Again he stated "out of the past is built the future. Look back therefore, as far as you can, drink deep of the eternal fountains that are behind, and after that, look forward, march forward and make India brighter, greater, much higher than she ever was" as he was convinced that it is out of this past that the future has to be moulded as this past will become the future. He was sure that "the more the Hindus study the past, the more glorious will be their future, and whoever tries to bring the past to the door of every one is a great benefactor to this nation. The degradation of India came not because the laws and customs of the ancients were bad but because they were not allowed to be carried to their legitimate conclusions". May the prediction of Swami Vivekanda about whom one of his western admirers commented as one who was young in age but eternal in wisdom, that "in future India would rise to great heights of prosperity and power far more than what she had attained in the past" come true.

Acknowledgement

I am deeply indebted to all the authors of books on the subject of ancient Indian wisdom, those who created websites on this subject and the innumerable great religious and spiritual masters who translated the original Sanskrit versions of the scriptures in to English particularly of the four Vedas namely, the Rig, Yajur, Sama and Atharva Vedas and their Upanishads, the *Ithihasas* or Epics namely Ramayana and Mahabharata and the eighteen Maha Puranas. The spiritual discourses of eminent spiritual masters also provided me with much information that I needed for writing this book. The material for writing the chapter that deals with the scientific findings on Universe is gathered from encyclopaedias, dictionaries, articles from various scientific magazines and websites dealing with this subject. The entire credit for writing this book, if any, goes to these highly learned scholars and religious and spiritual masters who made available all the resources needed for this book; my humble gratitude and thankfulness to each one of them.

My gratefulness to my husband Sri K C N Nair who is my pillar of strength, for all the moral support and help that he extended to me through out. My appreciation and blessings to my son Uday Gowri Shankar for giving me all encouragement, co-operation, and technical help that I needed from the starting of this book till its completion. I am also thankful to my daughter- in- law Roopa for her contribution. I hope this book will be read by my grandchildren Pranav Shankar and Gayatri Shankar when they grow up.

1
Introduction

Since time immemorial man has been seeking answers for the questions who, when, how and why the Cosmos or the Universe and the animate and inanimate Beings were created? What does this Universe contain? What is its future? And so on. Mythology, religion and spirituality and science have tried to answer these questions. But even today, in spite of the tremendous technological advancement many of these questions about the Universe are yet to find a complete and final perfect answer. While the findings of the ancient seers or saints and mythology are final, because they are being already pronounced in the past and it is certain that no new additions or changes or modifications can take place in this, the scientific discoveries cannot be taken as the final one since they are disproved or modified after a certain period of time as they are still advancing. It is also a fact that for the question why the Universe was ever created, there is no answer yet, as it has remained a mystery for mankind till today and in all possibility it will remain so eternally. Carl Sagan in his book on cosmos said, the size and age of cosmos are beyond ordinary human understanding. Lost somewhere between immensity and eternity is our tiny planetary home. The ancient prehistoric *Rishis* of India went further in stating, in all their humility (*Rig Veda*, the first document of the earth, (Book10-CXXIX), "who really knows? Who will proclaim it? Whence was it created? The Gods came after wards, with the creation of this Universe, Who then knows whence it has arisen? –Perhaps it formed itself, or perhaps it did not, the one who looks down on it in the highest Heaven , only He knows, or perhaps even He does not know". In Book 8 of *Rig Veda* it is stated, "Fain would not we learn to know thee (the creative principle or the creator) well, nor yet can we attain to thee". In *Srimad*

Bhagavatham it is said (canto 2, chapter 4), that the transcendental activities of creation, sustenance and annihilation of the Universe by the Supreme Soul are all wonderful and they appear inconceivable because even great endeavours by many learned scholars have still proved insufficient for understanding them. Again in the same Canto, in chapter- 6 it is said, that even *Brahma*, the creator, in spite of being an expert in mystic powers is unable to understand Him, the Lord who is the very source of *Brahma's* birth. Even *Brahma,* the creator can only wonder about the illusory external energy of the Supreme Lord as all beings can see only His manifold cosmos according to one's own ability. He the Supreme cannot be known fully. Again in Canto-5 Chapter-16, in the same *Purana* it is said that this material universe is a transformation of the material qualities, yet no one can probably explain it perfectly even in a lifetime.

The ancient Indian religion, the *Sanatana Dharma* or Hinduism to which all Indians once belonged to, like the other religions of the world and Science has tried to explain, if not accurately, or for certain, how and when the universe got originated and evolved, about its Astronomy, Astrology, Geography and so on. The ancient Indian view is synonymous with ancient *Hindu* discoveries because the ancestors of all Indians were *Hindus* once. Only later the other religions came up in India in which the founders were either once *Hindus* themselves originally as in the case of *Jainism, Buddhism* or *Sikhism* for example or where the other religions that were found at a much later period as compared to *Hinduism*, like Christianity and Islam entered in to India from elsewhere making the present India a secular one. India, the ancient land of the *Hindus* absorbed all other religions that were either born in India later or that came from other places and that got merged with the Indian blood in course of time due to several factors. The nation as well as the people had no hesitation in that act because such was the universal vision of the *Hindus*. Even today it is not rare to find the pictures of Jesus or Allah or of any other Gods of any other religion or the scriptures of other religions in Hindu homes. The ancient seers of India had taught us, to respect and absorb all that are sacred and that resulted in good to humanity. As Sri Aurobindo has stated " From the time of Rig Veda till today, India has been the home of different religions and the Indian genius adopted a policy of live and let live towards them". Perhaps this is because, as Sri Aurobindo had remarked, "that which we call the Hindu religion is really the eternal religion because it embraces all others". This again is because the Indians knew that there are many paths towards God, the divine, Energy, and all of them are equally valid. This conviction led to infinite tolerance of the Indians even from the distant past and made them broadminded and royal at heart.

While the scientific explanations as to how and when the Universe was formed, the Astronomy and Geography of the Universe are based on objective experiments, in India, the material, the religious, the philosophical and the spiritual knowledge about the Cosmos were totally based upon the inner vision of the seers of the bygone pre-historic days, in their subjective 'Supra conscious' meditative state.

Cosmos that is used as a synonym of Universe is a huge wide open space that holds everything in itself. It includes all matter and energy, planets, stars, galaxies, space, earth, beings and so on. It contains the original, fundamental Conscious energy, the *Purusha*; the centre of all consciousness that is even beyond the gross Space and Time, and that is the single truth or the Absolute or *Paramaatman* that contains all cosmic energy or *Prakruthi* which is the source of all material existence.

Cosmology deals with the nature of the Universe as a whole. The cosmologists try to understand the origin, evolution, structure and the ultimate fate of the Universe at large and the natural laws that keep the Cosmos in order. Before the advent of Science as a subject, Cosmology was a part of theology, religion and mythology. The different religions of the world had their own beliefs about the Universe. Modern scientific cosmology is dominated by the Big Bang theory. It brings together the Observational Astronomy and Particle Physics. In recent times Physics and Astro Physics are playing a central role in understanding the Universe through scientific observation, experiments and analysis.

Cosmos in the Mystic Vision of Ancient Indian Rishis

The ancient sages of India pondered over the Universe from different angles and they revealed many of their discoveries in very many different ways both explicitly as well as implicitly. They tried to find out particularly about the origin of the Universe, (Cosmogony) the creator and the beings and other objects and the worlds that are created, the future of the Universe, the short and long term concept of time, Astronomy, Astrology, the geography of earth with particular reference to *Bharatha Varsha*, and the relationship between the creator and the created. They revealed their findings both in concrete material terms as well as in abstract spiritual terms. Their materialistic explanations contained names not only for the worlds, the hells and so on but also for the very Absolute Principle from which the Universe came in to being. The ancient sacred scriptures of India analyse both the metaphysical or spiritual as well as physical realities. The seers in their supra conscious state understood that any study that separates these two aspects will only lead to a false or incomplete knowledge as all knowledge is based upon spiritual foundation which is both the source as well as the end. The study of the material universe sans spirituality, the seers understood was like a body without a soul. The spiritualistic explanations were found mostly in *Vedas* and *Upanishads* and the materialistic explanations found its place mostly in *Smrithis* for the easy understanding of the knowledge. However all knowledge has *Vedas* as the basis.

The earliest known models of the Universe are found in the ancient Indian *Vedas* that are the oldest scriptures on earth. Count Maurice Macterlinck a Belgian poet said that the sacred books of India contained knowledge about cosmogony which no European conception has ever surpassed. In ancient India spirituality and studies relating to material aspects of the Universe went hand in hand and so the study of the material universe in all its aspects went along with spirituality. The sages of yore found the answers for questions relating to material aspects including that of the Universe through spiritual quest and they also explained what they could know through religious and spiritual terms as well as in concrete material terms.

The ancient scriptures of religion of Hinduism that is also known as *Sanathana Dharma* and that is based upon the *Vedas* (Hinduism has no single founder as in the case of other religion), state, that the Universe goes through repeated cycles of creation, upkeep and destruction and then rebirth and hence the Universe actually has no beginning or end as the cyclical process of creation, upkeep, destruction and recreation occur endlessly. That means the Universe originates, grows and expands and finally dissolves into its subtle causal form only to reappear again. It is similar to the sprouting of the seed that becomes a seedling and then growing and becoming a big tree yielding fruits and flowers and finally when the fruit falls on the ground the seed enters in to the soil and after a certain period it sprouts in to a seedling. The process during the period from the time of its falling into the soil and its cropping up into a seedling is not visible to the naked eye. However it is certain that the seed goes through several process of transformation underneath the soil before it comes out of the earth as a small seedling. This again is similar to the birth, death and rebirth of a being. Once a person dies his physical body mingles with the earth in the form of ash on account of cremating the body or gets disintegrated in to the soil when the body is buried. In course of time the plants absorb these from the soil and yield leaves, and fruits that get into the body of a being as his food nourishing the body in the process and at an appropriate time when the seed is implanted in its female counterpart it grows in to a being. This act in the expression of the sages of the past was the intermingling of the *Purusha* with *Prakruthi* giving rise to creation. The *Rishis* therefore pointed out that whatever we see in microcosm can be extended to the Macrocosm as well.

In the waking stage or *Jagrat Avastha*, the beings are active and perform. This looks similar to the activity of *Brahma* during his day when he creates the beings, the world and so on. At this stage the mind is very active as otherwise the creator and similarly the beings cannot perform. When the being is in deep sleep or *Sushupthi*, the mind is lost as one cannot remember anything nor are there any thoughts that show that the mind is absent. This is the stage when the *Jivatma* temporarily, in a night's sleep merges with the divine as it becomes pure and untainted as the *Paramatma* that engulfs it. This is similar to the *Yoganidra* of Lord Narayana, the *Paramaatma,* the *Para Brahman,* the Absolute energy, the divine principle. At this time everything is in perfect equilibrium position and there is no creation although the seed of the Universe is contained in the Absolute Principle in potential form.

The *Rishis* also stated that nothing emerges out of nothing as something comes out of something only. After *Pralaya* or dissolution of the Universe all matter get absorbed by the Absolute energy. After a particular period of time during the process of creation matter that is inherent in the *Purusha* or the Absolute become visible in the form of Universe.

The sages were also aware of the five elements which they called as the *Pancha Bhoothas* with which the physical body of the beings and the Universe are composed of, the Cosmology and Astronomy of the universe, the behaviour of the Planets and their effects on the humans, the Geography of the earth, the other regions of the Universe that are not visible to the naked eye, and the celestial bodies and beings and so on. The ancient seers also explained about the long run and short period of time. And they even classified time in to human years and divine years, that is terrestrial time and celestial time in explaining *Yugas, Kalpaas,* and *Manvantharaas* and so on. They also spoke of eternal time and vast limitless space. They were definite in their pronouncement that the Supreme power of the Universe is that Absolute energy or Principle that is responsible for the creation, maintenance and destruction and recreation of the Universe and that all other Gods were the later creations of that Supreme. *Rig Veda* (1.164.46) says, "They (the men of wisdom) call Him (the supreme Absolute power) *Indra, Mitra, Varuna, Agni* and God (the supreme Absolute power) is the creator, the ruler, as well as the indweller. The various aspects of Gods and Goddesses exist within the body of this Lord in their subtle and causal form as *Prajapathi, Hiranya Garbha* and so on".

After explaining about Cosmology, Astronomy, Astrology, Geography and so on that related to the material objective knowledge about the Universe, the *Rishis* finally came to the conclusion that in the ultimate reality there is only that, the Absolute, supreme power or energy and the illusion of Universe and the beings are the same as that energy that is neither created nor destroyed and that is beginning-less and endless.

However it must be borne in mind that the Vedic knowledge as contained in the *Vedas* and *Upanishads* particularly may not be fully intelligible to a material mind as the material mind is conditioned by material reasonings, material space, time and intelligence. Those that are stated in these ancient scriptures should not be taken only as material happenings just like any other historical events or fictions but should be understood as the divine happenings that involve all the three dimensions namely, the material, celestial and divine and the two kinds of space and time namely the material and the celestial. This alone will make one understand the knowledge contained in the ancient scriptures of India.

The ancient Indian sages also stated that in the beginning there was neither non-existent nor existent. The supreme cosmogenic force by its sheer will produced the Universe first in the form of darkness enveloped in darkness. The cosmic waters, *Ambhaas* that filled the *Akaasa* or entire space then got manifested in the form of undifferentiated fluid in total darkness. From the cosmic waters combined with the will to move and probably as a consequence of friction, fire called *Arka* was generated. Due to the action of fire and water, wind was created and the combination of wind, fire and water gave rise to the froth that got solidified and subsequently formed the earth. The supreme soul, the *Brahman* is responsible for the emergence and movement of the Universe. The ancient Indian view also says that the cosmic fluid is created due to the will of the supreme soul. The undifferentiated atoms became the undifferentiated dark fluid. Due to the friction of motion, the dark fluid got heat and it gave rise to the embryonic state of the universe that can be compared to the Proto Star concept of the modern Cosmologists. Further motion of the cosmic fluid and that of the earth produced Sun and so on. There are also other explanations in the ancient Indian scriptures about the creation of the Universe.

The ancient sages of India most probably made a comparison between the individual creations that they termed as *Vyashti* with that of the creation of the Universe which they indicated as *Samashti*. The Universe that comes and goes in repeated cycles, perhaps, the *Rishis* thought is similar to the birth and death and rebirth of a being. That is why the sages called universe as *Jagat* that is the one that comes and goes. In *Shukla Yajur Veda* (20. 23) it is said that the earth comes again, the dawn, the Sun, the Universe all come again. In Hymn-8 in Book -11 of *Atharva Veda* it is said that the earth that was before this earth, which only the wisest sages know. Again in *Brihad Jabala Upanishad* of *Atharva Veda* it has been pointed out that the Universe has been burnt several times. These explain the cyclical process of creation annihilation and recreation of the Universe.

The ancient Rishis pointed out that *Purusha*, the universal energy acting upon *Prakruthi* due to its wish or will or *Ichcha* gave rise to *Brahmanda* and the varied objects with varied forms. In creation *Prakruthi* first generated the ego principle or *Ahamkara*. This in turn resulted in the subtle principles of mind and intelligence. These two in turn brought about the *Panchabhoothas* or the gross principles that created the universe with all names and forms. The will or the desire of the Absolute energy, the *Purusha* in combination with the material modes of nature, the *Prakruthi* that is bound by time created the Universe consisting of animate and inanimate beings and matter with different names and forms in this *Brahmaanda* or Universe and that after inducing the creation of the Universe the super soul or *Purusha* or the Absolute Principle withdrew and acted as a mere witness to everything as the process of creation was entrusted to *Prakruthi*.

The Rishis themselves had pointed out that the concept of *Virata Purusha* or the Universal form of the super soul or *Paramatman* that is found in the scriptures is only *Kalpana* or imagination as this concept is used by them to stress the all pervasiveness of the Universal soul. The concepts of *Jivaatma* the individual soul and *Paramaatma,* the Universal soul or energy are nothing but *Thattvaas* or principles or energy. In Canto-1, Chapter-3 in *Bhaagavatha Purana* it is stated that the notion *Virat* or the universal form of the super soul, that is, the material body conceptions of this Absolute is only imaginary and it is described in this manner for the easy understanding of the less intelligent to understand the extensive nature of that supreme energy as the Absolute Energy that has no form, is not gross but subtle, is without form or shape. It is unseen, unheard and unmanifest. He or that Universal energy that is within every being is that, that creates, maintains and destroys the Universe. Again this concept also makes one understand that the whole universe is the body of the Almighty.

This notion has made the ancient Indians who were originally Hindus to worship everything in the Universe as they saw god and the divinity in each and everything including the elements, mountains, seas, rivers, trees, flowers, plants, birds, animals and so on. Animals and birds are also the vehicles of the Gods. This is also because they could visualise the inconceivable *Purusha* , the super soul by looking at and by worshipping *Prakruthi* or nature (the Universe with forms) that is inherent in *Purusha*.

As per modern science Matter and energy are really different concepts of the same thing and that matter can be converted into energy and vice versa. This is what the famous equation of Albert Einstein, the father of modern Physics that $E=mc^2$ tells us. This equation demonstrates that energy (E) is equivalent with matter. This means that they are inter-convertible. From matter, energy is generated as in the case of generation of electricity from water or wind or generation of fire from friction of two Fire stones or of iron pieces and so on. That energy again activates matter as in the case of fans or lights operating with electricity. Energy and matter are the fundamental source of the physical Universe. The principle of *Ardha Nareeshwara* in which Lord *Shiva* is represented as half male (*Shiva)* and half female (*Shakthi* His counterpart) explains the equal participation of energy and matter that is inherent in energy in creation process and it shows that *Prakruthi* or nature with all the three modes or matter is inherent in *Purusha*. However matter has mass and volume and need space. It is dependent on energy and has value only when it is combined with energy. In the absence of energy in it, matter becomes dead. On the other hand when all matter becomes energy it becomes the Absolute, the most powerful, the Super Absolute soul, the *Para Brahman* or *Paramaatma*. That means matter has no independent existence. Also, matter can be created as well as destroyed but energy is independent of matter. It always remains the same whether it is with matter or not. Also, matter is inert and only along with energy it has existence. *Purusha* that is total energy is infinite but *Prakruthi* is finite as *Prakruthi* or matter is that which comes and goes, appears and disappears, has birth and death but *Purusha* the Absolute energy does not undergo any change. It is the same always. It has no birth or death. So the Universe that is nothing but matter is created and destroyed but the Absolute energy remains the same always. It is infinite, *Anantha*, birthless, deathless and is the *Paramaatman* or Para Brahman. All matter, the Universe as a whole is like the waves that appear and disappear but the ocean that is the *Purusha* or the Absolute principle is the substance from which waves, that is, the Universe or matter appear and disappear. The waves appear from the ocean and disappear or merge with the ocean after sometime. The waves have no independent existence. If the waves have to appear there must be an ocean but not otherwise. The ocean is the basis or substance of the waves that appear from the ocean and merge with the ocean. But the ocean is not dependent upon the waves that always remain the same whether the waves appear or disappear. The waves emerge and after sometime merge with the ocean. Similar is the case with the Universe as well as beings in the Universe. The individual beings as well as the Universe that are made up of the five elements or *Panchabhoothas* are created by the Absolute principle and after some time they are destroyed. This has been revealed by the Indian sages of antiquity even in the remote past. They had pointed out that the Absolute Principle that was, before the creation of the Universe, that was indeterminate or *Avyaktha* became determinate by acting upon *Prakruthi* or nature and created this Universe with different objects and beings with names and forms. At the time of destruction all matter get destroyed and get absorbed in the Absolute Energy that in course of time regenerates the Universe with its *Icchcha* or will through *Prakruthi*. Just as with the death of a person his physical body consisting of the five elements or the *Panchabhoothas* merge with elements or *Panchabhoothas* of the atmosphere or Space similarly at the time of *Pralaya* or destruction of the universe the *Pancha Bhoothas* that are nothing but all objects with names and forms merge with the Absolute energy and there will again be a complete total void as before that is *Avyaktha* or indeterminate. The *Panchabhoothas* that is contained in the physical form, whether it is a being, tree or Universe itself has birth, existence, death and rebirth. The Universe that is nothing but a combination of the *Panchabhoothas* after its manifestation into material things with names and forms, is created, maintained, destroyed and recreated. The world or the Universe is denoted by the term *'Prapancha'* in Sanskrit language. It means that, that shines with the *Pancha Bhoothas.* If any one of these elements is absent then there is no Universe or life for the beings that are created. All the material modes of nature that is contained in matter (the Universe with all matter in it including all animate and inanimate matter), after a period of time get destroyed (during *Pralaya)* and they get converted into energy and with the play of time again, a part of the energy get converted in to matter and the Universe then gets recreated. Before creation all matter as well as energy are contained in the Absolute Principle and in an unmanifest form and is indeterminate. Just as the tree that is in the seed is invisible or *Avyaktha* similarly the Universe that is matter contained in the *Purusha* that is energy is invisible. Once the tree in the form of a seedling sprouting from inside the earth becomes visible, in the same manner, the Universe that is already there in the *Purusha* in an unmanifest form becomes visible or manifest in various forms and names due to its creation by *Prakruthi.* Even after the creation of matter, the energy is not destroyed. So even after the creation of the Universe the Absolute remains as before. The *Rishis* also pointed out that creation, expansion, existence and destruction and recreation of the Universe is similar to the birth, growth, existence and death of a being. This pattern explains the cyclical nature of creation, destruction and recreation of all that exists in the Universe as well as the Universe itself, each following the other as night and day or the birth and death of beings and all matter. This revelation made the *Rishis* to conclude that the Universe has no beginning or end. They also stated that after the creation of the Universe the infinite, the Absolute Principle remains the same without undergoing any change as birth and death, creation and destruction belong to matter that is created by *Prakruthi.* It does not belong to the original principle cause that induced the process of creation. It remains the same always without undergoing any change. This understanding made the *Rishis* to declare (*Mandala Brahmana* of *Shukla Yajurveda*) that Brahman is infinite; the Universe is infinite. The infinite proceeds from the infinite, then taking the infinitude of the infinite, that is, the Universe, it remains as the infinite alone.

Albert Einstein, the father of modern Physics stated that "concerning matter, we have all been wrong. What we have called matter is energy, whose vibration has been so lowered as to be perceptible to the senses. There is no matter." That means matter and energy are two different aspects of the same as matter can be converted into energy and vice versa. This statement from a modern Scientist makes one to remember the root and essence of *Jagadguru Shankara's* philosophy, that *Aatman* (the Absolute energy) alone has real existence but not the objective world (*Prakruthi* or matter) with all its names and forms (*Brahmam Satyam Jagat Mithya.*) *Adi Shankara* says that the world or the Universe is only relatively real or *Vyavahaarika Sattah.* When the energy gets converted into matter the Universe comes into being with all forms and names and when all matter is destroyed only the energy remains. Even in this conversion of energy into matter and matter into energy, the cyclical process can be found. But then, to the question when and how did energy appear first- there is no answer. This may be because the original Absolute Energy, the Absolute Supreme Soul, the *Paramatman* that is only a bundle of energy was never created. It was there already even before the creation. It has neither birth nor destruction. Its existence cannot be traced back to a cause that results in some effect as any duality like cause and effect, birth and death, male and female, are limited only to physical aspects and not for that that is beyond physical or mundane. It is similar to the question- what made beings do good or bad in the very beginning. The theory of *Karma* and accordingly the theory of rebirth tells us that one will reap the benefit of one's past thoughts, words and deeds, but then who and why and what made or what is responsible originally for any being to be good or bad in thoughts, words and deeds ? The only answer for such questions lies in the fact that man knows only a little. What he does not know is far more when compared to what he knows about himself, the Universe and the Creator as logic and reasoning cannot help man in finding out answers for everything. The *Rishis* of the past were fully aware that logic and reasoning can lead one only up to a point- So also objective experiments. Beyond that it can be only subjective, mystical experience that cannot be proved or expressed in words but only be experienced. What all the *Rishis* revealed were their knowledge gained in their meditative, supra conscious stage when their mind became the most subtle. Beyond that stage even the *Rishis* could only experience the unlimited Bliss as they were in a state of no mind and this stage is beyond any understanding that can be expressed as the very mind loses its existence. There is no duality at that stage as the experiencer merges with the experience that means the *Jeevathma* merges with the *Paramaathma* or *Parabrahman* that is the source of all knowledge even though the Jeevathma still remains in the physical body. The Bliss experienced at such a stage is beyond the reach of human understanding. This can be compared to the temporary experience of a person in deep sleep when the mind itself is absent. This revelation has made the ancient sages to say 'who knows then who and when the Universe was created? Perhaps the one who is in the lofty heights of heaven knows it- Perhaps he too may not'. At this revelation one merely becomes spell bound and the only thing that he does at this point is to marvel, admire and enjoy the beauty of creation by that Absolute or power or energy or Universal soul, the universal energy, the *Chaithanya* that is the *Paramaatma*. Albert Einstein in his 'merging of spirit and science' commented that the most beautiful and most profound experience is the sensation of the mystical. It is the sower of all true science. He to whom this emotion is a stranger, who can no longer wonder and stand rapt in awe, is as good as dead. To know that what is impenetrable to us really exists, manifesting itself as the highest wisdom and the most radiant beauty which our dull faculties can comprehend, only in their primitive forms- this knowledge, this faculty is at the centre of true religiousness. The *Rishis* finally made it very clear that a human being is a part of the whole called by us Universe; a part limited in time and space.

Universe in *Vedas, Upanishads, Ithihasas* and *Puranas*

The ancient scriptures of India reveal much information about the Universe that shows the advanced level of knowledge of the ancient Indian seers.

Vedas that are considered as *Sruthis*, contain much knowledge about the Universe. However all hymns are not available to mankind now. Also the Vedic hymns are highly subtle and contain both external or material and inner or hidden spiritual, mystic meanings. So it becomes very difficult to understand their real meaning. However the *Smrithis*, namely *Ithihasa*s and *Puranas* explain all knowledge contained in the Vedas in simple language through tales. The *Rig Veda* that is considered as the oldest scripture on earth along with the three other *Vedas* contain immense knowledge about the origin, existence and destruction Universe and its recreation, Astronomy and Astrology. The *Upanishads* mainly speak about the relationship between the creator and the created and how the created that can be compared to the waves of the ocean who by merging with the ocean, the *Brahman*, can become the ocean, *Brahman* or the Absolute itself.

The *Ithihasas* particularly, *Ramayana* contains only a few facts about creation. This *Adikavya* describes the regions below the Earth, the various missiles and sophisticated weapons that are handled with *Manthras* and their nature, the nullifying missiles, the aircrafts of the celestial beings that are like cities in their shapes and sizes, some drawn by horses and some by elephants, the space stations and the cloned celestials created by sage *Viswamitra*, the story of creation of universe, the horizon and earth during eclipse, the physical world as perceived by Sugriva, the different categories of celestials and the mansions of the celestials and a few Kings and so on.

Mahabharatha that is considered as the biggest Epic in the world contains knowledge about the process of creation, the cyclical nature of creation, destruction and recreation of the universe, and description of celestial mighty weapons. It also contains the explanation of some of the subtle *Rigvedic* hymns on Astronomy, about those regions that are invisible to the naked eye like Mount *Meru* and the *Mandara Mountain*, Indra *Loka,* the mansion built by the *Asura* architect Maya, region north of *Kailash*, the celestial assembly room of *Indra, Yama, Varuna, Kubera, Brahma* and so on, the geography of the Earth, the celestial beings and their powers, *Indra*'s chariot, *Gandhamandana* and *Himalayan Mountains*, *Kailash*, the nature of *Yugaas,* the regions and peaks around *Himalayas*, greatness of Mount *Sumeru*, the countries beyond *Himalayas*, duration of *Yugas,* the process of *Pralaya* or destruction of the universe and its recreation, properties of the five elements or the *Pancha Bhoothas*, the regions of heaven, the nether regions, the Eastern, Southern, Western and northern regions of the universe, and the residents inhabiting there, attributes of the five elements, the island *Sudarsana*, the mountains stretching from east to west extending from eastern to western oceans and the inhabitants there, the height and width of *Meru Parvatha* that is supposed to bear the worlds above, below and transversely, the sun, Moon, and other constellations circumambulating Mount *Meru*, greatness of *Meru Parvatha* and *Gandhamandana,* the other mountains, the *Himalayan* regions, and beyond, the *Malyaavat* Mountains, the different *Varshaas, Bharatha Varsha*, the four *Yugaas* and their nature, the structure of earth including the islands and kingdoms on earth at that period of time, the Planet *Swarbhanu* (perhaps *Raahu),* the diameter of Moon and the Sun, about the unmanifest, the Absolute who is the creator, the knowledge obtained by the *Rishis* during ancient times called *Brahma Kalpa* about universe after their ascetic contemplation for a period of 1000 celestial years, the five elements or the *Pancha Bhoothaas* forming all creation, about death that is only destruction of the body and not of the spirit (as the spirit only changes form), measurement of time and *Yugaas*, process of universal dissolution, recreation and so on.

The eighteen major *Puraanas* explain the process of creation of the Universe, the four *Yugaas* and their features, the celestial beings, the world of sun, moon and stars, the nine planets, the seven great sages, the fourteen regions of the universe, the *Manvantharas*, the three types of destruction of the universe, the chariots of all the nine planets, the geography of earth, the limits of earth, the underworld, the twelve *Adihtyas* and their nature and number of rays, *Jambudveepa and Bharatha Varsha*, the chronological order of eras, *Brahma's* life span and His creation, the fourteen *Manvantharas*, the fourteen regions of the universe, measurement of units of time, *Ayanaas*, fortnights, seasons, the seven regions or *Dveepas* of the earth, regions or *Lokas* above *Bhoo Mandala*, the constellations and planets, human years and celestial or divine years, chariots of Planets, the regions north of *Himalayas,* the 28 hells the planets, and the relationship between the creator and the created beings and so on. However the names of regions, mountains and other places slightly differ from one *Purana* to the other. This may be due to the fact that the *Puranas* were written over a period of several centuries by many sages and as such many of the oceans, rivers, mountains, and so on might have totally disappeared in course of time and it is also possible that they were known by different names at different periods of time. In the *Vana Parva* of the great epic *Mahabharatha,* in section -148 it is stated by *Hanuman* that the ground, planets and rocks, Siddhas, gods, celestial sages and so on conform to time in harmony with the state of things in different *Yugaas.*

In *Srimad Bhagavatham* that is one of the major *Puraanaas,* in addition to all knowledge that is contained in the other *Puraanaas* some more knowledge about the Universe is revealed. This *Puraanaa* explains in detail the creative process of the universe, the relationship between the creator and the created, the nuclear weapons and their nature, the five elements constituting the gross body, parts of earth, nature of *Yugaas,* the universal form of the Absolute- the *Purusha,* the *Yogi* passing over the Milky way to other celestial regions, the fourteen planetary systems, the three divisions of the Planetary systems, the personality of Godhead, nine different kinds of creations, explanation of the material manifestation in scientific terms, measurement of atomic time and so on, the elements covering the universe, expansion of the universe, the *Bhoo Mandala,* the seven islands of earth, *Jambudveepa,* the nine *Varshaas, Bharatha Varsha,* Mountain *Sumeru* and other mountains and lakes surrounding it, the greatness of *Bharatha Varsha,* the measurements of the *Dveepas,* the seven islands and the *Lokaloka* Mountain, the location of sun and the distance between sun and the earth, the circumference and diameter of the universe, the region of Planets, the Sun's movements, location of Moon and its travel compared to Sun, location of stars, location of planet Venus, Mercury, Mars, Jupiter, Saturn, the *Saptha Rishi Mandala, Vaikunta,* Planets and stars revolving around the Pole star, Planets floating in the air in the sky resembling Dolphin in water, the planet *Rahu,* planets below *Rahu,* location of the Planet Earth, the seven Planets below the earth, the features of lower planetary systems, location of hellish Planets, the concept of Multiverse, *Brahmaa*'s life span, the *Sankhya* philosophy about creation and universe, nature of *Kaliyuga,* the time of re-emergence of *Sathya* or *Kritha Yuga,* the cycle of the four *Yugaas,* features of the unmanifest stage, and four types of cosmic annihilation and so on.

The Interpretaion of Some of the Ancient Views found in the Scriptures

The description of the 28 types of hells found in the *Puranas* probably at the subtle level indicate the physical and mental sufferings that one has to bear while living in this world depending upon the sins or bad that he had committed earlier or perhaps the worlds that were there actually in good old days.

Just as in the human body there are parts that are very gross like nails, hair, bones and so on which also grow similarly in the creation of Universe also the inanimate things like Mountains that also form part of the Universe that are very gross also possess Conscious energy that is in a very dormant state.

The concept of *Ardha Nareeshwara* and the emergence of Lord *Brahma*, the creator from the stalk of the lotus that emerged from the navel of Lord *Vishnu* or creation undertaken by *Brahma* for example, is in agreement with the Scientific findings that there were only identical chromosomes called Autosomes around 300 million years ago or even earlier and only later the X and the Y chromosomes appeared and the differentiation of the male and female sex came only later with the appearance of two X chromosomes in female and X and Y chromosomes in male .The creation of *Brahma* who is the creative principle in the Puranas and his creation of four *Maanasa Putras* prove that the sages were aware of this point even in good old days. Only later Lord *Brahma* created one male *Swayambhu Manu* and one female *Satarupa Devi,* who became husband and wife.

In Scriptures, the Universal principle is represented by Lord *Vishnu* and the creative Principle is represented by Lord *Brahma*. Again the trinity of Gods namely *Brahma, Vishnu and Maheshwara* in the *Smrithis* also represent the creative Principle or *Tattva*, the Principle of maintenance of the life force and the principle destruction of matter for a new beginning of another creation. The creation, maintenance and destruction all the three belong to matter and not the life spirit or the life energy. It is independent of all these and there is no birth or death for that Absolute whether it is in the *jeeva* as *Jeevatma* or the all-pervading energy the *Paramaatma*.

A basic understanding of the Hindu concept of the Universe that reflect the notions contained in the *Vedas* and *Upanishads*, and *Puraanas* that explain the basic philosophy contained in the *Vedas* and *Upanishads* mostly through stories, to help the ordinary men to understand, mainly reveal that the sages of India in the past, as a result of their understanding of the Universe, came to the conclusion that there were and are and will be many Universes as there are drops of water in the holy river Ganges. In *Srimad Bhagavatham* cato-6, chapter 16, hymn 37 it is said that there are innumerable Universes besides this one and although they are all large, they move about like atoms in the Absolute. In Canto10, chapter-14 it is stated again that the unlimited Universes pass through the pores of the Absolute just as particles of dust pass through the openings of a screened window. The same idea is expressed in canto 10, chapter-87 hymn 41 as well. The Universe was created by the divine will of the Absolute, supreme energy who in three different *Tattvas* or aspects as *Brahma, Vishnu* and *Maheshwara* create, maintain and destroy the world only to recreate it. Once the allotted time is over destruction or *Pralaya* comes and at that point of time, nothing is left out except a vast expanse of water. In that water Lord *Narayana*, (that means, the Absolute Energy that rests on water), and who reclines on the huge celestial snake called *Anantha*, and who is the Supreme energy, the Absolute principle alone remained, and from His navel a sacred huge Lotus with the brightness of innumerable suns propped up and from its stalk Lord *Brahma* appeared for creating the world and its beings. In each *Kalpa* the cyclical process of creation, upkeep, destruction goes on and gets repeated.

The ancient poet saints of India also talked about multiple Suns and the Sun as the source of light and warmth and at the centre of the solar system that clearly revealed the notion of heliocentricity. The hymns in the sacred scriptures also state that the Earth is flatted at the poles and bulging at the equator suggesting that the Earth is not perfectly spherical. *Rig Veda* also refers to the Earth as a bowl that suggests sphericity of Earth. Even the 12 Zodiacal signs were also known to the ancient *Rishis* as we find its reference in the *Rig Veda*. The Indian *Rishis* of the pre historic past also understood that gravitation held the solar system together and therefore the Sun had to be at its centre. The Vedic knowledge also made *Bhaskaracharya* to state that objects fall on the Earth due to one single force. The earth, planets, constellations, Moon and Sun are all held together in orbit because of that one force (*Surya Siddhantha* written by *Bhaskaracharya* in 400 A D). The modern Scientists confirmed after many experiments that the Sun's rays travel in a curved manner and not in a straight line. Thousands of years before this revelation, the *Vedas* stated that the chariot of *Soorya* is drawn by seven horses (that indicate the seven colours) led by snakes and we know snakes have wavy, crooked, and curved movements. Any number of such ancient revelations that are proved scientifically correct today can be found in the ancient sacred scriptures of India.

The sages of ancient India also understood that what is found at the individual level is the same as what is happening in the Universe. Just as beings are born, live and die and are again reborn similarly the Universe also is also created, maintained and destroyed and recreated in a periodical manner. This cyclical process can be witnessed in everything in the universe. For example when *Yagnaas* are performed the heat produced by the flames of the *Yaaga* fire and the vapour of the ingredients that are put in the *Yaga* fire go upwards that generate more heat in the Sun resulting in absorption of water from oceans, rivers and so on from the earth by the Sun and this in course of time form into clouds resulting in rain that comes back to earth. The *Rishis* of yore also were categorical in stating that creation, upkeep and destruction are only the play or *Leela* of the Lord or the Supreme power that results in illusion or ignorance since actually the Universe is neither created nor destroyed. Only the Absolute remains everywhere at all times.

The ideas contained in the great scriptures of the past particularly that are in the *Vedas* and *Upanishads* apparently may seem to be contradictory in many places. But it must be understood that the knowledge contained in the scriptures were imparted to suit the different levels of understanding and temperaments and different levels of consciousness of those disciples to whom they were imparted. It is also because the Vedic language and ideas are so hidden, subtle and abstract in their meanings and more often they give rise to multiple meanings that are beyond the comprehension of even of the scholars. Some deeper aspects of knowledge are also given in the Vedic hymns in coded form as the Vedic seers might have thought that there is possibility of misuse of such knowledge by some profane. This difficulty has given rise to innumerable explanations of the contents of the scriptures that has also resulted in multiple interpretations of the hymns. Further each word in the Sanskrit language is full of meanings. The words are to be interpreted as per the context in which they are used. The contradictions seem to appear also because different ideas are expressed through the same words that have different meanings and interpretations. It must be understood then that the same words have different meanings and are to be interpreted according to different contexts that of course is very difficult and beyond the reach of the mundane mind and words. A literal one to one word interpretation is therefore bound to create confusion in understanding the true meanings of the Vedic hymns. It is therefore possible that all the terms and words found in the ancient Indian scriptures particularly in *Vedas* are not interpreted properly due to lack of knowledge of Vedic Sanskrit and lack of proper understanding of the Scriptures the contents of which are understood, inadequately, or wrongly or understood out of the context. *Raja Ram Mohan Roy* the author of Vedic Physics writes, "The knowledge contained in the *Vedas* is very abstruse, and is well beyond the comprehension of ordinary human beings". The *Rig Veda* in 4.3.16 testifies that the hymns have hidden meanings. It is also a fact that all the scriptures are not available to mankind today in their complete form as they are lost to mankind due to repeated invasion by the outsiders or they are destroyed with the passages of time. Even if the *Vedas* had revealed great truths about Universe that science is yet to understand and prove, still these truths revealed by the ancient sages are not brought to light as many of those facts lie outside the imagination and competence of the people who interpret them and are also beyond the reach of science at least for now as the scriptures have subtle, hidden, multiple meanings both physical as well as Metaphysical. One must also keep in mind that the knowledge revealed in the Vedic hymns has outer or external as well as inner or subtle meanings. While the ordinary and materialistic mind understands the outer meaning and consider the hymns as childish and barbaric and so on, the inner meaning of each of the hymns could be understood by the enlightened mind is meant for the illumined souls. It must also be understood that the symbolic, mystic, hidden meaning of the Vedic hymns is primary. The external or outer meaning of the hymns is only secondary. For example, scholars have stated that the Vedic deities represent the forces of nature or the cosmic powers on the one hand and at the inner level they represent the subtle forces present inside the physical body of man. At the subtle level, the *Devathas* or Gods represent the positive energy in man and the *Asuraas* represent the negative tendencies of man. The hymns convey the truth that the real freedom lay in attaining freedom from all bondages by strengthening the divine, positive forces in one self and slaughtering the evil tendencies or forces inherent in man. *Agni* is supposed to be the Vedic fire God. At the subtle level it represents the inner fire, the divine spark, the illumined energy that elevates one. Similarly, *Mithra* symbolises the Lord of Love, the Sun God or *Soorya* is the power of illumination and energy, *Varuna* is the Lord of expansiveness, *Indra*, the Lord of senses that are kept under control (he, considered to be the Lord of heavens and of the Earth corresponds to the enlightened mind), *Vaayu*, the life force, *Soma*, the divine intoxicating bliss experienced by the enlightened souls, *Asuras,* the negative energy in man or of that of the entire Universe and so on. Last but not the least it must be stressed that the subject of Universe is so vast and complex, full of mystery and in our mundane understanding it looks that it was beyond the capacity of even the most enlightened *Rishis* of India to reveal all its secrets and to give a single description of all that is connected with the creation, maintenance and annihilation of the Universe with all its objects including the celestial bodies, planets and their nature, the underworld, the inhabitants and so on.

Still at a higher levels of consciousness the *Rishis* became aware of the fact, that the fundamental reality that all these changes that we seem to observe and the notion that the Universe, world and beings are different from that Absolute principle (that is the very cause of creation) is mere illusion caused by ignorance, that they termed as *Maya*, since all animate and inanimate creations are that same Absolute Principle or energy which they termed as *Para Brahman*, that is neither born nor dies, that is neither created nor destroyed. This Absolute or *Para Brahman* enters into the individual bodies and is then called as *Jeevatma f*or worldly purpose of understanding. It is like space that is the same whether it is outside a pot or inside a pot. The space that is limited to the physical form of the pot gets merged with the space outside it, once the pot is broken and then it is no longer the space of the pot as it merges with the all-pervading space. When the Supreme energy is all pervading, where and what else can exist other than this? *Swami Vivekananda* remarked that to know the ultimate reality we have to turn towards to our ancient roots of metaphysics, the *Upanishads* and ancient texts.

A Few Ancient Indian Views and the Findings of Modern Science on Universe

Scientific studies view the Universe in an objective manner. For them Universe is an object to be viewed as separate from man. They, in that process try to find out many things about the Universe- its origin and future, the celestial bodies, their nature, size, distance from earth, whether life exists in other planets and so on. In this study the Scientist's objective is to gain material knowledge for the material prosperity and welfare of man.

The ancient *Rishis* on the other hand viewed the Universe both objectively as well as subjectively. To them whatever we find in the Universe has its place at a subtle level, inside beings as well and what we find at the micro level can be extended to the macro level as well. They also meditated upon the relationship of the celestial bodies with that of man, how they influence the life of all created beings on earth and what is the relationship between the creator and the created and how man the created, can become God or the creator himself (*Aham Brahmasmi, Tatvamasi* and so on as stated in the *Mahavakyas* of the *Upanishads* that are the culmination or the crowning glory of the *Vedas).* From the ancient Indian scriptures it can be understood that the sages of distant past were not content with mere outer objective study of the Universe. They went deeper in to the subject of Universe and probed how beings were created, the relationship of the creator and the created. However they did not want to stop even there, they went deeper further and explained how man, the created can attain Godhood that is how man can become God –in which the creator and the created merge into one and become the same.

Unlike the Scientists, the *Rishis* had two objectives in their mind while probing into the Universe intuitively. The first objective was the same as that of the Scientist. But, for the sages of the past, their second objective was far more important and was the ultimate one. With the help of material knowledge that they gained they went deeper and further and tried to find out the relationship between the creator, the Absolute Energy and the created, the beings and the Universe and how man can elevate himself spiritually and can become one with the creator the Absolute. According to them the achievement of such non material or spiritual welfare is the ultimate purpose as well as goal of man. Beyond these two objectives which the *Rishis* had in their conscious mind it is also possible that in their state of no mind that was beyond any consciousness whatever knowledge they obtained from Space as vibrations resulted in their total inner Bliss which they could not reveal or express but could only experience.

There are a number of people who consider the revelations of ancient Indian seers as rubbish and they also ridicule those who say that the ancient *Rishis* of India revealed many things about the Universe that coincides with the modern scientific findings about Universe. Great scholars and scientists on the other hand have only marvelled at the high level of knowledge and wisdom of the ancient seers of India regarding the mysteries of the Universe. For instance Scientists like Carl Sagan have expressed their amazement at the accuracy of space and time description found in the ancient Indian scriptures. It has been admitted that the "*Rig Veda* shorn of its allegory and metaphorical camouflage is the oldest text book of modern astronomy". One must understand that the ancient *Rishis* were not only spiritual masters but also were great scientists. They were great astronomers, astrologers, and architects and so on. For example from the *Aadi Kavya* namely *Raamayana* that was composed by the *Aadi Kavi* namely *Vaalmiki* we come to know that a huge bridge was built across the ocean from India up to Sri Lanka even in *Tretha Yuga* by Sri *Rama* with the help of *Nala* and the *Vaanara* army. This bridge that is given the name of Adam's Bridge by the Britishers who ruled our India in the 19th and first half of the 20th century still seems to stand intact although it is being submerged in the ocean while some of the bridges constructed today with the help of advanced and sophisticated technology are crumbling down within a short period of time of their construction causing enormous damage and wastage of huge amount of resources including money. This is a real testimony to the advanced level of knowledge which the ancients Indians had. So any one who ventures to ridicule the ancient knowledge of India, undoubtedly exhibits and expresses his own ignorance and lack of knowledge only although they think that by such acts of theirs they will be considered as highly modern, sophisticated and knowledgeable.

According to Dr *Rajaram Mohan Roy*, a Physicist, the Vedic cosmology is quite different from the modern Scientific theories of Universe, and therefore there need not be any comparison between these two because *Vedas* were already given to mankind by the ancient seers of India while the modern Physics still goes on with research regarding the origin and evolution of the Universe. He further adds even the ancient commentator *Yaksha* who belonged to 3100 B C stated that even during his time scholars no longer had the intuitive grasp of Vedic hymns that the ancients possessed. Even the Vedic terminologies are also quite different from that of the modern scientific concepts. It must also be noted that the Scientists' objective in analysing and discovering the Universe is to know all about the creation, its existence and future of the Universe including those of the celestial planets and to make use of such knowledge for the material prosperity and welfare of human beings. The *Rishis* on the other hand had two objectives for their quest of the Universe. Like the Scientists the *Rishis* also probed Universe to gain material knowledge that would enhance the material welfare of the humans on Earth. The other objective that was more important to them related to non-material welfare of the humans. Therefore they went further and deeper to find out the relationship between the creator, the Absolute, and the created and how the created can become one with the Creator Himself. Because according to them any knowledge should not only result in material advancement and thereby the material welfare of the beings but knowledge should enable one to elevate himself spiritually as well and this second objective for them was far more important than the first.

However the scriptures of ancient India revealed many things about the Universe and it is astonishing to note that many of their revelations have been proved in modern times to be scientifically correct. The scriptures point out that the origin of creation is sound and light that are inseparable and that the first sound of the Universe according to them is the *PranavaManthra* denoted by *OHM'*. These three letters in English language that is expressed in a single letter in Sanskrit language represent the principles or *Thattavas* or the phenomenon of creation, maintenance and destruction of the Universe and these three *Tattvas* or principles are represented by the *Thrimoorthis* or the Trinities namely *Brahma, Vishnu and, Maheshwara*. The Trinities in Hinduism represent the three principles or *Tattvas* or aspects of creation, maintenance and destruction that follow each other in a set pattern. The word GOD in English also represents these three aspects of the Absolute soul as *Brahma, Vishnu and Maheshwara.* The letter G can be taken to be representing the generating principle that denotes *Brahma*, the letter O the principle of organisation or maintenance that is supposed to be done by the *Tatthva* or principle represented by Lord Vishnu and the letter D representing destruction can be said to indicate the principle or *Tatthva* or function of Lord Shiva the destroyer. The form of Lord Shiva as *Ardha Nareeshwara* also indicate the equal participation of Lord Shiva that is the *Purusha* or the Absolute Energy that is represented as Shiva, and his consort Parvathi, that is *Prakruthi* or nature or *Shakthi in* the creative process of the Cosmos. The cause of creation is the Super soul or *Paramaatman* or the Absolute that represents the original sound that by inducing *Prakruthi* or the light that comes together with the sound is supposed to have given rise to or created the *Hiranyagarbha*. The Big bang theory of scientists also says that the Universe (the *Hiranyagarbha)* appeared with a big bang (*Pranava Manthra* or *'OHM')*. The Indian scriptures also long ago pointed out that the Universe reappeared or was recreated (but not created for the first time as the scientists pointed out) with sound followed by light. The Rig Vedic hymn 4.50.4 states that *Brihaspathi*, the creator had his being from mighty splendour, with the noise of thunder and with His seven rays blew and dispersed darkness.

The ancient Indian scriptures provide us with a glimpse of the advanced level of knowledge possessed by the ancient *Rishis* of India. Many more of such revelations of the sages are yet to be proved. It has been pointed out by a scientist that "*Rig Veda* explains some unexplained phenomenon that is regarded by some as legends. These need to be investigated in the light of new knowledge of perpetual motion" that still remains a mystery to many. He says, the Vedic knowledge about perpetual motion for example is sure to become a powerful guide for the scientific progress of energy and power engineering in the present times of energy crisis. The ordered and ceaseless motion of planets around the Sun as found in the hymns of sage *Dirghtamas* is enough proof of the existence of perpetual motion. Canto 5- chapter-23; hymn 3 to 7 in *Srimad Bhagavatham* also explains the planetary orbits. It has been stated here that just as the bulls are yoked to a central post at different distances, the planets and the innumerable stars revolve around the Pole star in their respective orbits some higher and some lower. *Drightamas* also refers to *Vishuvat*, the solistic or equinox. However one should bear in mind the verses that deal with Sage *Dirghatama*'s celestial perpetual motion wheels are not easy to comprehend in the sense the *Rishi* wanted them to be interpreted as the symbols of the Vedic period were quite complex and is also different from the familiar symbols of technology and communication that we have in modern times. It has been accepted by the learned that "much of the knowledge contained in the Vedic hymns still need to be explored; if this can be achieved, then science is sure to progress by leaps and bounds". Canto-5; chapter-21; hymn 4, 5 and 6 in *Bhagavatha Purana* gives a detailed explanation of the Solstice Equinox in simple language. The *Vedas* also mention the use of perpetual driven vehicles that were built by *Maya* the architect of demons and also by the divine architect *Visvakarma*.

It is pointed out that the *Pancha Bhoothas* or the five elements namely *Akasa* or space, *Vayu* or air, *Agni* or fire, water and earth mentioned in the scriptures represent the nuclear state, gaseous state, Plasma state, liquid state and the solid state.

It must be stressed here that the laws and theories of Science are subject to revision in the light of new theories and therefore no comparison of the ancient revelations with scientific discoveries can be affected. It is also because while the ancient scriptures of India tried to explain the mysterious Universe both in material explicit terms as well as in subtle abstract, symbolic, spiritual terms the modern science explains the wonders of the Universe from materialistic point of view alone. It is also a fact that the ancient revelations of the prehistoric Vedic *Rishis* (that became the foundation on which the later Indian thinking and Hinduism, and that of the entire world as well) and the findings of modern science on Universe agree in certain cases, still in certain other points they disagree and in some cases they run parallel to each other with no meeting point.

There are some who criticise and condemn the ancient scriptures without realising and understanding their greatness. For instance some of these people point out that the *Vedas* mention that the Sun reflects the light of the Moon while the accepted fact is that the Moon shines with the light of the Sun. Perhaps this criticism is based upon a few hymns in the 9th Book of *Rig Veda* and also in *SaamaVeda t*hat state that it is the Moon (*Indu*) that gave splendour to the Sun. This criticism is due to lack of proper understanding of the hymns that are known to possess great hidden and subtle meanings. In *Rig Veda* and in *Atharva Veda* the Sun is described as a bride of the Moon. The Moon is also compared to a male and is considered as the fastest moving of all heavenly bodies that activates all the other heavenly bodies that come in to contact with it. Some of the *Samavedic* hymns state that *Soma Pavamaana* granted strength to *Indra* who in turn generated light in *Soorya*. At the subtle level probably it means that the mind (*Manas)* through its will and strength (*Indra*) brightened intelligence (*Buddhi*) because in *Vedas,* Buddhi or intelligence and mind or *Manas* are compared to the Sun and Moon. Further in Section-3 in the Epic *Mahabharatha* it is stated that the Moon converts the effects of solar heat into clouds and pour down the rain causing plants and herbs to spring up and grow and bring forth vegetables and fruits that yield food for all creatures on Earth. In this sense also it is the Moon that causes strength to the Sun. Again, in the *Taittareeya Samhitha* it is said that the 33 daughters of *Prajapathi* that also includes the Sun are given in marriage to Moon. But in many other Vedic hymns where the meaning is explicit but not hidden for example in hymn 33.2 of *Shukla Yajur Veda* the Sun is mentioned as self-luminous.

There are also hymns that may be analysed by Science for proving the greatness of the age old Indian wisdom. In the first book of *Rigveda* one of the hymns (*Rig Veda* 1.25.8) refers to 12 Moons and their progeny and the Moon of later birth. According to Science also the gas giant Planets have many Moons. In *Krishna Yajur Veda* the poet *Rishi* mentions the Moon that is born again. In *SaamaVeda* (Book-4, chapter- 1, decade-4-hymn3) mention is made about young Moon. In *Rig Veda* in 6.53.3 it is said that *Pusaan* in his chariot is set to go to *Surya* on an embassy. The *Shatapatha Brahmana (Kaanda-2; Adhyaaya-1; Braahmana-2*-the 18th verse) states that originally the *Nakshatras* were many different powers (*Kshatra)* just as the sun. But when the sun rose he took from them their energy, their power, therefore the sun is called *Aditya* and those that lost powers became *Na- Kshatras* or powerless. Science can take up and analyse these revelations of the seers in order to prove or disprove the facts mentioned by them.

In order to prove how advanced and accurate the ancient revelations are one need to make a comparison of these two wherever they meet and are in agreement with each other and analyse and find out the validity or otherwise of other subtle Vedic hymns on the Universe that are at present not analysed by science or seem to be beyond the scientific understanding of today.

It has been pointed out that the Vedic God *Indra* and his attribute that can be interpreted as a personification of the natural force of gravity, the plurality of the Universe - the Multiverse, Bending of sunlight under the influence of *Indra,* that may be interpreted as gravity and all about gravity, the knowledge about Sun in the *Vedas*, the *Ashvins* the fastest moving Gods, that can be interpreted as the electromagnetic force, their feats in medical sciences, in transportation and war, and in agriculture, they, as a personification of twin particles, the physical principles of force, energy and motion in the *Vedas*, effecting a comparison of Vedic science of heat with classical Thermodynamics with special emphasis of the principles of perpetual motion, *Agni* and energy, Perpetual motion in the hymns of creation in *Rig Veda*, *Drighatama's* hymns about the perpetual motion wheels that run parallel to the description of the Sun and the solar system especially the chariot of *Pusaan* that is equipped with technology to go to the Sun, the *Purusha Sooktha*, *Hiranyagarbha* the golden embryo, *Adithi, Vishvakarma and Maaya*, the concept of wheel of time, Astronomy and Astrology in the *Vedas*, the celestial bodies making a full circle, the celestial bodies being behind one another, the cyclical nature of creation and dissolution of the Universe, aerial vehicles, the flying chariots of *Asvins*, *Rbhus* and the celestials, kings and so on, and chariots that are the self-moving and moving with *Manthras,* the geometry of Vedic Altar, the descriptions found in the *Puraanas* about the *Lokaloka* mountains, the distance between Mount *Sumeru* and the *Lokaloka* Mountains as one fourth of the diameter of the universe or 125,000,0000 *Yojanaas* or one Billion miles, the representation of the four elephants like Mountains supporting the earth in the four directions, life and inhabitants in the other worlds and Planets, the astral travel, the story of *Indra* for example, slaying demon *Vratra* and disclosing the waters, whether Indra represents the Absolute energy and who is the demon *Vtratra?* Is he symbolic of any negative energy, what does the representation of the snake demon *Swarbhanu* swallowing or engulfing the Sun and Moon (during eclipses) are some of the Vedic notions that need to be taken up for scientific analysis and scientific discoveries as they seem to be either impossible or beyond the understanding of modern mind. In *Vedas* eclipse is explained as *Swarbhanu* the demon engulfing or swallowing the Sun and Moon. Later, in *Ithihasas* and *Puraanas* there is the mention of *Rahu and Kethu* engulfing the Sun and Moon along with the story of Lord *Narayana* slaying the *Asura* in to two pieces (of which the head became *Rahu* and the tail became *Kethu)* who was in the guise of a '*Devatha* trying to consume the nectar that was distributed among the *Devaas* after the churning of the Milk ocean. Later Varahamitra in his *Brihat Samhita* explained and *Rahu and Kethu* as the nodes of the Moon. The point where the Moon crosses the ecliptic that is the Sun's path, while travelling from South to North is known as Rahu and the north or the ascending node. The point where the Moon crosses the ecliptic, while travelling from North to South is known as Kethu, the southern or descending node. So the nodes are the two points 180 degrees apart. In *Surya Siddhanta* they are considered as the nodal points which now are known as shadowy planets without form. It has been pointed by Scientists now that the nodal points that is *Rahu* and *Kethu* mentioned in the scriptures are the clubs of magnetic and gravitational forces of the two celestial bodies, the Moon and the Earth and therefore influence the life of man on Earth and that these points influence the central nervous system and the sympathetic and parasympathetic nervous system. It is also indicated that these nodal points *Rahu and Kethu* govern the stress level of mind of all beings and the activities of the hormones, blood circulation and functioning of the heart and so on. This is perhaps the reason that least activities are undertaken on Earth by humans and it can be noticed that there is some sort of eerie feeling during eclipse when even the plants, birds, animals, ocean and so on behave in an abnormal way. This is a point to be noted and understood by those who ridicule each and every ancient Indian tradition and practice.

2

Cosmos in Vedas and Upanishads

VEDAS

The most ancient mystic vision of the ancient poet saints of India about Cosmos can be found in the *Vedas* that are supposed to be the oldest scriptures on earth. About Vedas Jawaharlal commented that "it is the first outpourings of the human mind".

Vedas that are considered as the towering monument of the earth as a whole contain some important ideas on Cosmology that shows that Cosmology formed an important part of ancient Indian thinking and wisdom. The Cosmic or divine vibrations that are normally inaudible were heard by the meditative Indian *Rishis* or sages of yore as actual sound waves. But all *Vedic Mantras* are not available to mankind today. What is available only form a fraction of what the ancient meditating *Rishis* could experience in their Supra Conscious state and revealed to the world in oral form even very many centuries before they were actually written down on palm leaves. Arthur Schopenhauer, the German Philosopher and Writer wrote that "I— encounter (in the *Vedas*) deep, original, lofty thoughts". Francois Voltaire stated that "everything has come down to us from the banks of the Ganges".

In Sanskrit language *'Vid'* means to know, or knowledge, or truth, or wisdom, or vision. The word Veda is derived from the word *'Vid'* that are the repository of all knowledge. They are however written in symbolic forms with deeply hidden and subtle meanings that are very difficult to understand and interpret because the true meanings of the Vedic hymns lie buried deep in Vedic symbolism. All *Vedas* are also not available to mankind today. Although each and every hymn of the *Vedas* contains a lot of meaning and knowledge, they are far from the grasp of people who have no knowledge of Vedic Sanskrit, Vedic History, and Vedic culture and customs. The hymns also are beyond the power of comprehension of those who are not endowed with deep understanding of spirituality.

Vedas come under the category of *Shruthi*, which means what is revealed or heard. The *Rishis* heard the *Vedas* that is knowledge as vibrations from space. They contain the spiritual experiences of the *Rishis* of ancient India. So they are super human and without authors. They are the earliest knowledge of the earth and the oldest scriptures on earth. The *Vedas* are known as *Prabhu Samhitas* that means commanding treatises with great authority. They are the roots of Indian culture and the basis of Hinduism or *Sanatana Dharma*, the ancient Indian religion. They were all written in Vedic Sanskrit.

It is believed that the knowledge (*Vedas)* discovered by the ancient *Rishis* of ancient pre historic India, as vibrations of space, as a result of their prolonged and continuous meditation that resulted in the mystic vision of seers about the ultimate immortal knowledge was passed on from one generation of seers to the others orally through word of mouth for a very long time. Later *Vedavyasa* the 28th *Vyasa* of the *Dwapara Yuga* who was known as *Krishna Dwaipayana*, who was the son of sage *Parasura* and *Satyavathi,* a fisher woman, classified the *Vedas*, the knowledge, into four categories and thus the four *Vedas* emerged. They are the *Rig Veda*, the *Yajur Veda*, the *Sama Veda* and the *Atharva Veda*.

Each *Veda* has four divisions. These are *Samhita, Brahmana, Aranyaka* and *Upanishads.* The *Samhitas* and *Brahmanas* correspond to the *Karma Khand*, that is, the ritualistic section of the *Vedas.* These relate to hymns, *Yagnas,* and Vedic rituals. The sections *Aranyakas* and *Upanishads* correspond to the *Upasana Khanda* and *Jnana Khanda* respectively. While the *Upasana Khand* is concerned with the different kinds of worships, and meditation as suitable to the *Vanaprasthin*, the forest dwelling *Rishis*, the *Jnana Khand*, the knowledge section tells about *Nirguna Brahman* the universal soul, the *Paramatman* and the spiritual knowledge to attain *Mukthi* or liberation that is freedom from all sorrows by realizing the ultimate truth or knowledge that is mainly for the *sanyasi* or monk who has renounced the world and all its related *Karmas*. The *Samhitha* is the main text of the *Vedas*. The *Samhithas* contain devotional hymns and are in verse form. The *Samhithas* form the basis for the *Brahmanas, Aranyakas* and *Upanishads*. It is said that there were 1180 branches of *Samhitas* in all the four *Vedas* and 20, 389 or even 20, 500 *Mantras* in the *Samhitha* portion of the *Vedas*. The Vedic Mantras are more than 70 million in number. The *Samhitha* portion of the *Vedas* is the oldest. *Brahmanas* explain the hymns of the *Samhithas* and are in prose and verse form. They deal with Vedic rituals. *Aranyakas* are forest books. They give the mystical, symbolic and philosophical interpretation in metaphysical and cosmic terms and contain the inner meanings of the *Mantras* or hymns contained in the *Samhitas* as well as the inner meanings of the rituals and sacrifices explained in the *Brahmanas*. It is called the Theological section. The *Upanishads* give the knowledge of *Brahman*, the supreme, the Absolute. They are considered as the *Shruthi- Siras* or the head or crown of the *Vedas*. This is called the philosophical section of the *Vedas*. The *Upanishads* are also known as *Vedantha* because they are the concluding portion of the Vedas or the ultimate knowledge itself. They teach *Atma Vidya,* the knowledge of the soul, and the means to realize *Brahman* the Absolute. This is the most important section of the *Vedas*. *Upanishads* are in the form of stories, dialogues, discourses, arguments, discussions, and chants. Some *Upanishads* like *Brihad Aranyaka Upanishad* are very long and some like the *Mandukya Upanishad* are very short. They are believed to have been composed over a very long period covering several centuries. The *Brihad Aranyaka Upanishad* and the *Chandyoga Upanishads* are considered as the earliest of all the *Upanishads* and are dated between 800 BC and 400 B C. The later *Upanishads* are said to belong to the period around the 5th century B C. Some of the *Upanishads* were written during and even after the period of Buddha. *Upanishads* mostly deal with the questions of self and its relationship with the cosmos, the nature of ultimate reality and so on.

The *Vedas* imparted knowledge mainly about the four *Purusharthas* or goals of life namely, *Dharma, Artha, Kama and Moksha*. It combines all knowledge about the material as well as spiritual. Sri

Aurobindo in his forward for the 'Commentary on the *Rig Veda*- The Planet's most ancient text' remarked that the Vedic thought reflected in Vedic hymns is the seeking after truth, light and immortality- the truth that is deeper and higher than the limits of outward existence, a light greater and higher than the light of human understanding that comes by revelation, and inspiration and immortality towards which the soul has to rise. He further says that the Vedic mystics had taught us that "we have to find our way to that, to get into touch with this Truth and immortality. To be born into the Truth, to grow into it, to ascend in spirit into the world of Truth and to live in it". The Vedas also declare that one has to gain material things that they termed as *'Artha'* for leading a happy life on earth. However the material things should be acquired by one only in accordance with *'Dharma'* or righteousness. Again they pointed out that after having the desire or *'Kama'* to acquire wealth and after enjoying all material wealth, too much of which in the long run lead to unhappiness and misery, one should aspire and should have the desire or *'Kama'* for *'Moksha'* that is release from the cycle of birth and death and achieve the final goal of freedom from all sorrows of life that is possible through spirituality that teaches how to know the mind, then transform the mind and finally transcend the mind for enjoying permanent happiness. It shows that *Vedas* covered knowledge physical or material as well as spiritual. The ancient scriptures of India taught both material knowledge as well as spiritual truths for the benefit of man. The *Vedas* and *Upanishads* therefore revealed all knowledge about the universe or *Jagat,* then about man whom they viewed as the *Jivatma* , that is the individual soul that is the supreme soul or *Paramatma* inside a being and finally about the relationship between the *Jivatma* and *Paramatma.*

The *Vedas* contain many important facts about the Universe. However the Vedic hymns are very difficult to understand and interpret in the way the *Rishis* of yore wanted them to be understood as the hymns contain subtle and hidden meanings. Not only that. Many of the Vedic hymns are lost to mankind today due to various factors and due to the ravages of time. Further the *Upanishads* were imparted by the sages to the disciples who were at different levels of consciousness and understanding. Also each word in the hymns contains different meanings and one has to understand the meanings as per the context in which the words are used. It is said that the great sage Bharadwaja was granted three lives only to study and absorb the *Vedas*. It is believed that Lord Shiva appeared before this sage and asked him if he were to be granted another span of life what will the sage do? The sage immediately replied that like his earlier births he would spend his whole life in the study of *Vedas*. In order to impress upon the sage about the depth and vastness of the *Vedas*, Lord Shiva with a wave of His hand created several huge mountains and He picked up a handful of mud from them and told the sage that what all he had studied and understood till then amounted to that handful of earth only and what he has yet to understand is a million times more than those mountains.

The basis or foundation or source for almost all material as well as spiritual knowledge and wisdom is the *Vedas*. The knowledge contained in the *Vedas* was expanded and explained in a simplified manner in the *Ithihasas* and *Puranas* and in later writings that came after the Vedic period.

A Few Symbolic and Esoterc Vedic Hymns describing the Cosmology, Astronomy and Astrology of the Universe

The *Vedas* describe Cosmology, Astronomy and Astrology of the Universe through symbolic and esoteric hymns. Vedic hymns are full of subtle and profound symbolism. The Vedic symbolism is reflected in *Puranas* through allegoric stories.

The *Vedas* declare that this Universe is infinite and the infinite proceeds from the infinite; taking the infinitude of the infinite (Universe) it remains as the infinite (*Brahman*). The Vedic concepts denoting infinity are *Ananta, Purnam*, and *Asamkhya* and so on. The *Isha Upanishad* of *Shukla Yajur Veda* states that from infinity is born infinity; when infinity is taken out of infinity, only infinity is left over. In *Atharva Veda* it is said that infinity can come out of infinity only and infinity is left over from infinity after operations on it.

In *Vedas* planets are associated with the names of *Rishi-Brihaspathi* with Jupiter, *Sukra* with Venus, and *Kashyapa* with Sun and so on. Again animals are also assigned to constellations in *Vedas*. The *Shatapatha Brahmana* states that when the creator created the stars He assigned each an animal/being of which there were originally five namely, goat, sheep, cow, horse and man. In *Vedas* zodiac is the wheel of the sun- the circle created by the sun's rays. The *Shatapatha Brahmana* states that the fire altar is also the sun. The regions are its enclosing stones and there are 360 of these because 360 regions encircle the sun on all sides and 360 are the rays of the sun.

In the Forward on commentary on the '*Rig Veda*- The Planet's most ancient text' Sri Aurobindo states "under pressure of the necessity to mask their meaning with symbols and symbolic words- for secrecy must be observed- the *Rishis* resorted to fix double meanings, a device easily manageable in the Sanskrit language where one word often bears several different meanings, but not easy to render in an English translation and very often impossible". For example the five Bulls of heaven mentioned in the *Rig Veda* refer to the five Planets.

The story of Prajapathy or *Hiranyagarbha* as the primal embryo of the egg refers to the primal atom that can be split into two halves. It is explained as the two off springs or forms of *Prajapathy* or *Hiranyagarbha* as the *Devas* and the *Asuras.*

In the legend of the discovery and rescue from the dark cave in mountain, of the Sun, the cows or herds of the Sun or the Sun world by the Gods and *Rishi Angiras,* the symbol of Sun is associated with the higher light and truth.

One of the Rigvedic verse in *Rig Veda* states that there is a truth covered by truth, where they unyoke the horses of the Sun, the ten hundred stood together, there was that One (the supreme Truth). The ten hundred here refers to the rays of the Sun. The unyoking of the horses of Sun refers to the revealing of the light of the Sun or knowledge so that the supreme may be seen.

The seven planets are referred to in the Vedic hymns as the seven half embryos forming the seed of the world.

In the *Vedas* the Moon's path is divided into 27 equal parts although the moon takes about 27 1/3 days to complete it. Each of these parts is termed as a *Nakshatra*. In *Rig Veda* it is said that *Nakshatras* are linked to the Moon's path.

One of the Vedic hymns states that seven yoke the chariot that has single wheel. One horse that has seven names carries it. The wheel has three naves undecaying and never overcome where all these beings are placed. (*RigVeda 1*.50.9; 1.164.2; 1.164.3; *Krishna Yajur Veda*-2.4.14(o) *Atharva Veda*- 9.9) Here the zodiac is the single wheeled chariot or circle yoked by the seven planets that are forms of sunlight. All beings are placed on the wheel of time. The Vedic horse symbolises energy.

In another hymn it is said, that 12 are its fellies, the wheel is one. It has three naves. Who has understood it? These are held together like spokes the 360, moving and non- moving. (*Rig Veda*-1.164.2; 1.164.11; 1.164.48; *Atharva Veda*- 9.9; 10.8; 13. 3)The 360 spokes referred to in the *Rig Veda* are the 360 degrees or the divisions of the zodiac. The 12 are the Vedic signs or *Rashis*. The three names mentioned are the three *Lagnas* or ascendants in Vedic tradition. These are the ascendant *Rashi* that is the position of birth star in the first house, *Chandra Rashi* or *Lagna* that is the position of *Chandra* or Moon in the star signs, and the *Surya Rashi* or Lagna that is the position of the Sun in the birth chart with regard to star signs. These three were later marked in *Sudarshana Chakra*, the astrological chart where all the three ascendants or *Lagnas* were marked in the zodiac.

In *Vedas*, the zodiac serves both astronomical purpose and also indicates the inner zodiac or the subtle body and the *Chakras*. The seven wheels mentioned in the *Vedas* are the seven subtle *Chakras i*n the subtle body. The sun that rules refers to the inner spirit, the soul or the life force. The *Jivatma* or the individual soul, the inner Sun creates time inwardly also, through the biological process of breathing, the energy that runs up and down the spine and flows through the seven *Chakras*..

Buddhi (intelligence) and *Manas* ((in a broad sense the mind) are often compared to the Sun and Moon and at a subtle level these are related to the higher *Chakras* of the subtle body.

Another Rig Vedic hymn suggests the Vedic numerology and says that the cosmic bull has four horns, three feet, two heads and seven hands, probably suggesting the great *Kalpa* number of 4, 32, 000, 000 years.(*Rig Veda* 4.58.3; *Shukla Yajur Veda*- 17.11)

The headless *Vritra* whom *Indra* won over as mentioned in the *Rig Veda* might be referring to the tail of the serpent *Ketu. Vritra,* also *Swarbhanu* is the Vedic serpent demon who was cut into two. It is said that his head became *Rahu* and his tail or trunk became *Ketu.* In *Rig Veda, Swarbhanu* is considered as the demon of solar and lunar eclipses. It is considered as the demon or darkness hiding the Sun. In *Rig Veda, Rishi Atri* describes a total solar eclipse.

One of the Rig Vedic hymns states that the chariot which the seven have mounted has seven wheels or chakras and is carried by seven horses. The seven sisters sing forth together where the hidden names of the cows are. (*Rig Veda* 1.164.3; 1.164.15; 1.164.36; *Atharva Veda* 9.9; 10.8). These hymns refer to the seven planets that create their seven rotations or seven wheels. Each is drawn by a horse with its energy and velocity. Each has its feminine power referred to as sisters with its power of expression. It carries its own hidden or secret knowledge (symbolically referred to as cows or rays). These hymns tell about the astrological influence of planets. The Rig Vedic hymn that says that the wheel of law with 12 spokes does not decay as it revolves around heaven, Oh, fire, here your 720 sons abide. The 12 spokes referred to here are the 12 signs of the zodiac. It has 720 half degrees or twins making a total of 360. Zodiac is the single wheeled chariot or circle yoked by the seven Planets. It is also the wheel of time on which all beings are placed.

Another Rig Vedic hymn (*Rig Veda* 1.164.12; *Atharva Veda* 9.9) states that the father with five feet and 12 forms, they say, dwells in the higher half of heaven, full of waters- others say that he is the clear seeing one who dwells below in a sevenfold wheel that has six spokes. Here the five feet of the father refers to the five Planets or the five elements. His 12 forms are the 12 signs. The sun in the higher half of heaven with the water is the sign Leo with Cancer ruled by Moon with the other five planets each ruling two signs. In Vedic thought Sun is the abode of water and in its proximity are the signs of cancer and Leo. The seven fold wheel is the zodiac with seven planets. The six spokes are the six double signs through which the Planets travel. The same is mentioned in the *Prasna Upanishad* where it is stated that the five spoken wheel is the zodiac ruled by five planets and five elements.

Still another Vedic hymn says that the undecaying wheel or circle together with its felly or circumference, ten yoked to the upwards extension carry it. The eye of the Sun moves encompassing the region. In it are placed all beings. (*Rig Veda* 1.164.13; *Atharva Veda* 9.9) This hymn also refers to the ten signs ruled by the five planets with each planet ruling two signs. The eye of the Sun refers to the sign of Leo through which the solar influence pervades the zodiac or Sun. The upward extension may be referring to the Polar Regions. According to David Frawley, the zodiac in Vedic thought is the wheel of the Sun. It is the circle created by the Sun's rays. In *Satapatha Brahmana* it is stated that the fire altar also is the Sun. The regions are its enclosing stones and there are 360 of these because 360 regions encircle the Sun on all sides and 360 are the rays of the Sun.

In the Rig Vedic hymn that states that of those that are born together, the seventh is born alone, the six are the twins, divine born *Rishis*- the six born together or are twins are the 12 signs where two each are ruled by one planet. Here the Sun and moon are taken as a single planetary influence. The seventh that is singly born is that single supreme light that illumines all planets. (*Rig Veda* 1.164.15; *Atharva Veda* 10.8)

David Frawley in his book on *Nakshatraas* and *Upa Nakshatraas* points out that "the Vedic altar is an image of time, year, the human being and the universe. In *Shatapatha Braahmana* the altar is equated with earth, atmosphere, heaven, sun, *Nakshatraas*, meters, year and the body of self of man and the entire universe. The fire altar thus seems to be an image of space, time and consciousness. Apart from mathematical accuracy it also linked the universe with common understanding". Again he says, "But indeed the fire altar also is the sun; the regions are its enclosing stones and there are three hundred and sixty of these because 360 regions encircle the sun on all sides; the rays are its *Yajushmati* bricks, for there are 360 of these and 360 rays of the sun". This suggests the zodiac or the belt through which the Sun travels. Further it is also stated "But indeed; that built *Agni* (the fire altar) is all being, all the Gods; for all the Gods, all beings are the waters, and that built Fire- altar is the same as those waters; the navigable streams (round the Sun) are its enclosing stones, and there are three hundred and sixty of these because three hundred and sixty navigable streams encircle the sun (and flow towards the sun) on all sides and the navigable streams indeed are also the *Yjushmati* bricks". The 360 streams encircling the sun and 360 streams flowing towards the sun indicate that the sun in its travel crosses over these that are the lines of longitude. In one of the Rig Vedic hymns the sun is figured as riding in a boat. These 720 (360 + 360) rays and directions or streams refer to the days and nights of a year and the spatial existence.

It is understood that there were three fire altars for performing Vedic *Yaagaas* symbolising Earth, Space and Sky. The fire altars were surrounded by 360 enclosing stones. Of these 21 were around the Earth Altar, 78 were around the Space Altar and 261 were around the Sky Altar. It means that the Earth, Space and Sky were symbolically assigned the numbers of 21, 78 and 261. The main Altar was built in five layers of a thousand bricks of specified shapes. According to *Subhash Kak* the construction of these altars required the solution to several geometric and algebraic problems. Two different types of bricks were used; the special and the ordinary. The total number of special bricks was 396 that refereed to the 360 days of a year and additional 36 days of intercalary month. By layers the first contained 98, the second 41, the third 71, the fourth 47, and the fifth 138. The sum of the bricks in the fourth and the fifth layers equalled 186 *Thithis* of the half year. The number of ordinary bricks was 10, 800 that equalled the number of *Muhoorthas* in a year (1 day= 30 *Muhoorthas)* or the number of days in 30 years. Of these 21 go to *Garhapatya*, 78 in to the 8 *Dhishnya* hearths and the rest go into the *Ahavaniya* s altar. The main altar had an area of 7 ½ units taken to be equivalent to the nominal year of 360 days.

Scientist *Subhash Kak* in his book on astronomy and its role in Vedic culture-(chapter—23) points out that in the *Mahaavedi*, the large trapezoidal area for *Yagnaas*, a brick altar is built to represent time in the form of a Falcon about to fly and in the *Pracnavamsa*, that is, the smaller triangular area to the west of the *Mahavedi,* there are three fire Altars in specified positions namely, the *Grahapathya*, the household fire that is round shaped, *Ahavaniya* and *Dakshinaagni*. The *Grahapatya* is the house holder's fire that is perpetual fire from which the other fires are lighted. *Dakshinaagni* or *Anvaharyapacana* is half-moon shaped where cooking is done. *Ahavaniya* is square shaped. During *Agnicayana* ritual the old *Ahvaniya* performed the function of *Grahapatya*. That is why their areas are identical although one is square and the other is round. In addition eight *Dishnya* hearths are built in the spacious ritual ground. Between the *Ahavanya* and the *Grahapatya* a space of a rough hourglass is dug out and strewn with grass. This is the *Vedi* that is meant for Gods to sit. The *Agnicayana* altars are supposed to symbolize the universe. *Garhapatya* represents the Earth, the *Dhisnya* hearths represent space and the *Ahavaniya* altar represents the sky. The last altar is made in five layers. The Sky that is supposed to represent the universe includes Space and Earth. The first layer represents the Earth; the third Space; and the fifth the Sky. The second represents the joining of Earth and Space and the fourth layer represents the joining of Space and Sky. At the subtle level the altar ritual in the words of *Subhash Kak* "is meant to symbolise the paradoxes or the magic of change of time in motion. — The *Yajamaana* or the patron who patronises the ritual symbolically represents the Universe. The ritual is a play or *Leela* dealing with paradoxes of life and death enacted for the *Yajamaana*. In this play symbolic deaths of animals and humans including the *Yajamaana* himself may be enacted."

He further says that in *Vedas* time is represented by a metaphor of a bird. The year as a bird has *Vasantha* (spring) season as its head, *Hemantha* (winter) and *Sisira* (freeze) as its body, *Sarada* (autumn) and *Griisma* (summer) seasons as its two wings and *Varsha* (Rainy) season as its tail.

The deities mentioned in the *Vedas* are identified with constellations.

Nearly 33 Gods are mentioned in the *Vedas*. Among these 11 Gods are supposed to be in heaven or space, 11 Gods in atmosphere or intermediary space and the remaining 11 Gods are supposed to be Gods belonging to earth or the observable space. The 33 Gods or entities are called *Devathas*. In the *Taittariya Samhitha* it is said that the 33 daughters of *Prajaapathi* that personifies time most probably are given in marriage to Soma, the Moon. These are the 27 *Nakshatraas*, the five planets and the Sun. The sun is described as a bride in *Rig Veda* and *Atharva Veda.*

The 34 lights mentioned in the *Rig Veda* include the Sun, the Moon, the five planets and the 27 *Nakshatraas.* These are taken as Gods in *Vedas.*

The rivalry between the families of Sages *Angirasas* and the *Bhrugus* mentioned in the *Rig Veda* most probably represents the motions of Jupiter and Venus.

The Moon is considered as the fastest moving of all the heavenly bodies. So in *Vedas i*t is compared to the male who activates the other heavenly bodies with which it comes into contact.

The 8 *Vaasus* mentioned in the *Vedas* are the elemental Gods representing aspects of nature that represent the cosmic natural phenomenon. *Vaasu* means 'dweller' or 'dwelling'. These are *Agni*, or Fire, *Prithvi* or Earth, *Vaayu* or Wind or Air, *Antareeksha* or Space, *Aadithya* or Sun, *Dyaus* or Sky, *Chandrama* or Moon, and *Nakshatraas* or stars. These are called '*Vaasus*' because they are the abode of all that lives, moves and exists.

The 12 *Aadithyas* represent the 12 months in a year. These are solar deities and represent the different forms of the sun. These are described as the 12 spokes of the wheel of time upholding cosmic law. These are also described as Gods that include *Mithra, Varuna, Aryaman, Dakshsa, Bhaaga, Amsa, Tvastri, Savitr, Pusaan, Sakra, Visvasvat and Vishnu.*

The 33 devas mentioned in the *Vedas* include the 8 *Vaasus,* the 11 *Rudras,* the 12 *Adithyas,* the all-pervading electrical energy called Indra, and *Prajaapathi* who benefits mankind by purifying air, water, rain and vegetation. These 33 deities are known as *Devathas.*

The *Vedas* mention a Vedic Goddess by name *'Prisni'*. *Prisni* means spotted. It probably refers to star clusters in the sky such as the Milky Way region. *Veda Prisni* is also referred to as the mother of Sky Gods, the *Maruts* that means the flashing ones that probably represent stars. *Prisni* is also associated with cow that yields milk and who is the mother of calves the *Maruts.* In this sense also *Prisni* may be referring to the Milky Way. She also represents sky in general. *Prsni* is also the night sky in general.

'Goddess *Adithi'* mentioned in the *Veda* may be referring to 'Black holes' that swallows or eats up everything that enters into it. *'Ad'* means to Eat and *'Adithi'* means eater.

The Vedic Gods or the *'Devas'* means shining ones. *Div* means to shine or illuminate. The *Devas* are supposed to be the sons of *'Dyaus'* meaning, sky or illuminated and also of *Adithi's*, meaning unbounded sky. So *Devas* probably refer to the constellations or *Nakshatraas*. The *Krishna Yajur Veda* elaborates upon this point and describes *Devas.*

'Shukra', (the effulgent), and *'Virochana'* (greatly effulgent) refer to planet Venus who is supposed to be the Guru or teacher of *Asuras* or Anti Gods. King *Vena* and the seer *Ushanas* mentioned in the *Vedas* may also be referring to planet Venus for their materialistic and blissful outlook.

The deity *Pusan* is also connected with wealth and Moon or *Soma.*

Brihaspathi' or *Guru* refers to planet Jupiter that is a positive star or planet and he is supposed to be the teacher of the *Devas* who are Demi Gods. He is also the deity of wisdom and inner illumination.

'Deva Soma' or *Indu t*hat means a circle or drop refers to Moon. *Soma* is the Vedic deity of *Chandra* or Moon or *Indu* and of delight. It also represents the immortal elixir that moon represents on an inner dimension.

Deva Bhaga, the deity of delight wealth and prosperity also refers to Moon and Venus.

Deva Agni refers to planet Mars or Aries that is fiery. It is the Vedic deity of fire. *Deva Agni* that is the Vedic deity of fire is represented as a youthful warrior called *Kumara* and *Karthikeya*. Agni also refers to the primal unborn self, the *Hiranyagarbha* and the child of cosmic waters.

Deva surya is the Sun. *Surya (Savitr)* is Sun God. He is the chief of the 12 *Adityas* or Vedic Solar Gods and is the ruler of the *Adithyas. Deva Surya* as king refers to inner illumination as well.

Deva Rudra is the conqueror of death. He is Saturn in his transcendental aspect. He is connected with *Varuna,* the Vedic deity of death and judgment and *Yama* the Lord of the underworld of later times. *Varuna* also refers to the cosmic waters from which the primal egg emerged.

The deity *Vishnu* is the Vedic deity of *Buddhi* or intelligence and inner wisdom and represents Mercury or *Budha* in the *Vedas.*

Indra refers to the all-pervading electrical energy.

The creator *as Brahmanaspathi* is mentioned to have created a blast or bang that resembles the big bang theory of the later scientists about the creation of the Universe.

The different types of celestial chariots mentioned in the *Vedas* resemble the modern day space ships or even orbital satellites. The chariots may also be similar to the unidentified flying objects (U F O) possessed by the Vedic sages or kings or the celestial beings. It may also mean a device like a weather balloon or Satellite technology that they possessed for each one of them that are controlled by chanting sacred *Manthras.* The chariots of *Pusan* or the chariot of *Soorya* probably relate to the solar powered space ships and Satellites that result in no pollution that are used by the ancients to go round the universe and explore the planets. It shows that humanity has only rediscovered what was there before and returning to more ancient devices and sources like solar energy that were used during Vedic times or *Sathya Yuga*. In *Rig Veda* it is said that *Indra*'s chariot runs by *Manthras* and has ten sides indicating a complicated structure. In a subtle sense the ten sides refer to the ten senses of the body; the five *jnanendrias* and the five *Karmendriyas.* The four yokes are the four regions, four *Vedas* and so on. The three whips are the three *Lokas* or the states of consciousness namely waking, dreaming and the state of deep sleep. The seven reigns may be referring to the seven *Chakras* in the subtle body. The Prayers are the Vedic hymns. This shows that even chariots were made as per universal principles such as the cosmic body of man which is the same as the model of the universe. It is also stated in the Vedic hymns that the chariots of *Aswini* Gods, the Gods of healing reach the heavens or the skies proving the technological brilliance of ancient Indians.

Pusan going to the Sun mentioned in one of the hymns in *Rig Veda* indicates the astralisation of the chariot and body of the astronauts, so as not to burn themselves on the fiery stars, and planets. They might have worn heat resistant great tempered steel suits. In another hymn it is stated that the *Vimaanas* fly like birds suggesting the bird like shapes of the *Vimaanas.*

Vedas state that when the time of creation came, the supreme soul, the *Paramathma* gathered extremely subtle particles namely *Paramaanus.* The first principle that is created out of the highly subtle elementary *Prakruthi* was named the *Mahaatatthva,* that is, the principle of wisdom. Out of the *Mahatattva* evolved *Ahamkaara,* the ego or the principle of individuality. The *Mahatatthva* and the *Ahamkaara* gave rise to the five subtle principles called *Pancha Bhoothas*; the five principles of sensation that are called *Jnanendriyas* and five principles of action called *Karmendriyas* and also the principles of grasping or understanding . The five subtle *Bhoothas* by passing through various stages of less subtle conditions of matter finally transformed into five least subtle states of solids, liquids etc. from which various kinds of trees, plants etc. sprang up. These became the source of food and out of food was produced the reproductive element that is the cause for the physical body. *Vedas* state that the universal soul or *Purusha* the super soul is the efficient cause and *Prakruthi* the primordial elementary matter is the material cause of this universe. However the first creation of bodies was not the result of sexual intercourse because it is only after the male and female bodies were created by the Almighty or the Supreme Soul, the *Parabrahman* or *Paramaatma* or the Absolute energy, and putting into them the souls, the *Jivaatma*, creation proceeded with the union of male and female.

The *Vedas* also declare that creation and dissolution of the universe follow a cyclical pattern and succeed each other in alternate succession similar to day and night.

The structure of the Universe in which God or the Absolute power is the efficient cause and *Prakruthi* as the material cause of the Universe is explained in the *Rig Veda.*

David Frawley (Pandit *Vamadeva*) in his 'Vedic origins of the zodiac: the hymns of *Drighatamas* in the Rig Veda' states that the Vedic hymns apart from containing a vision of the zodiac, that is astronomical, also reveal the inner subtle body and its *Chakras*. The seven that are mentioned in the hymns correspond to the seven *Chakras* of the subtle body and *Praana* is the inner Sun that creates time at a biological level through the act of breathing and this is the energy that flows up and down the spine and the seven *Chakras* that are strung like Lotus along it.

Rig Veda

The earliest Veda is the *Rig Veda* the date of origin of which is not known for certain as it was composed in the remote past. It derived its name from *'rk'* meaning *'Manthra'*. *Rig Veda* is the first book on earth. It has ten mandalas or books. It contains 1017 hymns consisting of approximately10, 315 verses (the number differs according to different estimates).

The hymns were composed by several Rishis over a period of long duration of time. Many of the Rigvedic hymns get repeated in the other three *Vedas*.

A Few Rig Vedic Verses on Universe

(Source—English translation of *Rig Veda* by Ralph T H Griffith, 1896)

BOOK—1

1.22.2

In this hymn the *Asvins'* chariot is stated to reach the heavens.

1.25.8

The sages are supposed to know the twelve Moons with their progeny and the Moon of later birth.

1.31.4

The hymn about *Agni* indicates the Sun who seems to move from East to West.

1.35.11

The Sun's pathway is supposed to have been established in the air's mid region".

1.38.4

Maruts are stated to be the sons of *Prsni.*

1.50.2

The constellations are supposed to pass away together with their beams before the all beholding sun.

1.50.7

The Sun Travels through the sky and wide mid-air.

1.50.8

About Sun

The Sun's chariot is supposed to have seven steeds (they also represent seven colours) harnessed to it.

1.50.9

Surya is said to be having the pure bright seven yoked to his chariot.

1.85.5

The *Maruts* are stated to have chariots drawn by spotted steeds

1.88.2

The *Maruts* here are indicated as red hued.

1.89.7

The *Maruts* are said here to be the sons of *Prsni*

1.118.1 and 1.119.1

The chariot of *Asvins* is described here as flying swifter than the mind of mortal, fleet as the wind and three seated.

1.139.11

The 33 Gods are mentioned here. Eleven Gods are supposed to have heaven as their home, eleven gods have their home on Earth and the remaining eleven gods are supposed to be residing in the waters.

1.143.1

Agni is mentioned here as the offspring of the waters.

1.157.3

The twin *Asvin's* chariot is mentioned here as having three wheels and drawn by fleet-foot steeds, thrice seated, opulent, bestowing all delight.

1.158.3

Asvin's chariot is supposed to be sea crossing, strong and equipped and set amidst waters.

1.160.1 and 2

The Heaven and Earth are supposed to be the two bowls, the two world halves.

1.164.2 and 3

The chariot of *Soorya* or Sun is described here.

"Seven to the one wheeled chariot yoke the courser; bearing seven names the single courser draws it.

Three naved the wheel is, sound and undecaying

Where on are resting all these worlds of being".

"The seven who on the seven wheeled car are mounted have horses, seven in tale,

Who draw them onward.

Seven sisters utter songs of praise together in whom the names of the seven cows are treasured".

1.164.11

"Formed with twelve spokes by length of time, unweakened rolls round the heaven this wheel of during order, here in established joined in pairs together, seven hundred sons and twenty stand".

1.164.12

"They call him in the farther half of heaven the sire five footed of twelve forms, wealthy in watery store., These others say that he, God with far seeing eyes, is mounted on the lower seven wheeled six spoked car".

1.164.13

"Upon this five spoked wheel revolving ever all living creatures rest and are dependent. Its axle, heavy laden, is not heated the nave from ancient times remains unbroken".

1.164.14

"The wheel revolves unwasting, with its felly; ten draw it, yoked to the far stretching car pole. The Sun's eyes move encompassed by the region on him dependent rest all living creatures".

1.164.15

"Of the co- born they call the seventh single born, the six twin pairs are called—is children of gods".

1.164.36

"Seven germs unripened yet are heaven's prolific seed:
Their functions they maintain by *Vishnu*'s ordinance.
Ensured with wisdom through intelligence and thought,
They compass us about present on every side".

1.164.48

"Twelve are the fellies, and the wheel is single; three are the naves. What man hath understood it?

There in are set together spokes three hundred and sixty, which is no one can be loosened".

1.183.1

Asvin's chariot is described here.

"Make ready that which passes thought in swiftness that has three wheels and Triple seat, ye, mighty where on you seek the dwelling of the pious where on three fold, ye fly like birds with pinions".

Flying like birds suggest the bird shaped flying space craft or air plane.

BOOK—2

2.18.1

Indra's new chariot is described here.

The rich new car of *Indra* is stated to have four Yokes, three whips, seven reigns to guide it, ten sided, friendly to mankind, light- winner and that is urged to speed with prayers and wishes.

2.34.3

The chariot of *Maruts* is supposed to have spotted deer

BOOK—3

3.1.3

The gods are supposed to have discovered *Agni* in the midst of waters.

3.5.3

Agni is said to be the friend and gem of waters

3.9.5

Agni is stated to have been brought by *Matarisvan* from far away from gods and produced by friction.

3.22.2

"That light of thine (Sun) in heaven and earth, O, *Agni*, in plants, O, Holy one, and in the waters, Where with thou hast spread wide the air's mid region- bright is that splendour, wavy, man- beholding".-Here the Sun's rays are said to be wavy.

3.58.1

The ancient's milch cow (the Milky Way) yields the things we long for.

BOOK—4

4.13.3

The Sun God who holds the universe, is supposed to be carried forward by seven strong and youthful coursers.

4.13.5

Here the poet sage seems to wonder, how that unbound and unsupported Sun does not seem to fall down at sunset although it seems to be going downwards (the sun setting in the west in the ocean)? In awe he asks, "By what self-power moves he? Who hath seen it? He guards the vault of heaven, a close set pillar".

4.43.5

In the wide open space *Asvin*'s chariot is capable of reaching the heaven-

4. 50.4

About creation it is said,

"*Brihaspathi*, when first he had his being from mighty splendour in super most heaven, strong, with his seven fold mouth, with noise of thunder, with his seven rays, blew and dispersed darkness".

4.58.3

"Four are his horns, three are the feet that bear him, his heads are two, his hands are seven in number. Bound with a triple bond the steer roar loudly, the mighty god entered into mortals".

BOOK—5

5.40.5

About total solar eclipse it is said that the *Asura*'s descendant *Svarbhanu* pierced the Sun through and through with darkness, and then all creatures looked bewildered, not knowing the place where they were standing.

5.40.9

The *Athris* found the sun again him, when *Svarbhanu* of the brood of *Asuras* had pierced with gloom. This none besides had power to do.

5.55.5

Maruts are supposed to uplift the rain through the vaporous moisture from the Oceans and pour the torrents down.

5.56.6

Maruts' chariot is supposed to be drawn by the bright red mares.

BOOK—6

6.53.3

Pusan's golden chariot is supposed to travel across the ocean, in mid-air, and go on an embassy to the Sun.

BOOK—8

8.80.3

"Fain would we learn to know thee (the universal principle who or which is the cause of creation) well, nor yet can we attain to thee".

8.80.6

"Let us praise him who made these worlds and creatures, all things that after him sprang into being".

BOOK—9

9.28.5

"This *Pavamaana* (*Soma*) swift and stray omniscient gave splendour to the Sun and all His forms of light".

9.37.4

"*Pavamaana* has made the Sun shine".

9.63.7

"Flow onward with that (*Soma Pavamaana*, the Moon) stream of thine where with thou gavest *Soorya* light urging on waters good to men".

9. 66.24

"He, *Pavamaana* has produced the lofty low, the brilliant light, destroying darkness of hue".

9.86. 29

"Thou reachest out beyond the Earth, beyond the heavens thine are the lights, o, *Pavamaana*, thine the Sun".

9.86.32

"He (the Moon) has assumed the rays of *Soorya* for his robe".

9.97.31

"Oh, *Pavamaana*, when born, thou madest *Soorya* rich with brightness".

9. 97.41

"*Pavamaana* granted strength to *Indra*, he, Indu, generated light in *Soorya*".

9.110. 3

"Oh *Pavamaana*, thou didst generate the Sun and spread the moisture out with power, hasting to us with plenty vivified with milk".

BOOK—10

10.5.2

"Great is that secret name and far extending, whereby thou (the supreme soul) makest all that is and shall be".

10.22.14

"That Earth, through power of knowing things that may be known, handless and footless yet might thrive". (It indicates the movement of Earth around the Sun)

10.55.3

"With four and thirty lights he looks around him"

The 34 lights are the Sun, Moon, the five planets and the 27 *Nakshathras*.

10.72.2

About creation it is said,

"These *Brahmanaspathi* produced with blast and smelting like a smith'

Existence, in an earlier age of Gods, from non- existence sprang".

10.72.3

Existence, the creation, sprang from non-existence and thereafter the regions came up from the productive power.

10.72.4

Earth also sprang from the productive power and the regions were born from the earth.

10.72.6 and 7

About creation

In the beginning from the feet of gods a thickening cloud of dust arose and *Soorya* who was lying hidden in the sea was brought forward.

10.73.9

About the Milky Way

"Thou *(Indra)* from the udder which over Earth is fastened hast poured the milk into the kine."

10.82.5

About the beginning of creation the poet saint in wonder asks,

"That which is earlier than this earth and heaven, before the *Asuras* and Gods had being-

What was the germ primeval which the waters received?"

10.82.6

About the cosmic waters from where Universe came up

"The waters, they received that germ primeval where in the gods were gathered all together.

It rested set upon the unborn's navel, that one where in abide all things existing".

10.82.7

It is stated that no one can find him, the Absolute Universal soul who produced all the creatures.

10.85.2

About Moon

"By *Soma* (the Moon) are the *Adihtyas* strong. By *Soma* mighty is the Earth. Thus *Soma* in the midst of all these constellations hath his place".

10.88.13

About Sun

"The ancient star (the Sun) that wanders forever, lofty and strong, lord of the living being".

10.90.1

About *Purusha*, the supreme soul, it is said,

"A thousand heads hath *Purusha*, a thousand eyes, a thousand feet.

On every side pervading earth, he fills a space ten fingers wide".

10.90.2

"This *Purusha* is all that yet hath been and all that is to be".

10.90.3

All creatures are one fourth of the *Purusha* the Absolute energy, the creator. The remaining three fourths of Him remains as eternal life in heaven.

10.90.4

"With three fourth a *Purusha* went up; one fourth of him again was here.

Thence he strode out to every side over that eats not and what eats".

10.90.8

He, the supreme created the creatures of the air, and wild and tame animals.

10.90.13 and 14

From the Universal Soul

"The moon was gendered from his mind, and from his eye the Sun had birth;

Indra and *Agni* from his mouth were born, and vayu from his breath".

"Forth from his navel came mid-air the sky was fashioned from his head

Earth from his feet and from his ear the regions. Thus they formed the worlds".

10.121.1

"In the beginning rose *Hiranyagarbha*
Born only Lord of all created beings
He fixed and holdeth up this earth and
Heaven".

10.121.2

"Giver of vital breath, of power and vigour,
He whose commandments all the Gods acknowledge
The Lord of death, whose shade is life immortal"

10.121.3

The poet saint asks in all humility,

"Who by His grandeur hath become sole Ruler of all the moving world that
breathes and slumbers; He who is Lord of men and lord of cattle,
What God shall we adore with our oblation"?

10.121.5

About the Universal Principle, the creator,
"By him the heavens are strong and
Earth is steadfast, by him lights' realm
And sky- vault are supported
By him the regions in mid-air were measured.
What god shall we adore with our oblation"?

10.121.7

The poet saint in all wonder asks,
"What time the mighty waters came
Containing the universal germ, producing *Agni?"*

10.121.10

The poet saint admits
"*Prajaapathi,* thou only comprehendest all
these created things and none beside thee".

10.129.1

About creation

"Then was not non- existent nor existent, there was no realm of air, no sky beyond it

What covered in, and where? And what gave shelter? Was water there?

Unfathomed depth of water?"

10.129.2

About creation

"Death was not then, nor was there aught immortal:
No sign was there, the day's and night's divider.
That one thing, breathless, breathed by its own nature,
Apart from it was nothing whatsoever".

10.129.3

About creation

Darkness there was: at first concealed in darkness
This all was indiscriminated chaos.
All that existed then was void and formless:
By the great power of warmth was born that unit.

10.129.4

About creation

"Thereafter rose desire in the beginning.
Desire, the primal seed and germ of spirit,
Sages who searched with their hearts' thought
discovered the existent's kinship in the non- existent".

10.129.5

About the two halves namely Earth and Heaven,
"Transversely was their severing line extended:
What was above it then and what below it?
There were begetters, there were mighty forces
Free from action here and energy yonder".

10.129.6

About creation

"Who verily knows and who can here declare it,
Whence it was born and whence comes this creation?

The Gods are later than this world's production
Who knows then whence it first came in to being"?

10.129.7

About creation
"He the first origin of this creation, whether he
Formed it all or did not form it
Whose eye controls this world in highest heaven, he verily
Knows it, or perhaps he knows not".

10.149.1

About Sun's attraction in holding Earth and other Planets it is stated,

that the Sun or *Savithar* supports this Earth with bands of rays to bind it, and made heaven steadfast where no prop supported.

10.153.5

About the Supreme Soul it is stated that
It is pre-eminent over all Creation in its might
pervading every place.

10.190.3

Dhatar, the great creator, formed in due order Sun and Moon and then He formed in order Heaven and Earth, the regions of air and light.

Rig Veda Upanishads on Universe

Aaitareya Upanishad

In the beginning there was only the Absolute Truth. There was nothing else. The Absolute Truth then wished and created the worlds namely, *Ambas, Marichi, Mara* and *Apah* (water). *Ambas* is beyond Heaven and Heaven is its support. *Marichi* is the sky. The earth is *Mara*. The worlds that are below are the *Apah*. Later, the self-created man by gathering a lump of the human form from water and gave a shape to it. Finally the Creator entered into man as the Self in all beings as consciousness that is *Brahman*.

All beings are the products of the five Elements namely, Space, Air, Fire, Water and the Earth.

All Beings that are born of eggs, of wombs, of moisture of earth, that which move or fly and which do not move at all have Consciousness. All these are impelled by Consciousness that is the Self. The Universe has Consciousness and Consciousness is *Brahman.*

Aatmabodha Upanishad

Only *Brahman* exists as the basis of the world.

The spirit is not destroyed with the body as the Sun that makes the pot shine is not destroyed along with the pot. This explains the immortality of the soul.

Bahvricha Upanishad

The creator in the form of Goddess was the only one in the beginning and she emitted the world Egg all alone. *Brahma, Vishnu, Rudra*, the wind Gods, nymphs, Semi humans, humans and all that are stationery and moving that are egg born, the sweat born, the seed born, the womb born and whatever breaths, were born from Her. She is the non-dual, supreme, the *Brahman*, the pure consciousness, the *Atman*, the Bliss that illuminates within, the Being- Consciousness- Bliss that is the *Sat- Chit- Aananda*, the *Maha Thripura Sundari* associated with space, time and objects. She has assumed all forms.

Kaushitaki Brahmana Upanishad

Whosoever departs from this world go to the Moon. In the earlier half of the lunar month the moon flourishes on their vital breaths. In the later half it causes them to be reproduced. The Moon allows the departed souls move upwards or causes them to be reproduced by becoming rain and are born as beings according to his past deeds.

Mudgala Upanishad

The *Purusha* (the *Chaitanya* or the Absolute Conscious energy that resides in the being) that is beyond the scope of name and form that is hard for people to understand took a form with a thousand parts that is beyond space and time by its own will. In that form He was beyond space and time and was the greatest. He made Himself in to four parts and with three of them He existed in Heaven. The fourth part of the Lord created *Prakruthi* or matter for creating the worlds and He imparted the knowledge of creation to the Creator to create all moving and non-moving things. Thus the single God that was unborn became many.

Nadabindu Upanishad

The *Bhuloka* is located in the *Virata Purusha's* feet; *Bhuvarloka* in its knees; the *Swarloka* in its loins; and the *Maharloka* in its navel. In its heart is the *Janaloka, Tapoloka* is in its throat, and the *Sathya Loka* in the centre of the forehead between the eyebrows.

Thripura Upanishad

In the beginning there was only a blazing light up above.

There was only gloom and motion that stretched far and wide before creation.

Yajur Veda

Yajur Veda gets its name from the word '*Yaj*' that means reverence, veneration or sacrifice. This *Veda* mainly deals with different types of *Yagnas*. There are two *Yajur Vedas*; the *Krishna* or dark or *Taittareeya Yajur Veda* that is older and the *Shukla* or white *Yajur Veda* that is the later one. This *Veda* is believed to have been written around 10th century BC. *Yajurveda* contains the knowledge of Sacrifice or Vedic *Yagnas*.

Shukla Yajur Veda

Shukla Yajur Veda is divided into 40 Books consisting of a total of approximately 1976 hymns with several verses in each book.

A Few Hymns of *Shukla Yajurveda* on Universe

(Source—English translation of *Shukla Yajurveda* by Ralph T.H. Griffith, 1899)

13.4

In the beginning of creation, *Hiranyagarbha* was born as the only Lord of all created beings. He fixed and holds this Earth and heaven.

17.11

Four are his horns, three are the feet that bear him; his heads are two, his hands are seven in number. Bound with triple bonds the Bull roars loudly; the mighty God hath entered into mortals. (Rig Vedic hymn)

17.19.

About the Supreme Soul it is said, that He has eyes on all sides around Him;

a mouth on all sides, arms and feet on all sides; He, the sole God, who produced the earth and heaven weldeth them with his arms as wings together.

17.26

The Supreme Architect, the creator of the Universe, the *Vishwa Karman* is mighty in mind and power. He is the maker, disposer, and most lofty presence.

17.27

About the Almighty, the creator the poet saint says,

"Father, who made us, he who as disposer, knoweth all races and all things existing. Even he alone, the deities 'name giver, him other beings seek for information".

17.30

The Cosmic waters received the primeval germ and it rested set upon the unborn's navel; that one wherein abide all things existing.

17.31

The poet- saint says that

"You will not find him who produced these creatures" as he is formless.

20.23

About the cyclical nature of creation, it is said,

"Earth comes again, the dawn, the Sun. This universe all comes again".

22.18

"Ye *Pavamaana*, thou didst generate the Sun and spread the moisture out with power. Basting to us with plenty vivified with milk". (Rig Vedic hymn)

23.1

"In the beginning rose *Hiranyagarbha* etc."—-

23.10

"Earth is a great receptacle".

23.51 and 59

"The poet saint seems to ask the creator,

What are the things which *Purusha* (the Universal Soul) hath entered?

What things hath *Purusha* contained within him?

This riddle we propound to thee, o, *Brahman-*

Why dost thou give no answer to my question"?

"Who knoweth this world's central point? Who

knoweth the heaven, the earth and the wide air between them?

Who knows the birth place of mighty *Soorya?*

Who knows the moon; when he was generated?"

23. 63

About creation of the Universe, the *Brahmaanda,*

The strong, the self-existent one, the first,

within the mighty flood (the cosmic waters)

Laid down the timely embryo from which

Prajaapathy was born".

31.1

About the all-pervading and extending Universal Soul, the *Virata Purusha,*

"*Purusha* hath a thousand heads, a thousand eyes, a thousand feet.

Pervading earth on every side he fills a space ten fingers broad". (Rig Vedic hymn)

31.2, 3 and 4

About the Universal Soul, the Lord of immortality, that is cause of repeated creation,

"*Purusha* is in truth this all, what hath been

and what yet shall be".(Rig Vedic hymn).

"All creatures are one fourth of him, three Fourths, eternal life in heaven". (Rig Vedic hymn).

"With three fourths *Purusha* rose up: one fourth of him again was here.

There he moved forth to every side over what eats not and what eats" (Rig Vedic hymn).

31.12 and 13

About creation from the Universal Soul or *Virata Purusha,*

"The Moon was generated from his mind, and from his eye the sun had birth.

Vayu and *Praana* from his ear, and from his mouth was *Agni* born". (Rig Vedic hymn)

"Forth from his navel came mid-air, the Sky was fashioned from his head,

Earth from his feet, and from his ear the quarters- Thus they formed the worlds".

32.2

About creation of the Universe,

Everything sprang from the twinkling of the eye lid of *Purusha*, the resplendent one and no one can comprehend him, above, across or in the midst.

32.4

About the universal principle, the cause of all creations,

"This very God pervadeth all the regions; yea born aforetime, in the womb he dwelleth".

32.11

About the Universal Soul the *Paramaatman* entering into the individual soul as *Jivaman,*

"He with his self into the self-hath entered".

Sukla Yajurveda Upanishads on Universe

Brihad Aranyaka Upanishad

There was nothing in the very beginning. It was covered by utter darkness.

He the Absolute created the mind first and started worshipping on this mind of His. As He was worshipping water or *Arka* sprang up. The froth like substance on the surface of water got solidified and became the cosmic egg, the embryonic state of the Universe. Then lustre that is fire emerged from Him. Then He that is known as *Viraj*, that is *Praana* differentiated Himself in three ways and then the directions came. Then with His will Time appeared. Then He created the horse. And later every other creation followed.

In the beginning this Universe was only the Self, the *Viraj* the *Purusha*. He parted His body into two. They became husband and wife and the descendants were born from them.

The Universe in the beginning was undifferentiated and the Self entered into all. It, the self, the *Brahman* was all in the beginning. As a spider moves along the thread it produces and as a fire tiny sparks fly in all directions, so also from this Self emanate all organs, all worlds, all Gods and all beings.

Brahman is infinite and this Universe is infinite; infinite proceeds from infinite.

There are five fold divisions of *Akasa* or space. They are, *Akaasa, Paraakasa, Mahaakasa, Suryaakasa, and Paramaakasa.*

Among the 33 Gods the 8 *Vaasus* are the Fire, Earth, Air, Sky, Sun, Heaven, Moon and Stars.

There are 12 *Adithyas* or Suns representing 12 months in a year.

Mandala Brahmana Upanishad

The five-fold divisions of *Akasa* or space are, *Akaasa, Paraakasa, Mahaakasa, Suryaakasa, and Paramaakasa.*

Brahman is infinite and this Universe is infinite. The infinite proceeds from the infinite, then taking the infinitude of the infinite, that is, the Universe, it remains as the infinite alone.

Niralamba Upanishad

Brahman is the ineffable spirit. It appears as *Mahat*, the ego, the elements, the microcosm, the macrocosm, actions, knowledge and ends. It is without beginning and end.

God, the veritable *Brahman*, due to its power called *Prakruthi* creates the world, and enters into them as the inner controller of *Brahma* and so on, He is *Eswara*. He is *Avyaktha* or unmanifest.

Prakruthi is only the power of *Brahman* that creates the world and enters into them as its inner controller, as *Eswara*.

Everything that we see in this Universe is that very spirit of *Brahman*.

Paingala Upanishad

In the beginning aloneness, *Avyaktha*, the indeterminate, the unmanifest alone existed. This was the *Brahman*, the Absolute Truth or Absolute Bliss, Knowledge and Bliss, the *Sat, Chit* and *Ananda*. In that existed the Primordial and indefinable *Prakruthi* with the *Pancha Bhoothas* or the five elements, that was the cause of creation, sustenance, and dissolution. It consisted of *Gunas* or nature (the *Sahtvik, Rajasic* and *Tamasic* qualities) that was in a state of balance. It was all *Avyaktha* or unmanifest.

From this unmanifest, from its will, the manifest, the *Mahat* was created. From it came the Ego and from it the *Virat*, the manifest body was created. From this Self arose Ether, then Air, then Fire, then Water and finally the Earth (the *Pancha Bhoothas* or the five elements). Each element got bifurcated and the halves of each were made fourfold. Each of the five halves was added to one eighth of the other four. With this the Self created endless microcosms with organs of senses and action. He made *Praana*, the organ of action, the inner organ, the organs of cognition and the sense organs. Then the creator, God entered into all by splitting the macrocosm, the crowns of beings and made them pulsate with life. The Creator, the Lord then together with *Maaya* or ignorance became the *Jeevatma* in individual bodies that revolved like a potter's wheel in the endless cycle of birth and death.

Subala Upanishad

In the beginning that is, before any creation, there was neither existence nor non-existence.

From that *Thamas* or laziness was born. From *Thamas, Prakruthi* or matter was born with the five elements or *Pancha Bhoothas*. First Space came, from Space came air, from Air came Fire, from Fire came Water and finally from Water, Earth appeared. This became the world Egg the *Hiranya Garbha*. It then split into two. One half became the Earth that is below and the other half became the Heaven that is above. Between these two was *Virata Purusha*, the Divine man with a thousand (meaning innumerable) heads, eyes, feet and arms. As *Brahma* He created everything.

Then when the time for destruction approached, He became *Visvanara*, the fire, and burnt all His creations. The created process then got reversed. The earth was absorbed in water, water in fire, fire in air, air in space or ether , ether in sense organs, and they in subtle elements, they into *Prakruthi*, and ultimately *Prakruthi* in *Mahat*, *Mahat* in *Avyaktha* or indeterminate, *Avyaktha* in *Tamas* and finally *Tamas* in God or the supreme Absolute culminating in *Pralaya* or deluge. This is delusion or *Pralaya* as stated in the *Vedas*. At that point, there is neither existence nor non-existence.

In the beginning there was nothing. The creatures were born without root and support.

This *Upanishad* speaks about several worlds like *Rasaatala, Bhu, Suvar, Mahar, Janas, Tapas, Prajapathi's* region, and *Brahma*'s region and says that all these are like gems in the string that is the base, the *Brahman*.

Trisikhi Braahmana Upanishad

Brahman gave rise to that which is not clear that is *Avyaktha a*nd *Avyaktha* gave rise to *Mahat*. *Mahat* gave rise to *egotism*. *Egotism* gave rise to five *Thanmatras* (these are the subtle elements and are the objects of the five senses. They are, the touch or perception of the skin, form or vision of the eye, taste of the tongue, odour or smell of the nose, and hearing of the ears) The *Thanmatras* gave rise to *Pancha Bhoothas* or the five elements namely, Earth, Water, Fire, Air and Space or Ether.

As a result of *Pancha Bhoothas* the earth came into existence embracing one thing with the other, pervading by crisscross connections gradually. In that earth or world all beings appeared.

Krishna Yajur Veda

Krishna Yajur Veda is divided in to seven *Kaandas*. Each *Kaanda* has several *Prapathakas* and each *Prapathaka* contains several hymns. Some of the *Prapathakas* contain prose completely or a mixture of hymns as well as prose. Approximately there are 305 hymns with 2941 verses and also Prose in this *Veda*.

A Few Hymns of *Krishna Yajur Veda* on Universe

(Source—English translation of *Krishna Yajur Veda* by Arthur Berridale Keith, 1914)

1.4.10-a

About the dwelling place of the 33 Vedic Gods it is stated that eleven of them reside in the sky, eleven on the Earth, and eleven in the waters.

2.4.14-o

About the seven forms or rays of energy represented by seven horses of Surya it is said that the Seven bays in the chariot of the Sun God bear Him.

4.2.3

About the photosynthesis

g—" In the waters oh *Agni,* thou enterest the plants; Being in the germ thou art born again".

h—-"Thou art the germ of plants, the germ of trees, the germ of all things, o, *Agni*, thou art the germ of waters".

4.4.11

The names of seasons are given here

a—*Maadha and Maadhava*— Spring

b—*Cukra and Cuci*—Summer

c—*Nabha and Nabhasya*—Rain

d— *Isa and Urja*—- Autumn

e— *Saha and Sahasya*— Winter

f—-*Tapa and Tapasya*—Cool season

7.4.18

d—"The Sun moveth alone the moon is born again".

Krishna Yajurveda Upanishads on Universe

Ekaakshara Upanishad

The Absolute engulfs everything in the Universe. He is *Prajaapathy* or the Lord of all beings. He is everything, the earth, the atmosphere, firmament, and the self and so on.

Garbha Upanishad

In this body whatever is hard is the Earth, liquid is Water, warmth is Fire, whatever moves is Air, and Space enclosed is Ether or *Akaasa.*

For everyone there is desire in the mind for enjoyment of objects. Blood is created by relishing food; from blood flesh is born then fat, bones and marrow. The foetus is born with the combination of semen and blood. Then in the warmth of the womb and belli, the seat of bile, *Praana* flows at the proper time ordained by the creator.

The embryo lying in the womb for a day and night is a confused mass. After seven days it becomes a bubble; after a fortnight, a mass; and in a month it hardens. In two months the region of the head develops; in three months the feet; in the fourth month the belly and the hip; in the fifth month the backbone; in the sixth month the nose and eyes and ears; in the seventh month the embryo quickens with life and in the eighth month it becomes complete. In the eighth month in conjunction with the five vital airs or *Pranas* like *Praana, Apaana, vayaana, udaana and samaana,* the *Jeeva* gets the capacity to know the past affairs of its past births. It conceives the imperishable Absolute or Atman through perfect knowledge and meditation. The body becomes complete in the ninth month and remembers its past birth. It embraces all its past good as well as bad actions and its results, the *Karma* or destiny and determines to be good and follow the righteous path with devotion to God, but touched by the all-pervading *Maaya* or delusion it forgets all about its past birth.

By the dominance of the father's semen, the child becomes male; by the mother's it becomes female; when equal, eunuch. If at the time of impregnation, the parents are agitated, then the child will be blind, crippled, hunch backed or of stunted growth. If the couple has vital air trouble, the semen enters in two parts resulting in twins.

Katha Rudra Upanishad

From the Self that is one with *Brahman* and which contains powers including *Maaya* emerged the unmanifest Ether or *Aakasa.* From Ether emerged the unmanifest Air or *Vaayu.* From Air, Fire emerged, from Fire, Water appeared and from Water the Earth came. After dividing and compounding all the subtle elements into five gross elements, the Lord, the *Brahman* created the cosmic egg or energy. Covered by this cosmic energy are the Gods, demons, *Kinnaraas*, humans, animals, birds and so on in accordance with their own past *Karmaas* or actions.

The physical body is made up of food. Within is the *Praana* or the Vital energy split in to five namely, *Praana, Apaana* and so on. Further within is the mind and further within is knowledge. In the interior it is Bliss.

The physical form is pervaded by the vital energy, the vital energy by the mind, mind by knowledge, and knowledge is pervaded by Bliss and the Bliss is finally pervaded by *Brahman*, the witness, the independent, the innermost of all and it is not pervaded by anything else. This pure *Brahman* is God, the individual self the knower, the means of knowledge, the object of knowledge as well as the result.

The Conscience devoid of *Maaya* or ignorance is pure *Brahman*. When it is related to the world it is known as God.

Katopanishad

It is said that the earth was formerly water upon the ocean of space.

There the sun does not shine, both the moon and the stars; nor do these flashes of lightning shine.

Maha Narayana Upanishad

The Lord of creation enters in to the shining intelligence of beings in seed form and acts in the foetus that grows gradually in to a living being.

Within that Lord all Universe exist together and into that it dissolves.

He, the Absolute that is the most subtle cause of the Universe is *Prajaapathi*. He is supported by His own imperishable nature- the Absolute Ether. The space between the heaven and earth and both heaven and earth are enveloped by Him. In Him all creatures abide.

From Him *Prakruthi* or nature was born with five elements. She created the world, the beings, from the five elements.

Nothing else exists apart from Him or subtler than Him. He alone sustains the Universe. The Universe therefore emerged from this *Viswa Karma* through the five elements.

In the beginning the world was engulfed in darkness and gloom. It received its brightness from Sun that shines in the glory of the *Paramaatman* or *Parabrahman.*

This self-luminous Lord pervades all quarters. It was born as *Hiranyagarbha* in the beginning. He the *Hiranya garbha* or the *Prajaapathi* became by His own nature the *Paramaatman,* the ruler and protector of the individual souls or the *Jeevatman.*

This *Prajaapathi* was born in the beginning of creation from the supreme potent with the power of *Maaya.*

The *Paramaatman,* the *Hiranyagarbha* supports the Earth as well as heaven. Having been born as *Hiranyagarbha* in the beginning He represented the Universe as the Womb. He alone is the manifest world of creation that sprang into existence and that causes the birth of the world of creation yet to come. He dwells as the innermost Self of all creatures. The Universe originated from Him and into Him the Universe would be absorbed.

This *Prajaapathi* or *Hiranyagarbha*, the creator of the mortal world and who pervades the world and all quarters and the intermediate quarters that is Space is the first born of Brahman. He by His own nature became *Paramaatman*, the unmanifest cause of creation, the ruler and protector of the individual souls. From this all illuminating Supreme, by His own resolve, after the creation of the oceans, time was generated and ordained Sun, Moon, Sky, Earth, Atmosphere, and Heaven just as they were in the previous cycle of creation. The Supreme *Brahman* also manifested Himself as *Bhuh* and *Suvah*. Beings born from *Prajaapathy* are not separate from Him.

Before their birth nothing existed other than Him. He entered into all creatures of the world as their innermost Self and He identified Himself with them.

Pancha Brahma Upanishad

In the very beginning *Parabrahma*, the *Paramaatman* took shape in stages of *Satyojatha*, the aspect of Earth and Sun, *Aghora*, the aspect of Water and Moon, *Vamadeva,* the aspect of Fire, *Tatpurusha*, the aspect of Air that is the basis of *Srushti, Sthithi and Laya*, that is creation, sustenance and dissolution and *Ishaana,* the aspect of Space or sky that is beyond sound, and the upper boundary of peace. This *Pancha* or five *Brahma* is everywhere and activates the actions of creation, upkeep, destruction, disappearance and blessing. Every form is the form of the *Pancha Brahma.*

Sareerika Upanishad

The body is a combination of five elements. What is hard is Earth, what is liquid is Water, what is hot is Fire, what moves is Air and what is porous is Space.

Svetasvatara Upanishad

The divinity that is within everyone as the Self luminous entity pervades all directions.

The *Hiranyagarbha*, the first born is inside all persons as the indwelling Self facing all directions. He pervades the entire Universe.

It is that, that existed alone at the time of creation and dissolution of the Universe. After projecting and maintaining all worlds He finally withdraws them into Himself. By that Being the whole Universe is filled. He dwells in the hearts of all beings as their inner Self. He is without beginning and created the Cosmos in the midst of chaos. This divinity later manifested into nature, time and so on. It is at His command, the command of that pure Consciousness who is omniscient, the master of all G*unas* and maker of time and who envelops everything that energy assumes various forms like Earth, Water, Fire, Air, and Ether.

He starts creation associated with the three *Gunas* or nature namely the *Sathva*, (goodness) *Rajas* (passion) and *Thamo Gunas* (ignorance).

Thus after setting the creation in motion, by bringing forth the agents of creation, the great soul pervades everything and then later,

He withdraws Himself from it. Finally in the absence of the *Gunas*, He destroys all created objects and after destruction remains aloof in His Essence. He is the Primordial cause of the union of energy with matter. He is the soul of the Universe. He in the beginning projected *Brahma*, the Universal Consciousness for purpose of creation.

Taittareeya Upanishad

From *Brahman* the supreme self, Space emerged. From Space, Air, from Air Fire, from Fire Water and from Water, Earth and from Earth came the herbs and food came and from food man came. This is the outer Self.

In the beginning everything was unmanifested, that is *Brahman*. *Brahman* created itself by itself. He was therefore self-creator. From that emerged manifested beings.

The Self or *Brahman* wished and He created all that exists and entered into each of them. Having entered there it became the formed and the formless, the defined and the undefined, the sustaining and non-sustaining, the sentient and the insentient, the true and untrue.

He that is inside the human form and He that is there in the Sun are one and the same.

Varaaha Upanishad

The real nature of all embodied objects is nothing but the Absolute Consciousness. The *Jeevas* and *Ishwara* are evolved out of the *Chidaakasa*, the Universal Consciousness.

Sama Veda

Sama Veda is derived from the word '*Sama*' meaning hymn or destroying sins. It also refers to that which brings tranquillity to mind and it contains the knowledge of chanted hymns. *Sama Veda* is divided in to two parts. The first part has six books each having two chapters. Each chapter has five decades. Each decade contains several hymns. The first part has approximately 59 decades with 585 verses. The second part is divided into several books, and there are two chapters in each book. Each chapter is further subdivided in to several subdivisions. Each subdivision contains many verses. In Part-2 of this *Veda* there are approximately 401 subdivisions with 1226 hymns.

A Few Hymns of *Sama Veda* on Universe

(Source—English translation of *Sama Veda* by Ralph Griffith, 1895)

PART—1

BOOK—1

CHAPTER—1—DECADE—1

Agni that is supposed to have been born due to friction

9—*Agni* was brought forth by Atharvan by rubbing from the sky.

CHAPTER—2—DECADE—2

9— *Agn*i came from the sky's farthest limit.

BOOK—4

CHAPTER—1— DECADE—4

About Moon

3—"The old hath waked the young Moon from his slumber who runs his circling course with many round him. Behold the God's high wisdom in its greatness: he who died yesterday today is living".

BOOK—6

CHAPTER—1—DECADE—5

2--About *Pavamaana*, the Moon, it is said that it begot and speeded up the Sun with splendour

CHAPTER—1—DECADE—5

10—About Moon or *Pavamaana* it is said that it granted strength to *Indra*, he, *Indu* in turn, generated light in *Soorya.*

PART—2

BOOK—3

CHAPTER—2—DECADE—22

About the splendour of the Sun

2— *Indra*, is supposed to have given splendour to the Sun.

BOOK—5

CHAPTER—1—DECADE—8

About Moon and splendour of the Sun

1. The Moon gave splendour to the Sun.

CHAPTER—2—DECADE—1

About Moon and Sun's splendour

3. He, *Pavamaana* granted strength to *Indra*, he, *Indu*, generated strength in *Surya.*

BOOK—6

CHAPTER—1—DECADE—7

About Sun and Moon

2 *Pavamaana*, did beget the Sun with might and rain in the supporting sky.

BOOK—7

CHAPTER—3—DECADE—8

1. *Indra* who has spread out Earth and Heaven, is supposed to have lightened up the Sun with his power.

***Sama Veda Upanishads* on Universe**

Aruneyi Upanishad

Bhur, Bhuvar, Svar, Mahar, Jana, Tapas and *Sathya* are the seven *Lokas* or worlds or upper spheres.

The seven underworld or Nether spheres are *Atala, Pataala, Vitala, Sutala, Rasaatala, Talaatala* and *Mahaa Tala.*

Avyaktha Upanishad

The three states of evolution in the beginning were *Avyaktha*, the indeterminate, *Mahatatthva*, or the determined indeterminate, and *Ahamkara,* the determinate.

Avyaktha is explained in the Nasadiya Suktha (in the Rig Veda). There it is stated that in the beginning there was nothing; no air, no sky and no beyond. There was no death, no deathlessness, and no change of night and day. That one breathed calmly, the Self sustained one. There was nothing else beyond it. Only gloom existed. Within that void, that chaos, desire that is the Primal germ of mind arose and this kindling ray shot across the dark and the dreariness. There was immense power and force in it with a self-supporting mass beneath and energy above.

Chandogya Upanishad

The light of *Brahman* that shines above everything and all is the light within the body of man. Verily all the Universe is *Brahman*. From Him all things originate, unto Him they dissolve and by Him they are sustained.

Never does the Sun set nor does it rise.

The Sun is *Brahman*. Before creation, there was no Universe. It is only later that it became existent. It then grew and turned in to an egg; it lay for a period of one year and then it burst open. Of the two halves of that egg shell, one was of silver that is earth and the other gold, the heaven. Its outer membrane became the mountains and the inner membrane became the mist with clouds. Its veins are the rivers; the water contained in it became the ocean; and then the Sun was born; after that sounds of the form of loud shouts and all beings and all desired objects came up.

Jabali Upanishad

Jeeva is nothing but God Himself acting the role of egotism.

Kundika Upanishad

From *Brahman* arose Ether, from Ether came Air; from Air appeared Fire, from Fire Water came and from Water Earth was formed.

Mahopanishad

In the beginning there was only the *Paramatman* or *Narayana*. There were no *Brahma, Shiva,* waters, fire, heaven, earth, stars, sun, and moon and so on. From His desire the *Yajnasthoma*, that is, *Avyaktha* the indeterminate arose. The Supreme Being employed him for creation and remained detached.

The Cosmos and the differences in the Universe are all the manifestation of that Being. He is existence itself.

Millions of particles undergo generation, sustenance and dissolution inside the Supreme Being by rotation. The Supreme Being is all pure consciousness.

From the desire of the *Paramaatman* arose all other things.

The cosmos is only the manifestation of the Supreme Being that is pure consciousness. All the differences in the Universe are His manifestation only.

The Universe is born only to die and it dies only to be reborn.

It is only for empirical purposes that the wise people have attributed name for the Supreme Being and the magical illusion of the Cosmos created by the Supreme Being.

Atharva Veda

It is the last Veda of all the four *Vedas*. This *Veda* is associated with the ancient poet saint *Atharvan* that means 'the wise old one' and *Angiras* and hence this *Veda* is also known as *Atharvangirasa Veda*. This was supposed to have been composed at a later period. It is said to have been written around 1500 B C. *Atharva Veda* contains knowledge of prayer, charm and spells. This Veda is divided into 20 books and contains nearly 731 hymns.

A Few Hymns of *Atharva Veda* on Universe

(Source—English translation of *Atharva Veda* by Ralph T.H. Griffith, 1895-96)

BOOK—2

HYMN—1

About the Milky Way
Prisni milked all life that has existence.

HYMN—31

About the cause of creation it is stated that the highest, the prime cause of all things lies hidden. It is from that hidden principle that all get forms.

BOOK—7

HYMN—107

The *Agni* or the rays of heat from the Sun causing evaporations of water cause rain.

BOOK—9

HYMN—2

Desire or will or *Ichcha* is the first cause of all creation.

HYMN—9

"The seven make the one wheeled chariot ready: bearing seven names the single courser draws it.

The wheel, three naved, is sound and undecaying there on these worlds of life are all dependent.

The seven, who on this seven wheeled car are mounted have horses, seven in tale who draw them onward.

Seven sisters utter songs of Praise together in whom the cow's seven names are held and treasured.

Who hath beheld at birth the Primal Being, when she who hath no bone supports the bony?

Where is the blood of earth, the life, the spirit? Who may approach the man who knows, to ask it?"

"Upon the five spoked wheel revolving ever, where on all creatures rest and are dependent.

The axle, heavy laden, is not heated the nave from ancient time remain unheated.

They call him, in the farther half of heaven the Sire fivefold, of twelve forms, wealthy in watery store

These other, later still say that he takes his stand upon a seven wheeled car, six spoked, whose sight is clear.

Formed with twelve spokes, too strong for age to weaken, this wheel of during order rolls round heaven

Here in established, joined in pairs together, seven hundred sons and twenty stand, o Agni.

The wheel revolves, unwasting with its felly; ten draw it, yoked to the far stretching car pole

Girt by the region moves the eye of *Soorya*, on whom dependent rest all living creatures.

Beneath the upper realm, above this lower, bearing her calf at foot the cow hath risen".

BOOK—10

HYMN—7

Men know the inexpressible *Hiranyagarbha* as the supreme.

HYMN—8

The heaven and earth, the world of life are upheld by the power of *Skambha*.

"One is the wheel, the tires are twelve in number, the naves are three, what man hath understood it?

Three hundred spokes have their upon been hammered, and sixty pins set firmly in their places

Discern then, this, o, Savitr, six are the twins, one singly born.

They claim relationship in that among them which is born alone

Though manifest, it lies concealed in the vast place they call the old

There in is firmly stationed all the moving, breathing universe.

Up, eastward, downward in the west it rolleth, with countless elements, one wheeled single fellied".

"The five horsed car moves onward side horses harnessed with the others draw it".

BOOK—11

HYMN—8

About the cyclical nature of creation

The earth is stated to have been in existence even before this earth in which we live now.

It is stated that Gods made the mortal their abode and entered and possessed the man.

Whoever knows the truth knows that man is none other than *Brahman*'s self since all deities reside in him.

BOOK—12

HYMN—1

The Earth came up from water in the ocean.

BOOK—13

HYMN—1

The Sun that was in waters ascended creating *Soma*, waters, plants and cattle—

Rohitha (a form of Sun and Fire) established earth and heaven firmly and by him ether and welkin were fixed. It is He who measured out mid-air and all the regions and it is by Him that the gods found life.

The refulgent and immortal bay steeds of the Sun draw His light-rolling chariot on forever and prepare the Milky Way, the god's never reluctant milch cow that teems with fatness.

HYMN—3

The Sun dwells in waters
This seven make the one wheeled chariot ready:
Bearing seven names the single courser draws it.
The wheel, three naved, is sound and undecaying
There on these worlds of life are all dependent". (Rigvedic hymn)

HYMN—4

All constellations including the Moon are subject to Sun's will.

BOOK—14

HYMN—1

Soma, the *Moon* makes the Earth mighty.

BOOK—19

HYMN—6

About the all pervasiveness of the Super soul, *Purusha*, the creator it is stated that-

"*Purusha* hath a thousand arms, a thousand eyes, a thousand feet.

On every side pervading earth he fills a space ten fingers wide.

He with three quarters rose to heaven here reappeared a fourth of him.

Thence he strode forth on every side to all that eats not and that eats.

So mighty is his grandeur, yea, greater than this is *Purusha*.

All creatures are one fourth of him, three fourths what dieth not in heaven.

Purusha is in truth this All; what hath been and what yet shall be.

Lord too of immortality."

The Moon was generated from his mind, and from his eye the Sun had birth.

Indra and *Agni* from his mouth were born and *Vaayu* from his breath.

Forth from his navel come mid-air the sky was fashioned from his head

Earth from his feet and from his ear the regions. Thus they formed the worlds.

In the beginning rose *Viraj.* As soon as he was born he spread westward and eastward o'er the earth.

HYMN—7

The *Nakshatras* mentioned as the lunar mansions are addressed in the following order in this hymn.

Kritthika, Rohini, Mrigasiras, Ardra, Punarvasu and Sunrita, Pushya. Aslesha, Magha, Svathi, Chitra, Fist Phalgunis, Hastha, Radhas, Visaakhas, Anuradha, Jyeshtha, Moola, Ashadhas, Abhijit, Sravana and Sravishthas, Dsatabhishak, the two Prosthapaadas, Trevathi, Asvayujas, and Bharanis.

HYMN—52

About creation it is stated that, Desire the primal seed and germ of spirit rose in the very beginning of creation.

HYMN—53

About Time or *Kaala-*

It is prolific, thousand eyed and undecaying, a horse with seven reins. It is Time that bears us onward.

"This Time hath seven rolling wheels and seven naves
Immortality is the chariot's axle
This time brings hither ward all worlds about us:
As primary deity is he entreated.
He carries from us all these worlds of creatures.
They call him *Kaala* in the loftiest heaven.
He only made the worlds of life, he only gathered
The worlds of living things together".
"No other higher power than he existeth
Kaala created yonder heaven, and
Kaala made these realms of earth

By *Kaala*, stirred to motion, both what is and what shall be expanded.

Kaala created land; the Sun in *Kaala* hath his light and heat
In *Kaala* rest all things that be: In *Kaala* doeth the eye discern.
In *Kaala* mind, in *Kaala* breath, in *Kaala*
Name are fixed and joined
These living creatures, one and all,
Rejoice when *Kaala* hath approached.
Kaala embraces holy fire, the highest *Brahma* in himself'
Yea, *Kaala*, who was father of *Prajaapathi*, is Lord of all
He made, he stirred the universe
To motion, and on him rests,
He, *Kaala* having now become *Brahma,*
Holds *Parameshthin* Up"..
Kala created living beings, and
First of all *Prajaapathi.*

Atharva Veda Upanishads on Universe

Atharva Siras Upanishad

From *Akshara*, the immortal, the deathless being, time is created. From time the all pervasiveness is created. From His breath the power of *Thamas* or darkness is created. From *Thamas* water emerged. Then the foam appeared. From foam the galaxy came up. From Galaxy *Brahma* the creator of beings emerged and from Him finally the world appeared.

Brihad Jabala Upanishad

The Universe has been burnt several times.

Garuda Upanishad

From the complete whole only the other complete whole rose. Still the complete whole remains unaltered and undisturbed.

Narada Parivarjaka Upanishad

This Universe is made up of five elements and remains in the five and becomes endless in varieties and is pervaded by the Self.

Mandukyoupanishad

(Mandukya Karika–The commentary on *Mandukya Upanishad* by *Gaudapada, Adi Shankara's Parama Guru* that is his teacher's teacher)

There is no dissolution, no origination.

The birth of that which exists occurs only through Maya or delusion or ignorance and not in reality. He who thinks that something is born in reality should know that, that which is already born is only reborn. That, that was there before cannot be born afresh and that which does not exist cannot be born. If so, then, when one is born from another it leads to *ad infinitum*.

From the relative plane of thinking everything seems to be born and is thought to be everlasting. From the Absolute level of thinking or perception, everything is unborn and therefore there is nothing like destruction or deluge.

Mundaka Upanishad

From Him, the Absolute originates the vital force, mind, all senses, space, air, fire, water and earth that support everything.

Sandilya Upanishad

The entire world is interwoven in *Brahman*. *Brahman* is that from which all originate and into which all merge or absorbed. He is everywhere and engulfs everything.

3

Cosmos in Ithihaasas

Ithihaasas or Epics

Ithihaasa means 'it happened thus'. It tells the stories of the past and present, about remote areas of the universe that cannot be perceived with the naked eye, the evolution of the universe, different *Yugaas*, units of time, astronomy and astrology, geography and so on. The Vedic philosophy is explained here through tales in a simple manner for the benefit of common men who cannot grasp the Vedic knowledge that is revealed in Vedic language. However *Ithihaasas* convey the same eternal truth or knowledge that is found in the Vedas. The *Ithihaasas* make use of the language of *Bhakthi* for conveying the truth through interesting historical tales of kings, sages, devotees and ordinary men and so on. The two great *Ithihaasas* are the *Ramaayana* and the *Mahaabharahta*. *Ramaayana* is however much earlier to *Mahaabharatha*.

Ramayana

It is known as *Aadi Kavya* and its author sage *Valmeeki* as *Aadi Kavi*. In *Vaalmeeki Raamayana* there are 24,000 verses divided in to six *Kaandas* in six books and an end piece or epilogue namely the *Uttara Kand*. In *Uttara Ramayana* there are seven *Kandaas* with 649 chapters with 24,253 verses. The *Valmeeki Raamayana* is dated around the 5$^{th\ to\ 4th}$ century B C. It is said that sage *Valmeeki* composed *Ramaayana* based on each of the 24 letters of the *Gayathri Manhtra*. It tells about the story of *Sri Rama* who is supposed to be the incarnation of Lord *Naarayana*. He was a descendant of *Ikshaavaku* clan belonging to solar dynasty. He and his brothers lived in *Treta Yuga*, the silver age. This epic tells how an ideal man particularly, a king should act. This epic tells the story of *Sri Raama* and his consort *Seetha*, *Raama's* three younger brothers namely *Bharatha, Lakshmana and Shatrugna*, their father king *Dasaratha*, their mothers *Kousalya, Kaikeyi and Sumihtra*. The seven *Kaandas* in *Raamayana* are, the *Baala Kaanda, Ayodhya Kaanda, Aranya Kaanda, Kishkinda Kaanda, Sundara Kaanda, Yuddha Kaanda, and Uttara Kaanda, the* epilogue.

Raamaayana on Universe

The epic *Raamaayana* contains a few hymns on the Universe. It stresses more on the life of *Sri Raama* who lived during *Tretha Yuga* rather than expounding facts about Cosmology. However there are a few hymns in this epic that give a few facts about the origin of this Universe, the creative process, about the geography of earth and so on.

Bala Kaanda

In this *Kaanda* the use of many sophisticated weapons like *Shatagni* that is a canon and a thorny weapon that can kill a 1000 people, and *Kshipani* another weapon (chapter—5) are mentioned. It also gives a detailed picture of the *Vaanaras* who are not necessarily monkeys but most probably monkey humans. *Vaanara* only means the one who moves around in the forests. It describes the regions underneath the surface of the earth up to its core. These regions are mentioned as *Atala, Vitala, Sutala, Talaatala, Mahaatala*, and *Rasaatala*. *Rasaatala* is stated to be the deepest subterranean plane. This *Kaanda* also tells about *Nala* who obtained a boon from his mother as per which whatever article he throws in to the water will float on water and this he made use of to build a bridge across the ocean to Lanka.

CHAPTER—4

The *Gandharvas* are celestial beings and performers of all kinds of performing arts and the divine singers with adorable personalities.

CHAPTER—14

The names of the seven sages in the *Saptha Rishi Mandala* are, *Atri, Angirasa, Pulastya, Pulaha, Krathu, Marichi and Vasishta* (The seven sages or the *Saptha Rishi Mandala* is the constellation of stars in the Ursa Major- the Great Bear.)

CHAPTER—17

The Gods procreated many thousands of *Vaanaras* and guise changing monkeys of immeasurable strength and bravery. They took birth in bears, monkeys, and sacred *langoors*.

The *Kinnaras*, great Sages, *Gandharvas*, eagles, *Yakshas*, reptiles, *Kimpurushas, Siddhas,, Vidyadharas, Uragas, Caaranas, Apsarasas and Naagas* and so on procreated several thousands of forest ranging and valiant *Vaanara* sons from their bodies endowed with guise changing faculties, with bodily might and are identical in strength and might with tigers and lions. They all assault with stones, with trees, and with their nails and claws as their weapons and are also experts in missiles and well versed in warfare.

CHAPTER—27

Several sophisticated weapons given by sage *Visvamihtra* to *Sri Raama* are mentioned here. These are, *Danda* disc, *Dharma* disc, *Kalaa* disc, *Vishnu* disc, *Indra* disc, *Thunderbolt* missile, *Shiva's* trident, *Brahamashira* missile, *Aishiika* missile (grass blade missile) and *Brahma* missiles that when invoked with *Manthras* become a projectile weapon, *Modaki,* the beater and *Shikari,* the tower of protection, three nooses namely *Dharma Paasha, Kaala Paasha* and *Varuna Paasha*, the unequalled missile *Varuna Astra*, two projectile bolts namely *Shushka* the drier and *Aardra* the drencher and missiles namely *Pinaaka* (the missile of God Shiva), missile *Shikari* (the tower), *Prathama* the blower, and missile of god of air namely Vayu *Bhagavan*, missiles namely, *Hayashira t*he horse head, *Krouncha,* the wrestler, two weapons one presided over by the power of *Vishnu* and the other by the power of *Rudra,* the missile *Vaidyadhara*, the gem sword *Nandana Mohana*, the missile *Prasvapana* that induces sleep, gentle *Prashamana,* the pacifier of enemy's anger, missiles *Varshana* the rainer, *Shoshana* the drainer, the *Santopana,* the humidifier, *Vilapana* the weep inducer, *Mohana*, the intoxicator (the missile of *Manmada,* the god of love), and the favourite missile of the *Gandharvas, Manava* the humane missile, the missile dear to *Pishaachas*, the monster missile, greatly powered *Tamasa* and *Saumana* missiles, the indomitable missiles like *Samvartha, Mausala, Sathya, Maaya missiles, Teja Prabha*, a solar missile that destroy' s other's brilliance, *Shishira* the cooler, the missile of Moon God deadly missile *Tvastha* and *Sudamana,* dangerous missile *Shita-isu*, and *Maanava* missiles of *Manu* the earliest ruler of mankind and so on. These weapons are greatly powered .These weapons and missiles are invoked with *Manthras*. It is stated that after *Sri Rama* received these weapons from sage *Visvaamitra, Sri Raama* invoked these weapons with *Manthras* and when all the missiles came and stood accessible to *Sri Raama* in their astral form along with their presiding deities, *Sri Raama* motivated them with *Manthras to* take leave and to return when he needed them and invoked them.

The nature of some of the weapons is also described here. It is stated that the *Brahmastra* contains air, fire and cosmic poison with two goat like fangs, full of poison, weighty, emits air, contains mercury , fiery, sparkling, and when invoked the sky will be filled with air. It is projected with three hymns, *Gayathri* at its centre.

The Time Disc renders a state with magical powers, ending in air, and is water filled and ends in craters with fire, and generates fire.

About another weapon it is said that this weapon sparkles at first with cosmic holes. It possesses high degree radiance with one lakh revolution per foot and very dangerous is its projection.

CHAPTER—28

In this chapter the nullifying missiles are mentioned by sage *Visvamithra.*

VERSE—28

The city of Lanka was built on the *Thrikoota* Mountains.

CHAPTER—30

The *Manava* missile is a cold arrow that takes away the enemy without killing him

The *Agneya Asthra* is supposed to be a very powerful fire missile.

CHAPTERS—39 and 40

It is stated here that King *Sagara*'s 60,000 sons hollowed out each and every area of the surface of the earth in the process of searching the sacrificial horse sent by them. In the process several serpents, *asuras*, demons and other beings living underneath the surface of the earth were killed. Thus they dug 60, 000 square *Yojanas* of the earth and reached *Rasaatala,* the 6th subterranean and the nethermost plane. There they saw a mountain similar to the easterly elephant named *Virupaaksha* that bore the eastern side of the earth with all its mountains and oceans on its head. On certain occasions when that great elephant moved its head desiring respite due to tiresomeness, the earth quakes occur on earth. When the princes split the southern direction, there also they saw an elephant namely *Maha Padma* that was similar to a very great mountain and that sustained the southern side of the earth on its head. Then they dug the western side of the earth. Even there they saw a mountain similar to that of elephant *Sumanasa* of the western direction. Then they dug the northern side of the earth. There again they saw *Bhadra*, a snow white elephant bearing the northern side of the earth.

CHAPTER—43

This chapter mentions the aircrafts of celestial beings and gods that are like cities in their shape and size, some drawn by horses and some by best elephants.

River *Ganga* plunged from the sky on to the matted locks of Lord *Shiva*. Shiva later released *Ganga* in *Bindu* Lake in the *Himalayas* and seven streams emerged out of it. Three auspicious *Ganges* flowed eastward. These are, *Hladini, Paavani, and Nalini (Brahma Putra).* To the westward direction streamed three other rivers namely, *Sucaksu, Seetha and Sindhu (the Indus*). The southward flow is known as *Bhageerathi.*

CHAPTER—47

The seven presiding deities of cosmic air divisions are the seven wind gods that are the seven segments of *Dihti*'s feats cut by *Indra*.

The seven wind Gods or *Maruts*, who are the sons of *Dithi a*re the seven presiding Deities of the cosmic air divisions. These are also called as *Gagana, Sparshana, Vaayu, Anila, Praana, Parameshwara, and Jeeva.*

CHAPTER—55

This chapter mentions the Turbo- jetting missiles.

CHAPTER—56

The missiles invoked by king *Vishvamihtra* against sage *Vasishta* are mentioned here. These are fiery missiles that are regulated by Gods like *Varuna, Rudra, Indra, Paasupatha and Ishhika* that is a projectile missile through grass blade, missiles named Humane, Rager, Stupifier, hypnotizer, yawner, intoxicator, humidifier, weep inducer, drainer, Ripper, Thunderbolt, missiles of *Brahma, Kaala* and rain gods, missiles of *Shiva*, monster, punisher, wrestler, Baffler, Bolter, Drier, drencher, discs of virtue, time and *Vishnu,* missiles with horse head, blower, Stirrer, Apari Poer (the power of *Vishnu* and *Shiva)* impeller, staggerer, lethal missile of time, and so on.

CHAPTER—60

In order to create another eternal heaven for king *Trishanku* who sought the help of the sage for reaching heaven with his physical body, Sage *Visvaamitra* replicated the *Saptha Rishi Mandala* in the south (the Ursa Major or the Great Bear is a prominent constellation in the northern sky containing seven bright stars in a pattern called the Plough, the Big Dipper). He also replicated the stocks of other galaxies and stars. The gods granted his wish but said that those amazing numerous stars created by the sage would remain in the firmament, but outside the path of stelliforms of cosmic person. *Trishanku* will also remain in the circle of stars created by *Visvaamitra* but upside down. Thus *Visvaamitra* perhaps created many space stations and cloned celestials.

Ayodya Kanda

CHAPTER—110

In his description of creation sage *Vasishta* tells *Raama* that in the beginning there was only water everywhere. It is from that the earth was formed. After that *Brahma* along with other Gods emerged. The earth at that time was submerged in water. *Brahma* therefore assumed the form of a boar and caused the earth to rise from water and created the world. The eternal, imperishable *Brahma* was begotten from ether and from Him creation started.

Aranyakanda

CHAPTER—23

In the proximity of the Sun there appeared a dark reddish disc (probably referring to eclipse). At an odd hour of the day the evening dusk appeared at an extremely fast pace to be followed by a sudden night fall; nothing could be discerned anymore; the birds and animals became awestricken and started howling at the top of their voice. The Sun was totally engulfed by *Raahu* and appeared to be totally dull, but a big halo was seen around the dark disc of the Sun; some stars and Planets became visible.

Kishkinda Kanda

CHAPTER—46

Sugreeva gives a description of the physical world viewed from above as per his perception. He says the earth looked like a circle of a fire ball that is encircled with fire like reddish, brownish minerals and ore resembling a cow-hoof.

In its eastern side (most probably the *Bharathavarsha*) were found various trees, enchanting mountains with caves and innumerable lakes. There was the mountain rich in ores namely *Udaya,* the Sunrise, and the Milk Water Ocean that is the abode of the *Apsaras*. In the south direction he saw *Vindhya* Range Mountain and different types of trees especially sandal wood trees. In the west were found different cities and the best mountain *Ashtagiri* and Mt. Dusk. In the northern direction were the *Himaalayaas,* the Mt. Meru.

Yuddha Kanda

CHAPTER—35

The *Kinnaraas* are a species of demi gods with human figure and the head of a horse or with the body of the horse and the head of a human being.

CHAPTER—36

Uragas are serpent demons

CHAPTER—37

The *Deityas* are giants

Daanavas are demons

CHAPTER—39

Raavana's mansion is described as thousand pillared mansion with a height almost touching the sky. It is built on top of the *Trikuta* Mountain. The *Trikuta* Mountain extends around 800 miles.

CHAPTER—41

Some *Vaanaras* have the strength of 10 elephants, some ten times of that and some equal to the strength of 1000 elephants.

Chapter—44

Mystic missiles that are equal to venomous serpents are mentioned here.

CHAPTER—90

The weapon presented by *Kubera* to *Lakshmana* had arms that resembled a pair of steel rods emitting a piercing sound like that of a pair of curfew cranes.

CHAPTER—93

Siddhas are demi gods who are endowed with mystic powers.

Yakshas are demi gods attending on *Kubera,* the God of riches.

CHAPTER—99

Mystic missiles like *Thaamasa*, the missiles that shine like sun, moon, comet, planet, and the lunar mansions, huge meteors, flashes of lightning, blazing thunderbolts are mentioned here.

CHAPTER—100

Naagas are semi divine beings with face of a man and tail of a serpent.

Mahaabhaaratha

Mahaabhaaratha was composed by *Veda Vyasa* in *Dwapara Yuga* (the Bronze Age). Originally *Vyaasa* composed this epic in 24, 000 verses. Later he composed an epitome in 150 verses consisting of the introduction with chapter contents. Then he taught his composition to his son *Sukha Brahma* and later to his disciples. Then again he composed 600,000 verses. The final form of this *Ithihaasa* is supposed to have been written around the 6th and the 9th centuries B C. This

Epic tells about the life of the descendants of the lunar race particularly from the period of King *Shaanthanu* and his descendants the *Paandavas* and the *Kauravas*. This Epic describes the childhood of the *Paandavas* and the *Kauravas*, their enmity, the exile of the *Paandavas*, the great *Mahabhaaratha* war at *Kurukshetra*, *Sri Krishna's* life, His divine protection of the *Paandavas*, the marvellous divine teachings of Lord *Krishna* that is known as the *Bhagavad Geetha*, the victory of the *Paandavas*, their reign, their departure to the *Himaalayas* and finally the end of *Krishna Avataar* and the onset of *Kali Yuga*. Linked with the main story, innumerable minor stories are also found in this Epic. The *Mahaabhaaratha* as it is available today contains 100, 000 verses that is divided into 18 *Parvas*. After the 18 *Parvas c*ome the *Khila* or Appendix *Hari Vamsa* and *Vavishya. Harivamsa* contains 12,000 Slokas. It is said that the epic of *Mahaabhaaratha* is eight times longer than Homer's Iliad and Odyssey put together. This epic covers almost all aspects of human life and knowledge both material as well as spiritual. It also tells many things about the universe. It is said that there is nothing that we cannot find in this epic. In the *Aadi Parva* of this epic it is stated that what is found in *Mahaaabhaaratha* may be found elsewhere but what is not found here may not be found anywhere else.

Mahaabhaarata on Universe

Aadi Parva

SECTION—1

When the universe was without brightness and light and was enveloped all around by total darkness, the primal cause of creation, a mighty egg that was the inexhaustible seed of all created beings came up. It was called *Maha Divya*, and was formed in the beginning of the *Yuga*. At that time the *Rishis* pointed out that there was only the true light of *Brahman,* the eternal one, the wonderful and inconceivable being that is omnipresent, the invisible and subtle cause. From this appeared Lord *Brahma* that was the first and foremost of all *Prajapathis*. Later, humans, the *Viswa Devas*, the *Adithyas,* the *Vasus*, and the twin *Aswins, the Yakshas, the Sandhyas, the Pisachas, the Guhyakas* and the *Pitri appeared.* After these came the wise and most holy *Brahma Rishis*, and the numerous *Raaja Rishis* endowed with all noble qualities. Then in due succession, water, the heavens, the earth, the air, the sky, the points of heaven, the years, the seasons, the months, the fortnights called *Pakshas* with day and night were all created.

All animate and inanimate things that are created in this Universe will at the end of the world and after the expiry Of the Yuga will be recreated again and at the commencement of other Yugas all things will be renovated. Thus the universe revolves perpetually without beginning and end.

Mighty weapons are mentioned here. *Aswathama* discharged the weapon called *Aishika* by which the embryo in the womb of Uttara was wounded. The weapon *Brahmastra* discharged by Aswathama was repelled by Arjuna with another weapon over which he pronounced the word "*Sasti*".

Time creates all things and it also destroys everything. All the good and evil in all the three worlds are caused by time. Time cuts short everything and creates everything anew. Time alone is awake when all things sleep. All past, present and future are the offspring of time.

From *Brahma*, the supreme soul the *Adhyatma* or *Purusha* appeared the universe with principles of generation and progression, birth and death and rebirth.

SECTION—3

The hymn in *Rig Veda* is explained here.

The 360 cows are represented by 360 days that produce one calf between them that is the year. The year is only the nave of the wheel to which is attached 720 spokes representing as many days and nights. The circumference of this wheel represented by 12 months is without end. The wheel of time represented by the year has a nave represented by the six seasons. The number of spokes attached to that nave is 12 as represented by the 12 signs of the zodiac. This wheel of time manifests the fruits of the acts of all things. The presiding deity of time or *Kaala* abides in that wheel.

The wheel whose circumference is marked by 24 divisions represents as many lunar changes furnished with 360 spokes. It is set in motion continuously by six seasons. These damsels representing universal nature are weaving without intermission a cloth with threads black and white (night and day) and there by ushering into existence the manifold worlds and the beings inhabiting them. The two damsels are *Dhaata and Vidhaata*, the black and white threads denoting night and day. The wheels of 12 spokes turned by the 6 beings are the 6 seasons of the year.

SECTION –17

Mountain *Meru* appears blazing and looks like a heap of effulgence. The rays of the sun falling on its peaks of golden lustre are dispersed by them. It is decked with gold and is exceedingly beautiful. This mountain is the haunt of the Gods and *Gandharvas*. It is immeasurable and unapproachable by men of sins. There are dreadful beasts wandering there and it contains many divine life giving herbs. It is very high and is the first of all the mountains. It is full of trees, streams, and resounds of the chirping birds.

SECTION—18

Mandara Mountain is adorned with cloud like pearls. It is the best of all the mountains. It is fully covered by herbs. There are beasts of prey as well as beautiful birds here. The Gods, *Apsaras*, and *Kinnaras* visit this place. It rises to a height of 11, 000 *Yojanas* and descends downwards in equal measure.

SECTION—19

The *Sudarsana Chakra* is the weapon of extraordinary lustre, effulgent as the blazing fire and dreadful and capable of destroying large areas.

SECTION—30

Various sharp edged weapons of terrible shapes with sparks of fire with smoke and sharp pointed missiles, maces furnished with iron spikes shinning like another firmament illumined by the rays of the sun are mentioned here.

SECTION—33

While explaining *Garuda (Suparna)* piercing through *Soma* (Moon) it is said that the weapon placed near Soma was a wheel of steel, keen edged and sharp as the razor revolving continuously. The fierce instrument of the splendour of the blazing Sun and of terrible form devised by Gods for cutting into pieces the attackers of *Soma*. Within the wheel *Soma* is guarded by two great snakes of effulgence of blazing fire with tongues bright as the lightning flash of great energy. The snakes have mouth emitting fire and blazing eyes containing poison very terrible looking in anger and with great activity.

SECTION—36

The serpent *Sesha* supports the earth with his head with everything in it.

SECTION—90

Yayathi, a great king who could reach high regions due to his meritorious deeds while explaining the higher regions says,

Indraloka is extraordinarily beautiful with 1000 gates and extending over a 100 *yojanas* all around. Still at a higher level is the region of perfect beatitude that has no decay. It is the region of the creator and the lord of earth and is very difficult to reach. Some dwell in these and still higher regions for 60,000 years, some for 80,000 years in heaven and after the expiry of the results of their good karmas they fall down to earth. There are seven gates through which one can get entry into heaven and these are asceticism, benevolence, tranquillity of mind, self-command, modesty, simplicity and kindness to all creatures.

SECTION—93

There are infinite worlds in heaven all blazing like lightning.

SECTION—135

Many terrible weapons are mentioned here like *Brahmasira* that can be hurled and withdrawn and has the right to burn the whole universe (to be used to a foe that is not human).

SECTION—137

Agneya weapon that creates fire, weapon *Varuna* that creates water, *Vayavaya* that creates air, *Parjanya* that creates clouds, *Bhauma*

that creates land, *Parvatya* that creates mountains and *Antardhana* that makes all that created to disappear are all mentioned here.

SECTION—139

The fire that covers the whole world has risen from the waters.

SECTION—169

Celestials like *Danavas* and *Yakshas* are mentioned here.

SECTION—172

The beings and celestials like *Gandharvas, Raakshasas, Pisachas,* and *Uragas* are mentioned here.

SECTION—189

The names of several other celestials are mentioned here.

SECTION—192

Weapons like *Brahma* and *Pauandara* are mentioned here.

SECTION—214

From this section it is understood that the celestials who are the inhabitants of other planets and the other worlds not only had contact but also had relationships and friendship with humans on earth.

SECTION—220

Various unknown regions of the earth are mentioned here.

SECTION—227

Wearing of leather gloves and the celestial weapons are mentioned here. Gods are also mentioned to have gifted humans with weapons and chariots. *Kaumodaka* was given by Lord *Varuna* to Lord *Krishna*; *Gandeeva*, the celestial weapon was given to *Arjuna* by Lord Brahma.

SECTION—229

Various celestial weapons like the spiked club of Lord *Kubera*, the death dealing mace of Lord *Yama*, the noose of Lord *Varuna*, the long lance of Lord *Skanda*, the respondent plants of the *Aswins*, the bow of *Dhatri,* the thick club of *Jaya*, the bright Dart of *Soorya,* the battle axe of *Mrityu*, the sharp discus of *Mitra* and so on are mentioned here.

Sabha Parva

SECTION—1 and 2

Maaya, the *Asura* is supposed to have built a mansion that is similar to a celestial palace, that surpassed *Brahma*'s mansion and that combined godly, *Ausuric* and human designs composed entirely of gems and precious stones gained from all the three worlds in 5000 cubic square. He completed the mansion in 14 months.

SECTION—3

A region north of *Kailasha* in the Mountain of *Mainaka* where there is a huge peak of gems and jewels called *Hiranya Sringa* near which is the lake *Vindu* is mentioned here.

SECTION—4

It is said here that the celestials like *Gandharvas*, *Apsaras* and *Kinnaras* and so on visited the humans on earth.

SECTION—6

Narada explains the wonders of the celestial assembly room of *Sakra* (*Satakkratu* or Indra) built by *Indra* himself that is capable of going everywhere at will. It is 150 *yojanas* in length and 100 *yojanas* in breadth and 5 *yojanas* in height and all the gods are present there. The *Rishis* and the celestial gods who travel by their chariots visit this place. It is called *Pushkaramalini.*

SECTION—8

The assembly hall of *Yama,* the son of *Vivasvat,* built by the celestial architect *Viswakarma* is as bright as pure gold. It covers an area of more than a 100 *yojanas.* It possesses the splendour of the sun and yields everything that one desires. It is neither very cool nor very hot. There is neither weakness nor grief there, neither hunger nor thirst; no ill feelings. All objects of desire either celestial or human are found there and all kinds of enjoyable articles and delicious edibles are provided with cold and hot water. The *Sanyasins, Gandharvas, Apsaras* and so on visit this place.

SECTION—9

The assembly hall of *Varuna* is unparalleled in splendour. Its dimensions are similar to *Yama*'s assembly hall. Its walls and arches are of pure white. It is built by *Visvakarma* within waters. It is surrounded by beautiful trees and plants with very many varieties of beautiful birds. It is neither cold nor hot. It is pure white in colour. It has many rooms and many seats like other celestial mansions.

SECTION—10

Kubera's (*Vaisravana)* assembly hall built by *Visvakarma* is 100 *yojanas* in length and 70 *yojanas* in breadth. It possesses the splendour of peaks of *Kailaasa*. It has high chambers of gold. It gives the fragrance of celestial perfume and is decked with innumerable costly jewels. It seems to float in air. It is provided with colours of celestial gold. The deities, *Gandharvas, Apsaras* visit and wait upon *Kuvera* or *Kubera. Kinnaras, Raakshasas, Yakshas* wait upon Lord *Kubera*. It looks attached to the firmament and is capable of moving along with it.

SECTION—11

Brahma's mansion is immeasurable, indescribable as regards form and shape and is with great splendour. Within moments it assumes different forms. It is neither cold nor hot. One does not experience hunger, thirst or any kind of uneasiness. It is made of brilliant gems of many kinds. It is not supported on columns. It has no deterioration and is eternal. It is self-effulgent and seems to surpass Moon, Sun and fire in splendour. It is stationed in heaven. All gods and planets and so on in their personified form wait upon Lord *Brahma* there.

SECTION—27

In the northern *Kuru* land that is the celestial region, nothing could be seen with human eyes.

SECTION—30

The Cole Mountain and *Surabhipatna* and the island called Copper Island and the mountain *Ramyaka* are mentioned here.

SECTION—50 and 51

The tribes some of whom possess two eyes, some three, some having eyes on foreheads and those called *Aushmikas, Nishadas, Romakas* and Cannibals, *Chins, Sakas, Udras, Vrisnis, Harahunas* and dusky tribes of *Himavat, Nipas, Valhikas, Tukhatas, Tukaharas, Kankas, Romakas* and men with horns, *Khashas, Ekasanas, Arkas, Predaras* and so on are mentioned here.

Vana Parva

SECTION—2

By virtue of their wealth of *Yoga*, the *Rudras,* the *Sandhyas, Aadityas, Vaasus* and the twin *Aswins* rule the beings on Earth.

SECTION—3

In days of old all living beings that were created were afflicted with hunger. Then *Savihar*, the sun took compassion upon them. First he went to the northern side and drew up water by his rays and then coming back to southern side the sun stayed over the earth with heat centred in it. While the sun stayed there the moon the Lord of the vegetable world converted the effects of solar heat into clouds and poured down rain that caused plants to spring up. Thus it is the sun drenched by the influence of moon transformed the sprouting of the seeds into vegetables that constituted the food of all creatures on earth Thus the food that supports the lives of creatures is the solar energy and hence the sun is considered as the father of all creatures.

The sun in short is all gods. It illumines the whole world. The sun is the beginning and end of a day of *Brahma.* When the time of universal dissolution comes, the fire *Samvarthaka* born of sun's wrath consumes the three worlds and exists alone and the clouds of various colours that come from the sun's rays accompanied by the elephant *Airavatha* and thunderbolt bring about the deluge and then dividing into 12 parts and becoming 12 different suns, the *Soorya* drinks up the ocean once more with its rays. The sun in all gods though addressed in different names such as *Indra, Prajapathi*, fire and the subtle mind. He is as swift as speed and destroyer of darkness and possessor of yellow steeds. He is the soul of all beings.

SECTION—10

The celestials and *Raakshasas* are able to assume any form at will.

SECTION—20

Bullets from barrels and rockets are mentioned here.

SECTIONS—21 and 22

Weapons like *Pragnastra* and *Sataghnis, Sharangas* the bow from which arrows of snake forms with intense energy and capable of going at a great height, weapons that are in the skies and are invisible with arrows of diverse forms and celestial weapons inspired by *Manthras*, thunderbolt of *Indra, Sudarsana Chakra* the sharp edged like razor, the weapon of fire blazing with irresistible force and energy and penetrating into everything and of great splendour are mentioned here.

SECTION—40

Brahmasira is the fierce celestial weapon. *Paasupata* is the weapon that can be held, hurled and withdrawn and that can destroy the whole Universe. It can be hurled by mind, by eye, by word and by bow.

SECTION—41

The celestials are both embodied and disembodied.

Antardhana weapon is endowed with the energy and power and splendour and capable of sending the foe to sleep.

The gods are capable of going everywhere at will and are endowed with the speed of the mind.

SECTION—42

Indra's chariot with great effulgence can illuminate the firmament. In that car with its rattle, as deep as the roar of mighty masses of clouds contains swords and missiles of terrible forms and maces of frightful description, winged darts of celestial splendour and lightning of the bright effulgence and thunderbolts and propellers furnished with wheels and worked with atmosphere expansion and producing sounds as loud as the roar of great masses of clouds and fierce and with huge bodied *Naagas* with fiery mouths and heaps of white stones. It is drawn by 10,000 horses of golden colour endowed with the speed of the wind, drawn with good speed that the eye could hardly mark its progress; with flag staff, and *Vyjayantha* weapon of blazing effulgence resembling emerald or dark blue lotus and is decked with golden ornaments.

The celestial chariots course through the firmament and there are thousands of chariots of extraordinary beauty. The region has no sun or moon or fire to give light, but blazed in self-light, generated by virtue of ascetic merit. They are seen from the earth in the form of stars, like lamps in the sky. They look so small due to their distance, but they are actually very huge. These are the places of ascetics, *Gandharvas, Rishis, Apsaras* and so on and other virtuous people who performed virtuous deeds during their life time. From earth they are seen as stars.

SECTION—43

Siddhas and *Charanas* reside in *Indra Loka*. In *Indra Loka* there are thousands of celestial chariots, capable of going everywhere at will. From *Indraloka* goes the large and extensive starry way called *Suraveedi*, where the *Sadhyas*, the *Viswas, Marutas, Twin Aswins*, the *Adityas, Vasus, Rudras, Brahmarishis, Raaja Rishis, Gandharvas* and great sages like *Tumvura* and *Naarada* are found.

SECTION—100

Vyjayantha is the weapon of Indra that is made of bones of *Rishi Dadhicha*. It is fiery and powerful and of six sides and capable of destroying even the most powerful enemies.

Twashtri is the celestial weapon maker.

SECTION—139

Mountain *Mandara* is inhabited by *Yakshas*. At this place 80, 000 *Gandharvas* and four times as many *Kimpurushas* and *Yakshas* of various shapes and forms, holding various weapons, attend upon *Manibhadra* the king of *Yakshas*. In these regions their power is very great and in speed they are equal to the wind. These mountains are inaccessible as these gods and *Raakshasas* protect them.

The Mountain *Kailasa* is 6 yojanas in height. It contains a gigantic *jujube* tree. Numerous gods, *Yakshas* and *Rakshasas, Kinnaras, Nagas, Suparnas* and *Gandharvas* pass this way.

SECTION—140

The domain of *Suvahu* located on the *Himalayas* is inhabited by *Kiratas* and *Tanganas, Pulindas* and visited by celestials. This region is full of wonders.

SECTION—141

Mandara is a celestial Mountain.

SECTION—142

Gandhamadana Mountain is inhabited by sages, *Siddhas* and celestials and visited by *Kinnaras* and *Apsaras.*

SECTIONS—143 and 144

On the *Himalayan* mountains are the *Mlecha* people, mines of diverse gems, hillocks with minerals. There the celestials like *Vidyadharas, Kinnaras, Kimpurushas,* and *Gandharvas* are also seen residing.

Kailasa contains many wonders. It has the hermitage of *Nara-Narayana.* The celestial *Jujube* tree is visited by great sages. There are the holy lakes *Vinda* and several other beautiful lakes and also the mountain *Mainaka* of golden summits. This region is extremely difficult to reach. The peaks there are full of trees, creepers with black rocky base and frequented by celestials and are full of minerals, plants with flowers, beasts, birds of various colours and they appear like the up raised arm of the earth adorned with an entire set of ornaments.

SECTION—148

Hanuman tells *Bhima-*

That form of mine no one can behold, since in *Treta Yuga* the state of things was different and they do not exist in *Dwapara Yuga*. In *Kritha Yuga* the states of things was one, in the *Tretha Yuga* another, and in *Dwapara Yuga* still another. Diminution is being witnessed at the passing of each *Yuga*. The ground, planets and rocks, and *Siddhas*, gods, celestial sages conform to time in harmony with the state of things in different *Yugas*. "Therefore do not desire to see my former shape— I am conforming to the tendency of the age. Verily, time is irresistible".

In *Krihta Yuga* the best of *yugas*, eternal religion was present. Everyone had religious perfection and hence there was no need for religious acts. There were neither gods, nor demons, no *Gandharvas*, no *Yakshas*, no *Raakshasas* nor *Naagas*; no buying and selling. There were no *Vedas*, no manual labour. By mere wish of thought all necessaries of life could be obtained. There was no disease, no decay of senses, no malice, no pride, no hypocrisy, no discord, no ill will, cunningness, fear, misery, envy or covetousness. Even supreme *Brahma* was attainable by all. *Naarayan*, the soul of all creation wore white colour. The sole objective of the people was to attain the supreme. There was only one *Manthra* namely *AUM* and there was only one law. All people practised only one religion. In *Treta Yuga* sacrifices were introduced. Virtue decreased by one fourth. *Naarayana* the supreme soul of the universe assumed a red colour. Men practiced truth and devoted themselves to religion and religious rites. People began to device means to attain an object and attained it through acts and gifts but they never deviated from *Dharma* or righteousness. In *Dwapara Yuga* virtue was decreased by half. *Naarayana* wore yellow colour. *Vedas* were divided in to four. Men began to perform many activities. Intellect decreased and only a few adhered to *Dharma*. Disease, lust, anger, and natural calamities and so on began to appear. Afflicted by these people began to perform austerities and penances. People became impious and degenerated. In *Kali Yuga* only one fourth of *Dharma* remains. In this age *Naarayana* wears black colour. Virtue, *Vedas,* sacrifices, religious observances gradually disappear. Diseases, laziness, anger, deformities, natural calamities, anguish, and fear of scarcity become widespread. Thus as the *Yugas* wane, virtue dwindles; creatures degenerate so they undergo deterioration.

SECTION—152

In the vicinity of *Kailaasa* is the *Saugandhika* Lake with celestial golden lotuses, guarded by the *Raakshasas* and frequented by the *Gandharvas Apsaras, Kimpurushas*, and *Kinnaras* and protected by *Kubera.*

SECTIONS—157 and 158

The cliff *Sweta* in the *Himaalayas* is like a mighty mass of clouds and it is abundant in streams and contains a mass of gold and gems.

Gandhamadana is the abode of *Kimpurushas a*nd is frequented by *Siddhas, Charanas, Viudyadharas, and Kinnaras*. There are several plants and trees full of beautiful flowers and fruits, various birds and lakes with aquatic creatures, lakes transparent like crystal with several minerals, waterfalls, beautiful woods, and beasts and snakes. Sages subsisting on air come to this mountain traversing through air. Beyond this is the sporting region of the celestials. To this region mortals cannot go.

Beyond the summit of *Kailasa* is the path of celestial sages.

SECTIONS 159 to 162

On Mount *Sumeru* sits *Brahma*. Next to it is the abode of Lord *Vishnu* to the east of *Meru*. None except *Yatis* have access here. The Sun and the Moon go round *Meru* Mountain every day in opposite direction and so also the other luminaries. Having set, the Sun takes a northerly course. Then again nearing Mount *Meru* the Sun again goes facing east. Similarly, the Moon and the stars go round this Mountain dividing the months into several sections. When the Sun goes towards south it becomes winter for all creatures. Then turning back, the Sun draws up the energy from all creatures. By his rays and the humans become subject to perspiration, fatigue, drowsiness, and laziness. Then the Sun returns through unknown regions and causes shower and there by revive beings and then he resumes his former course dividing time into day and night.

SECTIONS—164, 168 and 170

Various weapons and *Astras* are mentioned here namely, *Sthunakarna*, *Varuna*, *Salava*, *Asmavarsha* weapons, the *Pasupathastra*, the weapons of *Nivita Kavachas* like *Satagni*, and *Visoshana* the celestial dreadful flaming weapon.

SECTION—172

The unearthly city of *Paulamas* and *Kalakanjas* known as *Hiranyapura*, is guarded by *Asuras*. It is an aerial city that goes anywhere at will. It has the effulgence of the Sun or fire. It has trees composed of gems. There are many wonderful and unearthly birds there. It is made up of all sorts of jewels. This city is invisible even for sages, *Yakshas, Gandharvas, Asuras* and *Raakshasas*. Here there is neither grief nor disease.

SECTION—176

Many countries beyond the Himalayas like China, *Takhara, Darada*, *Kulinda* and *Suvahu* are mentioned here.

SECTION—187

Kritha Yuga is 4000 years; *Tretha Yuga* 3000 years; *Dwapara Yuga* 2000 years and *Kali Yuga* 1000 years. After *Kali Yuga, Kritha Yuga* comes again. A cycle of all these four *Yugas* put together comes to 12, 000 years. A full 1000 of such cycle would constitute a day of *Brahma* when the entire universe is withdrawn into its source-- the creator. The disappearance of all things is known as the Universal destruction. Towards the end of *Kali Yuga* men will become addicted to falsehood. People will not follow their *Dharma*. These signs foreshadow the universal destruction. People who govern will become sinful. People will have less span of life, have less strength, energy and power, and will be small made. Animals will increase enormously. Human population will decline. There will be famines. Cows will yield less milk, trees will bear less fruits, people will be burdened with more taxes and they will become deceivers. There will not be proper rains. Men will be full of envy and malice and earth will become full of sins and immorality. He that is virtuous will not live long and they will not be prosperous. Traders will use false weights and measures. Virtue will lose its strength while sin will become very powerful. People will resort to cheating. Even girls of seven or eight years of age will conceive while boys of ten or twelve will beget offspring and in the 16th year decay will start and then more youths will act like the aged. On the other hand all that should be observable in youth may be noticed in old people. Woman will be marked by evil manners and wrong conduct and will not be loyal to their husbands and will forget themselves with menials, slaves and even animals.

At the end of these, drought extending over many years will occur and men and creatures will die by thousands. Then seven blazing suns that appear in the firmament will drink up all waters of the earth that are in rivers and seas and everything in the universe would be reduced to ashes. Then the fire called *Samvartaka* impelled by the winds will appear on the earth that had already been dried up by the seven suns. That fire then will penetrate through the earth by making its appearance. Even in the nether regions also that tremor will strike in the hearts of gods, *Danavas* and *Yakshas*. Thus the fire will destroy everything by consuming the earth and the nether regions. This fire

Samvartaka aided by the terrible wind will consume the universe by extending for hundreds and thousands of *Yojanas*. This fire will consume the universe with all its gods, *Asuras, Gandharvas, Yakshas, snakes, Raakshasas* and so on. Deep masses of clouds will appear on the sky that would look like herds of elephants decked with wreaths of lightning. Some of the clouds will have colour like the blue lotus and some will be like water lilies. Some would resemble the filaments of the lotus flower and some purple, some yellow and some like the crow's egg. Some will be as bright as the petals of the lotus and some will be red in colour. Some resemble palatial cities in shape and some the heads of elephants. Some will be like lizards; some like crocodiles and sharks. The clouds will look terrible with lightning and will roar frightfully. The masses of vapour charged with rain will soon cover all the regions, the earth, her forests, mines and so on. Then it will flood the entire surface of the earth. The rain will continue for twelve years. Then the oceans will submerge the continents and the mountains and the earth will sink under the increasing flood. Then moved on a sudden by the impetus of the wind, the clouds will wander along the entire expanse of the firmament and would disappear from the view. Then the Super Soul, the Lord, the first cause of everything, with his abode in the lotus will drink the terrible wind and will go to sleep. Thus when the universe becomes one dead expanse of water, when all mobile and immobile creatures have been destroyed, when there are no more gods or *Asuras, Gandharvas or Raakshasas* or men, beasts or trees and when the firmament itself ceases to exist then the universal soul will take within itself all that are in the universe.

SECTION—189

The features of *Kaliyuga* are explained here.

SECTION—210

The five elements, Earth, Water, Fire, Air and Sky have properties inter-lapping each other. The earth has all the five the properties of sound, touch, forms, odour and taste; Water has four properties of sound, touch, form and taste; Fire has three properties of sound, touch and form; Air has two properties namely sound and touch and Sky has one property namely sound. These 15 properties inherent in the five elements exist in all substances of which this universe is composed of. They are not opposed to each other. They exist in proper combination. The universe arises and perishes by the play of time in due order. The entire mobile and immobile world is composed of the five elementary substances. Whatever is perceptible by the senses is called *Vyaktha* or comprehensible and whatever is beyond the reach of the senses and can only be perceived by imagination or intuition is known to be *Avyaktha* or incomprehensible.

SECTIONS—230 and 243

Some of the celestial weapons like *Satagnis, Prasas and Parighas, Kshurapras, Bhallas*, and weapons made of bones and steel, *Sthunakarna, Indrajala, Saura, Agneya, Saumya, Sabda Veda*, are mentioned here.

SECTION—259

The region of heaven tower high and has excellent paths and are ranged by celestial chariots. This place is obtainable only through virtuous acts and piety. A number of beautiful, shining, resplendent worlds that bestow all objects of desire are owned by celestial beings like gods, *Sadhyas, Vaiswas*, great sages, *Yamas, Dharmas, Gandharvas* and *Apsaras*. There, the golden Mountain *Meru* extends over a space of thirty three thousand *Yojanas*. There are very many sacred celestial gardens along with the supreme celestial garden *Nandana*. There is no hunger, thirst, laziness, or fear there. In short there is nothing that is disgusting or inauspicious. All odours are delightful and the breeze is delightful to touch. All sounds are captivating to the ear and heart. The inhabitants there look resplendent and happy due to their virtue. There is no sweat, no smell, no dust or no urine there. Their excellent garlands with the divine fragrance never fade. They possess beautiful chariots. There is no grief, misery, fatigue or envy, ignorance or malice there. Higher above are regions that are endowed with higher celestial virtues where the meritorious *Rishis* dwell. The beings there are called *Ribhus*. These regions are supremely blessed and are adored even by the deities. These regions shine by their own light and bestow every object of desire. The *Rishis* there have no passion, do not possess worldly wealth and are free from guile. They have celestial forms and cannot be perceived by the senses. These eternal gods of the celestials do not desire happiness for the sake of happiness, nor do they change with each *Kalpa*. For them there is no ecstasy, joy or happiness or misery, anger or aversion. They are the embodiments of crowning emancipation that is hard to achieve. The number of such deities is 33. However the inhabitants here after the expiry of the fruits of their past good deeds are subjected to fall and take birth among men according to their *Karma*. The region that is free from any fall, which is above the abode of *Brahma*, the supreme seat of Lord *Naarayana* is pure, eternal, and luminous. Only extremely meritorious and virtuous can reach this region.

Section—270

Creation from the lotus of Lord *Naarayana* is described here.

Virata Parva

Indra's chariot has gems of every kind and is capable of going anywhere at the will of the rider. Its roof is upheld by a hundred thousand pillars of gold with a central one made entirely of jewels and gems.

Udyoga Parva

SECTION—51

Many types of weapons are mentioned here.

SECTION—98

In the nether regions is the Lord of the waters- *Varuna*. Here *Nagas* dwell. It is delightful and full of riches. The abode of *Varuna* is made entirely of gold and is full of the wine called *Varuni* with which the gods attained their godhood. The *Daityas* have various kinds of weapons that are blazing. These weapons when hurled at the foe return to the hand that hurled them. These weapons can be used only by the one possessing considerable mental energy. The blazing fire of flames and the lustrous disc of Lord *Vishnu* and the bow that destroys the world having the strength of 100, 000 bows and endowed with great energy are found in *Varuna*'s lake.

SECTION—99

In the centre of the world of *Nagas* is *Patala* that is worshipped by *Daityas* and *Danavas*. Here the fire known as *Asura* fire blazes forth continuously. Because all watery forms such as moon and others shower their water on this region it is called *Patala*. The waxing and waning of the moon are seen from here. Various kinds of aquatic animals dwell here. Many creatures die here during day time due to the heat of the sun but revive again in the night with the rays of the moon. Here lies an egg in these waters that blazes with beauty. Since the commencement of creation it has been here. It neither moves nor bursts. When the end of the universe comes, mighty fire bursts from within it that spreads and consumes all the three worlds with all the mobile and immobile objects and beings.

SECTION—100

In *Pataala* is the city of *Hiranyapura* that possesses a hundred different kinds of illusion. The city here was built by the *Danava* architect *Maya*. Here *Daanavas* and *Asuras* called *Kalakhanjas* endowed with terrible teeth and impetus, speed and power of the wind and possessing great energy and power of illusion and *Rakshasas* called *Yatudhanas* and *Nivatakavachas* who are invincible in battle dwell. The residences of the *Nivatakavachas* are made of silver and gold and are well adored with decorations. All mansions are decked with precious gems, corals, and marbles or excellent wood. They all possess the radiance of the Sun or blazing fire and have great architectural beauty. They use costly beds, costly utensils with precious stones and are exceedingly beautiful. There are also beautiful retreats for recreation and sports. The hills there look like clouds or fountains of water. The trees move on their own and yield all fruits and flowers that one may ask.

SECTION—102

Rasaatala in the nether region is the seventh stratum below the earth. Here the celestial cow *Surabhi* that is born of *Amritha*, the nectar, resides. She, the mother of all kine yields milk that is the essence of all the best things on Earth. A single jet of her milk falling on the Earth created the 'Milky Ocean'. Four kines born of her support the four quarters of the Earth. The Eastern quarter is supported by *Sumpa*; the Western quarter ruled by *Varuna* is *Subhadra*; the southern quarter is supported by *Hansika* and the northern quarter consisting of the region of virtue and of *Kubera* is supported by the cow *Sarva Kamadirgha*. The inhabitants of *Rasaatala* consider *Rasaatala* as the happiest of all places.

SECTION—103

In the nether region, the city of *Bhogavathi* resembles the celestial city of *Amaraavathi* and is ruled by *Vaasuki*- the king of *Nagas*. His body like a white mountain supports the Earth. He has a 1000 heads and he is decked in celestial ornaments. His tongue blazes like flames of fire and he is endowed with great strength. Here innumerable *Nagas* possessing different forms reside. They are decked with ornaments of different varieties that bear the signs of gems, *Swasthika* circles and drinking vessels. They are fierce and possess great strength. Some have 1000 heads, some 500 heads. Some of them have three faces, some two and some five and some have seven faces. They possess huge bodies resembling mountains. They are numerous in number.

SECTIONS—108 to 111

The eastern, the southern, western and the northern regions of the universe are described here. The eastern or the *Poorva* is said to be the gate of the three worlds. All goods things start from here. In the southern or *Dakshina* the *Pitris* and that group of celestials who subsist on smoke alone reside and those known as *Viswadevas*. This is called the second door of *Yama*. In this region the fruit of all *Karmas* of the dead are reaped. Here all the forms come and are then dissociated into their constituent elements. Here is the city called *Bhogavathi* that is ruled by *Vasuki*, by *Takshaka* and *Airavata*. From the western quarter night and sleep spread themselves. From here the roots of *Himavat* stretch towards the eternal *Mandara* Mountain. From this region the Sun's course begins to deviate from the straight path and it is in this direction that all the luminous bodies, the constellations enter the solar sphere. Having moved for 28 nights with the Sun, they come out of the Sun's course to move in accompaniment with the Moon. All the rivers have their source here. Here in this abode of *Varuna* are the waters of the three worlds. In this is the abode of *Ananta*, the prince of snakes and that of Lord *Vishnu*. The northern quarter is considered superior to all quarters. The celestial stream *Mandakini* and the

Mountain *Mandara* are seen here. From here the *Saptha Rishi* and *Swathi* constellations can be seen.

Bhishma Parva

SECTION—5

The elements are Space, Air, Fire, Water, and Earth. Their respective attributes are sound, touch, vision, taste and scent. Every one of these elements possesses in addition to what is its own, the attributes of that or those coming before it. The earth therefore possesses the attributes of all the other four elements besides its own. Water has four attributes except smell. Fire has three attributes sound, touch and vision. Air has the attributes of sound and touch and Space has only sound. These five attributes exist in the five principal elements depending upon which all creatures exist in the Universe. They exist separately and independently when there is homogeneity in the Universe. When they exist with one another then creatures are created furnished with bodies. The elements are destroyed in the order of the one succeeding, merging in to the one that precedes it and they spring in to existence one arising from the one before it. All of these are immeasurable and all creatures have these five elements.

The island *Sudarsana* that has the esoteric meaning, the mind, is circular and of the form of a wheel. It is covered with rivers, with mountains and looks like masses of clouds and is with cities and many delightful provinces. It is also full of trees with flowers and fruits and with crops of different kinds and other wealth. It is surrounded on all sides with the Salt Ocean. This island is seen in the lunar disc. Two of its parts seem to be a Peepul tree, while two others look like a large hare. It is surrounded by assemblage of all kinds of deciduous plants. Besides these portions the rest is all water.

SECTION—6

Six mountains stretch from East to West that extends from the eastern to the western Ocean. These are *Himavat, Hemakuta, Nishada, Nila, Sweta* and *Shringavat*. Here *Siddhas* and *Charanas* reside. The space between each of these measures a 1000 *Yojanas* and there many kingdoms called *Varshas* are seen. The land where we live is *Bharata*. To its north is the *Varsha* called *Himavat*. The land beyond *Hemakuta* is *Harivarsha*. South of the *Neela* range and on the north of the *Nishada* is *Malyavat* Mountain that stretches from East to West. Beyond *Malyavat*, towards north is the mountain called *Gaandhamadana*. Between *Malyavat* and *Gaandhamadana* is a globular mountain called *Meru* of gold. It is like fire without smoke. It is 84, 000 *Yojanas* high and has a depth of 84, 000 *Yojanas*. It bears the worlds above, below and transversely. By the side of *Meru* there are four islands namely, *Bhadraswa, Ketumala, Jambudvipa* or *Bharatha* and *Uttara Kuru* that is the abode of those who achieve the merit of righteousness. The Sun, Moon with the attendant constellations and the wind god circumambulate *Meru*. This Mountain has celestial fruits and flowers and have mansions made of gold. Here the *Gandharvas*, the *Asuras* and *Raakshasas*, and *Apsaras* always sport. This region is visited by *Brahma, Rudra, Indra, Tumvru, Naarada* and *Viswavasu* and high souled *Rishis* and the *Usanus* who are the poets and their disciples the *Daityas*. *Kubera* enjoys one fourth of the wealth here. On the northern side of *Meru* is an excellent fort called *Karnikaras* that has a range of hills. Here Lord *Shiva* accompanied by His consort Goddess *Uma* sport. From the summit of this mountain *Ganga* that is known as *Bhageerathi* flows like a stream of milk on the lake of *Chandramas* that is formed by *Ganga* herself. On the western side of *Meru* is *Ketumali*. Here is *Jambu khanda*. Both are great regions for human beings. Here humans live for 10, 000 years. The men have golden complexion and women are like *Apsaras*. There is no sickness or sorrow here. Her men possess the effulgence melted gold. In *Gaandhamadana* the span of human life is 11,000 years. Men are very cheerful and have great energy and strength. Women are like lotus in complexion and very beautiful. Beyond *Nila* Mountain is *Sweta* and beyond *Sweta* is *Hiranyaka Varsha*. Beyond *Hiranyaka* is the *Varsha* called *Airavata* with provinces. This is the *Varsha* in the extreme north and *Bharatha* Varsha is in the extreme South. These two are in the form of a bow. The five *Varshas* namely *Swetha, Hiranyaka, Elavritha, Harivarsha* and *Himavat Varshas* are in the middle, of which *Elavritha* is in the middle of all. The huge Mountains of *Hemakuta* are called *Kailaasa*. Immediately to the north of *Kailaasa* and near the Mountain of *Mainaka* there is a huge and beautiful Mountain called *Manimaya* endowed with golden summits. Besides this Mountain there is a large, beautiful, crystal clear and delightful lake, the *Vindusaras* with golden sands on its beach. Here Lord *Shiva* with His attendants is adored. Here the celestial *Ganga* flows from the region of *Brahman* in three currents and then divides into seven streams and become *Vaswokasara, Nalini, Saraswathi, Jamvunadi, Seetha, Ganga and Sindhu. Raakshasas* reside on *Himavat, Guhyakas* on *Himakuta*, serpents and *Naagas* on *Nishaadha*, and ascetics on *Gokarna. Swetha Mountain* is the abode of the celestials and *Asuras*; *Gandharvas* reside on *Nishadas* and *Rishis* on *Nila*. The celestials also reside on the mountains of *Srinavat*. These are the seven *Varshas* of the world. In the extreme north and south of the regions, the two *Varshas* have two islands, *Nagadveepa* and *Kashyadweepa* like the two ears of a hare. The beautiful *Malaya* has rocks like plates of copper that form another part of *Jambudveepa* that resembles the shape of a hare.

SECTION—7

On the south of *Neela* Mountain and the northern side of *Meru* are the sacred northern *Kurus*- the residence of *Siddhas*. The trees here bear sweet fruits and are always covered with fruits and flowers. All flowers are fragrant and the fruits are very tasty. Some of these trees yield fruits according to the will of the plucker. There are also trees called milk- yielding trees. These always yield milk and six different kinds of food that has the taste of nectar or *Amritha*. These trees also yield clothes and in their fruits there are ornaments. The place has golden sands. A portion of this region is extremely delightful and possesses the radiance of ruby or diamond or other gems. The tanks have crystal clear water. All beings are extremely handsome here. They are free from illness and are cheerful. They live nearly 1000 years to 10, 000 years. This is the region of northern *Kurus*. In the Eastern side of *Meru* is *Bhadraswa* the foremost of all regions here. Here there is a large forest namely *Bhadra Salas* and a huge tree called *Kalamra* that is always full of flowers and fruits. It is one *Yojana* in height and is adored by *Siddhas* and the *Charanas*. The men here are of white complexion, have great energy and strength. Women are like lilies in complexion and are very beautiful. They are good singers and dancers and they have the radiance of the Moon and their bodies are as cool as the rays of the Moon. Their longevity is 10, 000 years. They drink the juice of

Kalma tree and remain youthful always. On the south of *Neela* and north of *Nishadha* the huge *Jamvu* tree that is eternal can be seen. This is adored by the *Siddhas* and *Caranas* and this tree is supposed to fulfil all wishes. After this tree this region is known as *Jambudveepa*. The *Jambu* tree is 1100 *Yojanas* in height. The circumference of a fruit of that tree is 2500 cubic measure. The fruits burst when they become ripe and fall down on earth making a loud noise and then a silvery juice come out of them. It flows like a river around Mount *Meru* and then comes to the region northern *Kurus*. The juice of the fruit is conducive to peace of mind and no thirst is felt after drinking it. Here a species of gold called *Jamvunad*a used for celestial ornaments is produced. The men here possess complexion of the morning sun.

On the summit of *Malyava*t Mountain is the fire known as Samvarthaka that blazes at the end of universal destruction. Towards the east of *Malyavat* summit there are very many small Mountains. *Malyavat* Mountain measures 11,000 *Yojanas*. All men here have a golden complexion and they all go through severest of ascetic austerities. They number around 60, 000. To protect the beings they advance to the sun and get heated with the sun's rays for 60, 000 years and then they enter the lunar disc.

SECTION—8

On the south of *Swetha* and North of *Nishaada* is the *Romanaka Varsha*. Men here have white complexion and have handsome features. They have no enemies and are ever cheerful. They live for 11, 500 years. On the south of *Nishaada* is the *Hiranmaya Varsha* where the river *Hiranwathi* flows. This is the place where *Garuda*, the vehicle of Lord Vishnu reside. The people here are followers of *Yakshas* and are wealthy, handsome, cheerful and strong. They live for 12, 500 years.

The Mountains of *Shringavat* have three beautiful summits. One of these is made of gems and jewels, another with gems and adorned with palatial mansions. On the north of *Shringavat* and up to the margin of the sea is the *Airavat Varsha*. This *Varsha* is superior to all because it has a mountain of jewels. The sun does not give heat here. Men have no decay here. The only source of light here is the Moon and the stars. The people here possess the radiance and complexion of lotus and are endowed with eyes resembling lotus petals. They have wink-less eyes and agreeable scent emanate from their bodies. They go without food and have controlled senses. They commit no sin. They live for 13,000 years.

On the north of Milky Ocean is the dwelling of Lord *Hari*. His chariot made of gold, has eight wheels with numerous supernatural creatures on it and has the speed of the mind. It blazes like fire and has great strength. It is adorned with *Jambunaada* gold.

SECTION—9

Bharatha Varsha contains seven Mountains namely, *Mahendra, Malaya, Sahya, Suktimat, Rakshavat, Vindhya* and *Paripatra*. Besides these there are thousands of Mountains that are unknown, that are hard, huge and with excellent valleys. Many other smaller Mountains here are inhabited by tribes. It has many sacred rivers like *Ganga, Sindhu* and so on and there are innumerable big and small rivers and provinces here in all the four directions.

SECTION—10

There are four *Yugas, Krihta Yuga, Tretha Yuga, Dwapara Yuga* and *Kali Yuga*. In *Kritha Yuga* people live for 4000 years; In *Tretha Yuga* for 3000 years, in *Dwapara Yuga* for 2000 years and in *Kali Yuga* there is no fixed time period for human life. They die even while in womb. In *Kritha Yuga* men begot children by hundreds and thousands of great strength, power, wisdom and strength and they possessed wealth and handsome features and were great sages. They were virtuous and honest. In *Tretha Yuga Kshatriyas* had long life and were skilled in warfare. In *Dwapara Yuga* all the four orders of men possessed great energy and desired to conquer each other. In *Kali Yuga* people have little energy; they are highly wrathful, covetous, and untruthful with pride, jealousy, anger, deceit, malice and so on.

SECTION—11

The earth possesses many islands. There are many kingdoms here that are adorned with gems, corals, and the mountains here have different varieties of metals. It is inhabited by innumerable *Siddhas* and *Charanas*. The *Jamvudveepa* has *Jamvu* Mountain extending 14,

600 *Yojanas*. The salt ocean is located here and it is twice the area of the island of *Jambudveepa*.

SECTION—12

The islands in the north have the ocean of clarified butter or curd. Next is the ocean of wine and then there is the ocean of water. Each island is double the area of the one that is before it as one proceeds towards north and the islands are surrounded by the oceans.

The planet *Swarbhanu* is globular in shape. It is 12, 000 *Yojanas* in diameter and its circumference is 42, 000 *Yojanas*.

The diameter of the Moon is 11,000 *Yojanas* and its circumference is 38,900 *Yojanas*.

The diameter of the Sun is 10,000 *Yojanas* and its circumference is 35, 800 *Yojanas*.

The planet *Rahu* because of its greater bulk envelops both the Sun and Moon in due time during eclipses.

SECTION—15

The celestial powers described here includes excellent celestial apprehension, sight beyond the range of visual sense and hearing from great distance, knowledge of other people's hearts and of past and future, knowledge of origin of all persons beyond the ordinances, the power of travelling through the skies and the non-effectiveness of weapons on the celestials during wars.

SECTION—26

Here Lord *Krishna* says that before birth all beings were unmanifest. Only between birth and death, in the interval, they are manifest and then again when death comes they become unmanifest. But none understands it truly. But the embodied soul in each one's body is ever indestructible.

SECTION—31

Lord *Krishna* says the Earth, Water, Fire, Air, Space, Mind, Understanding and Consciousness —this eightfold nature is His (that of the Supreme soul's) lower nature. Different from these there is a higher form of His nature by which the Universe is held and by which all beings are created.

SECTION—32

Lord *Krishna* says that those who know a day of *Brahma* to end after a thousand of *Yugas* and a night of His are persons who know the day and night. On the advent of *Brahma*'s day everything that is manifest springs forth from the unmanifest and when the night comes in to that same unmanifest all things disappear. Those assemblages of beings, springing forth again and again dissolves on the advent of night (*Pralaya* or destruction of the Universe) and appears again when the day (when the creative activity begins) comes. There is however another entity that is the unmanifest and eternal, which is not destroyed when all the entities are destroyed. This is the highest.

SECTION—33

Lord *Krishna* says that the entire universe is pervaded by the unmanifest. All entities are in that but the unmanifest is not in them. The unmanifest supports all entities and produces them. It is like the great atmosphere occupying the entire space. All entities attain the nature of the unmanifest at the close of the *Kalpa*. In the beginning of the *Kalpa* they are created again.

SECTION —38

Lord *Krishna* says, He, the supreme soul places the living gem in the womb of Lord *Brahma* and then all creatures are born.

Santhi Parva

SECTION—166

In ancient times the Universe was one vast expanse of water, motionless and skyless and without this earth. Everything was enveloped in darkness. There was utter silence everywhere that was immeasurable. When the appropriate time came the grandsire created the wind, fire, sun, sky, heavens, nether regions, earth, directions, the firmament with the Moon and stars, constellations, planets, the year, the seasons, months, the two fortnights and smaller divisions of time. Then creation proceeded further.

SECTION—183

In very ancient times called *Brahma Kalpa*, the high souled *Rishis* began to ponder over the creation of the Universe. They refrained from speech, remained immovable, and engaged in ascetic contemplation. They gave up all food and subsisted upon air alone. In this manner they all remained for a period of 1000 celestial years. At the end of the period, certain sacred words they heard from the firmament and the celestial voice said, "Formerly there was only infinite space, perfectly motionless and immovable. It seemed to be asleep without the Sun, the Moon, stars and wind. Then water sprang up into existence like something darker within darkness. Then from the pressure of water arose wind. As an empty vessel without a hole appears first to be soundless, but when filled with water air appears and makes a great voice, similarly, the infinite Space was filled with Water and the Wind arose with great noise, penetrating through the water. That wind thus generated by the pressure of water in the ocean of water, still moves. Later due to the friction of water and wind fire of great might and blazing energy sprang into existence with flames directed upwards. That fire removed the darkness that had covered everywhere. Assisted by wind the fire drew space and water together. And combining with wind, fire got solidified. While falling from the sky the liquid portion of fire solidified again and became earth.

SECTION—184

All creation that belongs to the infinite receives the appellation of the great five elements. Activity is Wind. Sound is Space. Heat is Fire. The liquid juice in it is Water. The solidified matter, flesh and bones are Earth. The bodies of all living creatures are thus made up of the five primeval elements. The ear partakes the properties of space, the nose, that of earth, the tongue that of water, touch that of wind and the eye that of fire or light. Though possessed of density even the trees have space within them because flowers and fruits appear in them. Due to the heat within them, the leaf, the bark, fruit and flower droop and they also sicken and dry up. It shows that they have the perception of touch. Through sound of wind and fire and thunder the fruits and flowers drop down. Sound is perceived through ear. So trees have ears and can hear. A creeper unlike a blind thing finds its way and winds up around a tree and goes about all its sides. It shows that trees have vision. Trees also recover vigour and bring forth flowers due to odours, good as well as bad. The trees have scent. They drink water by their roots. They also catch different kinds of diseases. From this it is clear that trees have the perception of taste. Just as water is sucked through the lotus stalk, similarly trees also with the aid of wind drink water through their roots. They are also susceptible to pleasure and pain and grow. So trees also have life. They are not inanimate. Fire and wind cause the water that is sucked up to be digested. According to the quantity of water drawn, the tree grows and becomes humid. Similarly in the bodies of all mobile things also the five elements are seen. However, in each the proportions are different. Because of the presence of these five elements the mobile objects are able to move their bodies. The skin, flesh, bones, marrows and the arteries and veins that are in the body are made up of earth. Energy, wrath, eyes, internal heat, and the heat that digests the food, these constitute the fire in the body of all creatures. The ears, nostrils, mouth, heart and stomach all these constitute the elements of space. Phlegm, bile, sweat, fat, and blood are the water in the mobile bodies. Through the first kind of Prana known as breath all living creatures move; through the second *Prana*, the Vyana there is strength for action; the third, the Apana moves downwards, the fourth Samana resides within the heart and through the fifth kind of Prana namely, Udana one is able to speak due to its piercing through the lungs, the throat and mouth. These winds or Pranas enable the creatures to live and move. Through the earth element the creatures are able to realise the properties of smell and scent. From the water element one perceives taste. From the fire element, represented by the eyes, one perceives forms and from the wind element he gets the perception of touch. Scent, touch, taste, vision, and sound are the general properties of every mobile and immobile object.

SECTION—187

All creatures that seem to die actually do not perish but only change form. The living being does not perish with his physical body. Upon leaving the body the creatures live in space and are not seen because they are subtle.

The physical body is made up of the five elements. The soul that is inside is the one that perceives smell, taste, sound, touch and form and other external properties. That soul is the witness of the mind, pervading the entire body and resides in the body that is composed of the five elements.

SECTIONS—188, 194 and232

The process of creation of the beings is explained here.

SECTION—231

Measurement of time, the days and nights, fortnights, seasons, the life span of humans during different *Yugas,* the period of each *Yuga*, the nature of humans in each *Yuga* and the cyclical nature of the universe are all explained in this section.

SECTION—233

The process of universal dissolution is explained here.

SECTIONS—312

This section explains the process of creation of the super soul along with *Prakruthi.*

SECTIONS 313 and 343

The process of destruction of the Universe is explained here.

Aswamedha Parva

SECTION—40

From the unmanifest first sprang *Mahat*, the great soul endowed with great intelligence and that is the source of all qualities. This is said to be the first creation. This great soul is signified by words like intelligence, *Vishnu, Jishnu, Sambhu*, understanding, means of acquiring knowledge, means of perception, fame, courage, and memory. It has hands and feet and ears on all sides. It pervades everything in the Universe and is stationed in the hearts of all.

SECTION— 41

That *Mahat* that was produced first is called egoism. When it sprang up as 'I', it came to be called as the second creation.

SECTION—42

From egoism, the five great elements namely, Earth, Air, Ether, Water and light were born. When at the close of destruction of these elements the annihilation of the Universe takes place. Every existent object gets dissolved into that from which it sprang. The dissolution takes place in an order that is the reverse of that in which creation took place.

4

Cosmos in Puranas

Puranas

Puranas are friendly treatises that contain the essence of *Vedas*. As Sri *Aurobindo* put it the *Puranas* are the extension of *Vedas*. Hence they are known as the fifth *Veda*. These were written during different *Yugas*, when the need for highlighting right conduct became highly essential as people were falling from righteousness to unrighteousness with the passage of time with every succeeding *Yugas*. It is said that several *Puranas* were composed approximately between 100AD–1000AD. They were written to impress the teachings of the *Vedas* upon common men who cannot grasp the wisdom contained in the *Vedas* and also to highlight *Bhakthi Marg* or the path of *Bhakthi* or devotion that is the easiest path for peace and happiness on earth for one and all. The *Puranas* give a detailed account of the process of creation, the division of time in to *Kalpas, Manvantharas, Yugas*, the gods and sages in each *Kalpa*, the geography of earth as well as the entire universe, and astronomy besides explaining the several incarnations and names of gods, and how the Gods rescues the devotees in times of need, the metaphysics of religious worship, stories of gods, goddesses, sages, kings, demons and ordinary men, historical events , the code of conduct in life, rituals, places of pilgrimage, *Thirthas*, future predictions, spiritual instructions, hymns, and the struggle between good and evil and how god triumphs over evil ultimately and so on.

It is believed that there were many *Puranas* but many are not available due to the ravages of time. It is believed that there are a total number of 64 *Puranas* now. There are 18 major or *Maha Puranas* and 18 primary *Upa* or minor *Puranas* and the rest secondary *Puranas*. The

Maha Puraanas contain approximately 400,000 *Slokas*. They are four times the size of *Maha Bharatha*. In these six are *Satvik* or *Vaishnava Puraanas* that highlight the glory of Lord *Vishnu*, six of them are *Rajasic* and highlight the glory of Lord *Brahma* and the remaining six *Puranas* are *Taamasic* that glorify Lord *Shiva*.

According to *Matsya Purana* and *Bhaagavatha Purana* the *Maha Puranas* have a total of 4 lakh *Slokas* altogether. The number of verses in each *Maha Purana* is given in *Matsya Purana, Bhagavatha Purana and Skanda Purana*. The *Matsya Purana* says that the *Brahma Purana* was originally recited by Lord *Brahma* to sage *Marichi,* and it has 13,000 *Slokas* (according to *Srimad Bhagavatha Purana* and *Skanda Puranas* the number is 10, 000), the *Padma Purana* has 55,000 *Slokas*. *Vishnu Purana* was originally recited by Sage *Parasara* and has 23,000 *Slokas*, *Vayu Purana* was first recited by Wind God *Vayu* and has 24,000 *Slokas*, *Srimad Bhagavatha Purana* contains 18,000 *Slokas*, *Narada Purana* was first recited by sage *Narada* and has 25,000 *Slokas*, *Markandeya Purana* has 9000 *Slokas*, *Agni Purana* that was first recited by the fire God *Agni to* sage *Vasishta* has 16,000 *Slokas* (according to *Srimad Bhagavatha Purana* the number of *slokas* is 15,400), *Bhavishya Purana* recited originally by *Brahma* has 14, 500 *Slokas*, *Brahma Vaivartha Purana* that was first recited by *Savarni Manu* to sage *Narada* contains 18,000 *Slokas*, *Linga Purana* that was recited by Lord *Brahma* originally contains 11,000 *Slokas*, *Varaha Purana* that was recited in the beginning by Lord *Vishnu* to earth or *Prithvi* has 24,000 *Slokas*, *Skanda Purana* that was composed by Lord *Skanda* contains 81,000 *Slokas*, *Vaamana Purana* that was recited by *Brahma* originally has 10,000 *Slokas*, *Kurma Purana* that was originally recited by Lord *Vishnu* in His form as turtle contains 18,000 *Slokas,* the *Matsya Purana* that Lord *Vishnu* recited first as a form of a fish or *Matsya* to King *Manu* contains14,000 *Slokas, Garuda Purana* that Sri *Krishna* recited first has 18,000 *Slokas* (according to *Srimad Bhagavatham*, the number of verses here is 19, 000) and the *Brahmanda Purana* that Lord *Brahma* recited first contains 12, 200 *Slokas*. (This list includes *Vayu Purana* but excludes *Shiva Purana*) The *Bhagavatha Purana* includes *Shiva Purana* in *Maha Puranas* and according to this Purana there are 24,000 verses in *Shiva Purana*

It is said that *Maha Puranas* deal with five features mainly. As per *Matsya Purana* the five characteristic features of a *Maha Purana* are, *Sarga,* that is, the process of creation, *Prathi Sarga*, that is the periodical process of destruction and then a new creation, *Manvanthara*, that is the various eras, *Vamsa*, that is the histories of the solar and lunar dynasties and *Vamsanucharita*, that is, the royal lineage. According to *Vamana Purana* the ten features that are found in all *Puranas* are, Sarg, dealing with description of the Universe or *Jagat*, *Visarg*, the explanation as to how a living thing transforms itself from one species to another, *Sthan*, *Poshan*, *Uti, Vrithi*, all dealing with the description of various means employed by man for his survival, *Raksha*, the various incarnations of Lord *Vishnu* for the protection of mankind, *Manvanthara*, the description of long-term time, *Vansh*, the description of the lineage of all kings including that of Lord *Brahma*, and *Upashraya*, that is, enlightening the real meaning of *Brahm*a. According to *Brahma Vaivartha Purana* the ten features of a *Purana* are that they explain about creation, preservation, *Pralaya* or destruction, *Karma*, *Kaama* or lust, the 14 *Manus,* the rulers of the earth and their dynasties, salvation, virtues of Lord *Naarayana*, and glories of Gods. *Vaamana Purana* also says that there are *Puranas* with the features of *Sarga* or creation, *Prathi Sarga* or periodical process of destruction, *Vamsa,* the description of solar and lunar dynasties and their kings, and the description of the 14 *Manus*.

It is said in *Matsya Purana* that *Vyasa* composed *Puranas* after composing *Maha Bharatha*. It is said that *Veda Vyasa* wrote the *Purana Samhitha* originally and he then taught this to his disciple *Roma Harshana* or *Loma Harshana*. From him the *Puranas* passed on orally for a long time to the sages of successive periods of time and in the process the sages added their own compositions to the already available *Puranas* there by increasing the number and volumes of the *Puranas*. Therefore the date of composition of the *Puranas* cannot be ascertained with precision as they were all composed at different periods of time. In the view of some scholars, the final form of the *Puranas* is believed to have come between 300 AD and 1000 AD. But it is quite possible that in their original form they were composed hundreds of years earlier.

Puranas explain creation of Universe, the periodical process of creation and destruction and recreation along with the histories of the Solar dynasty, Lunar dynasty and royal genealogies, the geography of earth and the regions above and below the earth, about time, duration of *Yugas,* and nature of human beings in different *Yugas*, astronomy and so on. *Puranas* describe numerous worlds, planets and planes of existence or *Lokas*. They also mention the seven levels of nether regions. *Puranas* also state that life exists in other Planets and that there are varieties of living beings in other Planets. (As per modern astronomers there is no life on any other planet except earth). The *Puranas* state that that there are at least 40, 0000 human like beings living on various planets. In the *Puranas* planet Venus is described with lovely gardens, trees, flowers, fruits, birds and so on. The Moon also is considered to be having elevated inhabitants who are like demi gods. *Bhu Mandala* probably refers to the planetary orbits of our Solar system. *Bhu Mandala* therefore may mean the 'circle of the Sun' that refers to all the planets along the plane of the solar system that are on the same orbital plane. This has been stated by Dr Richard L Thompson, the Great scholar and writer of Hindu Cosmology and Astronomy, in his book on 'mysteries of the sacred universe'. Perhaps there is no life on the surface of the planets but may be life exists in the interior of the planets that could not be detected by the astronomers.

Universe in *Puranas*

Vishnu Purana

This *Purana* tells about the creation of the Universe, the four *Yugas*, beings like demons, *Yakshas, Gandharvas*, sheep, horses and so on, the geography of Earth and the under worlds, The world of Sun, Moon, Stars, the nine planets or *Nava Grahas*, the *Saptha Rishis* or the seven sages, the 14 regions of the Universe, *Manvantharas* and the cyclical process of creation and dissolution of the Universe and the three types of annihilation of the universe and so on.

According to *Vishnu Purana* before creation the Universe was full of water. In that water a huge egg that was like a water bubble emerged. The egg gradually became bigger and bigger in size. That egg, the *Brahmaanda* contained all mountains, land, oceans, seas, gods, demons, humans and stars. The egg was surrounded by the elements of Water, Fire, Wind and Sky. Inside that egg Lord *Naarayana,* meaning the one who rests on water (*Nara* means water and *Ayana* means resting place) that is the Conscious energy, took the form of *Brahma* and started creating the Universe. When the Universe is to be destroyed finally, (*Pralaya*) Lord *Naarayana* takes the form of Lord *Maheshwara (Shiva)* and performs the act of destruction.

About the factor 'Time' it is told that the long period of time is divided into four *Yugas* namely, *Kritha* or *Sathya Yuga* or Golden age or era consisting of 4000 years, *Treta Yuga* or the Silver era consisting of 3000 years, *Dwapara Yuga* or Bronze age consisting of 2000 years and *Kali Yuga* or the Iron era consisting of 1000 years. All these put together comes to 10, 000 divine years. When all the eras pass 1000 times each then it is one day of *Brahma,* the creator that is roughly 10 million years. It is said that *Kaliyuga* will last for three lakh and sixty thousand years. It is estimated that at the end of each day of *Brahma* (a *Kalpa*) all the sages, Gods, and kings are destroyed in the deluge or *Pralaya* and recreated again after one night of sleep of *Brahma* that lasts for another 10 million years. The deluge or *Pralaya* or the process of destruction marks the commencement for a new cycle. At the time of Pralaya the world gets burnt. There are three types of *Pralayas.* The first type is called *Brahma* or *Naimitthika Pralaya.* It takes place after each *Kalpa,* that is, one day of *Brahma* that is after 14 *Manus.* Before this *Pralaya* the earth would become weak and there will not be rain for 100 years. Then Lord *Vishnu* would adopt Lord Rudra's form and would drink all waters of the rivers, the oceans, the seas and the mountains. The seven rays of the Sun would manifest themselves as seven different Suns. These Suns would burn up all the three worlds and all the three worlds namely, the *Bhuloka, Bhuvarloka*, and *Svarloka* would be destroyed. There will be dark and thick clouds everywhere. There will be continuous rain and winds for 100 years. Everywhere there will be darkness. Lord *Vishnu* will then sleep on water that is all around until the worlds are recreated. The second type of *Pralaya* is known as *Prakrutha Pralaya.* The perfect balance of the three *Gunas* or nature, namely the *Sattva, Rajas and Tamo Gunas* is known as *Prakruthi.* When *Prakruthi* gets assimilated in to *Paramatman* it is known as *Prakrutha Pralaya*. The third type of *Pralaya* is known as *Atyathika Pralaya*. In this *Pralaya* the three types of distress the *Adhyatmika,* consisting of physical and mental ailments, the *Adhidaivika*, that is suffering due to cold and heat and *Adhi Boudhika* that is, suffering due to other living beings like ghosts, snakes and so on would disappear.

A cycle of creation and destruction is known as one *Manvanthara*. Each one of the *Manvantharas* is ruled by a ruler called *Manu*. When Lord *Naarayana* desired to recreate the world He adopted the form of a Boar or *Varaaha* and went to the underworld and by using His tusks, He lifted the earth from the underworld and placed the earth again on water and the earth floated on water. Lord *Vishnu* levelled the earth and placed the mountains. Till now there has been six such *Manvantharas* ruled by six different *Manus* namely, *Svayambhu Manu, Svarochasha, Outtami, Tamasa, Raivata and Chak shusha*. The present is the 7th *Manvanthara* ruled by the son of the sun who is known as *Vaivasvata*. Each *Manvanthara* has its own gods and *Rishis*. The gods of the present *Manvanthara* are the *Adithyas, the Vasus, the Rudra*, and *Purandara* who holds the title of *Indra*. The seven *Rishis* of the present *Manvanthara* are *Vasishta, Kashyapa, Atri, Jamadagni, Gauthama, Vishwamitra, and Bharadwaja*. There are seven more *Manvantharas* that are yet to come that would be ruled by seven more *Manus* namely, *Savarni, Dakshasavarni, Brahmasavarni, Dharmasavarni, Savarna, Rouchya* and *Bhoutya Manus*. At the end of each four cycles of *Yugas Vedas* or the knowledge gets destroyed and in each *Sathya Yuga* the respective *Manu* rewrites the sacred scriptures. *Manu*, the seven sages, *Indra*, gods and kings are created again in each *Manvanthara*. Fourteen such *Manvantharas* make one *Kalpa* and then comes *Brahma*'s night. During that night Lord *Vishnu* in His form as *Brahma* sleeps on all surrounding waters.

Later *Brahma* created beings through the power of His mind. First He created the *Asuras* or demons then came gods or *Devas*, then the *Pitris* or ancestors and then human beings and later on He created the other things of the world that included the *Yakshas*, snakes, *Gandharvas*, birds, animals and so on and then came plants.

In *Kali Yuga* the norms of *Varna* and *Ashrama* will not be followed by the people. The good relationship between the teacher and the disciple will cease. Women will take care of their hair all the time. Wealth will be everything. People will spend on building houses but not for *Dharma*. Money will be spent for one's own happiness only as men will become selfish. Money will be earned through selfish means. There will be drought. Man will not bathe before meals. Both men and women will become shorter. Kings will not take care of their subjects but will impose more taxes. Women will not listen to their husbands. People will become old even when they reach the age of twelve and they will not live for more than twenty years. Evil will flourish. Worship and prayer will cease. The only good in *Kali Yuga* is that while in *Satya Yuga* one had to do a lot of *Tapasya* or meditation to earn its good effects, in *Kali Yuga* the good effects can be acquired even through a little *Tapasya*. Ten years of *Tapasya* in *Kritha Yuga* is equal to one year of *Tapasya* in *Tretha Yuga* that is equal to one month of *Tapasya* in *Dwapara Yuga* that is equal to one day of *Tapasya* in *Kali Yuga*.

About geography of earth this *Purana* says that in the beginning the world was divided into seven *Dveepas* namely, *Jambu, Shalmali, Krouncha, Palksha, Shaka, Pushkara* and *Kusha*. These *Dvipas* were surrounded by seven oceans namely *Lavana, Ikshu, Sura, Sarpi, Dadhi, Dugdha* and *Jala* (containing salt water, sugar cane juice, wine, ghee, curd, milk, and water respectively). *Jambudveepa* (also known as *Sudarshanadveepa)* was at the centre of all and in the middle of *Jambudveepa* is Mount *Sumeru* the figurative axis of the Universe, separating and uniting all worlds or planes of existence. (It is the spiritual, psychic and the physical levels). To the south of Mount *Meru l*ay the *Brahmavarsha*, then *Kimpurusha Varsha* and then *Hari Varsha*. To its north are *Ramyaka*, then *Hiranmaya* and *Kuru Varsha*. On all the four sides of Mount *Meru* are four mountains; to its east the *Mandras*, to its south the *Gandhamadna*, to its west *Vipula* and to its north *Suparshva*. These Mountains had lot of *Jambu* or *Jamun* trees. Hence it was called as *Jambudweepa*. Around Mount *Meru* there are four beautiful lakes. They are *Arunoda, Mahabhadra, Asitoda and Namasa. Brahma Loka* or *Brahma*'s abode is on the peak of Mount *Meru*. River *Ganga t*hat is originated from the feet of Lord *Vishnu* after flowing around the Moon falls on *Brahma Loka*. It then divides itself in four rivers namely, *Seetha*, flowing eastwards, *Alaknanda* flowing southwards, *Chakshu* flowing westwards and *Bhadra Varsha* flowing northwards. The *Alaknanda* then divides itself into seven rivers. The region around Mount *Meru* is considered as the heaven on earth. All the gods, goddesses, *Gandharvas, Yakshas, Raakshasas,* deities and *Daanavas* live there. The sons of *Bharatha* live in *Bharatha Varsha*. There are seven major mountains in *Bharatha Varsha* namely, *Mahendra, Alaya, Sahya, Shukthimana, Riksha, Vindhya* and *Paripatra*. To the east *of Bharatha Varsha* the *Kirtas* or hunters live. To its west the *Yavanas* live. From the *Himaalayas* the rivers *Shatadru* and *Chandra Bhaga* flow. The main rivers mentioned in the *Vedas* flow from mount *Paripatra* and from mount *Vindhya* the rivers *Narmada* and *Surasa* flow. *Bharatha Varsha* is the best part of *Jambu Dweepa. Jambu Dweepa* is surrounded by the ocean *Lavana*. The earth has seven underworlds. They are, *Gabghstimata, Mahatala Atala, Vitala, Nitala, Sutala* and *Patala*. The demons namely *Danavas, Daityas, Yakshas*, and *Naagas* live there. It is said that Sage *Narada* went to *Patala* once and saw that *Pataala* was more beautiful than heaven. The place was full of jewels and during the day sun provided light without heat. So also during night the moon provided light without cold. There were also many rivers, forests and lakes. The inhabitants there wore beautiful clothes, apply sandal paste on their bodies and loved music. At the bottom of *Paatala* lay Lord *Vishnu* in the form of a 1000 headed snake known as *Aadi Sesha*. Under the earth and water are several hells for sinners. There lay the kingdom of *Yama* or the God of death. The hells were known as *Rourava, Rodha, Shukara, Tala, Taptakunda, Tapta louha, Mahajvala, Lavana, Vimohana, Krimibhaksha, Lalabhaksha, Vedhaka, Vishasana, Adhomukha, Puryavaha, Rudhirandha, Vatarani, Krishna, Asipatravana, Vanhijvala, Shvabhojana, and Niraya*. Sinners are made to suffer in any of these hells as per the different sins committed by them.

The world of Sun is far away from the Earth. There are several worlds of the Moon, Stars, Mercury, Venus, Mars, Jupiter, Saturn, the *Saptha Rishis* (the great Bear Constellation) and *Dhruva*. At the centre of all stars is *Dhruva*.

There are seven *Lokas* or worlds. Above *Dhruvaloka* is *Janaloka* where the sons of *Brahma* live. In the *Tapoloka* that is above *Janaloka* gods live. Still higher is *Sathya Loka*. It has *Brahmaloka*, that is, the abode of *Brahma* and *Vaikunta Loka*, the abode of Lord *Vishnu*. At the end of each cycle of creation the inhabitants of *Dhruvaloka, Janaloka, Tapoloka* and *Sathyaloka* are not destroyed whereas the inhabitants of other three Lokas are destroyed. The first of these is earth or *Bhurloka*, and then comes *Bhuvarlok*a where the sages live. This is the region between the Earth and Heaven. The third is *Svarloka* that is the region from the sun to *Dhruva*.

The sphere of *Bhur loka* consisting of it oceans, mountains and rivers extends as far as it is illuminated by the rays of Sun and Moon. To the same extent the *Bhuvar loka* spreads above it up to *Swar loka*. *Bhur loka* is that region wherever earthly substance exists that may be traversed by feet. This is the seventh of the 14 planes. *Bhuvar loka* is the region that extends from the earth to sun where *Siddhas* and other celestial beings move. It is the sixth loka. It is near earth space including earth's atmosphere- the region where air crafts fly. (It can be equated with Geo space that is, the space dominated by earth's magnetic field).

The Universe consists of 14 regions that include the *seven Lokas* and the seven *Pataalas* or the underworlds. *Patala* is called *Bhuvana* and there are 14 such *Bhuvanas* in this Universe. The *Bhuvanas* are surrounded by darkness and around the darkness there is water and around water there is fire. Beyond fire there is wind and beyond wind there is *Akaasa* or ether or sky or space.

About tides this *Purana* says, that in all oceans, the water remains at all times the same in quantity and never increases or decreases; but like water in a cauldron, that in consequence of its combination with heat expands, so the waters of the ocean swell with the increase of the Moon. The waters although really neither more or less, neither dilate nor contract as the Moon increases or wanes in the light and dark fortnights.

Garuda Purana

Garuda Purana explains about the Lord of creation, who is the creator, maintainer and destroyer of the universe and about the process of creation in various Sargas, astrology and so on.

In the beginning of creation on account of His will, the imperceptible or subtle matter of nature came into being. The *'Atma'* or the *'Purusha'* owes its very existence to Him. Subsequently, *Buddhi* or intelligence manifested itself from the subtle matter of nature, the mind or *'Manas'* manifested from intelligence, the space or *'Akasa'* from mind, air or *'Vayu'* from space, Fire or *'Teja'* from air, water from *'Teja'* and finally the earth or *'Bhoomi'* from water. Then an egg of an enormous size appeared. Lord *Vishnu* and other deities, the whole universe was inside that egg. The Almighty who in the form of *Brahma* created and He in the form of *Vishnu* nurtured and He in the form of *Shiva* annihilated the universe at the end of each *Kalpa*. First He created the *Mahat Tattva* that symbolized His gross quality. This was called the first '*Sarga*' (creation). Secondly He created the five basic elements or *Pancha Tanmatras*. They were *Prithvi* (earth), *Jala* (water), *Teja* (fire), *Vayu* (air) and *Sabda* (sound). Matter is made out of these. In the third *Sarga* the Almighty created Sense organs and organs of actions that were intelligence oriented. All these three *Sargas* come under *'Prakrit' Sarga* or natural creations. The fourth Sarga is known as the *'Mukhya Sarga'* or the main creation. It consists of creation of immovable things like mountains, trees and so on. The fifth *Sarga* is known as *'Tiryak Sarga'*, namely the creation of animals and birds. In the sixth Sarga the deities and other celestial beings were created, and is known as *'Deva Sarga'*. The seventh stage consisted of creation of human beings and hence it was called *'Manush Sarga'*. The eighth Sarga also called as *'Anugrah Sarga'* that consisted of creation of both *'Satvik'* that is pure and *'Tamasic'* that is dark in nature or *Gunas*. The ninth Sarga is *'Kaumar Sarga'* when Lord *Brahma* started His creation of Supreme entities through His will and the ten *'Manasa Putras'* were manifested from Him. Subsequently He created many other entities like deities, (*Devas*), demons (*Daanavas*) and so on.

This *Purana* describes the chariots of all the nine planets. It is stated here that the chariot of *Surya Deva* or the Sun has an unbelievable expanse stretching up to 9000 *Yojanas*. The axle of the chariot is one crore and fifty seven lakh *Yojanas* long and wheels are fixed at both its ends. The wheels have six circumferences symbolising the six main seasons and five spokes symbolising the five different units of time measurements in them. The chariot of *Surya* is pulled by seven horses. These horses symbolise the seven *Chandas*, the stanzas used in poetry namely, *Gayatri, Vrihati, Ushnik, Jagathi, Trishtup, Anushtup* and *Pankthi*. The chariot of Moon has three wheels in it. It is pulled by 10 white horses. The colour of the chariot of *Mangal* or Mars is golden and is pulled by horses of dark red colour. The chariot of *Buddha* or Mercury is of brown colour and is pulled by eight horses of the same colour. The chariot of *Brihaspathi* or Jupiter is made of gold and is pulled by eight horses of yellowish colour. Jupiter remains for a period of a year in each of the twelve zodiacs. The chariot of *Shukra* or Venus is well escorted by his army. This chariot has a mast on its top and is pulled by horses that are found on earth. *Shani*'s or Saturn's chariot is pulled by horses that are of different colours. The chariot of *Rahu* is pulled by eight horses with the colour of smoke and the chariot of *Kethu* is pulled by eight horses that has red colour.

Brahma Purana

This *Purana* tells about the creation process, *Manvantharas*, geography of earth, hells, earth's limits, 12 *Adithyas* that are different forms of *Soorya* or Sun that shines each month and about the southern ocean that is known as *Lavana Samudra*, the underworld, hell, and so on.

In the beginning there was water everywhere and *Brahman*, the divine essence slept on this water in the form of Lord *Vishnu*. He was also known as '*Naraayana*' that is the one who rested on water. In the water a golden egg or '*Anda*' appeared. *Brahma* was born from that egg. Since He created Himself He is called the self-creator or '*Swayambhu*'. For one full year *Brahma* lived inside that egg. He then split that egg into two and created the heaven (*Swarga*) and the earth (*Prithvi*) from the two parts of the egg. In both Heaven and Earth He created skies, directions, time, language, senses and so on. From the power of His mind He then created the seven great sages namely *Marichi, Atri, Angua, Pulastya, Pulaha, Kratu*, and *Vasishta*. He also created *Rudra* and the sages *Sanat Kumaras*. For continuing the process of creation, *Brahma* created a man and a woman from His body. That man was *Swayambhu Manu* and the woman was *Satarupa*. Humans emerged from this *Manu* and hence they are called as '*Manava*'. Then the creation continued.

Regarding the cycle of 'time', this purana says there are four *Yugas* or eras namely, *Sathya* or *Kritha Yuga, Tretha Yuga, Dwapara Yuga and Kali Yuga*. Each cycle of all the four *Yugas is* called a *'Maha Yuga'*. A *'Maha Yuga'* consists of 4,320,000 human years. 71 *Mahayugas* constitute one *'Manvanthara'*. 14 'Manvantharas' is equal to one cycle to one *'Kalpa'*. One *'Kalpa'* is equal to one day of *Brahma* and the Universe is destroyed at the end of each *Kalpa* only to be recreated again. Each *Manvanthara* is ruled by a *'Manu'*. In the present *Kalpa* six *'Manvantharas'* are over. We are in the seventh *'Manvanthara*. It is ruled by *'Vaivasvata Manu'*. The Gods, the title of *Indra*, the seven great sages change from one *Manvanthara* to the other. Before the Universe is destroyed there will be seven more *Manus* and *Manvantharas* in the present *Kalpa*.

The Earth is divided in to seven regions or *Dveepas* namely, *Jambudveepa, Plakshadveepa, Shalmaladveepa, Khushadveepa, Krounchadveepa, Shakadveepa* and *Pushkaradveepa*. These seven regions are surrounded by seven oceans namely *Lavana, Ikshu, Sura, Sarpi, Dadhi, Dugha and Jala*. In the middle of these seven regions is the *Jambudveepa* and in its centre is the Mount *Sumeru*. To the south of *Sumeru* is the mountains of *Himavana, Hemakuta, Nishada*, and to the north of *Sumeru* are the mountains of *Neela, Shveta, and Shringi. Jambudveepa* is divided in to several regions or *Varshas. Sumeru* is in the middle of *Ilavrithavarsha. Bharatha Varsha* is towards the south of *Sumeru*. To its east is *Bhadrash Varsha* and to the west is *Ketumala Varsha. Hari Varsha* lies to the south and *Ramyaka Varsha* to the north. Still further north is *Hiranmaya Varsha* and beyond that *Uttarakuru Varsha. Brahma*'s city is on the peak of *Sumeru*. Here *Ganga* descends from heaven and gets divided into four tributaries. *Seetha* flows eastwards, *Chakshu* westwards, *Bhadra* northwards and *Alaknanda* southwards into *Bharatha Varsha*. There are seven major mountain ranges in *Bharatha Varsha* and their names are, *Mahendra, Malya, Sahya, Shukthimana, Rikasha, Vindhya and Priyatra. Bharatha Varsha* is divided into nine regions or *Dveepas*. These are *Indradveepa, Kaserumana, Tamraparna, Gabhastimana, Nagadveepa, Soumya, Gandharva and Varuna* and the ninth region is completely surrounded by ocean in all directions (Probably the present

Sri Lanka). To the east of *Bharatha Varsha* live the *Kiratas* and to the west are the *Yavanas.*

The seven regions of the underworld (*Patala*) lie below the Earth. They are *Atala, Vitala, Nitala, Sutala, Talaatala, Rasaatala, and Paatala*. The *Daithyas, Daanavas,* and *Sarpas* or snakes live there. The underworld is more beautiful than heaven. Below the underworld the thousand hooded great serpent known as *Sesha* or *Anantha*, who is considered to be one of the forms of Lord *Vishnu* sleeps. Part of this world consists of hells or *Naraka*. It is presided over by *Yama*, the God of Death.

The Earth or *Bhooloka* or *Prithvi* extends up to those parts of the sky that can be lit up by the rays of Sun and Moon. The space from there to the solar circle is the *Bhuvarloka* and the holy sages live there. Above the solar circle is the lunar circle and beyond it in succession are the regions of Mercury *(Budha)*, Venus (*Shukra)*, Mars (*Mangala*), Jupiter (*Brihaspathi* or *Guru*), Saturn (*Sani)*, the great Bear Constellation (*Saptha Rishi Mandala*) and the Pole Star (*Dhruva).* The region from the solar circle to *Dhruvaloka* is known as heaven. (*Svarloka* or *Swarga)*, Beyond *Bhuvarloka* is *Mahaaloka* and further beyond is *Janaloka* where *Brahma*'s sons live. Beyond *Janaloka* are *Tapoloka* and *Satyaloka.* At the end of each *Kalpa* all the three *Lokas* or worlds namely the *Bhooloka, Bhuvarloka*, and *Svarloka* are destroyed. But the *Maharloka, Janaloka, Taploka* and *Sathyaloka* are not destroyed.

The 12 *Adithyas* are the different forms of *Soorya* or sun. As *Indra* with 2, 200 rays he destroys the enemies of Gods, as *Dhata* with 1, 100 rays he creates living beings, as *Parjanya* with 72 rays he showers rain, as *Tvashta* with 1, 100 rays he lives in the trees and herbs, as *Pusha* with 900 rays he makes food grains grow, as *Aaryama* with 1300 rays he is in the wind, as *Bhaaga* he is in the body of all living beings, as *Vivasvana* with 72 rays he is in fire and helps to cook food, as *Vishnu* with 1200 rays he destroys the enemies of gods, as *Amshumana* with 15 rays, he is in the wind, as *Varuna* with 1300 rays he is in the waters, and as *Mitra* with 1000 rays he is in the moon and in the oceans. In each month of a year different *Aadithyas* shine. *Soorya* has 12 other names namely, *Aaditya, Savitha, Soorya, Mihira, Arka, Prabhakara,*

Marthaanda, Bhaaskara, Bhaanu, Chitrabhaanu, Divakara and *Ravi.* In addition *Soorya* has 108 sacred names as well.

Padma Purana

Padma Purana describes the geography of earth, the sequence of creation, geographical expansion of *Bharatha Varsha*, the chronological order of eras, *Brahma*'s life span and His creation, and the 14 *Manvantharas*, the sanctity of *Bharatha Varsha* and its geography and so on.

Initially Lord *Brahma* created the *Mahatatthva*. Then the three types of ego called *Satthva, Rajas* and *Thamas* were created by Him. From these three types of ego originated all five sense organs, organs of action and all the basic elements namely Space, Water, Fire, Air and Earth. With the permutation and combination of these five elements an enormous egg came in to existence. The entire Universe is within this egg- the mountains, islands, oceans, planets, deities, and human beings. The elements are also covered by the *Mahatatthva* that in turn is enveloped by *Prakruthi* or nature. At the end Lord *Vishnu* annihilates the Universe in the form of *Rudra*. He then takes rest on the *Adisesha*.

Lord *Brahma*'s life span is 100 celestial years. Four *Yugas* are equivalent to 12,000 years of the deities that is 4000 years of *Sathya* or *Kritha Yuga*, 3000 years of *Tretha Yuga*, 2000 years of *Dwapara Yuga* and 1000 years of *Kali Yuga*. Each *Yuga* is followed by the hibernation period or *Sandhya* that comes to the total of 1000 years. The four *Yugas* are collectively known as one *ChathurYuga*. Brahma's day equals 1000 such *Chathur Yugas*. Altogether fourteen *Manus* in fourteen *Manvantharas* appear during the entire period of 1000 *Chathur Yugas* that is equal to one day of *Brahma*. Each *Manvanthara* is named after a *Manu* and it is equivalent to a little more than 71 *Chathur Yugas*. A *Manvanthara* is equal to 30, 67, 20,000 years. *Brahma*'s day is equivalent to 30, 67, 20,000*14=4, 29, 40, 80,000 years. After one day of *Brahma* is over deluge or *Pralaya* comes when all the three worlds become devoid of life due to intense heat. Then Lord *Brahma* takes rest for the same period, that is, 4,29,40,80,000 years and that is His night. After the night *Brahma* commences His creation again. Thus the process continues for the entire life span of Lord *Brahma*.

At the end of the previous *Kalpa*, when Lord *Brahma* woke up from His sleep He found that the earth was under water. He meditated upon Lord *Vishnu* who took the form of *Varaaha* or boar to retrieve the earth and placed it in its original position. Then *Brahma* created the four worlds. *Bhooloka, Bhuvarloka, Swarloka,* and *Maharloka* and divided the earth into seven regions. To start with, *Brahma* created the *Maha Tatthvas*. After that He created the *Tanmatra*, sense organs or *Indriyas*, then mountains, rivers, animals, deities, demons and human beings and so on.

Narada Purana

Narada Purana explains about the process of creation, the concept of time, the geography of earth, *Bharatha Varsha*, Hells, and Rebirth of souls after undergoing punishments in hells, the *Manvantharas*, the different *Manus* in different *Manvantharas,* and the features of *Yugas.*

Prior to creation there was only the Godhead, the supreme everywhere. When the time of creation came He expanded Himself into three forms. Lord *Brahma* was created from the right side of Godhead, and His task was creation. Lord *Shiva* was created from the centre of the Godhead and He looked after destruction. Lord *Vishnu* was created from the left side of the Godhead and He performed the act of preservation. *Shakthi is* the female counterpart of Godhood. She divided Herself into two, namely *Vidya* or knowledge and Avidya or ignorance. Knowledge is the knowing of the identity between *Brahman* and the Universe. Ignorance is absence of such knowledge and it is the cause of miseries in the world. Goddess *Shakthi* becomes *Lakshmi* when She is identified with Lord *Vishnu*, Goddess *Uma* or *Parvathi* when She is identified with Lord *Shiva* and Goddess *Saraswathi* when She is identified with Lord *Brahma*. But actually these three are one and the same. This unified *Shakthi* or energy is referred to as the *Mahaamaya* or *Prakruthi*.

The Universe is made up of five elements or *Bhoothas* namely, the *Kshiti* that is Earth, *Apa* or Water, *Teja* or Fire or Energy, *Marut* or Wind and *Vyoma* or Sky or Space.

The Universe is divided into 14 regions or *Bhuvanas* or *Lokas*. Seven of them form the upper regions. These are the *Bhooloka,*

Bhuvarloka, Svarloka, Maharloka, Janaloka and *Sathyaloka*. There are seven more regions that form the lower regions or the underworld. They are, *Atala, Vitala, Sutala, Talaatala, Mahaatala, Rasaatala* and *Paatala*. *Patala* sometimes refer to the entire underworld. Each of the 14 regions has its own inhabitants, mountains, and rivers.

The Earth is *Bhooloka* and is split into seven regions or *Dveepas* namely, *Jambudveepa, Plakshadveepa, Shalmaladveepa, Kushadveepa, Krounchadveepa*, *Shakadveepa* and *Pushkaradveepa*. *Bhooloka* has also seven oceans namely, *Lavana, Ikshu, Sura, Sarpi, Dadhi, Dughadha* and *Jala*. *Bharathavarsha* is in *Jambudveepa*. It is that part of land that is bounded by *Lavana* Ocean on the south and *Himalaya Mountains* on the north. *Bharathavarsha* is a wonderful place to live and even gods desire to be born here. It is also known as *Karma Bhoomi*.

The smallest unit of time is a *Nimisha*. 15 *Nimishas* constitute one *Kastha*. 30 *Kasthas* make a *Kala* and 30 *Kaalas* is equal to one *Kshana*. There are 6 *Kshanas* in one *Danda*, two *dandas* in one *Muhoortha*, and 30 *Muhoorthas* in a day.

There are 30 days in a month and each month is divided into two *Pakshas* of 15 days each. Two months constitute a season or *Rithu* and three *Rithus* constitute one *Ayana*. There are therefore two *Ayanas* and six seasons in a year. The two *Ayanas* are, the *Uttarayana* and *Dakshinayana*.

One year of humans is equivalent to one day for the gods. *Uttarayana* corresponds to day for the gods and *Dakshinayana* is night for them. 12, 000 years of gods is known as a *Maha Yuga*. Each *Maha Yuga* is divided in to four sub periods or *Yuga*s namely, *Sathya Yuga* or *Kritha Yuga*, *Tretha Yuga*, *Dwapara Yuga* and *Kali Yuga*. Four *Yugas* constitute one *Maha Yuga* and a *Maha Yuga* lasts approximately for 12, 000 years of gods. In *Sathya Yuga* Dharma reigned supreme and people were righteous as gods. With the passing of each *Yuga, Dharma* declined and people began to be dishonest and anger and hate became common. *Kali Yuga* is the worst of all the four *Yugas*.

There are 14 Eras or *Manvantharas* in each of *Brahma*'s days. *Brahma*'s nights are as long as his day. During *Brahma*'s night the world is destroyed and flooded with water. One day of *Brahma* is called *a Kalpa*. Each *Manvanthara* is ruled by a *Manu*. The names of gods, sages and *Manus* change from one *Manvanthara* to another.

Shiva Purana

Shiva Purana deals with the process of creation, the units of time, duration of *Yugas*, hells, geography of earth, astronomy, *Manvantharas, Manus* and the gods in each *Manvanthara.*

In the beginning there was nothing. There was no Universe. There was only the divine essence or energy, the *Brahman* that was everywhere. It was neither hot nor cold, nor thick or thin, and had no beginning or end. There was only water everywhere. Then Lord *Vishnu* manifested Himself in a form and slept on the water. While He was sleeping a Lotus flower sprouted from His navel. It had many petals and the stem was shining like innumerable Suns. From the Lotus Lord *Brahma* was born. He began to wonder about His origin and the purpose of His birth as He found only water everywhere. In order to find out everything about Himself He went down the stem of the Lotus for 100 years. But in spite of wandering around for another 100 years He could not find the centre of the Lotus. When He became tired, He gave up His quest and rested. Suddenly He heard a voice asking Him to do *Tapasya* or meditation. *Brahma* then meditated for twelve years. At the end of twelve years Lord *Vishnu* appeared before *Brahma* holding *Shankha* (Conch) and *Chakra* (discus), *Gada* (mace) and *Padma* (lotus) in His four hands. When Lord *Vishnu* told Lord *Brahma* that He was created by *Vishnu, Brahma* was not convinced. So He began to fight with *Vishnu*. While they were fighting a shining *Linga* emerged there. So to find out about the *Linga, Brahma* adopted the form of a swan and flew upwards to find out its top. *Vishnu* then assumed the form of a boar and went down to find out its base or origin. But even after 4000 years both could not succeed in their mission. So, both of them began to meditate for one hundred years. At the end of the period they heard the sound of *'AUM'* and a Being with five faces and ten arms appeared before them. This was Lord Shiva. *Shiva* told *Vishnu* and *Brahma* that all the three of them are parts of the same entity- *Brahma* meant for purpose of creation, *Vishnu* for the upkeep and *Shiva* or *Rudra* for destruction of all that are created.

In the water Lord *Vishnu* created a huge egg or *Anda*. He then entered into that egg. *Brahma* in the meantime started to pray. From His mental power He created many sages or *Rishis*.

The smallest unit of time is *Nimisha* that is, the amount of time taken to blink once. Fifteen *Nimishas* make one *Kashtha* and 30 *Kashthas* constitute one *Kaala*. 30 *Kaalas* make one *Muhoortha* and 30 *Muhoorthas* are one day. 30 days are one month and each month has two lunar fortnights, *Shukla Paksha* and *Krishna Paksha*. 6 months constitute one *Ayana*. 360 human years are equivalent to one year for the gods.

The duration of *Yugas* are defined in terms of the divine years but not human years. Of the four *Yugas, Sathya Yuga* lasts for 4000 divine years, *Tretha Yuga* for 3000 years, *Dwapara Yuga* for 2000 years and *Kali Yuga* for one thousand years. So the total is 10,000 years. The *Sandhyas* and *Sandhamshas* are the intervening periods between *Yugas* and these add up to 2000 divine years. Thus the four *Yugas* put together comes to 12, 000 years. In a *Kalpa* each of the four *Yugas* occurs a thousand times. A *Kalpa* consists of 14 *Manvantharas* or Eras. In a *Manvanthara* each of the four *Yugas* occurs 71 times. One *Kalpa* is equal to one day of *Brahma*. One year of *Brahma* is equal to 1000 *Kalpas* and 8000 of *Brahma*'s years make one *Brahma*'s *Yugas*. One thousand such *Yugas* make up one *Savana* and *Brahma* lives for 3000 *Savanas*. This period is known as *Trivrita*.

The Earth is divided in to seven regions or *Dveepas*. They are *Jambudveepa, Plakshadveepa, Shalmalidveepa, Kushadveepa, Krounchadveepa, Pushkaradveepa* and *Shakadveepa*. These seven regions are surrounded by seven oceans namely, *Lavana, Ikshu, Sarpi, Dadhi, Dugaha, Jala* and *Rasa*. Mount *Sumeru* is right in the middle of *Jambudveepa*. To the north of *Sumeru* are the mountains *Neela* and *Shvethabhangi* and to the south of *Sumeru* are the *Himavana, Hemakuta* and *Nishada*. *Jambudveepa* is divided into many parts or *Varshas*. Right at its centre is the *Ilavritha Varsha*. To the south of *Sumeru* are *Bharathavarsha, Kimpurushu Varsha* and *Hari Varsha*. To the north of *Sumeru* is *Ramyaka Varsha*. Next to this is *Hiranmaya Varsha* and further north is *Uttarakuru Varsha*. There are four major mountains in *Ilavritha Varsha* namely, *Mandara* towards east, *Ghandamadana* towards south, *Vipula* towards west and *Suparshva* towards north of *Sumeru*. On the top of Mount *Sumeru* is *Brahmaloka* or the city of *Lord Brahma*. The holy river *Ganga* flows through the sky and divides into four tributaries namely, *Seetha, Alakanada* or *Nanda, Chakshu* and *Bhadra*.

Bharatha Varsha is bounded by mountain ranges on the north and sea on the south. *Bharatha Varsha* is divided in to eight parts of land and one part of island. They are *Indradyumna, Kaseru, Tamaraparani, Soumy, Gabhastimana, Nagadvipa, Gandharva and Varuna*. The ninth part that is island is surrounded by ocean. On the east of *Bharatha Varsha* live the *Kiratas*, on the west the *Yavanas*, on the southern the *Andhras* and the northern the *Turaskas*. The seven major mountains of Bharatha Varsha are *Mahendra, Malaya, Sahya, Shukthimana, Riksha, Vindhya* and *Pariyatra*. Several rivers originate from these mountains. It is said that *Bharatha Varsha* is a highly sacred place and only those who have accumulated good deeds or *Punya* over a 1000 human lives get to be born in *Bharatha Varsha*.

The boundaries of *Bhoo Mandala* or Earth extend to the furthest points where the rays of sun and moon fall. *Soorya loka* is situated one lakh *yojanas* above *Bhooloka*. The moon's region is one lakh *yojana* above that of the *Soorya loka*. All constellations and planets are spread over 10, 000 *yojanas* above moon. This is followed in succession by regions of *Budha* or Mercury, *Shukra* or Venus, *Mangala* or Mars, *Brihaspati* or Jupiter, *Shani* or Saturn, and the *Nakshatras* or stars. Then is the *Saptha Rishi Loka*, the circle of the seven great sages or the constellation of Ursa Major that is above Saturn at a distance of one lakh *yojana*. The *Dhruva loka* is at a distance of one lakh *yojana* above *Saptha Rishi Mandala*. All planets are located between earth and *Dhruva* star in three lokas namely *Bhur loka, Bhuvar loka* and *swarga loka*. These regions beyond the earth are known as *Bhuvarlok*a. Beyond it is *Suvarloka* or *Swarga* or heaven. *Bhurloka, Bhuvarloka and Suvarloka* are destroyed in the deluge or *Pralaya* that comes at the end of each *Kalpa*. But the regions beyond these three are not destroyed at the end of each *Kalpa*. They are, *Dhruvaloka*, the circle of Pole star, *Maharloka, Janaloka, Tapoloka and Sathyaloka/. Mahar* *loka* is beyond *Dhruvaloka*. This is the *Loka* where the four *Manasa Puthras* (born from mind) namely, *Sanaka* and so on of Lord *Brahma* reside. *Janaloka* is above *Mahar loka*. Above *Mahar loka* at a distance of six lakh *yojanas* is the *Tapoloka*. *Sathya loka* is six times the distance between *Maharloka* and *Tapoloka*. *Sathya loka* is *Brahma loka*. Beyond *Brahma loka* is *Vaikunta loka* of Lord *Narayana*. So including earth there are seven regions. Under the earth is the underworld or *Paataala*. It is divided in to seven regions. They are, *Paataala, Sutala, Vitala, Nitala, Mahaatala, Agrayasutala and Rasaatala*. There are also several hells namely, *Rourava, Shukara, Taptalouha, Krimibhaksha, Lalabhaksha, Vishasana, Rudhiandha, Vaitarani, Krishna, Asipatravana, Vahnijvala, Agnimaya, Sandamsha, and Shavabhojana*.

Each *Manvanthara* is ruled by a *Manu* and there are 14 *Manvantharas* in any *Kalpa*. The Gods or the *Devas*, the seven great sages or the *Saptha Rishis*, and *Indra* change from one *Manvanthara* to another. Now we are in the seventh *Manvanthara*. The seventh *Manu* is called *Vaivasvata*. In future there will be seven more *Manvantharas*.

Lingapurana

Linga Purana tells about creation, the duration of *Yugas*, characteristics of each *Yuga*, the concept of time, *Yugas*, geography of the Universe, and Astronomy.

The divine essence is known as *Brahman*. Before any creation only the divine essence was present everywhere. There was nothing else. *Brahman* divided the divine essence into three, namely, *Brahma* for creation, *Vishnu* for preservation and *Shiva* for carrying out destruction. In the beginning before creation of the Universe there was only water everywhere. In the water a gigantic egg appeared and *Brahma* emerged from the egg. Inside the egg there were all the worlds that would eventually be created. Creation takes place during *Brahma*'s day. During *Brahma*'s night there is destruction or *Pralaya*. When *Brahma*'s day dawns, creation takes place again.

Time is divided into four *Yugas* namely, *Sathya Yuga, Tretha Yuga, Dwapara Yuga* and *Kali Yuga*. *Sathya Yuga* lasts for 4000 years of Gods, *Tretha Yuga* for 3000 years of Gods, *Dwapara Yuga* for 2000 years and *Kali Yuga* for 1000 divine years. All the four *Yugas* put together constitute one *Maha Yuga*. It lasts for 10,000 divine years. The intervening period called *Sandhyamsha*, between *Sathya Yuga* and *Tretha Yuga* is 700 years, between *Trehta Yuga* and *Dwapara Yuga* is 500 years and between *Dwapara Yuga* and *Kali Yuga* is 300 years and between *Kali Yuga* and the new *Sathya Yuga* is again 500 years. This comes to another 2000 years. So a *Maha Yuga* actually lasts for 12, 000 years of gods or divine years.

The smallest unit of time is *Nimisha* that takes to blink once. 15 *Nimishas* constitute one *Kastha*, 30 *Kasthas* constitute one *Kaala*, and 30 *Kaalas* make up one *Muhoortha*. There are 15 *Muhoorthas* during day and 15 *Muhoorthas* during night. Therefore 30 *Muhoorthas* make up one day and one night known as *Ahoratra*.

One human year is equivalent to one *Ahoratra* for the gods. Six months that constitute one day for gods is known as *Uttarayana* and six months that constitute one night for gods is known as *Dakshinayana*.

360 Human years is equivalent to one divine year. 12,000 divine years are equivalent to 4,320,000 human years and this is equivalent to one *Maha Yuga*. *Sathya Yuga* lasts for 1,440,000 human years, *Tretha Yuga* 1,080,000 human years, *Dwapara Yuga* 720,000 human years and 360,000 human years for *Kali Yuga*. It comes to a total of 3, 600, 000 human years. The *Sandhyamshas*, that is, the intervening period is 720,000 years. So, the total comes to 4,320,000 human years in a *Maha Yuga*. There are a little more than 71 *Mahayugas* in a *Manvanthara*. 71 *Maha Yugas* comes to 296,720,000 human years. But there are actually 306,720,000 human years in a *Manvanthara*. 1000 *Maha Yugas* make up one *Kalpa*. There are thus 4,320,000 human years in a *Kalpa*. 14 *Manvantharas* constitute one *Kalpa*. One *Kalpa* is equal to one *Brahma*'s *Ahoratra*. 1000 *Kalpas* make up one year to *Brahma*, 800 such years are one *Yuga* for *Brahma*. 1000 of *Brahma*'s *Yugas* are equivalent to one day of *Vishnu*. 9000 *Vishnu*'s days are equivalent to one day for *Shiva*.

At the end of one of *Brahma*'s day the entire Universe and all beings are destroyed with the exception of *Brahma, Vishnu* and *Shiva*. Then there is darkness everywhere. *Vishnu* or *Naarayana* then sleeps on this water. At the end of the period of one night *Brahma* and

Vishnu heard the sound *AUM'* and it echoed all around and the *Linga* of *Shiva* appeared from within in the form of a sage named *Vedanama*. He told them that the *Linga* was the origin of the universe and that the universe was created from that Primordial egg or *'ANDA'*.

The Universe is divided in to 14 regions, seven of them forming the upper regions and seven other regions forming the nether regions. The seven *Lokas* of the upper regions are *Bhooloka* the earth, *Bhuvarloka, Suvarloka or Swar loka, Maharloka, Janaloka, Tapoloka and Sathyaloka*. The seven regions of the underworld are *Mahatala, Hematala, Rasatala, Talatala, Sutala, Atala* and *Paataala*. The demons and the *Nagas* live in the underworld. There are also many hells or *Narakas* in this universe.

The earth has got many oceans and mountains. The land mass of the Earth is divided into seven regions or *Dveepas* namely; *Jambudveepa, Plakshadveepa, Shalmalidveepa, Kushadveepa, Krounchadveepa, Shakadveepa* and *Pushkaradveepa*. The great seven oceans that surround the land masses are *Lavana, Ikshu, Sura, Ghrita, Dadhi, Jala* and *Sarpi*.

Agnidhara was the ruler of *Jambudveepa*. He had nine sons and one of them was *Nabhi*. After *Agnidhara, Jambudveepa* was divided into nine regions and *Nabh*i ruled over *Hemavarsha*. *Nabhi* and his wife *Meru* had a son by name *Rishabha* and his son was *Bharata*. It was after *Bharata* that the region that *Nabhi* ruled came to be known as *Bharatha Varsha*. To the north of *Bharatha Varsha* are the *Himalaya* Mountains and in its south is the ocean. Right at the centre of *Jambudveepa* is Mount *Sumeru* or *Meru* and there are many other peaks that surround *Sumeru*. Mount *Sumeru* is very high as to touch the solar circle. Many gods live there. *Amaravathi*, where *Indra* lives is on the eastern slopes of *Sumeru*. At another corner, the abode of fire god or *Agni* is located. It is known as *Tejasvini*. Towards its south is *Vaivasvati*, the residence of God of death or *Yama*. Right at the centre of *Sumeru* is *Brahmaloka, Brahma* or the creator's residence. Near that river *Jambu* flows. *Jambudveepa* acquired its name from this river. There are many Mountains around Mount Sumeru. *Neelachala* mountain to its north, *Shveta* Mountain still further north and the

Shringi mountain still beyond. The Mountains *Jathara* and *Devakuta* are towards the east of *Sumeru*. In the south are the *Nishadha* Mountains. The *Hemakuta* Mountains are further south and the *Himalaya* Mountain is farther south. To its west are the Mountains *Malayavana* and *Gandhamadana*. There are four beautiful lakes around *Sumeru* namely, *Arunodaya* to its east, *Manasa* to the south, *Sitoda* to the west and *Mahabhadra* towards its north. *Kiratas* live towards the east of *Bharatha Varsha* and *Yavana*s live towards its west. There are 28 hells below the underworld.

In *Sathya Yuga* people were equal and happy. The climate was neither hot nor cold. There was no hatred or jealousy, hunger or thirst. The earth yielded abundant supply of juices and mankind lived happily on earth. There were no houses. People lived on the shores of the oceans and mountains. There was no need for houses to reside. The concept of *Punya* or merit *Papa* or sin, heaven or hell was unknown to people as all were righteous. In *Tretha Yuga* clouds formed in the sky and it started raining heavily. The earth did not yield plenty of juices. But there was plenty of rain and trees began to grow and people began to live on the sap of these trees. But slowly people began to fight over possession of trees. The trees also gradually stopped yielding sap and began to dry up, wither away and disappear but they yielded fruits. The barks of the trees were used for clothing. There was pronounced heat as well as cold. Since trees became scarce people turned towards agriculture for living. But the land had enough water. The evils of jealousy, hatred and quarrels began to appear in *Dwapara Yuga*. Famines and draughts began to be experienced by the people. *Kaliyuga* became the worst of all *Yugas* as far as righteousness was concerned. All evil practices began to appear and flourish. Life expectancy began to decline with each *Yuga*. When the duration of *Kali* is over *Pramiti* or *Kali* will be reborn to re-establish righteousness on Earth.

The 28 hells are located below the Earth.

12 Months constitute one year. Two months constitute a season or *Ritu*. There are therefore six seasons in a year namely, *Greeshma* or summer, *Varsha* or monsoon, *Sharat* or early autumn, *Hemanta* or later autumn, *Sheetha* or winter and *Vasantha* or spring.

Just as *Indra* rules over *Devas*, the Sun rules over the planets and Moon rules over the stars and herbs. All these revolve around *Dhruva*, the Pole star. The sun's chariot was built by *Brahma*. It is made completely of Gold. In every season, two *Adityas*, two sages, two *Gandharvas*, two *Apsaras*, two *Raakshasas* ride over the Sun's chariot to keep the Sun company. The Moon has a chariot that has three wheels and is drawn by three horses that are white in colour. The Sun drinks up the energy of the Moon for 15 days that is known as *Krishna Paksha* (the waning period of the Moon). Then the Sun replenishes the Moon's energy over the next 15 days that is called *Shukla Paksha* (waxing period of the moon). *Budha* or Mercury is *Chandra*'s, (the Moon's) son and rides a chariot that is drawn up by 8 horses. These horses are yellow and the chariot is made of gold. *Brihaspathi* (Jupiter) also has a chariot that is made of gold and is drawn by 8 horses. *Shani*'s (Saturn) chariot is made of iron.

All the three worlds are burnt up at the time of *Pralaya*. Dark clouds full of thunder appear on the sky at that time. For a hundred years there will be continuous rain. The rain will put out the raging fires. The wind from *Vishnu*'s mouth would drive away the clouds. But there will be water everywhere. For an entire *Kalpa* Vishnu will sleep on these waters and later all the three worlds would be recreated.

Skanda Purana

It is the largest *Purana*. This Purana tells about creation, the prominent Mountains, features of Kali Yuga, and hells.

Lord *Shiva* commenced His creation by His own will. Lord *Vishnu* manifested from the left side of His body and Lord *Brahma* from His right side and Lord *Brahma* took the responsibility of creation, and *Vishnu* and *Shiva* became the preserver and the destroyer of the Universe.

To the north of *Himalayas* are the mountains like *Sumeru, Himavan, Mandarachal, Vindhyachal, Pariyatrak, Mahendra, Malay, Simhachal, and Gandhamadana. To the south of the Himalayas are the Arunachal, Hasti, Grdhachal and Ghatikachal.*

In *Kaliyuga* there is a rapid decline of moral values.

There are 28 types of hells. They are, *Atighora, Raudra, Ghoratma, Dhukhajanani, Ghorrupa, Tarantara, Bhayanaka, Kalaratri, Ghatotkata, Chanda, Mahachanda, Chundakollahala, Prachanda, Varagnika, Jaghanya, Avaraloma, Bhishni, Nayika, Karala, Vikarala, Vajravinshti, Asta, Panchakona, Sudhirga, Parivartula, Sapthabhuvana, Ashtabhuvana* and *Deerghamaya*. Each of the latter hell where the sinners go is more horrible than the preceding one.

Agni Purana

Agni Purana describes the creation process, the geography of the earth, astrology, *Manvantharas*, the *Manus* and *Indras* in different *Manvantaras,* hells, and about *Pralaya* or deluge at the end of every 4000 *Yugas*.

Before creation there was only *Brahman*. There was no day or night. First *Vishnu* created waters. He sowed the seeds of *Brahmanda*, the great egg in water. From the seed emerged a golden egg that floated on water. From that egg *Brahma* created Himself. Since He created Himself *Brahma* is known as *Svayambhu*. Then He stayed inside the egg for a year. At the end of one year He split the egg into two. One part became heaven and the part became the earth and in between these two, sky was created. Then *Brahma* created earth on the waters and made the ten directions. He created time, lighting, thunder, clouds, rainbow, words and anger. *Vedas* emerged from His body. From the power of His mind He created seven *Manasa Putras* or sons namely *Marichi, Atri, Angira, Pulastya, Pulaha, Kratu and Vasishta.*

The world is divided in to seven regions. These are *Jambu, Plaksha, Shalmali, Kusha, Krouncha, Shaka* and *Pushkara*. The seven regions were known as the seven *Dveepas*. The seven *Dveepas* are surrounded by seven oceans namely *Lavana, Ikshu, Sura, Sargih, Dadhi, Dughda* and *Jala*. Right at the centre of *Jambu Dveepa* is Mount *Meru*. To its south are the Mountains of *Himavana, Hemakuta, and Nishada*. To its north are *Neela, Shveta*, and *Shringi* mountains. In *Jambudveepa* there are a lot of *Jambu,* that is, *Jamun* trees and hence its name. On the top of Mount *Meru* is Lord *Brahma*'s city.

Under the Earth there is underworld. It consists of seven regions namely *Atala, Vitala, Sutala, Talatala, Mahatala, Rasatala*, and

Patala. *Daithyas* and *Daanavas* live in the underworld. Lord *Vishnu* is also there in the form of the great snake known as *Sesha*. This snake holds the earth on its hood. There are 28 circles of hells with many hells located in each circle.

Above the Earth is the Sun. Above the Sun is the Moon, the stars. Above the stars are Mercury, above that Venus, then Jupiter, and then the constellation of the Great Bear, known as the *Saptha Rishi Mandal*. Beyond all these is the world of *Dhruva*.

Each *Manvanthara* is ruled by a *Manu*. Periodically *Pralaya* or destruction takes place. A pralaya comes at the end of 4000 *Yugas* of earth. Just before *Pralaya* or destruction for a period of 100 years there will not be rains and there would be widespread draught. Then all waters of earth would get dried up. The three worlds namely, heaven, earth and the underworld would be burnt up. The Earth would become flat as the back of a Turtle. The great snake *Adisesha*, also would burn up all the three worlds. After the three worlds are burnt, dark clouds full of thunder and lightning would appear on the sky. Then for another 100 years it would rain continuously. The rain would then put out the fires. The winds would drive away clouds. But water will be there everywhere. Then Lord *Vishnu* will sleep on the waters for the period of an entire *Kalpa*. Then after that recreation would take place.

Sky or Space was created by *Brahma*; from the Sky came Wind; from Wind came Fire; from Fire came Water and from Water came the Earth.

Matsya Purana

Matsya Purana tells about creation, the *Manvantaras*, geographical and astronomical details, measurement of time, and characteristics of *Yugas*.

In the beginning there was nothing. There was only darkness and the divine essence. Then at the beginning of creation *Brahman* the supreme energy, the Absolute, removed the darkness and it divided into three namely, *Brahma, Vishnu* and *Shiva*. The first object that was created was water and *Vishnu* slept on it. A golden egg or *Hiranya Garbha* or *Anda* then appeared on water. It shone with the brilliance of innumerable suns. Inside the egg *Brahma* created Himself. Since He created Himself He is called *Swayambhu*. Since the egg was golden and *Brahma* emerged from inside it He came to be known as *Hiranyagarbha*. For a 1000 years *Brahma* stayed inside that egg. He then split the shell of the egg into two and emerged out of it. One half became heaven and the other half the earth. All the land masses, oceans, rivers and mountains were inside that egg in embryonic form. *Brahma* made them to manifest. The sun was the first to be born. So He is known as *Adithya*. Since the Sun was born when the egg (*Anda*) died, he is also known as *Marthanda (Mrita* means dead). *Brahma* then meditated and the *Vedas* emerged from His mouth. Ten sons were also born to *Brahma* then. They are *Marichi, Atri, Angira, Pulastya, Pulaha*, *Kratu, Pracheta, Vasishta, Bhrigu* and *Narada*. Others like *Daksha, Dharma* and so on were also born in succession from *Brahma*. To carry on procreation *Brahma* then created a male and one female from His body. They were known as *Swayambhu* and *Satarupa*.

One day of Lord Brahma is one *Kalpa* and there are 14 *Manvantharas* in each *Kalpa*. At the end of each *Kalpa* that is a day of *Brahma* the Universe is destroyed and created afresh the next day. In the present *Kalpa*, six *Manvantharas* are over and the present one is the seventh *Manvanthara*. There will be seven more *Manvantharas* before the end of this *Kalpa*. The Gods, the *Saptha Rishis* and the one who holds the title '*Indra*' change from one *Manvanthara* to another.

The 12 *Aadityas* are the sons of *Adithi*. *Maruts* are the seven parts of the foetus of *Diti* that were cut into pieces by *Indra*.

Vishva Karma shaved off some of the Sun's energy. This made the Sun's rays more bearable. However the feet of *Surya* or Sun were not touched by *Vishvakarma*. It is said that the one who prays on *Surya* should not look at his feet as it is not bearable. It is also said that the one who looks at the feet of the Sun would suffer from Leprosy. with the shaved off excess energy, many weapons of gods like the *Sudarsana Chakra* of *Vishnu,* the *Trishoola* or the Trident of *Shiva* and so on were made.

At the end of the last *Kalpa* the Universe was destroyed and it was flooded with water. *Vishnu* in the form of *Naarayana* slept on water.

When the time for creation of the universe came *Brahma* appeared inside an egg. The entire universe was contained in that egg. The Earth was then created first for beings to live. But it was full of mountains and the Earth began to sink into the water and went down to the underworld as it could not bear the weight of the huge mountains. The Earth then prayed to Lord *Vishnu* to rescue her. Lord *Vishnu* then took the form of a Boar or *Varaaha* and lifted up the Earth with His tusks and placed it on water and then levelled up the mountains.

The smallest unit of time is *Nimisha*, the time taken to blink once. 15 *Nimishas* constitute one *Kastha*, 30 *Kasthas* constitute one *Kaala*, 30 *Kaalas* make one *Muhoortha*, and 30 *Muhoorthas* are equal to one *Divarata* that is one day and one night of 15 *Muhurthas* each. One month of humans is equal to one day for the ancestors, 30 human months is equal to one month for the ancestors, 360 human months is equal to one year for the ancestors, and one human year is equal to one *Divaratrara* for gods. The lunar fortnight when the Moon waxes, is called *Shukla Paksha* and the lunar fortnight when the Moon wanes is called *Krishna Paksha*. There are two *Ayanas* in one human year. *Uttarayana* corresponds to the day for gods and *Dakshinayana corresponds* to the night for the gods. 30 Human years are one month to gods; 360 human years are equal to one year for the gods.

The period of time is divided in to four *Yugas* namely the *Kritha Yuga, Tretha Yuga, Dwapara Yuga and Kali Yuga*. *Kritha Yuga* lasts for 4000 divine years, *Tretha Yuga*, 3000 divine years, *Dwapara Yuga* 2000 divine years and *Kali Yuga* 1000 divine years. One cycle of all the *Yugas* put together is called a *Maha Yuga* that is roughly equals 10, 000 years of Gods or divine years. But there are intervening periods between any two *Yugas* known as *Sandhyamshas*. For *Sathya* or *Kritha Yuga* the *Sandhyamsha* is 400 years, for *Tretha Yuga* it is 300 years, for *Dwapara Yuga* it is 200 years and for *Kali Yuga* it is 100 years. So when these *Sandhyamsa*s are added up a *Maha Yuga* comes to 12, 000 years of Gods. 71 *Maha Yugas* make up one *Manvanthara* and 14 *Manvantharas* make up one *Kalpa* that is one day of *Brahma* when creation takes place. At the end of it *Pralaya* takes place. After night, the duration of which is equal to that of a day, at the dawn of another of *Brahma*'s days another cycle of creation starts again.

As one moves from *Sathya Yuga* to *Tretha Yuga* and then to *Dwapara Yuga* and finally to *Kali Yuga* the power of righteousness diminishes and evil flourishes. In *Sathya Yuga* there was no poverty and there was no need for houses. People lived on top of the mountains and near the shores of the oceans. There were no villages or cities. As time passed the need for houses and occupation cropped up. So the villages and towns came up. Evil became glaring in *Dwapara Yuga*. To bring people back to righteousness the great knowledge that is *Veda*s had to be imparted to the people. So *Vyasa* divided the supreme knowledge into four categories under the four *Vedas* and there was need for various other scriptures like *Ithihasas* and *Puranas* as well. So they were composed. There was widespread hatred, jealousy and fighting. People became unrighteous and diseases became widespread.

Varaha Purana

This *Purana* tells about the process of creation in each *Kalpa*, about *Purusha* and *Prakruth*i, the sustenance the dissolution of the Universe, the order of the four *Yugas*, how they are calculated, and the geography of earth and so on.

Purusha is the supreme energy or Almighty, Lord *Narayana* and *Prakruth*i is the medium through which *Purusha* manifests His power.

In the beginning of creation ego or *Ahamkara* and the five basic elements Space, Water, Earth, Air and Fire manifested themselves from the supreme Almighty. Subsequently, the great element, the *Mahatatthva*, nature and collective consciousness manifested themselves. The collective consciousness combined with each of the three basic qualities of *Sathva* (the pure), *Rajas* and *Tamas* (the dark). The different permutations and combinations of all the three *Gunas* with the collective intelligence resulted in the creation of different *Tanmatras,* the subtle form of matter. From *Tanmatras* the *Indriyas* or sense organs are created. Then all living creatures are created by the Almighty with the help of the five basic elements.

In the beginning there was nothing but empty Space. Subsequently various natural elements like *Shabda*, or Sound, *Akasha*, or Ether, *Vayu* or Air, *Teja* or Light, *Jal* or Water emerged. Each of the latter got manifested from the former. Then Earth was created by the supreme almighty to provide base for all living beings. The combination of Earth and Water resulted in an egg or *Anda*. As the egg grew in size, the supreme manifested Himself as *Naarayana* within it. During each *Kalpa* a Lotus manifests from the navel of *Narayana* upon which *Brahma* emerges. He is asked to commence creation by the Supreme Almighty. At the end of each *Kalpa* each Universe is engulfed in darkness. At that time *Narayana e*nters himself in *Yogic* sleep. After He wakes up creation begins anew. First of all five types of *Avidya* or false knowledge manifests from *Naarayana* namely, *Tamas* or darkness, *Moha* or attachment, *Mahamoha* or absolute attachment, *Tamisra* or jealousy, and *Andhatamisra* or anger. After this the immovable things like mountains, trees, and so on are created. This is known as the primary creation or main creation or *Mukhya Sarga*. Then *Brahma* creates species that are superior to the earlier creations like animals in the 3rd, 4th and the 5th *Sargas. Brahma*'s sixth creation is known as *Satviksarga* that consists of deities. The creation of human beings is the seventh in order and is known as *'Arvaaaksrota Sarga'*. *Brahma*'s eighth creation is called *'Anugrah Sarga'* in which He creates Sages and Hermits. The ninth creation of *Brahma* is called *'Kaumar Sarg'*, that is the creation of adolescent beings.

Bhuloka is located on the surface of the earth. In order to create the three *Gunas* or qualities namely, *Satvik, Rajasic* and *Tamasic*, the Almighty created water first and went into *Yoganidra* or divine sleep. Then a Lotus manifested from His navel on which *Brahma* originated. He then created His *Maanasa Putras* or mental sons and creation then proceeded.

The prominent islands or *Dveepas* on Earth are the *Jambudveepa, Shakdveepa, Kushadveepa, Krounchadveepa*, and *Shalmalidveepa*. *Jambudveepa* is spread over one lakh *Yojana*. It is inhabited by *Siddhas* and is blessed with great natural beauty. *Jambudveepa* is surrounded by many oceans on all its sides. Towards its east and west are the salt water oceans. Some important mountains in Jambudveepa are the *Himalayas, Sumeru, Hemakut*, and the *Nishadha* mountains. There are nine parts in *Jambudveepa*. The area of *Shakdveepa* is twice as that of *Jambudveepa*. It is inhibited by virtuous people who are prosperous and they enjoy a long life. They are free from the sorrows of old age. This island is covered by oceans on its two sides; the salt water ocean on one side and *Ksheer Sagar* or the ocean of Milk on the other. The mountain range on the northern part of this island is known as *Vidyachal*. There are also mountains like *Rajatgiri, Pambikey* and so on here. There are also the seven mountain ranges known as '*Kula Parvatas*' in this island. There is a large tree named '*Shak*' in the central part of this island; and hence its name *Shakdveepa*. The island of *Kushadvieea* is twice the area of *Shakdveepa*. There are seven prominent Mountain ranges in this region. In its central part '*Kush*' grass is seen in abundance and hence its name '*Kushadvipa*'. The *Krounchadveepa* is twice the area of '*Kushdveepa*'. It also has seven prominent mountain ranges. This *Dvipa* is surrounded by an ocean of clarified butter or ghee on all its sides. The *Shalmalidvipa* is double the area of *Kraunchadvipa* and is enclosed by the clarified butter ocean on all its sides. There are seven prominent mountains and seven prominent rivers here.

Vamana Purana

Vamana Purana tells about *Jambudveepa, Bharathee Varsha* and hells.

Jambudveepa is a very large island. It is subdivided in to nine parts. *Ilavritvarsha* is at its centre. The important regions around it are; *Bhadraasvvarsha* towards its east, the *Hiranyakvarsh* towards north east, *Kinnarvarsh* towards south east, *Bharatavarsh* towards south, *Harivarsha* towards southwest, *Ketumalvarsh* towards west, *Ramyakvarsh* towards northwest and *Kuruvarsh* towards its north. All these nine *varshas* are full of natural beauty. The inhabitants of all the eight varshas except *Bharatavarsha* never face old age or death. *Bharathavarsha* has nine sub islands. All these islands are surrounded by oceans on all sides. These are, *Indradveepa, Kaseruman, Tamravarna, Gabhastiman, Nagadveep, Karaha, Sinhal, Varun* and *Kumar*. The *Kiratas* live towards its east and *Yavan* live towards its west. The seven prominent mountain ranges here are, *Mahendra, Malay, Sahya, Shukthi, Manriksh, Vindhya* and *Pariyatra*.

Brahma Vaivartha Purana

Brahma Vaivartha Purana describes creation, *Manvantaras* and the sages and *Manus* in each *Manvanthara*, the geography of the earth, the underworlds, hells, and the boundaries of earth.

In the beginning there was Water everywhere. *Brahma*, the divine essence slept on this water in the form of *Vishnu*. In the water a golden egg or *Anda* emerged. *Brahma* was born inside that egg. For one whole year *Brahma* remained inside that egg. He then split the egg into two and created Heaven or *Svarga* and the Earth or *Prithvi* from the two parts of the egg. From the powers of His mind *Brahma* created seven great sages. To continue with the process of creation *Brahma* created a man and a woman from His own body. They are known as *Swayambhu Manu* and *Satarupadevi*.

A *Manvanthara* is an era. There are four smaller eras or *Yugas* namely, *Satya,* or *Kritha Yuga*, *Tretha Yuga*, *Dvapara Yuga*, and *Kali Yuga*. Each cycle of these four *Yugas* put together is called a *Maha Yuga*. A *Mahayuga* consists of 12,000 years of Gods or 4,320,000 human years. 71 *Mahayugas* constitute one *Manvanthara* and 14 such *Manvantharas* constitute one *Kalpa* that is one day of *Brahma*. The Universe is destroyed at the end of each of His day. In the present *Kalpa*, six *Manvantharas* are over and the present *Manvanthar*a is the seventh one. Each *Manvanthara* is ruled by a *Manu*.

This Purana asks who will search through the wide infinities of science to count the universes side by side each containing its *Brahma, Vishnu* and *Shiva*. Who can count the *Indras* in them all?

The Earth is divided into seven regions namely, *Jambudveepa, Plakshadveepa, Shalmaladveepa, Kushadveepa, Krounchadveepa, Shakadveepa* and *Pushkaradveepa*. These regions are surrounded by seven oceans and their names are *Lavana, Ikshu, Sura, Sarpi, Dadhi, Dugdha, and Jala*. *Jambudveepa* is in the centre and right in the middle of *Jambudveepa* is Mount *Sumeru*. To the south of *Sumeru* are the mountains of *Himavana, Hemakuta*, *Nishadha*, and to the north of *Sumeru* are the mountains of *Neela, Shveta*, and *Shringa*. *Jambudveepa* is divided in to several regions or *Varshas*. *Sumeru* is in the middle of *Ilavritavarsha*. Brahma's city is on the peak of Mount *Sumeru*. It is here the sacred *Ganga* River descends from heaven and gets divided into four tributaries. There are seven major mountain ranges in Bharathavarsha. *Bharathavarsha* is divided into nine regions or dvipas. The ninth region is surrounded by oceans on all sides. Below the earth there are seven regions of the underworld that is collectively known as *Patala*.

The Earth extends up to those parts of the Sky that can be lit up by the rays of the Sun and Moon. The expanse from there up to star circle is known as *Bhuvarloka* and holy sages live there. Above the solar circle is the lunar circle and beyond it in succession come the regions of Mercury or *Budha,* Venus or *Shukra*, Mars or *Mangal*, Jupiter or *Brihaspathi*, Saturn or *Sani,* the great Bear Constellation known as *Saptha rishi Mandal* and the pole star or *Dhruva*. The region from the solar circle to *Dhruvaloka* is known as Heaven or *Swarga*. Beyond *Dhruvaloka* is *Maharloka*. Further above are *Janaloka, Tapoloka* and *Sathyaloka* in succession. At the end of each *Kalpa* all the three lokas or regions namely, *Bhooloka, Bhuvarloka* and *Svarlok*a get destroyed. But the four lokas that are beyond namely, the *Maharloka, JanalokaTapoloka* and *Satyalo*ka are not destroyed.

Brahmanda Purana

Brahmanda Purana tells about the five types of the process of creation of the Universe, *Manvantharas, Kalpas, Yugas, Jambudveepa, Bharatha Varsha*, and the three types of dissolution or annihilation of the Universe. It also tells about the compound of precious stones.

There are three types of *Pralayas* or deluge namely, *Avaantara Pralaya, Maha Pralaya* and *Kaama Pralaya*. In every *Kalpa* these three *Pralayas* take place in a cyclical pattern.

The last of the seven oceans namely the *Jala Samudra* is now dried up.

The Earth is divided into many plates nearly 14 of them in the present *Manvantara*.

Kurma Purana

Kurma Purana tells about creation and describes the four *Yugas,* the metaphysical knowledge, history of creation in the four *Yugas*, measurement of time, the Boar *Avatar* of Lord *Vishnu,* the *Yugas*, geography of earth, the 14 regions in the universe, the seven seas, mountains surrounding the seven *Dveepas*, *Manvantharas* and the *Manus* and gods in each *Manvanthara*.

When it was time for creation, *Brahman*, the Absolute, created water throughout. Before that there was nothing. In the water a golden egg or *Hiranmaya Garbha* or *Anda* emerged. The egg grew in size and *Brahma* the creator appeared inside the egg. Everything that there is in the Universe was already there inside the egg in the embryonic form. Since *Brahma* originated from inside the golden egg He came to be known as *Hiranyagarbha*. *Brahma* was the first being in the universe.

Each *Kalpa* is one day of *Brahma* and there are 14 such *Manvantharas in* each *Kalpa*. That means there are 1000 *Maha Yugas* in every Kalpa. 360 *Kalpas* make one Brahma's year 100 times of this period that is 100 years of Brahma is known as *Parardha*. At the end of this period the whole universe is destroyed. At the end of destruction creation known as *Sarga* begins again afresh. *Prathi Sarga* is a minor destruction that takes place at the end of each *Kalpa*. The present *Kalpa* is known as *Varaha Kalpa*. The one that preceded the present *Kalpa* was *Padma Kalpa*.

In the beginning only *Brahman* that is indescribable was there. *Brahma, Vishnu* and *Shiva* are derived from *Brahman*; *Brahma* for performing creation, *Vishnu* for its upkeep and *Shiva* for its destruction for a new beginning. After destruction of the Universe, when it was time for recreation, *Brahma* found the earth to be submerged in water. Lord *Vishnu* then slept on water for 1000 *Maha Yugas*. While the Lord slept on water a wonderful lotus emerged from His navel. It was gigantic and was shining like the Sun. Its fragrance spread in all directions. *Brahma* then appeared inside the lotus. Therefore he came to be known as *Padma Yoni*. In order to restart creation *Brahma* requested Lord *Vishnu* to bring up the earth from water. So Lord *Vishnu* adopted the form of a boar and went underneath the water to the underworld and lifted the earth with His tusks and placed it on water. The earth then floated on the water like a huge boat.

Manu had a son by name *Priyavrata*. He had 10 sons. But three of them had no material desires. So *Manu* divided his kingdom among the seven of his remaining sons. The earth was therefore divided into seven regions or *Dveepas*. Among his sons, *Agnidhara* ruled *Jambudveepa*. *Agnidhara* had nine sons. So he divided his kingdom in to nine regions or *Varshas*. The region where *Nabhi*, one of *Agnidhara*'s sons ruled later went to one of his descendants by name *Bharata*. After his name this region came to be known as *Bharata Varsha*.

After each *Kalpa* or day of Brahma night falls and there is destruction and a new creation starts again in the next *Kalpa* or day of *Brahma*. At the time of last *Kalpa* there was water everywhere. Heaven, earth and the underworld were flooded with water. There were no sages or gods then. Only the Supreme, the Absolute, *Naarayana* rested on water with innumerable eyes, arms and feet. At that point a *Lotus* sprouted from the navel of *Naarayana*. The Lotus was gigantic and it shone like innumerable suns. *Brahma* was inside the lotus. He is therefore referred to as *Padma Yoni*.

Paramatman or *Brahman*, the Supreme or the divine soul, the only one is pure. The universe is created out of that and into it the universe will merge at the time of destruction. This *Paramatman* is present in the individual soul or *Jeevatman*. Both are one and the same.

Bhavishya Purana

Bhavishya Purana predicts about many things about the future happenings. Though this text was written thousands of years ago, Veda *Vyasa* through his mystic vision could predict the future history that is the happenings in the modern period. He says in this *Kaliyuga* 3000 years are already over.

Vaayu Purana

Vaayu Purana explains about creation, the four *Yugas* and their features, *Varaaha Kalpa*, units of measurement, *Manvantharas* and gods and sages in different *Manvantharas*, the geography of earth, upper Lokas and the under worlds, and units of time and so on.

In the beginning there was nothing in the Universe except the divine *Brahman*, the essence that was present everywhere. This *Brahman* was the origin of all that was desired to be created in the Universe. There was darkness and water everywhere. When it was time for creation, *Brahman*, the Absolute, divided itself into three, namely, *Brahma*, the creator, *Vishnu*, the sustainer and *Shiva* the destroyer. In the water a golden (*Hiranya*) egg (*Anda*) formed and floated like a gigantic bubble. *Brahma* was born inside that egg. So He came to be known as *Hiranyagarbha*. Since He created Himself He came to be known as '*Swayambhu*'. Inside the egg were all worlds that would be created in an embryonic form. The earth, mountains, land, oceans and rivers, moon, sun, stars and planets, gods, demons, humans and other beings were contained in it. This was the original creation of the Universe.

At the end of each one of *Brahma*'s days a minor destruction takes place. The Universe gets flooded with water during *Brahma*'s night or sleep. But *Brahma, Vishnu* and *Shiva* are not destroyed. At the end of last *Kalpa* the minor destruction took place and the world was flooded. *Naarayana* alone slept balanced on the hood of *Adisesha* on the water. A lotus then appeared from the navel of *Vishnu*. It was very huge and extended over 100 *Yojanas* and shone like innumerable sons. Then *Brahma* came and *Vishnu* went inside *Brahma*. There He saw the entire universe inside. *Vishnu* spent 1000 years inside *Brahma*'s stomach. Then He came out of *Brahma*'s mouth and He asked *Brahma* to enter into His stomach. *Brahma* entered and He too saw many worlds there. He also spent several years inside the stomach. In the meantime *Vishnu* closed all exit points and *Brahma* could not come out. So He came up through the stalk of the Lotus.

Each of *Brahma*'s days is known as a *Kalpa* or a cycle. There are 14 *Manvantharas* in each *Kalpa*. Each *Manvanthara* lasts for duration of 30, 67, 20, 000 years. Six *Manvantharas* are over and we are in the seventh *Manvanthara*. *Vaivasvata* is the present *Manu*.

After destruction or *Pralaya*, with the dawn of another day *Brahma* starts the creation process again. This periodical process of destruction and recreation is known as *Pratisarga*. The present *Kalpa* is known as *Varaaha Kalpa*. In each of the 14 *Manvantharas* there are 28 crores of gods. In 14 *Manvantharas* therefore there are 392 crores of Gods.

With the passage of time the power of righteousness fall and evil start gaining strength with each successive *Yugas*. So in each *Dwapara Yugas Veda Vyasas* are born. *Krishna Dwaipayana* happens to be the 28th *Vyasa* in the *Dwapara Yuga* of the present cycle of creation. He is credited with the classification of the supreme knowledge or *Vedas* and composing *Purana Samhitha*. He also composed *Mahaabharata* the great Epic.

Each day of *Brahma* is called a *Kalpa* and 1000 *Kalpas* constitute one year for *Brahma*. 8000 such years constitute Brahma's *Yuga* and in a *Kalpa* there are, 4,320,000,000 years. 1000 of these *Yugas* constitute a *Savana;* 2000 *Savanas* constitute a *Trivrita* and this is the life span of *Brahma*.

Day and night are equal twice a year. They are the precise mid points of early autumn, that is *Sharat* and spring that is *Vasantha*. 15 days make one *Paksha* or fortnight and there are two *Pakshas* in each month. Two months form one *Rithu* or season and three *Rihtus* constitute one *Ayana*. There are two *Ayanas* in a year namely, *Dakshinayana* and *Uttarayana*.

In *Sathya Yuga*, winter, summer, and monsoon were unknown. All were equally prosperous and pleasant. As people were naturally righteous, there was no concept of *Dharma* or righteousness or *Adharma* or evil. People did not live in a fixed place. They freely lived on the sea shore or on the mountains. People lived on juice that came out from earth. This juice was so miraculous that old age and diseases were totally unknown to people. There was neither hatred nor jealousy as all were equal. People had the divine mental power to get whichever object they desired by mere thought. There was no scarcity for anything. In *Tretha Yuga* the picture changed. The strong and divine mental power disappeared and people engaged in meditation or *Dhyana*. Thick clouds appeared on the sky and it rained. It helped the growth of plants and trees. People lived on the fruits of trees. They also used the bark of the tree for clothing. The trees were so wonderful that they were known as *Kalpavrikshas*, that is, they provided whatever one wished for. As *Tretha Yuga* progressed, people became narrow minded and began to fight over possession of trees and consequently trees began to wither away. So people began to build dwelling places on mountains and near rivers. Consequently, villages and cities emerged. Units of measurement became necessary now with the change of time. The houses were built on trees. Trees and herbs sustained people. But people began to fight for possession of rivers, lands, mountains, trees and herbs. The might became powerful and the weak suffered. The rare trees and herbs disappeared and thick forests came in its place.

Brahma created the five elements or *Panchabhoothas* namely, Earth, Water, Fire, Air, Sky, and then the directions, heaven, oceans, rivers, mountains, trees, time, night and days. Through His mental powers He created three sons namely, *Sanandana, Sanaka and Sanatana*. Then He created ten sons namely, *Bhrugu, Pulastya, Pulaha, Kratu, Angira, Marichi, Daksha, Atri, Vasishta* and *Rudra*. The first nine of *Brahma*'s sons became sages. Then *Brahma* divided His body into two halves. The male half was known as *Swayambhu* and the female was known as *Shatarupa* and they became man and wife.

Sumeru is in *Jambudveepa*. It is at a very high altitude and gold is found there in abundance. *Meru* was formed out of the stalk of the Lotus in which *Brahma* appeared in the beginning. *Brahma*'s city is located here.

Bharatha Varsha is bounded by *Himalayas* in the north and ocean in the south. To the east of *Bharatha Varsha* live the *Kiratas* and to the west are the *Yavanas*.

There are seven regions in the underworld namely, *Atala, Sutala, Vitala, Gabhastala, Mahaatala, Shritala*, and *Paatala*. The ground in *Atala* is dark in colour, in *Sutala* it is pale, *Vitala* has red ground, *Gabhastala*'s ground is *yellow* and the ground in *Mahaatala* is white. In *Shritala* there are numerous stones and boulders. *Paatala* has ground laced with gold. Snakes and demons live in the underworld. Similarly there are seven upper *Lokas* as well. They are *Bhooloka, Bhuvarloka, Svarloka, Maharloka, Janaloka, Tapoloka*, and *Sathyaloka*.

The Moon, Sun, stars and planets revolve around *Dhruva* the Pole star. The sun's chariot, made of gold is drawn by seven horses namely *Gayathri, Trishitupa, Anushutupa, Jagati, Pamkti, Vrihata* and *Ushnika*. The Moon's chariot is drawn by ten horses namely *Yayu, Trimana, Vrisha, Raji, Bala, Vasa, Turanya, Hamsa, Vyomi* and *Mriga*. *Budha*'s or Mercury's chariot is drawn by eight horses, Venus or *Shukra*'s by ten horses, Mar's or *Mangala*'s by eight horses and *Brihaspathi*'s or Jupiter's and *Shani*'s or Saturn's by eight horses.

Bharathavarsha is bounded by *Himalayas* on the north and by oceans to the south. It is divided into nine regions namely, *Indradvipa, Kaseruman, Tamraparani, Gabhastimana, Nagadvipa, Soumya, Gandharva* and *Varuna*. The ninth region is an island surrounded by an ocean. The southern part of `*Bharathavarsha* is known as *Kumarika*.

5

Cosmos in *Srimad Bhagavatha Purana*

The description of the cosmos in *Bhagavatham* baffles the modern man. It deals with the mystery of creation and annihilation of the Universe with its animate and inanimate creations beginning with the unmanifest stage of the Absolute energy. It also describes how the creation is effected by the agitation of the three modes of material nature, the different stages of evolution by elemental transformations, the construction of the Universal egg from which the Universal form of the Supreme Lord emerges. It also explains the subtle and gross movements of time, the generation of lotus from the navel of *Garbhodakasayi Vishnu*, the planetary systems, the astronomical calculations, astronomy, the geography of earth, the different *Yugas* and their characteristic features, the arrangement of celestial spheres and about the subterranean regions and hell, the concept of continuity in the creative process and the process of annihilation, the inhabitants in different planets and so on along with the description of the Supreme Lord *Naarayana*, His various incarnations, the path to *Mukthi* or *Moksha* and so on.

This Purana has 12 cantos each of which contains many chapters.

Srimad Bhagavatham on Universe

CANTO—1

CHAPTER—1

Hymns 30, 31, 32, 33 and 34

In the beginning of the creation of the Universe the Absolute, the *Parabrahman*, created the energies of cause and effect by His own internal energy and after creating the Universe, the Absolute soul entered into all beings of the universe. This Absolute soul, the *Paramatman*, pervades everything in the Universe just as fire permeates wood. The Super Soul after entering into the beings that have the three modes of nature namely *Sattva* or goodness, *Rajas* or passion and *Thamas* or ignorance, makes them, through their mind that is subtle, enjoy or suffer the effects of these triple modes.

CHAPTER—3

Hymns 1, 2, 3 and 5

In the beginning of creation the Absolute, the Super soul expanded Himself in the Universal form for purpose of material creation. Later a part of this

Purusha lay down on the cosmic waters of the universe and from His navel a lotus sprouted and from the flower on top of the stem *Brahma,* the creator, manifested. All the planetary systems are located inside His extensive universal body, but His body is always in eternal supreme state of spiritual excellence as He is independent of the material ingredients that are created.

Hymns 30, 32 and 36

The concept of the *Virat* or Universal form of the super soul is only imaginary but not real. It is only to enable the common man to understand the extensive infinite nature of that Supreme energy because in reality that Absolute energy has no form. This Absolute energy is subtle, has no form or shape, is unseen, unheard and unmanifest and resides within every being. This Absolute Soul that is the total energy creates maintains and destroys the universe but He remains totally independent although He or that is within every being.

CHAPTER—5

Hymn 10

The cosmos or the Universe emerged from the Supreme soul. In Him it rests and unto Him it gets merged after annihilation or *Pralaya*.

CHAPTER—6

Hymns 9 and 30

At the end of each millennium, Lord *Narayana*, the supersoul, reclines in the cosmic waters motionless. After 4,300,000,000 solar years the creative principle, *Brahma* enters into Lord *Naarayana* with creative elements and He recreates the universe as per the will of the Supreme Soul.

CHAPTER—7

Hymns 27, 28, 30 and 31

The nuclear weapons (*Brahmhastra)* that can be counteracted by another *Brahmastra* only are mentioned here. It is stated that when the two *Brahmhastras* collided (of *Arjuna* and *Aswatthama*) a great circle of fire like the disc of the Sun covered the outer space and the whole firmament of planets and all the beings of the three worlds were scorched by the combined heat of the *Brahmastras.* At that point of time every one was reminded of the *Samvartaka* fire at the time of *Maha Pralaya* or the great deluge.

CHAPTER—10

Hymns 21, 22 and 24

The Absolute, the Supersoul alone existed before all the manifested creation and finally in Him all creations merge, their energy being suspended. His internal potency induces *Prakruthi* that is inherent in Him, the *Purusha* to create the Universe. *Purusha* the supersoul creates maintains and annihilates the Universe but He himself does not partake in that process but remains aloof.

CHAPTER—13

Hymn 46

Kala, the eternal time, *Karma*, the action, and *Guna*, the modes of material nature, these three control the physical body that is made up of *Panchabhoothas* or the five elements.

Hymns 51 and 52

In the southern region of the *Himalayas* that is known as *Sapta srota* (divided by seven) great sages inhabit. It is here the sacred *Ganges* divides itself into seven.

CHAPTER—15

Hymn 12

In this hymn *Arjuna* says that he was able to reach the heavenly planet with his body.

Hymn 37

Kali Yuga is characterised by increasing avarice, falsehood, cheating and violence.

CHAPTER—16

Hymn 12

This hymn mentions all parts of the earth namely, *Bhadrasva, Ketumala, Bharatha, northern Kuru, Kimpurusha* and so on.

Hymn 22

In this hymn the features of *Kaliyuga* when there is widespread evil is explained.

CHAPTER—17

Hymn 24

The features of *Sathya Yuga* are austerity, cleanliness, mercy and truthfulness.

CHAPTER—18

6—*Kaliyuga* started with the disappearance of Lord *Krishna* from the Earth.

CANTO—2

CHAPTER—1

Hymns 24 to 36

The gigantic material Universe is the body of the Absolute wherein the past, present and future of material time is experienced. This *Virat* or Universal form is covered by several fold material elements. The planet *Patala* is the bottom of the feet of the Universal form; His heels and toes are the *Rasaatala* planets; His ankles are the *Mahatala* planets and His shanks are the *Talatala* planets; His knees form the planetary system of *Sutala* and His two thighs are the *Vitala* and *Atala* planetary systems; His lips are the *Mahatala* and outer space is the depression of His navel, the chest of this gigantic universal form is the luminary planetary system; His neck the *Mahar* planets; His mouth the *Janas* planets and His forehead the *Tapas* planetary system; *Sahtyaloka,* the top most planetary system is His thousand heads; His arms are the demi Gods headed by *Indra;* the ten directional sides are His ears and the physical sound is His sense of hearing; His nostrils are the two *Asvini- Kumaras*; the material fragrance His sense of smell; and His mouth the blazing fire; the sphere of outer space His eye pits and His eyeball is the sun as the power of seeing; His eyelids are both day and night and the movement of his eyebrows shows the residences of the *Brahm*a and similar supreme personalities; His palate the source of water; *Varuna* is His tongue that is the juice or essence of everything; the Vedic hymns are His cerebral passage; His jaws of teeth are *Yama*, the God of death; His heart the seat of affection, and the most alluring illusory energy is His smile; His very glance is the great ocean of material existence; the nature of modesty is the upper portion of His lips, hankering His chin; religion His breast; irreligion His back; *Brahma*, His genitals; and *Mitra- Varuna*, His two testicles; the ocean is His waist and the hills and mountains are the stacks of His bones; Rivers are His veins, trees are the hairs of His body; air His breath; passing ages are His movements; His activities are the three modes of material nature; Clouds are the hairs on His head; His mind is the moon that is the reservoir of all changes; the principles of matter or *Maha Tatthva* is His consciousness; *Rudradeva* is His ego; Horse, mule, camel and elephant etc. are His nails; and wild animals and the other fore legged ones are in His belt zone; the varieties of birds indicate His artistic nature; the ruler of mankind, *Manu*, is the emblem of His intelligence; humanity, is His residence; The celestial human beings like the *Gandharvas, Vidyadharas, Carnas* and angels represent His musical rhythm; and the demonic soldiers represent His prowess.

CHAPTER—2

Hymns 22 and 24 to 31

There are millions of planets in this Universe and *Brahma Loka* is the topmost planet. The *Yogi* or mystic due to his devotion, austerity, mystic powers and transcendental knowledge is able to pass over the Milky Way and reach *Brahma Loka*, the highest planet. First he goes to *Visvanara,* the planet of the Deity of fire and there he gets completely cleansed of all his contaminations. Then he goes still further upwards to the circle of *Sisumara*. This *Sisumara* is the pivot for the spiralling of this Universe and is supposed to be the navel of *Vishnu*, the *Gabhodaka Sayi Vishnu*. The Yogi alone can cross this circle of *Sisumara* and reach the planet *Maharloka* and here the purified saints enjoy duration of life of 4,300,000, 000 solar years. At the time of final devastation of the entire Universe, that is, the end of *Brahma*'s life span, a flame of fire emanates from the mouth of *Anantha*, that is, from the bottom of the Universe. The *Yogi* at that time can see all planets of the Universe burning to ashes and he goes to *Sathya Loka* where his duration of life is 15,480,000,000,000 years. In the planet of *Sathya Loka* there is no misery, no bereavement, old age or death. There is no pain of any kind and hence there are no anxieties. After reaching *Sathya Loka* the *Yogi* is able to move with his subtle body like that of his gross body and gradually he attains the existence from earthy to watery, then fiery, glowing and airy and finally he reaches the ethereal stage. There he surpasses the different senses like sight, smell etc. Thus after surpassing the gross and subtle forms of covering he enters the plane of egoism. There he becomes devoid of all material modes of existence like ignorance, passion and goodness and reaches the point of neutralization. After this stage he merges with *Mahat Tattva* and reaches to the point of pure self or *Atman* realization. He never returns to the material world again.

CHAPTER—4

Hymns 6, 8 and 12

The wonderful acts of creation of the Absolute soul, the *Paramatman* who is although residing inside every being is inconceivable even to the great Demi Gods and great scholars and so on.

CHAPTER—5

Hymns 11 and 14

11—*Brahma* created by the Supreme Soul, created this Universe as per the commands of the Supreme soul, by the effulgence known as *Brahma Jhyothi* just as the Moon, the firmament, the planets and stars manifest their brightness due to the Sun's fire and light.

Hymns 18 to 22

The Absolute the *Paramatman,* that is the *Brahman*, exhibited His external energy, the material modes or qualities of nature namely,

Sattva, (goodness), *Rajas* (passion) and *Thamas* (ignorance) for purpose of creation. The first incarnation of the Absolute Soul is known as the *Karanarnvasayi Vishnu*. After this the *Mahat Tattva* or the principle of material creation takes place, then the time is manifested, and in the course of the eternal time the three qualities or nature appear and finally they transform in to activities.

Hymns 23 and 24

The material creations happen when the *Mahat- Tattva* is agitated. The ego or *Ahamkara* gets transformed into the three modes namely, goodness, passion and ignorance, and result in matter.

Hymns 25 to 33

From the darkness of the false ego, the first of the five elements namely Sky is generated. Its subtle form is the quality of sound. From sky, Air got generated with the quality of touch. The Air is also full of sound, sense perception, mental power and body strength. From Air, Fire is generated and with its transformation Water is produced. It has also form, touch, and sound. Water then transforms into all vegetables on Earth. It is also full of touch, sound and form. From the mode of goodness mind is created. The transformation of the mode of passion results in sense organs like ear, skin, nose, eyes, tongue, mouth, hands, genitals, legs and outlet for evacuation together with intelligence and living energy. When the *Panchabhoothas* or the elements, senses, mind and modes of nature combine then the body gets a form. So also when all these namely the elements, senses, mind and the modes of nature combine universe is created by the pure Absolute energy.

Hymns 34 to 39

The Universe remained under water for thousands of eons and the Lord of all living beings entered into them. Later the Lord came out of water as *Hiranya Garbha* and entered into each Universe by assuming the universal form or *Virataroopa* with thousands of, that is, innumerable legs, arms, mouths, heads and so on. The planetary system of the Universe displays the different upper and lower limbs of the universal body of the Almighty. Men came out of His mouth, arms, thighs, and legs. In His legs are located the lower planetary systems up to the limit of the earthly stratum. The middle planetary systems beginning from *Bhuvarloka* are supposed to be located in His navel. Demi Gods and sages are supposed to be occupying still higher planetary systems and finally the highly evolved sages are supposed to occupy the chest portions of this Supreme Lord or energy. From the forefront of the chest up to the neck of the universal form of the Lord, the planetary system called *Janaloka* and *Tapoloka* are located. *Sathya Loka*, the top most planetary system is located on the head of this Universal form. The spiritual planets are however eternal.

Hymns 40 to42

There are a total of 14 planes of existence. Out of these, seven are the lower planetary systems. In these lower planetary systems, the first one, *Atala* is located on the waist of the *Virat,* the Universal form; *Vitala* is located on His thighs; *Sutala* on the knees; *Talatala* on the shanks; *Mahaatala* on the ankles; *Rasaatala* on the upper portion of the feet; and the seventh *Paatala* on the soles of His feet. The whole planetary systems can also be divided into three divisions. The lower planetary system on the legs that is up to earth; the middle planetary systems on the navel; and the upper planetary systems from the chest up to the head of the Supreme personality.

CHAPTER—6

Hymns 13 to 18

All phenomenal manifestation of the universes namely the planets, stars, asteroids, luminaries, lightning, thunder, and the inhabitants of the different planetary systems namely, the *Gandharvas, Apsaras, Yaksas, Raksas, Bhutaganas, Uragas, Pasus, Pitas, Siddhas, Vidyadharas, Caranas*, and all other different varieties of living beings including birds, beasts, trees and all other things are all enveloped by the Universal form of the Lord at all times namely the past, present and future. He, the Supreme is transcendental to all of them and He exists eternally in a form not exceeding nine inches. The Universal Soul maintains everything in the Universe just as the Sun that illumines all by its radiation. He, the Universal soul is beyond everything, including death, and results of *Karmas* or actions of the phenomenal Universe.

Hymn 20

The spiritual world that contains three fourths of the Lord's energy is located beyond this material world and it is meant for those spiritually elevated beings that are never reborn. Others must live in these three material worlds.

Hymn 22

All the innumerable Universes emerge with all the material elements, qualities and senses from the supreme *Purusha* who is independent of all these like the Sun that is independent of its rays and heat.

Hymns 31 to 33

All the material manifestations of the universes are contained in His material energies. But He is eternally independent of all these three material modes of existence although He is the powerful controller of the three energies of creation, upkeep, and destruction of everything.

Hymns 35 to 41 and 43 to 45

Even *Brahma*, the creator in spite of being an expert in mystic power is unable to understand Him, the Lord, who is the very source of *Brahma*'s birth. The Sky or Space cannot estimate its limits of expansion. Similarly, even the Supreme Lord Himself cannot fathom His own limits. All including *Brahma*, the creator can only wonder about the illusory external energy of the Supreme Lord as all beings can see only this manifested cosmos according to one's own ability. He, the Supreme Lord cannot be comprehended fully. Creation takes place because of Him and the material substance and manifestations are all only Himself. He maintains them for some time and absorbs everything unto Himself again.

The Supreme Absolute Soul is pure and is free from all contaminations of material tinges. He is Truth. He is the embodiment of full and perfect knowledge. He is all pervading with no beginning and end. He is the one without a second; only when one is beyond his senses one can understand Him. All that we see in this Universe is only a fragment of the infinite transcendental potency of the Lord.

CHAPTER—7

Hymn 1

The Supreme Lord assumed the form of a boar and lifted up the Earth that was drowned in the great ocean of the Universe called *Garbhodaka.*

Hymn 20

Sathya Loka is the top most planetary system in the Universe.

Hymn 37

After fully understanding Vedic scientific knowledge the atheists annihilate the inhabitants of different planets by flying unseen in the sky on well-built rockets prepared by the great scientist *Maaya.*

Hymn 40

It is impossible for anyone including the scientists who might have counted the particles of atoms of the universe to describe the prowess of the Lord.

Hymn 47

The Absolute power or energy, the supreme, the *Purusha* is complete consciousness or energy only that is devoid of matter.

Hymn 49

Even after annihilation of the material elementary bodies, the living entity exists, exactly like the air within the body.

52—The Absolute energy or power or Brahman is the basis of all energies.

CHAPTER—8

Hymn 2

This hymn mentions about living beings in all planets.

Hymn 10

The Supreme, the Absolute, the Lord of all energies is untouched by His external energy.

Hymn 23

The Godhead by His internal potency enjoys His pastime in the activity of creation and at the time of annihilation He gives them up to His external potency and remains a witness to all.

CHAPTER—9

Hymns 10 to 14

The Supreme planet above all others is *Vaikunta* –the abode of the Supreme. The inhabitants of *Vaikunta* planets are said to be having a glowing sky- bluish complexion. Their eyes resemble lotus flowers; their dress is of yellowish colour and their bodily features are very attractive. They are always very youthful; they possess four hands, are nicely decorated beings with lots of ornaments and appear effulgent. Some of them are effulgent like coral and diamonds even in complexion and have garlands around their heads and they bloom like lotus flowers. Some also wear earrings. The *Vaikunta* planets are also surrounded by various airplanes all glowing brilliantly. These airplanes belong to the great *Mahatmas* or devotees of the Lord. The ladies are very beautiful due to their celestial complexion. It is also the abode of Goddess *Lakshmi*. Both the Lord and His consort Goddess *Lakshmi* look as the embodiments of all glory, charm and beauty.

Hymn 21

The living being is created due to the external energy of the Lord and he misconceives thinking himself in terms of 'I' and 'mine'. Once he starts enjoying the transcendence beyond time and material energy, he gives up these two misconceptions and becomes the Supreme, pure Self, the *Atman* itself.

Hymn 23

The *Paramatman* or the Absolute ordered *Brahma* (when *Brahma* was perplexed about his duty of creation) to do penance for a period of 1000 years and then after that period of penance *Brahma* heard the transcendental vibrations from the sky imparting the knowledge of creation to Him.

Hymn 24

The Lord, the supreme soul or the *Paramatman*, as a result of His great penance creates, maintains and destroys the cosmos as *Brahma,*

Vishnu and *Maheshwara* that are the three forms of the same super energy.

Hymn 33

The *Paramatman* or *Purusha* alone existed before creation. Then there was nothing but only Himself. The material nature which is the cause of creation of the Universe also was absent then.

Hymns 34 and 35

All creations are the product of the illusory nature or *Maaya* created by the Supreme Soul. It is similar to the reflection that appears in darkness.

The Universal elements enter into the cosmos and at the same time do not enter into the cosmos. Similarly the *Super Soul* exists within every creation but at the same time He is outside and independent of everything.

CHAPTER—10

Hymn 3

The elementary creation of 16 items of matter namely, the five elements, sound, form, taste, smell, touch and the eyes, ears, nose, tongue, skin, and mind is known as *Sarga*. The subsequent resultant interaction of the modes of material nature is called *Visarga*.

Hymns 6 and 7

Pralaya or destruction of the Universe or winding up of the cosmic manifestation is nothing but the merging of the living entities along with his conditional material living tendency with the Super Soul. The Supreme Soul or the Absolute Truth or energy is the Supreme source of all cosmic manifestation as well as its maintainer as well as destroyer.

Hymn 10

After separating the different universes the gigantic Universal form of the Lord that came out of the causal ocean, that was the place of appearance for the first *Purusha*, entered into each of the separate Universes.

Hymns 11 and 15 to 19

The Supreme personality of Godhead is *Nara* or Person. The Cosmic or the transcendental water created by the supreme *Nara* is known as *Naara.* Since the Lord rests on water in mystic slumber He is called *Naarayana.*

From the sky or Space located within the transcendental body of the Supreme Soul, the sum total of all living energy that includes the sense energy, mental force and body strength, are created. When the total energy is in motion, all living beings move and when the total energy stops all living entities stop all sensual activities. All the organs that sprang up from the *Virat Purusha* or universal form were suspended when He lay in water.

Hymn 34

The transcendental manifestation that is finer than the finest form is beyond the gross manifestation. It has no beginning, no intermediary stage and no end. So it is beyond the limits of expression or mental speculation and is quite different from the material conception.

Hymns 37 to 40

All living entities are created by this Supreme according to their past deeds or *Karmas.*

Hymn 41

All created beings including the Demi Gods, human beings and hellish living entities are created according to the different modes of material nature (goodness, passion and ignorance). The nature of each kind of living creature is a mixture of a particular mode of nature with the other two modes and then divided into three.

Hymn 42

After creating the Universe, the Lord, the *Paramatman* maintains them and at the end of the millennium, the Lord in the form of *Rudra,* the destroyer annihilates the entire creation.

Hymn 45

Actually the *Paramatman,* the creator or the fundamental cause of creation, does not act directly in the creative process of the Universe and its beings. .

CANTO—3

CHAPTER—5

Hymns 5 and 6

The Absolute or the Super soul, the Lord is the controller of all energies and it is He who by His will created the cosmic manifestation. He spreads Himself in the form of Space and places the whole creation in that Space. He expands Himself into many beings that are being manifested in different species.

Hymns 23 to 36

The Purusha, the Absolute, the creator of all beings, the one without a second, the Supreme who is called by different names was there even prior to creation. Through His will creation takes place and again ultimately everything merges into Himself.

In the beginning before the cosmic manifestation, only the Supreme existed and nothing else. The material cosmic energy was dormant then. But there was that internal potency in Him. This Supreme energy then worked both as cause as well as effect in cosmic manifestation. Through His external energy that is called *Maaya*, the entire manifestation of the material world happened. The Supreme, as the transcendental incarnation or *Purusha*, that is the Lord's plenary expansion, brought about the material nature of the three modes and the living beings were created by the influence of time. Thus the Supreme, the *Mahattatthva* sowed the seeds of universal manifestation out of His own body and the sum total of matter known as the *Mahathtatthva* got manifested. In course of time the *Mahath Tatthva* differentiated itself into many forms. This *Mahath Tatthva* transformed in to false ego that is represented in the three different modes namely, goodness, passion and ignorance, got manifested as the cause, the effect and the doer. With the interaction of the mode of goodness the false ego transformed in to mind. The senses are the results of mode of passion in false ego. Sky is the transformation of egoistic passion. Then the touch of sensation was created from which air generated. Air interacting with space generated the form of sense perception and the perception of form transformed into light or fire. Fire or light interacting with air resulted in water and taste was created. When water was mixed with the eternal time the external energy gave rise to earth that is qualified by smell.

Hymn 51

The material forms are created out of *Mahath Tatthva* that is the total cosmic energy.

CHAPTER—6

Hymns 3 to 6

The supreme through His energy entered into the elements. All the elements were motivated into action by the will of the Supreme gigantic form, the *Virata Purusha*, or *Vishva Roopam* or the universal form of the Lord. As the supreme entered into the elements of the Universal creation they transformed into a single gigantic form in which all plenary systems and all creations existed. This *Virata Purusha*, known as *Hiranmaya* lived for 1000 celestial years on water of the universe with all the entities in Him.

Hymn 8

The gigantic universal form of the Supreme Soul is the first incarnation and is the plenary portion of the Super Soul. He is the self of all living entities and in Him the aggregate creation rests.

Hymn 11

He, the Super Soul after His manifestation as the universal form became the various forms of Demi Gods.

Hymns 27 and 28

From the head of the gigantic universal form the heavenly planets were manifested and from His legs the earthly planets came and from His abdomen the sky got manifested. Within them the Demi Gods and others were manifested as per the modes of material nature. The Demi Gods because of their super excellent quality of the mode of goodness are located in the heavenly planets whereas the human beings because of their modes of passion and ignorance inhabit the earth along with their subordinates.

CHAPTER—7

Hymn 4

By His internal potency of the three modes of material nature the Lord caused creation of the Universe and by that He maintains and dissolves the creation in a repeated manner.

Hymns 21 and 22

After creating the total material energy, the *Mahath Tatthva* manifesting His gigantic Universal form with senses and sense organs, the Supreme Lord entered into it. The original *Purusha* is that lying on the causal ocean. All planets and their inhabitants live in His *Virat* form.

CHAPTER—8

Hymns 11 and 12

When the three worlds were submerged in water *Garbhodakasayi Vishnu* alone was there lying on *Anantha*, the celestial snake with half closed eyes. He was in His own internal potency and free from the action of the external energy. He contained within Himself all living entities in their subtle bodies. The Lord lay in the cosmic waters with self-invigorated energy called *Kaala* or time. The Lord lay for 4000 *Yug*a cycles in His internal potency and by His external energy He appeared to be sleeping within water. When the time for creation came, He saw His transcendental body as bluish.

Hymns 13 to 22 and 33

When the subtle principles or *Tatthvas* were agitated by the material mode the subtle form of creation pierced through His abdomen. Then the sum total of all living entities took the shape of the bud of a lotus flower that was generated from the personality of Godhead, Lord *Vishnu*. His supreme will illuminated everything like the Sun and dried up the vast waters of devastation. In that universal lotus flower the Supersoul got impregnated with all modes of material nature. *Brahma* then came out of the lotus. But He could not know anything. So He circumambulated all space by moving His eyes in all four directions. Still He could not understand anything about the lotus, Himself or how he came into being. At the end of the millennium the air of deluge caused water and the lotus moved in circular waves. *Brahma* began to ponder about His birth. In order to know His source, He went deep into the stalk of the Lotus from which He emerged. But in spite of going near the navel of the Lord, *Brahma* could not make out anything about His root or origin. Not able to understand anything *Brahma* came out of the stem of the lotus and then He began to concentrate His mind on the Supreme Lord, the Absolute. At the end of 100 years of *Brahma* the required knowledge entered into His mind and He could visualize the Supreme power within Himself. *Brahma* saw the transcendental body that is unlimited in length and breadth occupying the three planetary systems, the upper, middle and lower.

Then the inclination to create came up in His mind and he began to offer prayers to the Lord.

CHAPTER—9

Hymns 16, 20 and 21

The Absolute Soul is the root or origin of the planetary systems. All the planets of the Universe are stationed within the transcendental abdomen of this supreme power when he is in *Yoga Nidra* or transcendental sleep.

CHAPTER—10

Hymns 6 to 9

After the Almighty blessed and disappeared from His view, *Brahma* drank the wind completely along with water. *Brahma* then contemplated upon how to create all the planets. He then entered into the lotus and as it spread all over the Universe, He divided the Universe in to three divisions and later in to 14 divisions for the inhabitation of different types of living entities.

Hymns 10 and 11

Eternal time is the primeval source of the interactions of the three modes of material nature. It is unchangeable and limitless and it works as the instrument of the supreme for His pastime or play or *Leela* during His material creation.

Hymn 13

The cosmic manifestation as it is now was the same in the past and will continue to be the same in future also.

Hymns 14 to 29

There are nine different kinds of creations besides the one which naturally occurs due to the interactions of the modes of nature. There are also three kinds of annihilations. Of the nine creations, the first one is the creation of *Mahatatthva* or the sum total of all material ingredients in which modes interact due to the presence of the supreme. In the second the false ego is generated in which the material ingredients, material knowledge and material activities arise. In the third creation, the sense perceptions are created and from these the elements are generated. The fourth creation is the creation of knowledge and of working capacity. The fifth creation is that of the controlling deities by the interaction of goodness, of which the mind is the sum total. The sixth creation is the ignorant darkness of the living entity. These are the six natural creations by the external energy of the Lord. The seventh creation is that of the immovable entities which are of six kinds namely, the fruit trees without flowers, trees and plants which exist until the fruit is ripe, creepers, pipe plants, creepers without support and trees with flowers and fruits. All the immovable trees and plants seek their subsistence upwards. They are almost unconscious but have feelings of pain within. The eigth creation is that of the lower species of life. They are 28 different varieties. They are extensively ignorant. They know what they want by smell but are unable to remember anything within the heart. There are animals with two hooves, one hoof, and five nails. There are also birds of different types. The humans are of one species only and this is the ninth creation. In the human race the mode of passion is very prominent. The last three creations and the creation of Demigods that is the 10th creation are called *Vaikrata* creation and are different from the *Praakrutha* or natural creations. There are eight varieties in the creation of Demi Gods. They are namely, Demi Gods, forefathers, *Asuras* or demons, *Gandharvas* and *Apsaras*, Yakshas and *Rakshasas, Siddhas, Caranas* and *Vidyadharas and the Bhutas, Pretas* and *Pisachas* and the Super human beings, celestial singers etc.

CHAPTER—11

Hymns 1 and 2

The material manifestation's ultimate particle that is indivisible and not formed into body is called the atom. It exists as an invisible entity even after the dissolution of forms. The material body is a combination of atoms. Atoms are the ultimate state of the manifest universe. When they stay in their own forms without forming different bodies they are called the unlimited oneness. But in physical forms they are different bodies. These atoms therefore form the entire manifestation.

Hymn 3

One can estimate time by measuring the movements of the atomic combination of bodies. Time is the potency of the Supreme, the invisible power, the creator who controls all the physical movements.

Hymns 4 to 9

Atomic time is measured according to its covering a particular atomic space. That time which covers the unmanifest aggregate of atoms is called the great time. In the case of gross time calculations, two atoms make one double atom; three double atoms make one hexatom. This Hexatom is visible in the Sunshine that enters through the holes of a window screen. The Hexatom goes upwards in the sky.

Hymns 10 to 12

There are four *Praharas* or *Yamas* in the day and four in the night of human beings. 15 days and nights make a fortnight and there are two fortnights white and black in a month and that period is one complete day and night for the '*Pita*' Planets. Two of such months comprise one season and six months comprise one complete movement of the sun from south to north. Two solar movements make one day and night of the Demi Gods that is one complete calendar year for the humans. The duration of life for the humans is 100 years.

Hymn 13

The stars, planets, luminaries, and atoms in the Universe rotate in their respective orbits under the direction of the Supreme represented by 'Time' or '*Kaala*'.

Hymn 14

There are five different names for the orbits of Sun, Moon and the stars and the luminaries in the firmament and they each have their own calendar years.

Hymn 15

The Sun moves in the firmament with great velocity. He maintains all living entities with His unlimited heat and light.

Hymns 18 to 21

The four millenniums are known as *Sathya, Tretha, Dwapara* and *Kali Yugas.* The total of all these *Yugas* comes to 12,000 years for Demi Gods. The transitional period before and after every millennium that are a few hundred years are known as *Yuga Sandhyas* or the conjunctions of the two *Yugas.* In *Sathya Yuga* man followed all principles of religion but it began to decline with the arrival of each succeeding *Yugas.*

Hymns 22 to 27

The four *Yugas* multiplied by one thousand make one day on the planet of *Brahma*. Similar period is the night of *Brahma* during which *Brahma* goes to sleep. After the end of *Brahma*'s night the creation of the three worlds begins again during the day of *Brahma* and this cycle of creation continues through the life periods of 14 successive *Manus* who are the fathers and rulers of mankind. After the dissolution of each *Manu* the next *Manu* comes along with His descendants to rule over the different planets. The seven sages, Demi Gods like *Indra* and their followers like the *Gandharvas* also appear with each *Manu.* In the creation, during *Brahma*'s day, the three planetary systems *Swarga, Martya* and *Paatala* revolve and the inhabitants including the lower animals, human beings and Demi Gods and *Pitris* appear and disappear as per their past *Karmas* or actions. With each and every change of *Manu*, the Supreme, the Absolute appears by manifesting His internal potency in different incarnations as *Manu* and others.

Hymns 28 to 33

At the end of *Brahma*'s day, due to the mode of darkness, the universe, merge in the darkness of the night. By the influence of eternal time, the innumerable living entities remain merged in that dissolution and everything is silent. During the night of *Brahma* all the three worlds are out of sight and the Sun and the Moon are without light and it is all like an ordinary night. *Pralaya* or destruction takes place due to the fire emanating from the mouth of *Sankarshana* and the great sages and other inhabitants of *Maharloka* transport themselves to *Janaloka* not able to bear the heat of the blazing fire that engulfs the three worlds below. At the starting of deluge or *Pralaya,* all the seas over flow and hurricane winds blow very violently. The waves of the sea become ferocious and in no time all the three worlds get submerged in water. The Supreme power then lies down in that causal waters on *Ananta,* with His eyes closed and the inhabitants of the *Janaloka* Planets offer their prayers to the Lord. Thus, the process of destruction after the duration of life happens for all living beings including Lord *Brahma*.

Hymns 34 to 38

At present we are in the second half of *Brahma*'s life as the first half of His duration of life is already over. In the beginning of the first half of *Brahma*'s life there was a millennium called *Brahma Kalpa* when Lord *Brahma* appeared along with Knowledge or the *Vedas*. It is also known as *Varaha* Millennium since the Super soul appeared as the *Varaha* or Boar incarnation in that millennium. The second millennium is known as *Padma- Kalpa* because in that millennium the universal Lotus flower grew out of the navel of, Lord *Vishnu* or *Naarayana*. The duration of the two parts of *Brahma*'s life is said to be equal to one *Nimisha* (less than a second) for the Supreme Soul who is the source of the entire creation.

Hymn 39

External time is the controller of different dimensions from the atom up to *Brahma*'s life but it is controlled by the Supreme and time can control only those who are body conscious.

Hymn 40

The phenomenal material world, the universe has a diameter of four billion miles.

Hymn 41

The layers or elements covering the universe are each ten times thicker than the one before and all the universes clustered together appear like atoms in a huge combination.

CHAPTER—12

Hymns 2 to 4

Brahma first created self-deception, the sense of death, anger and frustration, sense of false ownership and illusory bodily conception or forgetfulness of one's real identity. Feeling dissatisfied and unpleasant with these creations Brahma began to meditate on the Supreme and He then began another term of creation. He then created four sages named *Sanaka, Sananda, Sanatana* and *Sanat Kumara*. Since they had an elevated mind they were unwilling to enjoy material life.

Hymns 7, 21, 22, 25 and 27

When *Brahma* understood that His sons were unwilling to generate progeny, He became angry. His anger came out from between His eyebrows and a child mixed with blue and red was immediately generated and this child began to cry as soon as it was born. *Brahma* called this child '*Rudra*' and gave eleven other names also to Him and later *Rudra* created many beings just like Him in all respects and they began to destroy everything. So *Brahma* asked Him to meditate. Then *Brahma* begot ten sons from various parts of His body for procreation. Then religion manifested from *Brahma*'s chest, irreligion appeared from His back, Lust and desire from His heart, anger from the space between His eyebrows, greed from His lips, power of speaking from His mouth, ocean from His penis, low and abominable activities from His arms and so on. Thus *Brahma* manifested all either from His body or mind.

Hymn 37

All the four *Vedas* or Knowledge and *Puraanas* that are known as the fifth *Veda* were manifested from *Brahma* originally.

Hymn 48

Brahma is the personal representation of the Supreme.

Hymn 54

Finally *Brahma* created *Swayambhu Manu* a male and *Satarupa Devi*, a female to carry on procreation.

CHAPTER—13

Hymns 17 to 19

While *Brahma* was engaged in creation, the world went down to the depth of the ocean and when *Brahma* was pondering as to how to lift it up, a small form of a boar emerged out of *Brahma*'s nostrils and lifted up the Earth.

CHAPTER—14

Hymn 29

Brahma is the controller of all material energy that causes the creation of the material Universe.

CHAPTER—15

Hymns 13 and 17

Beyond the Universe where there are material planets there is the spiritual sky where there are spiritual planets known as *Vaikuntas* where Lord *Vishnu*, the Supreme Personality resides. In these planets the inhabitants fly in their airplanes.

CHAPTER—16

Hymn 37

The Lord, the Super Soul is the controller of the three modes of material nature and is responsible for creation, upkeep and dissolution of the Universe.

CHAPTER—17

Hymn 1

The Demi Gods are the inhabitants of the higher planets.

Hymn 14

At the time of birth of the demon *Hiranyaksha*, it is told that the planets Mars and Saturn shone brighter and surpassed the auspicious ones such as Mercury, Jupiter and Venus. The planets also came in conflict with one another by taking seemingly retrograde courses.

Hymn 27

Vibhavari is the home of *Varuna* who is the Lord of all aquatic creatures and guardian of the lower regions of the Universe where the demons usually live.

CHAPTER—19

Hymn 12

When the equilibrium of the three modes of nature gets disturbed the Supreme creates the material elements by the force of time.

Hymns 15 to 19, 22, 23, 29, 38 to 50 and 52

For over thousand years the shining egg lay on the waters of the causal ocean in lifeless state. Then the Lord entered into it as *Garbhodakasayi Vishnu*. From the navel of the Supreme Soul, the *Garbhodakasayi Vishnu*, a lotus flower effulgent like a thousand blazing Suns sprouted. This lotus flower is the reservoir of all conditioned souls and the first living entity that came out of the lotus flower was Lord *Brahma*. When the Supreme who was lying on the causal ocean entered the heart of *Brahma, Brahma* through His intelligence began to create this Universe as it was before. First of all *Brahma* created from His shadow 'ignorance' or *Agnana* of the conditioned souls that were namely, *Tamisra, Andha- Tamisra, Tamas, Moha and Maha Moha*. Out of disgust *Brahma* threw away the body of ignorance and the *Yakshas* and the *Raakshasas* who existed in the form darkness, hunger and thirst were born. Later *Brahma* created the Demi Gods who were embodiments of goodness and they existed in the form of day time. The demons came out of the body of *Brahma*'s back were very lustful. To protect Him from the lustful urge of the demons *Brahma* cast off His body as advised by the Supreme Soul. The body that was given up by *Brahma* took the form of twilight of the evening that kindles passion- and the *Asuras* who are passionate and dominated by the quality of '*Rajas*' were born. Later *Brahma* gave up that form and it was taken up by the *Gandharvas.* Later *Brahma* evolved from His sloth the ghosts and fiends. They took possession of the body thrown off by *Brahma* in the form of yawning. Then *Brahma* evolved from His navel, the hosts of *Sadhyas* and *Pitris.* The *Pitris* took possession of the invisible body of *Brahma*. Then *Brahma* created *Siddhas* and *Vidyadharas* and gave His wonderful form known as *Antardhana*. Then *Brahma* looking at His reflection in water and admiring Himself evolved *Kimpurushas* and *Kinnaras* out of His reflection. They took possession of the shadowy reflected form of *Brahma*. Then *Brahma* stretched His body in full length and in a sullen mode He gave up that body. The hair dropped from that body transformed into *Nagas* and serpents. When *Brahma* felt that the object of His life had been fulfilled, He evolved from His mind the *Manus* who rule to promote the welfare activities of the universe and *Brahma* gave them the human form. Then through His austere penance, adoration and mental concentration and absorption in devotion, with dispassion and control over His senses *Brahma* evolved great sages as His beloved sons.

CHAPTER—21

Hymn 2

The Earth consisting of seven islands is ruled by the sons of *Swayambhu Manu*.

Hymn 19

The Lord creates, maintains and withdraws the Universe that is under the control of His second energy called *Yoga Maaya* just as a spider creates a cobweb by its own energy and again winds it up.

Hymn 25

Swayambhu Manu, the son of *Brahma* who is supposed to reside in *Brahmavartha* rules over the Earth with its seven oceans.

CHAPTER—23

Hymn 33

The supreme Soul is powerful, independent, and transcendental and the Lord of the aggregate of all matter created as well as the element of time. He maintains all the Universes under the three modes of material nature and absorbs the material manifestations after *Pralaya* or deluge.

Hymn 39

The Supreme Self Effulgent Soul dwells in the hearts of all beings.

Hymn 41

Sage *Kardama* and *Devahuthi* travelled through various planets in the flying aerial mansion.

Hymn 43

The Supreme, the *Para Brahman* is beyond cause and effect. He manifests the three modes of material nature and at the same time is beyond the three modes.

Hymn 46

The Supreme, the Super Soul, the *Paramathman* resides in everyone's heart and everyone exists in Him.

CHAPTER—26

Hymns 3, 4 and 5

The Supreme soul has no beginning. He is beyond the three material modes of nature and also beyond the existence of this material Universe. He is found everywhere and He is self-effulgent and He maintains this creation by His Self-effulgent lustre. As His pastime the Absolute Principle accepts the subtle material energy that has the three material modes. The three fold modes divides material nature into varieties and creates the living entities with various names and forms.

Hymns 7, 8, 9 and 10

The total energy of the *Mahath Thattva* that is in the form of the gigantic *Virat-Roopa* divided Himself by Himself into the consciousness of the living entities, the life of activity and self-identification. The gigantic universal form of the Supreme Lord is the plenary portion of the Super Soul. He is the Self in all living entities. In Him rests the entire creation.

The Supreme Lord is the Super Soul.

Hymn 12

There are five gross elements namely earth, water, fire, air and sky or ether or Space. The five subtle elements are smell, taste, colour, touch and sound.

Hymn 13

There are five organs of senses and five organs of action. These are the organs of the sense of hearing, taste, sight, smell, and touch, and the organs of speaking, walking, moving, generating and evacuating.

Hymn 14

The internal subtle senses have four aspects namely, mind, intelligence, ego and contaminated consciousness.

Hymn 17

Time factor as the Supreme creates this Universe due to the agitation of the neutral unmanifested nature.

Hymns 19 and 20

The Absolute Principle impregnates material nature with His internal potency and the material energy creates the sum total of cosmic intelligence that is known as *Hiranmaya*.

Hymns 22 to 29

The material ego springs up from the *Mahath Thattva* that evolved from the Absolute energy. The material ego is endowed with three qualities namely goodness, passionate, and ignorant. From these three material ego, the mind, senses of perception, organs of action and gross elements evolve for which ego is the cause. It is known as *Sankarshana*- the Lord *Anantha* with a thousand heads. From the transformation of false ego of goodness evolves mind called *Aniruddha*, the supreme ruler of senses, whose thoughts and reflections give rise to desire. By transformation of false ego in to passion, intelligence takes birth. It gets knowledge by activating the senses.

Hymn 27

From the head of the gigantic form the heavenly planets were manifested and from His legs the earthly planets and from His abdomen the sky were manifested.

Hymn 28

The Demi Gods because of their *Sathvik* (goodness) nature are located in the heavenly planets and the humans due to their nature of passion (*Rajasic* nature) live on earth along with their subordinates.

Hymns 50 to 53

The universal egg or the universe that is in the shape of an egg is the manifestation of material energy. Its layers of Water, Air, Fire, Sky, Ego and *Mahath Thattva* increase in thickness one after another. Each layer is ten times bigger than the previous one and the final outside layer is covered by what is known as *Pradhana*. Within this egg is the Universal energy within which the 14 planetary systems are contained. The *Virat Purusha*, the Supreme Soul or the *Parabrahman* located in that golden egg that was lying in water divided itself into many organs and their power.

CHAPTER—29

Hymn 38 and 45

The Supreme is the time factor. It is the representative of the Super Soul that has no beginning or end.

CANTO—4

CHAPTER—6

Hymn 43

The Supreme creates this cosmic manifestation, maintains it and annihilates it by expansion of His personality just as a spider creates, maintains and winds up its web.

CHAPTER—7

Hymn 21 and 25

The Pole star (Lord *Naarayana* told *Dhruva*) would exist even after the dissolution of the Universe. It will be surrounded by all the solar system, planets and stars. All luminaries in the sky would circumambulate this Planet. This planet (the Pole star) is located above the planets of the *Saptha Rishis* (the bear constellation)

CANTO—5

CHAPTER—7

Hymn 3

Formerly *Bharatha Varsha* was known as *Ajanaabha Varsha*. Only since King *Bharatha*'s reign it came to be known as *Bharatha Varsha*.

CHAPTER—16

Hymn 1

The radius of *Bhoo Mandala* or Earth extends as far as the Sun spreads its light and heat and as far as the Moon and all stars can be seen.

Hymn 2

There are seven oceans around the seven islands of the earth.

Hymn 4

This material Universe is a transformation of the material qualities, yet no one can probably explain it perfectly even in a life time.

Hymns 5 to 14

The Earth resembles a lotus flower and its seven islands resemble the whorl of that flower. The length and breadth of *Jambudveepa* that is located in the middle of the whorl is one million *Yojanas* (8 million miles). *Jambudveepa* is round like the leaf of the lotus flower. In *Jambudveepa* there are nine divisions of land each with a length of 9000 *Yojanas* (72, 000 miles). There are eight mountains that mark the boundaries of these divisions. Amidst these divisions or *Varshas* is the *Ilavrta Varsha* that is located in the middle of the whorl of the Lotus. Within *Ilavrta Varsha* is the *Sumeru* Mountain that is made of gold. *Sumeru* Mountain is like the pericarp of the lotus like *Bhoomandala* planetary system. This mountain's height is nearly the same as the width of *Jambudveepa*, that is, 100,000 *Yojanas* or 800,000 miles. Out of that 16,000 *Yojanas* or 128,000 miles are within the earth and therefore the mountain's height above the earth is 84,000 *Yojanas* or 672,000 miles. The Mountain's width is 32,000 *Yojanas* or 256,000 miles at its summit and 16,000 *Yojanas* at its base. North of *Ilavrata varsha* and going further northwards one after the other, there are three mountains namely, *Neela, Sveta*, and *Sringavan*. These mark the borders of the three *Varshas* namely, *Ramyaka, Hiranmaya*, and *Kuru Varsha*. These mountains separate the *Varshas* from one another. The width of these mountains is 2000 *Yojanas* (16,000 miles). Length wise they extend east to west up to the beaches of the ocean of salt water. Going from south to north the length of each mountain is one tenth that of the previous mountain but the height of all of them are equal. South of *Ilavrta Varsha* and extending from East to West there are three great mountains named from North to South. They are, *Nishada, Hemakuta* and *Himalaya*. Each of them is 10,000 *Yojanas* (80,000 miles) high. They mark the boundaries of *Hari Varsha, Kimpurusha Varsha* and *Bharatha Varsha*. Towards the west and east of *Ilavrta Varsha* are two great mountains named *Malayavan* and *Gandhamadana* respectively. These two mountains which are 2000 *Yojanas* (16,000 miles) high extend as far as Nila *Mountain* in the north and *Nishadha* in the south. They indicate the boundaries *of Ilavrta Varsha*, *Ketumala* and *Bhadrasva*. On the four sides of the great mountain *Sumeru* are the four mountains of *Mandhara, Merumandara, Suparsva*, and *Kumuda*. The length and height of these mountains are around 10,000 *Yojanas* (80,000 miles). On the summits of these Mountains are a mango tree, a rose apple tree, a *Kadamba* tree and a banyan tree with a width of 100 *Yojanas* or 800 miles and a height of 1,100 *Yojanas* that is 8,800 miles. Their branches spread to a radius of 1,100 *Yojanas*. Between these four mountains are four huge lakes. The water of the first tastes like milk, the water of the second like honey, the water of the third like sugarcane juice and the water of the fourth is pure water. These lakes are enjoyed by celestial beings like *Siddhas, Caranas*, and *Gandharvas* who are Demi Gods. They have *yogic* power to become smaller than the smallest or greater than the greatest. There are also four celestial gardens namely, *Nandana, Caitraratha, Vaibhrajaka* and *Sarvatobhadra*. These are also used by celestial beings.

Hymns 16 to 27

On the lower slopes of *Mandara* Mountain is a mango tree named *Devacuta*. It is 1,100 *Yojanas* high. Mangoes as big as mountain peaks and as sweet as nectar fall from the top of this tree. The juice cascades from the mountain in waterfalls and becomes a river called *Arunoda* that flows through the eastern part of *Ilavrta Varsha*. Similarly, the fruits of the *Jambu* tree also fall. They are of the size of elephants and the juice gliding from the mountain becomes the river *Jambu Nadi*. This river flows for a distance of 10,000 *Yojanas* from the summit of

Merumandara to the Southern side of *Ilavrta Varsha*. The mud on the river banks of *Jambu Nadi* moistened by the juice and later dried by air and sunshine produce huge quantities of gold called *Jambu Nada*. This gold is used by celestials for making ornaments. On the side of the *Suparsva Mountain* stands the big tree *Maha Kadamba*. From the hollows of this tree five rivers of honey flow all around *Ilavrta Varsha* saturating the entire land area with the fragrance. The rivers extend 100 *Yojanas*. On the *Kumuda Mountain* there is a great banyan tree called *Satavalsa* as it has a 100 main branches. From those branches many roots come, from which many rivers flow towards the north of *Ilavrta Varsha*. The residents who enjoy the products of these flowing rivers have no wrinkles on their bodies and no grey hair and are with no marks of old age. They are always fresh and not afflicted by old age or diseases or untimely death or suffer on account of extremes of temperatures and they keep their lustre of the body and are happy with no anxiety till death. The other mountains around the foot of Mount *Meru* are like the filaments around the whorl of the lotus flower. On the eastern side of *Sumeru* Mountain are two mountains named *Jathara* and *Devakuta* that extend to the north and south for 18,000 *Yojanas* or 144,000 miles. On the western side of *Sumeru* are two mountains named *Pavana* and *Pariyatr*a which also extend to the north ånd south for the same distance. On the southern side of *Sumeru* are two mountains named *Kailas*a and *Karavira* that extend east to west for 18,000 *Yojanas* and on the northern side of *Sumeru* extending for the same distance east to west are two mountains named *Trisinga* and *Makara*. The width and height of all these mountains is 2000 *Yojanas* or 16,000 miles. *Sumeru,* a mountain of solid gold is surrounded by these eight mountains.

Hymns 28 and 29

In the middle of the summit of *Meru* is the abode of Lord *Brahma*. Each of its four sides extends for 10 million *Yojanas* or 80 million miles. It is made entirely of gold. Surrounding *Brahma Loka* in all directions are the residences of the eight principal rulers of the planetary systems, beginning with King *Indra*. These are similar to *Brahmapuri* but are one fourth of its size.

CHAPTER—17

Hymn 1

The Lord in His *Vaamana Avatar* extended His left foot to the end of the universe and pierced a hole in its covering with the nail of His big toe. Through the hole the pure water of the causal ocean entered this universe as the *Ganges* River. Before touching the Universe the water touched the feet of the Lord. Hence she came to be known as *Vishnupadi*. Later she came to be called as *Janavi* and *Bhageerathi.* After one thousand millenniums the water of the *Ganges* descended on *Dhruva Loka*, the topmost Planet in the Universe.

Hymns 3 to 10

The seven great sages reside on planets just beneath *Dhruvaloka*. After purifying the seven planets near *Dhruva Loka* the Pole Star, the *Ganges* water flows through the space of the Demi Gods in billions of celestial air planes. Then it inundates the Moon and finally reaches *Brahma*'s abode on top of Mount *Meru*. On top of Mount *Meru Ganges* divides into four branches- gushing through the four directions-east, west, north and south. These branches are *Seetha, Alakananda, Caksu* and *Bhadra* that flow down to the ocean. *Seetha* flows through *Brahmapuri* on top of Mount *Meru*, and then it runs down to the nearby peaks of *Kesarakala* Mountain that is almost as high as Mount *Meru*. From *Kesarakala* Mountain the *Ganges* falls on the Peak of *Gandhamadana* Mountain and then flows into the land of *Bhadrasva Varsha*. Finally it reaches the ocean in the west. *Caksha* falls on the summit of *Malayavan* Mountain and from there cascades on to the land of *Ketumala Varsha* and finally reaches the ocean in the west. *Bhadra* flows from the northern side of Mount *Meru*. Its waters fall on the peaks of *Kumuda* Mountain, mount *Neela, Svetha* and *Sringavan* in succession. Then it flows through the province of *Kuru* and finally it reaches the ocean in north. The *Alaknanda* branch of *Ganges* flows from the southern side of *Brahmapuri* passing over various mountain peaks and falls with fierce force on the mountain of *Hemakuta* and *Himakuta*. Then it falls on the land of *Bharatha Varsha* and finally reaches the ocean in the south. Many other big and small rivers also originate from the top of Mount *Meru* inundating the lands below with hundreds of their branches.

Hymns 11 and 12

Among the nine *Varshas* the region of *Bharatha Varsha* is understood to be the sacred land. The other eight *Varshas* are meant for very highly elevated pious persons for enjoying results of their past pious activities in these earthly regions after they return from the heavenly planets. In these eight *Varshas* humans live 10,000 years according to earthly calculations. All inhabitants here are like Demi Gods. They have the bodily strength of 10, 000 elephants. They enjoy all material comforts and pleasures of life.

CHAPTER—19

Hymns 16 to 18

In the region of *Bharatha Varsha*, as in *Ilavrta Varsha*, there are many mountains and rivers.

Hymn 23

A short span of life in *Bharatha Varsha* is preferable to a life achieved in *Brahmaloka* for millions and billions of years because even if one is elevated to *Brahmaloka*, he must return to repeated births and deaths. Although life in *Bharatha Varsha* is very short, one who lives there can elevate himself to supreme consciousness and he can free himself from repeated births and deaths.

Hymns 29 and 30

Eight islands surround *Jambudveepa*. These appeared when the earth was dug by the people of sons of King *Sagara* to find out their lost horse. These are *Svarnabrastha, Chandrasukla, Avartana, Ramanaka, Mandarahairna, Panchajanya, Simhala and Lanka.*

CHAPTER—20

Hymn 2, 3 to 11

As *Sumeru* is surrounded by *Jambudveepa*, *Jambudveepa* is surrounded by an ocean of salt water. The breadth of *Jambudveepa* and salt water ocean is 100,000 *Yojanas* (800,000 miles).

The salt water ocean surrounding *Jambudveepa* is itself surrounded by *Plakshadveepa* ruled by one of the sons of *Priyavrata*. The breadth of *Plakshadveepa* is twice that of the salt water ocean, that is, 260,000 *Yojanas* or 1,600,000 miles. On *Plakshadveepa* there is a tree shining like gold and as tall as the *Jambu* tree on *Jambudveepa*. At its root is a fire with seven flames. It was one of the seven islands governed by a son of *Priyavrata*. There are seven mountains and seven rivers. The inhabitants of *Plakshadveepa* are the *Hamsas, Patangas, Urdhvayanas,* and *Satyangas* who live for 1000 years. They are beautiful like Demigods. They worship sun, whom they consider as the reflection of the Super Soul. In all the five islands headed by *Plakshadveepa* the inhabitants are endowed with longevity, sensory prowess, physical and mental strength, intelligence, bravery. *Plakshadveepa* is surrounded by an ocean of sugarcane juice equal in breadth of the island.

The island *Salmalidveepa* is twice as broad as *Plakshadveepa* (400,000 *Yojanas* or 3,200,000 miles) and surrounded by an equally broad body of water called *Suurasagara*, the ocean that tastes liquor. On *Salmaladveepa* there is a *Salmali* tree that is broad and tall as the *Plaksha* tree that is 100 *Yojanas* or 800 miles broad and 1,100 *Yojanas* or 8,800 miles tall. It is considered as the residence of *Garuda*, the vehicle of Lord *Vishnu*. The king of that island divided the island into seven regions that he gave to his seven sons. These regions are *Surochana, Saumanasya, Ramanaka, Deva Varsha, Paribhadra, Apyayana* and *Avinjnata*. There are seven Mountains and seven rivers here. The inhabitants here are *Srutidharas, Viryadharas, Vasundharas,* and *Isandharas*. All of them worship *Soma* the moon that they consider as representing the Supreme Soul.

Hymns 13 to 16

Outside the ocean of liquor there is another island known as *Kushadveepa* that is 800,000 *Yojanas* or 6,400, 000 miles wide, twice as wide as the ocean of liquor. *Kushadveepa* is surrounded by an ocean of liquid ghee as broad as the island itself. Here plenty of *Kusa* grass is seen. The king divided this island into seven parts for his seven sons. In those seven islands there are seven boundary mountains and seven rivers. The inhabitants here are *Kusalas, Kovidas, Abhiyuktas* and *Kulakas*. They worship fire as the aspect of the Supreme.

Hymns 18, 20 to 22

Outside the ocean of clarified butter is another island known as *Kraunchadveepa* that has a width of 1,600,000 *Yojanas* or 12, 800, 000 miles, twice the width of the ocean of clarified butter. *Krounchadveepa* is surrounded by an ocean of milk as broad as the island. On this mountain is the mountain *Krouncha*. The king of this island divided his kingdom into seven among his seven sons and like his brothers he also named them as per the names of his sons. There are seven mountains here that form the boundaries of the seven regions. There are also seven rivers here. The inhabitants here are *Purusas, Rsabhas, Dravinas*, and *Devakas*. They worship *Varuna* as the form of the Supreme.

Hymns 24 to 27

Outside the ocean of milk is the island of *Sakadveepa* that has a width of 3,200,000 *Yojanas* or 25,600,000 Miles. This Island is surrounded by an ocean of churned yogurt as broad as the island itself. In *Sakadveepa* there is a big *Saka tree*, from which the island has its name. The king of this island like his brothers divided his kingdom, the island into seven regions among his seven sons in each of their names. There are seven boundary Mountains and seven rivers here. The inhabitants here are *Rtavrata, Satyavrata, Damavrata* and *Anuvrata*. They practice *Pranayama* and mystic Yoga and they worship *Vayu* as the Supreme Lord.

Hymns 29 to 32

Outside the ocean of *Yogurt* is the island *Pushkaradveepa* that is 6,400,000 *Yojanas* or 51,200, 000 miles wide, that is twice as wide as the ocean of Yogurt. It is surrounded by an ocean of very tasteful water as broad as the island itself. On this island there is a great lotus flower with 100, 000, 000 pure golden petals as effulgent as the flames of fire. In the middle of that island is the great mountain *Manasotthara* that forms the boundary between the inner side and the outside of the island. Its height and breadth are 10,000 *Yojanas* or 80,000 miles. On that mountain Demi Gods like Indra reside. The sun travels on top of this Mountain in an orbit called *Samvatsara* encircling Mount *Meru*. The sun's path on its northern side is called *Uttarayana* and its path on the Southern side is called *Dakshinayana*. The ruler of this island had two sons. He gave two sides of the island to his two sons. The inhabitants here worship *Brahma* as the representative of the Supreme power.

Hymns 34 to 37

Beyond the ocean of sweet water and fully surrounding it is a mountain named *Lokaloka* that divides the countries into those that are full of sunlight and those that are not lit by sun. Beyond the ocean of sweet water is a region as broad as the area between the middle of Mount *Sumeru* and the boundary of *Manasotthara* Mountains. Many beings live there as well. Beyond it, extending to *Lokaloka* Mountain is another land that is made of gold. Because of its golden surface it reflects light like the surface of a mirror and any physical article that falls on that land can never be found again so all living beings had abandoned that golden land. Between the lands that are inhabited by living beings and those that are uninhabited, there is a great mountain that separates the two and is therefore known as *Lokaloka.* This *Lokaloka* Mountain stands as the outer border of the three worlds, *Bhooloka, Bhuvarloka* and *swarloka.* It controls the rays of the Sun throughout the Universe. Because it is extremely high extending even higher than *Dhruvaloka* it blocks the rays of the luminaries without permitting further extension.

Hymn 38

With great deliberation the learned scholars have described the planetary systems and their symptoms, measurements and locations. They have also established the truth that the distance between Mountains *Sumeru* and the *Lokaloka* is one fourth of the diameter of the Universe or in other words 125,000,000 *Yojanas* or one billion miles.

Hymn 39

On top of the *Lokaloka* Mountain are the four elephants established in the four directions. These elephants are, *Rsabha, Pushkarakuda, Vamana* and *Aparajitha.* They are responsible for maintaining the planetary systems of the Universe.

Hymn 42

Outside *Lokaloka* is the region known as *Aloka Varsha* that extends for the same breadth as the area within the Mountain, that is,

125,000, 000 *Yojanas* or one billion miles. Beyond *Aloka Varsha* is the destination of those who aspire for liberation from the material world. Since it is beyond the jurisdiction of the material modes of nature it is completely pure.

Hymn 43

The Sun is located (vertically) in the middle of the Universe in the area between *Bhooloka* and *Bhuvarloka* that is called *Antariksha* or the outer Space. The distance between the Sun and the circumference of the Universe is 25 *Koti- Yojanas* or 2 billion miles.

Hymn 45

The Sun God and the Sun planet divide all the directions of the Universe. Because of the Sun we are able to know about the Sky, the higher planets, this world, the lower planets, the places of material enjoyment and the places for liberation and those that are hellish and subterranean.

CHAPTER—21

Hymn 1

The diameter of the Universe is 50 crore *Yojanas* or 4 billion miles.

Hymn 2

Just as a grain of wheat is divided into two parts and one can estimate the size of the upper part of the grain by knowing that of the lower, so also the expert geographers point out that one can understand the measurements of the upper part of the Universe by knowing those of the lower parts. The sky between the earthly sphere and the heavenly sphere is called *Antareeksha* or the outer space. It adjoins the top of the earth's sphere with that of the bottom of heaven.

Hymn 3

In the midst of that region of outer space or *Anthareeksha* is the Sun, the king of all planets that emanates heat. By the influence of its radiation the sun heats the universe and maintains its proper order. It also gives light and removes darkness. According to its movements in rising above, going beneath or passing through the equator and correspondingly coming in touch with the various signs of the zodiac, headed by *Makara* or Capricorn, days and nights are short or equal to one another.

Hymn 4

While the Sun passes through *Mesha* (Aries) and *Tula* (Libra) the duration of the day and night are equal. When it passes through the five signs headed by *Vrashabha* (Taurus) the duration of the days increase until Cancer, and then it gradually decreases by half an hour each month until day and night again become equal in Libra.

Hymn 5

When the Sun passes through the five signs beginning with *Vrichchika* (Scorpio) the duration of the days decrease until the sign of Capricorn and then gradually it increases month after month until day and night become equal in Aries.

Hymn 6

Until the Sun travels to the south the days grow longer and until it travels to the North the nights grow longer.

Hymn 7

According to scholars the Sun travels over all sides of *Manasothara* Mountain in a circle whose length is 95,100, 000 *Yojanas* or 760,800,000 miles. On the *Manasothara* Mountain towards east of mount *Sumeru* is the place *Devadhani*. In the south is the place *Samyamani*, in the west is the place *Nimalochani* and in the north is *Vibhavari*. Sunrise, midday, sunset and midnight occur in all those places according to specific timings.

Hymn 9

On the *Sumeru* Mountain the climate is always very warm as at midday because the Sun is always over head for the Mountain. The Sun moves anticlockwise facing the constellations with *Sumeru* Mountain on its left but it also moves clockwise and appears to have the Mountain on its right side because it is influenced by the *Dakshinavarta* wind. People living in countries diametrically opposite where the Sun is first seen rising will see the sun setting and if a straight line were to be drawn from a point where the Sun is at midday, the people in countries at the opposite end of the line would be experiencing midnight.

Hymn 10 to 19

When the Sun travels from *Devadhani* that is the residence of *Indra* to *Samyamani* that is the residence of *Yamaraja*, it travels 23,775,000 *Yojanas* or 190,200,000 miles in 15 *Ghatikas* that is in 6 hours. From *Samyamani* the Sun travels to *Nurilochani*, the residence of *Varuna*, from there to *Vibhavari*, the residence of the Moon God and from there again to the residence of *Indra* that is *Devadhani*. In a similar manner, the Moon along with the other stars and planets becomes visible in the celestial sphere and then sets and again becomes visible. Thus the chariot of the Sun God called *Trayimaya* worshipped by the three worlds *Bhur, Bhuvah* and *Svar* travels through the four residences of Indra, Yama, *Varuna* and Moon at a speed of 3,400, 800 *Yojanas* or 27, 206, 400 miles in a *Muhoortha*. The chariot of the Sun God has only one wheel, namely, the *Samvatsara*. The twelve months are its twelve spokes, the six seasons are the sections of its rim, and the three *Chaturmasa* periods are its three sectioned hub. One side of the axle carrying the wheel rests on the summit of Mount *Meru* and the other rests on *Manasothara* Mountain. Affixed to the outer end of the axle, the wheel continuously rotates on *Manasothara* Mountain like the wheel of an oil pressing machine. The first axle, like an oil pressing machine is attached to a second axle, that is 3, 937, 500 *Yojanas* or 31,500,000 miles long. The upper end of this second axle is attached to *Dhruvaloka* by a rope of wind. The carriage of the Sun God's chariot is estimated to be 3, 600, 000 *Yojanas* or 28, 800, 000 miles long and 900, 000 *Yojanas* or 7, 200, 000 miles wide. The chariot's horses are harnessed by *Arunadeva* to a yoke that is 900,000 *Yojanas* wide. This chariot carries the Sun God. Although *Arunadeva* sits in front of the Sun God and is engaged in driving the chariot and controlling the horses he looks backward towards the Sun God. 60,000 saintly persons called *Valikhilyas* each of a size of a thumb located in front of the Sun God offer prayers to Sun God. 14 other saints, *gandharvas, Apsaras, Nagas, Yakshas, Rakshasas*, and Demi Gods who are all divided in to groups of two assume different names every month and continuously perform different types of ceremonial worship to the Sun

God as the supreme power or energy. In His orbit through earth or the *Bhoomandala* the Sun God traverses a distance of 95,100, 000 *Yojanas* or 760,800, 000 miles at the speed of 2000 *Yojanas* and two *Krosa*s or 16,004 miles in a moment.

CHAPTER—22

Hymn 2

The signs and constellations with Sumeru and *Dhruvaloka* on their right move with the wheel of time and the Sun and other planets move with them. The sun and planets are however seen in different signs and constellations at different times. This indicates that their motions are different from the Zodiac and the wheel of time itself. It is similar that when a potter's wheel moves and small ants (in this example, the Sun) located on that big wheel move with it, one can see that their motion is different from that of the wheel because they appear sometimes on one part of the wheel and sometimes on another. That is why the Sun God that travels around *Dhruvaloka* with both *Dhruvaloka* and Mount *Sumeru* on His right but at the same time the Sun faces the signs of the zodiac with *Sumeru* and *Dhruvaloka* on His left.

Hymns 5 to 7

The Sun God who is the Super Soul, the soul of all the worlds is located in outer space between the upper and lower portions of the Universe. Passing through twelve months on the wheel of time, the Sun comes in touch with twelve different signs of the zodiac and assumes twelve different names according to those signs. The total of these twelve months constitute a *Samvatsara* or year. According to lunar calculations two fortnights, one of the waxing Moon and the other of the waning make one month. That period is one day and night for the planet *Pitrloka*. When the Sun travels two months a season is over. The period the Sun takes to rotate through half of the outer Space is known as *Ayana* or its period of movement. The Sun God has three speeds- the slow, fast and moderate. The time the Sun takes to travel around the spheres of Heaven, Earth and Space at these speeds is known by five names namely, *Samvatsara, Parivatsara, Idavatsara, Anuvatsara and Vatsara.*

Hymns 8 and 9

Above the rays of the sunshine at a distance of 100,000 *Yojanas* or 800,000 miles is the Moon that travels at a speed faster than that of the Sun. In two lunar fortnights the Moon travels through the equivalent of a *Samvatsara* of the Sun, in two and a quarter days it passes through a month of the Sun and in one day it passes through a fortnight of the Sun. When the Moon is waxing, its illuminating portions increase daily creating day for the Demi Gods and nights for the Pitris. When the Moon is waning it causes night for the Demi Gods and day for the *Pitris.* In this manner the Moon passes through each constellation of stars in 30 *Muhoorthas* that is one full day.

Hymn 11

Many stars are located 200,000 *Yojanas* or 1,600,000 miles above the Moon. Their motions are different from that of the Sun. They rotate with Mount *Sumeru* on their right. There are 28 important stars.

Hymn 12

Around 1, 600,000 miles above this group of stars is the planet Venus that moves at almost exactly at the same pace as that of the Sun. Sometimes Venus moves behind the Sun, sometimes in front and sometimes along with it. Venus cancels the influence of planets that hinder rainfall. Consequently its presence causes rainfall.

Hymn 13

Mercury is similar to Venus. It also sometimes moves behind, sometimes in front and sometimes along with the sun. It is 1, 600,000 miles above Venus or 7, 200,000 miles above the Earth. Mercury is considered as the son of the Moon. When Mercury does not move along with the Sun it forebodes cyclone, dust, irregular rainfall and waterless clouds resulting in inadequate or excess rainfall.

Hymn 14

The planet Mars is 1, 600, 000 miles above Mercury or 8,800,000 miles above Earth. If this planet does not travel in a crooked manner, it crosses through each sign of the Zodiac in three fortnights and in this way it travels through all twelve zodiac signs one after the other.

It mostly creates unfavourable conditions regarding rainfall and other things.

Hymn 15

The planet Jupiter is 1,600, 000 miles above Mars or 10,400, 000 miles above Earth. It travels through one sign of the Zodiac within the period of a *Parivatsara.*

Hymn 16

The planet Saturn is located 1,600, 000 miles above Jupiter or 12,000,000 miles above Earth. It passes through one sign of the Zodiac in 30 months and covers the entire Zodiac circle in 12 *Anuvatsaras.* This planet is usually considered inauspicious.

Hymn 17

Above 8,800,000 miles of Saturn or 20,800,000 miles above Earth are the *Saptha Rishis.* They circumambulate the *Dhruvaloka* or the Pole star.

CHAPTER—23

Hymns 1 and 2

The abode of Lord *Vishnu* is 1,300, 000 *Yojanas* or 10, 400, 000 miles above the planets of the seven sages. *Dhruva* also resides there.

The Pole star, the planet of king *Dhruva* constantly shines as the central pivot for all the stars and planets. The invisible, most powerful time factor causes the luminaries to revolve around the Pole Star without cessation.

Hymns 3 to 7 and 9

Just as the bulls are yoked together and tied to the central post to thrash rice, treading around the pivot without deviating from their path- one bull being closest to the post, another in the middle and the third on the outside, the planets and all the hundreds and thousands of stars revolve around the Pole Star in their respective orbits, some higher and some lower. These planets float in the air within the vast sky just as clouds with hundreds of tons of water floating in the air. This great mechanism consisting of stars and planets resembles the form of *Sisumara* or Dolphin in water. This form of *Sisumara* has its head downward and its body coiled. On the end of its tail is planet *Dhruva*, on the body of its tail are the planets of the Demi Gods and at the base of its tail are the planets of some other Demi Gods. On the hips are the seven saintly sages. The coiled body of the *Sisumara* turned toward its right side is the location of the first 14 constellations. The next 14 Constellations are on its left side. Thus its body is balanced because of equal number of stars that are on its either side. On the back of the *Sisumara* is another group of stars. On its abdomen *Ganges* flows in the sky in the Milky Way. On the right and left side of the loins of *Susumara* are two stars. Two other Stars are on its right and left foot; two other stars on its right and left nostrils; two other stars on its right and left eyes; two other stars on its right and left ears. Another eight stars are that mark the southern course are on the ribs of the left of its body; and another set of eight stars that mark the northern corner are on the ribs on its right side and two other remaining stars are on the right and left shoulders.

On the upper chin of the *Sisumara* is *Agasti-*, lower chin *Yamaraja*, on its mouth Mars, on its genitals Saturn, on the back of its neck is Jupiter, on its chest the Sun; and within the core of its heart is the Super Soul. Within its mind is the Moon. On its navel Venus and on its breasts the *Asvini Kumaras*, within its life force, *Pranapana* is Mercury, on its neck is *Rahu*, all over the body are comets and in its pores are the numerous Stars. The body of the Supreme Lord that forms the *Sushumara-Chakra* is the resting place of all Demi Gods, Stars and Planets.

CHAPTER—24

Hymns 1 to 3

The Planet *Rahu* that moves like a star is 10, 000 *Yojanas* or 80,000 miles below the Sun. The Sun globe extends for 10, 000 *Yojanas* or 80, 000 miles. The Moon extends for 20, 000 *Yojana*s or 160, 000 miles and *Rahu* extends for about 30, 000 Yojanas or 240,000 miles. It is stated in scriptures that previously when nectar was being distributed, an *Asura Rahu* sat between the Sun and Moon to get a share of the nectar that was being distributed among the *Devas* or Demi Gods by Lord *Vishnu* as *Mohini*, a beautiful damsel. Seeing this *Asura* Lord

Vishnu cut him into two pieces and, since then he covered the sunshine and moon shine on the New Moon day and full Moon night. At that time Lord *Vishnu* protected both the Sun and the Moon from *Rahu* with His disc- the *Sudarshana Chakra*. When the *Rahu* disturbs the Sun or Moon, eclipse occurs.

Hymns 4 and 5

Below *Rahu* by 10, 000 *Yojanas* or 80, 000 miles are the planets known as *Siddha Loka, Carana Loka* and *Vidyadhara Loka*. Beneath *Vidyadhara Loka, Carana Loka* and *Siddha Loka* in the sky called *Anthareeksha* are the places of enjoyment for *Yakshas, Raakshasas, Pisachas,* and *ghosts* and so on. *Antariksha* extends as far as the wind blows and the clouds float in the sky. Above this there is no more air.

Hymn 6

Below the abodes of *Yakshas* and *Raakshasas* by a distance of 100 *Yojanas* or 800 miles is the planet Earth. Its upper limits extends as high as swans, hawks, eagles and similar large birds can fly.

Hymns 7 to 14

Beneath this Earth are the seven planets known as *Atala, Vitala, Sutala, Talaatala, Mahaatala, Rasaatala* and *Paatala*. The width and length of the seven lower planetary system are known as the same as those of Earth.

In these seven planetary systems that are also known as the Subterranean heavens the *Bila Swarga*, there are very beautiful houses, gardens and places of enjoyment that are even more beautiful than that are found in the heavenly planets. The residents in these are the *Daithyas, Danavas*, and *Nagas*. They are totally after material pleasures. There are also many gates, assembly houses, temples, yards and hotels here. However there is no sunshine here, so, time is not divided in to day and night here. Many serpents with gems on their hoods live here. The residents here drink and bathe in juices and elixirs from wonderful herbs, so they are all freed from anxieties and physical diseases. They have no grey hair, wrinkles and diseases. Their body lustre does not fade and they have no fatigue due to old age.

Hymns 16 to 18 and 28 to 31

One of the lower planetary systems is *Atala*. Below *Atala* is *Vitala*. Below *Vitala* is *Sutala*. Beneath *Sutala* is *Talaatala*. Below *Talaatala* is *Mahaatala*. It is the residence of many hooded snakes. Beneath *Mahaatala* is *Rasaatala* planetary system. The residents here are enemies of Demi Gods, and they reside like snakes in holes. Beneath *Rasaatala* is *Paatala* or *Naagaloka* where there are many demons like serpents. They are extremely poisonous and possess many hoods.

CHAPTER—25

Hymns 1 and 2

Approximately 240,000 miles beneath *Paatala* resides *Anantha*- who is Lord *Vishnu* Himself. The great Universe rests on one of the 1000 hoods of *Aadisesha* or *Anantha* and looks like a white mustard seed.

Hymns 10 and 12 to 15

The manifestation of subtle and gross matter exists within the Supreme. The entire Universe filled with its many great Mountains, rivers, oceans, trees, and living entities is resting just like an atom on one of the many hoods of *Anantha Deva*, the *Aadisesha*, who is none other than the Supreme Soul itself. In His form as *Ananta*, the Supreme resides under the lower planetary systems and easily sustains the entire Universe. The conditioned souls who are full of material desires achieve various situations in different planetary systems and in this way they live with in this material creation. They also get different types of bodies in higher and lower planets as per their *Karmas* performed according to their desires.

CHAPTER—26

Hymn 5

All the hellish planets are located in the intermediate space between the three worlds and the celestial *Garbhodaka* Ocean. They lie on the southern side of the Universe beneath *Bhumandala* and slightly above the water of *Garbhodaka* Ocean. *Pitrloka* is also located in this region between the *Garbhodak*a Ocean and the lower planetary systems.

Hymns 7 to 36

According to a few there are 21 hellish Planets and according to some others the number is 28. The different hells are, *Tamisra, Andhatamisra, Raurava, Maharaurava, Kumbhipaha, Kalasutra, Asi-Patravana, Sukaramukha, Andhakupa, Krimibhojana, Sandamsa, Taptasurmi, Vajrakanthaka-Salmali, Vaitarani, Puyoda, Pranarodha, Visasana, Lalabhakshaka, Sarameyadana, Avichi, Ayahpana, Ksarakardama, Raksoganabhojana, Suta prota, Dandasuka, Avata-Nirodhana, Parya vartana,* and *Suchimukha*. All these planets are meant for punishing the sinners. Those who commit various crimes have to undergo great suffering depending upon the severity of the crimes committed by them; the pious ones who are free from crimes enter the planets of Demi Gods. However after the expiry of punishment in the hell or enjoyment in other planets, that is, after the expiry of the results of their impious actions or pious actions they are born again on Earth.

CANTO—6

CHAPTER—4

Hymns 47 and 48

Before creation only the Supreme energy existed with all its Spiritual potencies. Consciousness was then unmanifested just as one's consciousness is unmanifested during deep sleep. From the material cosmic energy of this Supreme, the cosmic manifestation appeared.

CHAPTER—9

Hymn 21

The three worlds are created by the five elements and controlled by various Demi Gods.

CHAPTER—16

Hymn 36

The Super Soul exist in the beginning, middle and end of everything-from the most minute particle of the cosmic manifestation, the atom, to the most gigantic Universes and the eternal has no beginning, middle or end. When the cosmic manifestation does not exist, the Supreme exists as the original potency.

Hymn 37

Every Universe is covered by seven layers- Earth, Water, Fire, Air, and Sky, the total energy and false ego. Each is 10 times greater than the previous one. There are innumerable Universes besides this one and although they are ultimately large, they move about like atoms in the Absolute. Hence the Super Soul is called *Anantha*, the unlimited.

CANTO—7

CHAPTER—9

Hymn 33

The cosmic manifestation, the material world is the body of the Super Soul. This total lump of matter is agitated by the potent energy known as the *Kaala Sakthi* of the Super Soul, that is, the power of the element of time, and thus the three modes of material nature are manifested. When the Supersoul wakes up from sleep, a small transcendental seed is generated. From this seed the lotus flower of the gigantic Universe is manifested. From that lotus *Brahma*, the creative energy was generated.

CANTO—8

CHAPTER—1

Hymn 4

In the present *Kalpa* already the period of rule of six *Manus* are over.

CHAPTER—3

Hymn 5

In due course of time when all the causative and effective manifestation of the Universe, including planets is annihilated, there is a situation of dense darkness.

CHAPTER—13

Hymn 1

Sraddhadeva is the present *Manu*.

CANTO—9

CHAPTER—4

Hymn 56

The innumerable Universes and their inhabitants come into existence and are annihilated by the command of the Lord.

CANTO—10

CHAPTER—3

Hymn 25

At the time of cosmic annihilation, everything, manifest and unmanifest is destroyed by the force of time, the five gross elements enter into the subtle conception and the manifested categories enter into the unmanifested substance. At that time only the Absolute will remain.

CHAPTER—14

Hymn 11

Unlimited Universes pass through the pores of the Absolute Principle, the Supreme Soul just as particles of dust pass through the openings of a screened window.

CHAPTER—40

Hymns 13 to 15

Fire is said to be the face of the Supreme personality of godhead, the Earth His feet, the Sun His eyes, the Sky His navel, Directions His sense of hearing, the chief Demi Gods His arms, the Oceans His abdomen, Heaven His head, the Wind His vital air. His physical strength, the trees and planets, the hairs on His body the clouds, the hair on His head the mountains, His bones and nails the passage of day and night, the blinking of His eyes the progenitor of mankind, His genitals and the rains His semen. All the worlds originate from Him. All these worlds travel in Him.

Hymn 21

The causes of cosmic manifestation namely Earth, Water, Fire, Air, Ether and its source the false ego, the *Mahath Thattva* the total material nature and her source, the *Purusha* expansion of the Supreme-the mind, senses, the sense objects are all born from the transcendental body of the Supreme.

CHAPTER—87

Hymn 15

The perceivable world is identified with the Supreme Soul because it is the foundation of all existence. It remains unchanged as all created beings are generated from it and at last dissolved into it just as clay remains unchanged by the products made out of it and again merge with it.

Hymn 41

Each of the countless Universes enveloped in each of its shell is compelled by the wheel of time to wander within the Super Soul like particles of dust blowing about in the sky.

CANTO—11

CHAPTER—3

Hymns 3 to 16

The Primeval Soul activates the material elements and creates all living beings in higher or lower species. The Super Soul then enters the material bodies and activates the senses and mind. At the time of destruction the Supreme, in His form of eternal time withdraws the manifest cosmos consisting of gross and subtle features and the entire Universe vanishes into non manifestation.

When the cosmic annihilation approaches a terrible drought will take place on earth for a period of 100 Years. At that time the heat of the sun also will increase and the blazing heat will begin to torment the three worlds. Beginning from *Paatala Lok*a, a fire will grow emanating from the mouth of Lord *Sankharshana*. Its flames will shoot upwards driven by high speed winds scorching everything in all directions. Hoards of clouds called *Samvartaka* will pour torrents of rain for 100 years. This deadly rainfall then will submerge the entire universe in water. Then *Vairaja Brahma*, the Soul of the universal form would give up His Universal body and will enter into the unmanifest nature like fire that has run out of fuel. The element of Earth then will be transformed in to Water and the Water due to wind would merge into Fire and then would dissolve in to the element of Air. When the Air loses its quality of touch it will merge into Space and then finally Space will merge into false ego in the mode of ignorance. Then the total false ego will merge in to *Maha Thattva*.

This creation, maintenance and destruction show the illusory energy of the Supreme Soul. This illusory potency consisting of the three modes of nature is empowered by the Lord for creation, maintenance and annihilation of the material Universe.

CHAPTER—9

Hymns 20 and 21

According to great sages that which is the basis of the three modes of material nature and which manifests the multi-fold Universe is called the *Sutra* or *Mahat Thattva*. This Universe rests within that *Mahat Tattva* and due to its potency; the living entity undergoes material existence. Just as from within Himself the spider expands thread through its mouth, plays with it for some time and eventually swallows it, similarly, the Supreme Lord expands His personal potency from within Himself displaying the network of cosmic manifestation, and utilizes it according to His purpose and eventually withdraws it completely within Himself.

CHAPTER—10

Hymn 30

Brahma possesses the supreme life span of 311,040, 000,000,000 years.

CHAPTER—16

Hymn 39

Even though over a period of time one might count all the atoms of the Universe none can count all the opulence of the Supreme Soul that He manifests within innumerable universes.

CHAPTER—22

Hymn 12

Nature exists originally as the equilibrium of the three material modes- goodness, passion and ignorance. These are the effective causes of creation, maintenance and destruction of this Universe.

Hymn 15 and 16

The five knowledge acquiring senses are hearing, touch, sight, smell and taste. The five working senses are speech, hands, genitals, anus and legs. Mind belongs to both these categories. Sound, touch, taste, smell and form are the objects of knowledge acquiring senses. Movement, speech, excretion, reproduction are the functions of the working senses.

Hymn 29

The manifest creation undergoes constant transformation as it is founded upon the agitation of the modes of nature.

Hymn 43 and 45

Material bodies are constantly undergoing creation and destruction by the force of time. It is like the illumination of a lamp consisting of innumerable rays of light undergoing constant creation, transformation and destruction.

CHAPTER—24

Hymns 2 to 14

As per the *Sankhya* philosophy after annihilation of the Universe the Super Soul alone exists. Later, that one Absolute Truth that remains free from material dualities and beyond comprehension divides Himself into two categories, the material nature and living entities who try to enjoy the manifestations of *Prakruthi* or material nature. Of these two one is material nature that contains both subtle causes and the manifest products of matter. The other is the conscious living entity who is the enjoyer of material nature. When material nature is agitated by the glance of the Super Soul, the three material modes- goodness, passion and ignorance, become manifest to fulfil the desires of the conditioned Soul, the enjoyer. From these modes, the false ego is generated by the transformation of *Mahat Thattva*. The false ego encompasses both spirit and matter and manifest in three varieties- goodness, passion and ignorance. From false ego in the mode of ignorance arise the physical perception from which the gross elements are generated. From false ego in the mode of passion comes the senses and from false ego in the mode of goodness comes the Demi

Gods. Due to the power of the Super Soul all these elements combine to function in an orderly manner and together they bring about the Universal egg that is the residence of the Super Soul. The Super Soul resides within that egg that floats on the causal water. From the navel of the Super Soul arise the Universal lotus, the birth place of *Brahma*. Endowed with the mode of passion *Brahma*, the Soul of the Universe perform great *Tapas* or austerities and due to the mercy of the Super Soul, He creates the three planetary divisions called *Bhur, Bhuvar* and *Svar* along with their presiding Deities. The *Swar Loka* or the heaven is the residence of Demi Gods. *Bhuvarloka* belongs to the ghostly spirits and the *Bhur* or Earth is the place of humans and other mortal beings. The mystics who strive for Mukthi or liberation are promoted beyond these three divisions. The region below the Earth is meant for the Demons and *Nagas* or snakes. By mystic *Yoga,* great austerities and renunciation, the destinations of *Mahar Loka, Jana Loka, Tapoloka* and *Sathyaloka* are attained. By devotional or *Bhakthi Yoga* one is able to reach and achieve the transcendental abode of the Absolute, the Supreme.

Hymns 17 to 19

The ingredients of a product are inherent in the beginning, in the middle phase and at the end of a product that has a form and also a name assigned just for convenience, as in the case of gold that is the basis or ingredient for different types of gold ornaments. The ingredient supporting the product, that is, with which the product is made, is the basis of its reality. In this way one material object becomes the cause for another material object. Similarly, the material Universe has nature as its original ingredient and ultimate stage.

Hymns 20 to 27

As long as the Supreme Personality of Godhead continues to glance upon nature, the material world will continue to exist. The Super Soul is the basis of the Universal form that displays endless varieties through repeated creation. It has within itself all planetary systems in a dormant state. At the time of annihilation everything merges ultimately with the unborn Supreme Soul who remains alone established within Himself from whom all creation and annihilation manifest.

CANTO—12

CHAPTER—2

Hymns 1 to 18

During *Kali Yuga* all good qualities will disappear. Wealth alone will be considered the indicator of a man's good birth, proper behaviour and good qualities. Law and justice will be applied on the basis of one's power. Men and women will live together merely because of superficial attraction. Success in business will depend on deceit. Womanliness and manliness will be judged according to one's sexual capacity. A man will be known as *Brahmana* just by wearing a thread. A man's spiritual position will be judged merely according to external symbols and on that same basis people will change from one spiritual order to the next. A person's propriety will be questioned if he does not earn a good living. One who is very clever in the jugglery of words will be considered a learned scholar. A person will be considered unholy if he does not have money. Hypocrisy will be accepted as a mark of virtue. Marriages will be arranged simply by verbal agreement. A person will consider himself fit to appear in public if he merely takes a bath. A sacred place will be the one where a reservoir of water is located at a distance. Beauty will depend on one's hair style. Filling the belly will become the goal of life. One who is audacious will be considered as truthful. The one who maintains a family will be regarded as an efficient person. The principles of religion will be observed only for the sake of reputation. The earth will become crowded with corrupt people. The strongest will gain political power. The rulers will be merciless and will behave like ordinary thieves. Citizens will be forced to flee to the mountains and forests. There will be famines and excessive taxes. People will therefore be forced to eat leaves, roots, flesh, wild honey, fruits, flowers and seeds. People will be ruined due to drought. People will also suffer greatly from cold, wind, heat, rain and snow. There will be quarrels, hunger, thirst, diseases and severe anxiety. Maximum duration of life for a man being in *Kali Yuga* will be 50 years. By the time *Kali Yuga* ends, people will become small in size. The path of the *Vedas* will be completely forgotten in human society. The so called religion will be mostly atheistic. The rulers will be mostly thieves. The main occupations of the people will be stealing, lying and unnecessary violence. Cows will become like goats, spiritual hermitages will be like mundane houses. Family ties will be limited to immediate bonds of marriage. Most plants and herbs will become tiny. Trees will be short and small. Clouds will be full of lightning. There will be no piety and all humans will become like asses. At that time the Super Soul will appear on Earth for rescuing eternal righteousness. Lord *Kalki* then will appear.

Hymns 23 to 34

When the Supreme Lord appears on Earth as *Kalki, Sathya Yuga* will begin again. When the moon, sun and *Brahaspathi* are together in the constellation of *Karkataka* and all the three enter simultaneously in to the lunar mansion *Pushya*, at that moment *Sathya* or *Krita Yuga* will begin again. The age of *Kalki* will begin when the constellation of the seven sages passes through the lunar mansion *Magha*. It consists of 12, 00 years of Demi Gods. When the *Saptha Rishi* constellation passes from *Magha* to *Purvasadha*, *Kalki* will have his full strength, beginning from King *Nanda* and his dynasty. Actually the influence of *Kaliyuga* started the day when Lord *Krishna* left this Earth. After 1000 celestial years of *Kali Yuga*, the *Sathya Yuga* will manifest again. At that time the minds of all men will become self-effulgent.

Hymn 39

The cycle of the four *Yugas*- the *Sathya, Tretha, Dwapara* and *Kali* continues perpetually among living beings on earth and this cycle gets repeated.

CHAPTER—3

Hymns 19 to 25

During *Sathya Yuga* people were self-satisfied, merciful, friendly, peaceful, sober and tolerant. They understood the Bliss from within themselves and treated everything in an equal manner and sincerely tried for spiritual perfection. In *Tretha Yuga*, violence, dissatisfaction and quarrels cropped up gradually. People performed severe austerities. They were not excessively violent or very passionate for sensual pleasure. In *Dvapara Yuga* dissatisfaction, untruth, violence and enmity cropped up gradually. However the people at large were very noble. They enjoyed life with vigour. During *Kali Yuga* people tend to be greedy, ill behaved, and merciless and they fight with one another without any reason.

Hymns 27 to 45

When the mind, intelligence and senses are firmly fixed in the mode of goodness, then that period is *Sathya Yuga*, the age of Truth. During this age people take pleasure in knowledge and austerity. When the conditioned souls become devoted to their duties but with ulterior motives seek personal prestige then that is the indication of *Tretha Yuga* where passion dominates. When greed, dissatisfaction, false prestige, hypocrisy, and envy become prominent, along with the attraction for selfish activities, then that is the mark of *Dwapara Yuga* that is dominated by the mixed mood of passion and ignorance. In the age of *Kali,* there is predominance of the mode of ignorance. It is characterised by the predominance of cheating, lying, sloth, sleepiness, violence, depression, lamentation, bewilderment, fear and poverty. Due to the influence of *Kali* humans will become short sighted, unfortunate, gluttonous, and lustful and poverty stricken. Women will become unchaste. Cities will be dominated by thieves, atheists will misinterpret *Vedas*, political leaders will exploit the citizens and the so called priests and intellectuals will be devotees of their bellies and genitals. The *Brahmacharis* or bachelors will become unclean, the householders will become beggars, the *Vanaprasthas* will live in villages and the *Sanyasins* will become greedy for wealth. Women will become much smaller in size. They will eat much, will have more children than they can properly take care of and lose all shyness. They will speak harshly and will exhibit qualities of deceit and unrestrained audacity. Businessmen will amass wealth by cheating. People will consider any degraded occupation quite acceptable even if it is not due to necessity. Servants will abandon their masters if they lose wealth even if the master is an exemplary person. Masters will also abandon an incapacitated servant even if the servant has been working for the master's family for generations. Cows will be abandoned or killed when they stop yielding milk. Men will be wretched and controlled by women. They will reject their parents, siblings and relatives and friends and instead will associate themselves with the sisters and brothers of their wives. Thus sexual ties will predominate in relationships. Uncultured men will amass wealth in the name of God and will earn their livelihood by making a show of austerity and wearing a mendicant's dress. Even those who know nothing about religion will mount on a high platform to speak on religious principles. In *Kali Yuga* people's mind will always be agitated. They will suffer due to famines and high taxes. They will have the fear of drought. They will have no adequate clothing, food and drink, will have no proper rest, have too much of sex, will have no ornaments to decorate their bodies. They gradually come to appear like ghostly, haunted creatures. Men will develop hatred for each other even over petty sums of money. They will even lose their own lives and kill relatives. Men will not protect their elderly parents, their children or their wives. Instead they will try to satisfy only their bellies. People's intelligence will be diverted towards atheism, and they will not worship God. Terrified about death, man will collapse on his bed. Objects, places and individuals will all get polluted in *Kali Yuga*.

CHAPTER—4

Hymn 2

One thousand cycles of the four *Yugas* constitute a single day of *Brahma*. It is known as a *Kalpa* in which 14 Manus, the rulers, come and go.

Hymns 3 to 19

At the end of the day of *Brahma*, annihilation occurs during night that is of the same duration as the day. At that time all the three planetary systems will get destroyed. This is called *Naimittika* or occasional annihilation, during the period of which the Super Soul lies upon *Anantasesha* and absorbs the entire universe within Himself while Lord *Brahma* sleeps. Upon the destruction of the material elements, the universal egg, consisting of the elemental amalgamation of creation is confronted with annihilation. As annihilation approaches, there will be no rain upon the earth for one hundred years. Drought will lead to famine and the starving population will be forced to eat one another and the inhabitants of the earth will be gradually destroyed. The sun will absorb all water in the ocean gradually. But there will be no rain. Then the fire of annihilation will flare up from the mouth of Lord *Sankarshana*. The wind that blows on fire will burn the entire universe, scorching the lifeless cosmic shell. Burned from all sides, from above by the blazing sun and from below by the fire of Lord *Sankarshana*, the universal sphere will glow like a burning ball of cow dung. The terrible wind of destruction will blow for more than one hundred years and the sky covered with dust will turn grey. Then groups of multi coloured clouds will gather, roaring terribly with thunder and will pour down floods of rain for one hundred years. At that time the shell of the Universe will fill up with Water forming a single cosmic ocean. As the entire universe is flooded, the Water will take away the unique quality of fragrance of the Earth, and the element of Earth will be dissolved. The element of Fire then will seize the taste from the element of Water and the Water deprived of its taste will then merge with Fire. Then Air will seize the quality of Fire, the form, and fire will merge with Air. The element of Ether will seize the quality of touch from Air and Air will enter into Ether. Then the false ego in ignorance will seize sound, which is the quality of Ether or Space and Ether will merge in to the false ego. False ego in the mode of passion will take hold of the senses and false ego in the mode of goodness will absorb the Demi Gods. The false ego will then be seized by *Maha Tattva* and the *Maha Tattva* itself will be seized later by the three basic modes of nature namely, goodness, passion and ignorance. Impelled by time these modes will then be taken over by the original unmanifest form of nature. The unmanifest nature however is not influenced by the time factor as it has no beginning or end. It is the unmanifest eternal cause of this Universe.

Hymns 20 to 22

Neither in the unmanifest stage of material nature called *Pradhana* there is any expression of words, mind and no manifestation of the subtle elements beginning from *Mahat* nor are there the three modes of goodness, passion, and ignorance. There is no life air or intelligence nor any senses or Demi Gods. There is no definite arrangement of planetary systems, nor are there the different stages of consciousness-namely, wakefulness, sleep and dreamless sleep. No Ether, Water, Earth, Air, Fire, or Sun. This situation is just like complete sleep or voidness. Actually this stage cannot be described. This *Pradhana* is the original substance, the actual basis of material creation.

Annihilation at this stage is called *Praakritha* during which the energies belonging to the Supreme personality and His unmanifest material nature, disassembled by the force of time are deprived of their potencies and merge together totally.

Hymns 23 to 34

It is the Absolute Truth that manifests in the form of intelligence, senses, and the objects of sense perception. A lamp that is viewed by the eye and its light both are basically non different from the element Fire. Similarly, intelligence senses and the sense perceptions have no existence apart from the Supreme reality although that Absolute Truth remains totally distinct from them. Even the three states of wakefulness, dream state of sleep and deep sleep are only different experiences created for the being. Actually these three states are only an illusion. Just as the clouds come together and disperse after some time, due to the amalgamation and dissolution of their constituent elements, similarly, the material Universe is created and destroyed within the Absolute by the amalgamation and dissolution of its elemental constituent parts. The manifested products in this Universe of the Supreme are just like the threads that are interwoven in a cloth. Actually, creation and dissolution are only unreal and is an illusion because anything experienced in terms of general cause and specific effect must be an illusion because such causes and effects exist only relative to each other. Even the transformation of a single atom of material nature has no ultimate definition without reference to the Absolute, the Supreme Soul. To be accepted as real, anything must possess the same quality as the Absolute- the eternal, the unchanging existence itself. Actually, there is no material duality in the Absolute Truth. The difference perceived by the conditioned soul is like the difference seen in the air outside the empty pot and the Air that is inside the pot or the difference between the reflection of the Sun in water and that seen in the Sky or the vital Air within one's body and in another's body. Gold is used in different ways and as such it is perceived in various forms. Similarly, the Supreme, who is inaccessible to human senses and understanding, is described in various terms by different people. Cloud that is a product of the Sun and is made visible by the Sun creates darkness for the viewing eye that is another partial expansion of the Sun. Similarly, the material false ego that is a product of the Absolute Truth is made visible by the Absolute Truth and at the same time obstructs the individual soul that is another partial expansion of the Absolute Truth from realizing the Absolute Truth. When the cloud produced from the sun is torn apart the eye is able to see the Sun. Similarly, when the material covering of false ego disappears the original spiritual awareness by inquiry into the transcendental science becomes known. When the false ego is cut off with the sword of discriminating knowledge, one is able to know the Supreme Soul, the *Avyaktha* or the ultimate or the indeterminate.

Hymns 35 to 38

It is understood that creation and annihilation of the Universe with all its created beings and things take place continuously. All material activities undergo transformation by the mighty currents of Time or *Kaala*. The perpetual cause of generation and annihilation is the various stages of existence of the material things. These stages of existence created by the perpetual Time, the impersonal representative of the Supreme are not visible to the naked eye just as the infinitesimal momentary changes of position of the planets in the sky cannot be observed directly. In this manner, the progress of time is described in terms of the four kinds of annihilation, namely, continuous, occasional, elemental and final.

CHAPTER—7

Hymns 11 and 12

From the agitation of the original modes within the unmanifest material nature, the *Mahath Thattva* arises. From the *Mahath Thattva* comes the element, false ego that divides in to three aspects. This threefold false ego further manifests as the subtle form of perception, as the senses and as the gross sense objects. The generation of all these is called creation.

The secondary creation is the manifest amalgamation of the desires of the living entities. Just as a seed produces additional seeds, activities that promote material desires in the performer produce moving and non-moving life forms.

Hymns 17

There are four types of cosmic annihilation- occasional, elemental, continuous and ultimate.

Hymns 20

Although material objects may assume various forms and names, its essential ingredient is always present as its fundamental basis of existence. Similarly, the Supreme Truth is also present with the created material body throughout its phase of existence, and destruction.

CHAPTER—11

Hymns 29 and 32

The Sun travels among all planets and thus regulates their movements.

The Supreme Soul as the Sun God travels about in each of the twelve months to regulate the planetary motion within the Universe.

6

Cosmos—A Few Findings of Modern Science

The Cosmos in the sense 'Universe' contains everything from the tiniest subatomic particles to galactic super clusters that are the largest structures known so far. Scientists say that the entire observable Universe with about 100 billion galaxies, each with about 100 billion stars stretching out more than about 10 billion light years in all directions was once squashed into an infinitesimally small space, far smaller than a single electron. (As per the vision of ancient Indian seers the Absolute Universal soul contained the Universe within itself in an unmanifested form before its creation into visible Universe.)

According to Science, the evolution of the Universe, since it began, can be divided in to three phases. In the very early stages the Universe was so hot and particles had high energy. In the second phase the first protons, electrons and neutrons were formed and then nuclei and finally atoms. In the final stage when matter started to aggregate and later, stars, galaxies, clusters of galaxies and super clusters started to form. (According to ancient Indian view in the beginning before creation of the Universe there was only the Absolute, Supreme energy, the *Paramathman* or the *Parabrahman*. Later the *Ichcha* or the will or the desire of the *Paramatman* resulted in the creation of Universe with varied names and forms).

The most popular and broadly accepted theory of the origin and evolution of the Universe that dominated cosmology is the theory of Big Bang.

According to this theory, the scientists state that that the Universe appeared in a cosmic event that is termed as the Big bang with a tremendous violent explosion at some finite time, about 13.7 billion years ago when an unimaginable heat and density exploded and the Universe continues to expand to this day. The big explosion that was about trillions of degrees in temperature that was infinitely dense, created the fundamental matter, energy, space and time.(The *Rig Veda* of the ancient Indians declare that before creation, in the unmanifested stage, there was only total darkness utter chaos and void without the realm of air or sky and so on. The *Brahmanaspathi* the Supreme soul recreated (but not created for the first time) the universe with a blast) The scientists say that the Universe erupted from a primordial, infinitesimally hot and dense initial condition from one singular point known as Singularity. All matter and energy were squeezed in to this singularity of infinitely small volume. (It resembles the notion of the ancient Indian sages that originally only the Universal soul or *Paramatma* alone existed and all energy and matter were contained in that Super Soul or Absolute potential energy in unmanifested form. What was unmanifested became manifested with creation). From this Singularity the Universe exploded and released an incredible amount of matter, energy, space and time.

Scientists point out that for an infinitely small fraction of a second, after the explosion it was infinitely dense and was a hot fire ball. There was only energy due to the tremendous heat of the explosion. A peculiar form of energy came out of space and time and it lasted only for one millionth of a second. This process came out from the forces of nature. The fire ball moved away from the singularity in all directions and after the first second, the early universe expanded and cooled to 100 billion degrees and from this came the elementary particles like Neutrons, Protons and Electrons. These particles spread out across at an incredible rate and about three seconds after the Big Bang, because of the nucleon synthesis, the Protons and Neutrons began to form simple elements mostly hydrogen and small atomic nuclei took shape with the interaction of Protons and Neutrons. As the Universe expanded the temperature dropped and the Universe cooled. After about 300,000 years the temperature of the Universe dropped below 3000 degrees and neutral atoms were formed due to the combination of Electrons and Atomic Nuclei. At this stage some of the Hydrogen fused to form

Helium. The Universe at this point of time was 25% Helium and 75% Hydrogen. The Hydrogen and Helium served later as the building blocks for stars and planets. But for the first 100,000 years after the first explosion there was no matter as we see them today. Instead there was only radiation everywhere. Matter in the form of atoms was formed and this matter began to dominate energy. (According to ancient Indian view also before creation of the Universe all was only energy known as *Paramatman* or *Parabhraman*. When matter that was inherent in the Absolute energy manifested, it became Universe, that is, creation happened.).This period is known as the Radiation era. Thus the Universe that was supposed to be infinitesimally very small, hot and dense and only a few millimetres across, in the very beginning of its formation, later, cooled down and expanded rapidly from the hot dense state in to vast and cooler Cosmos and the galaxies and planets were formed.

The Big Bang theory stated that initially the Universe was very hot. Initially it was a very hot, dense fire ball of expanding and cooling gas. After a million of years the gas might have started to condense to form Protogalaxies. During the next five billion years these Proto galaxies continued to condense and formed into galaxies in which stars were born. Remnants of this have been discovered by Radio Astronomers in 1965. With the help of the instrument called Spectroscope the scientists are able to say that the Universe is still growing in all directions. The galaxies also appear to be moving away from us at speeds that are proportional to their distance. This observation known as 'Hubble's Law' supports the expansion of the Universe as stated by the Big Bang Theory. There is an abundance of light elements like Hydrogen and Helium in the observable Universe. This evidence supports the Big Bang theory.

Some modern scientists question the correctness of the Big Bang theory and they have postulated alternative models and theories. It is pointed out that this theory is still largely a sketchy theory with blank spaces, mysteries and enigmas. Some even feel that all that are stated by science regarding the origin and the changes that are said to have taken place in the Universe could probably be a matter of mathematical fiction and speculation and are based upon hypothetical theories.

Astro Physicist George F.R. Ellis says, "People need to be aware that there is a range of models that could explain the observations—- For instance, I can construct you a spherically symmetrical universe with earth at its centre, and you cannot disprove it based on observations— You can only exclude it on philosophical grounds. In my view there is absolutely nothing wrong in that. What I want to bring in to the open is the fact that we are using philosophical criteria in choosing our models. A lot of cosmology tries to hide that". The Bang theory that was originated by the well-known scientist Gamow, who was also a Science fiction writer, is pointed out by some, as nothing more than a science fiction.

The modern view of Cosmology is that there was a cloud of slowly rotating hot gaseous material that was the starting point of the Universe. As it got cooled it shrank and rotated more rapidly. The cloud got compressed gradually at the polar regions into a lens shaped disc that gradually released masses of gases that cooled down into a liquid state and then into a solid state that gave rise to the planets. According to Kuupier's 'protoplanet hypothesis' the solar system originated from a hot gaseous cloud of Nebula, may be one tenth as massive as the Sun, that surrounded a large dark central mass that subsequently formed into a star. As the Nebula contracted and flattened, it became unstable and got divided into a number of separate clouds of Proto Planets. The solid particles accumulated into a central core in each Proto Planet and became surrounded by a very large gaseous covering. The Nebula was mainly composed of Hydrogen, some Helium and 1 to 2 % of heavier elements. The Proto planets were of different sizes but all were far larger and more massive than the present planets. The Satellites too were formed in a similar manner but they were relatively closer. When the central mass had contracted enough it became a star. As the Sun's temperature increased, its radiation and ejected particles ionized the gases around it. These gases interacted with the Sun's rotation and transferred most of its momentum to the particles in the Nebula and they moved faster due to their transfer. This Solar wind of radiations and ejected particles gradually swept off into space the remaining portions of the Nebula and most of the lighter gases of the Proto Planets. Thus according to the modern theory of cosmology, there was the pre-existing rotating hot gaseous Nebula, but it is not known how this came into being and which motivated the rotation.

Some cosmologists say that there was and is only a continuous expansion in the formation of the Universe but no giant explosion. Again, it is thought that in the beginning the Universe appeared as a fire ball in space. A few scientists argue that space did not exist prior to Big Bang. According to Astro physicists, time and space had a finite beginning that corresponds to the origin of matter and energy. (According to ancient Indian view Space and time in its limited, gross or physical sense appeared only after creation. But before creation that is, manifestation of the Universe, Space and Time did exist as the unmanifested, subtle and unlimited. So the ancient Indian point of view is that space and time became visible after the creation of the Universe. But before the creation of the Universe everything including space and time, and the Universe itself were inherent in a latent hidden manner in the Absolute potential energy and with the release or expression of that energy, the Universe, space, time, directions, animates and inanimate matters were born in concrete forms).

Whatever may be the claims or otherwise what Science has discovered till today is no humble achievement and the claims and counter claims only prove the progress of science.

Stars

Scientists point out that Gravity and the other fundamental forces of the Universe that were created in the big explosion caused the early atoms to pull together in to dense clouds called Nebulae. Later on Nebulae collapsed in to massive objects called Stars that range greatly in size mass and temperature. Their diameters vary from about 450 times smaller to over 1000 times bigger than that of the sun. Masses range from about a 28th to over 50 solar masses and the surface temperature may vary from about 5,000 degree C to over 50,000degree C. The colour of the stars depends upon their temperature. The Sun with a surface temperature of 5,500 degree C appears yellow. The energy emitted by a shining star is produced by nuclear fusion in the star's core.

Stars are born in the clouds of dust and gas that is mostly hydrogen. Scientists point out that Stars that are big balls of gas that emit both heat and light appeared at the end of this era. The first stars contained only hydrogen and helium. The first generation of stars was called population-2 stars and the later generation of stars was called as Population-1 stars. The tremendous pressure of the gravity of stars squeezed the atoms in it together. The stars converted the light elements of hydrogen and helium in to heavier elements like carbon, nitrogen, oxygen and so on. It is also pointed out that as the stars become more massive the amount of energy created in their cores grows at a faster rate than the force of gravity that holds them together. This energy would eventually become so powerful that the Stars are thrown apart. In July 2010 the biggest star named R136a1 with a mass 320 times greater than the Sun has been discovered at the edge of our galaxy by the British Astronomers. This Star is believed to have a surface temperature of more than 40,000 degrees Celsius and is 10 million times brighter than the Sun. Among the largest known stars previously known were the Pistol Star between 80 to 150 solar masses and Eta Carinae around 100 solar masses. The Pistol Star radiates as much energy in 20 seconds as the Sun does in a year. Previously the heaviest known stars were around 150 times the masses of the Sun.

From the Earth the northern sky usually appears less bright than the southern sky. The northern sky has the constellations Ursa Major (the great Bear Constellation or the *Saptha Rishis* in Indian terminology) and Orion. The Moon and planets move against the background of stars because stars are much more distant. The nearest star outside the solar system is more than 50,000 times further away than Jupiter. In the southern sky there is a huge population of star clusters and Nebulae. Stars make fixed pattern in the sky called Constellations. However this sight is only apparent as the distance to the stars in a Constellation varies enormously. The movement of the Constellations across the sky is due to the earth's motion in space. The daily rotation of earth causes the constellations to move across the sky from east to west, and the orbit of earth around the Sun causes different areas of the sky to be visible in different seasons. The visibility areas of the sky also depend upon the location of the observer on Earth.

The Protostar is a star that is in the very earliest stage of development in the process of star formation.

Galaxies

Galaxies are huge masses of stars, nebulae and interstellar material which in course of time cluster together to form mini galaxies that are clusters of matter. Then the mini galaxies merge to form mature galaxies that include the spiral galaxies like our milky way. Billions of galaxies that are clusters of stars form most of the visible mass of the Universe. According to estimates there are more than 100 billion galaxies in the Universe each consisting of an average of 100 billion stars like our Sun or bigger or smaller, newer or older, hotter or colder and so on and consisting millions of planets like ours that are bigger, smaller, colder, hotter and so on. The smallest galaxies contain around 100,000 stars while the largest ones contain around 5000 billion stars. The Gravity condenses the atoms in to galaxies that are islands containing billions of stars. They are separated from other galaxies by a vast ocean of almost empty space. It is after 200 billion years that galaxies and stars were formed. One particular galaxy is the Milky Way, in which we live.

The scientists say that there are three types of galaxies according to their shapes-elliptical, which are oval shaped; spiral which have arms spiralling outwards from a central bulge and irregular that has invisible shape. They have shapes like toothpicks or even rings. Sometimes the shape of the galaxy is also distorted because of the collision with another galaxy. The furthest known ordinary galaxies are about 10 billion light years away.

Quasars

Quasars that are quasi-stellar objects are far away and their nature is not known yet. They are compact and highly luminous objects in the outer reaches of the known Universe. The furthest known Quasar is about 15 billion light years away. It is believed that some of them are even larger than our Solar system. They emit huge amounts of energy and can even be a trillion times brighter than the Sun.

Supernova

After billions of years when the galaxies become old and exhaust all their nuclear fuel they end their life with an explosion called Supernova as the galaxies gain heat that generate nuclear fusion (The process by which two or more atomic nuclei fuse together to form a single heavier molecule that is accompanied by release or absorption of large quantities of energy.) in the outer layers of the stars that fall and explode. The Super novae shine brighter than the whole galaxy for a few days. They are also extremely hot. The new atoms are released back to the galaxy and join together to form cosmic dust by becoming tiny crystals that form grains of cosmic dust. The dust grains blown out of the dying stars mix with the original gas of the galaxy and form the dust clouds that make the disc of the galaxy thick with dust and molecules, (the smallest particle of a substance that retains the chemical and physical properties of the substance and is composed of two or more atoms.) This process spreads the star's matter back in to space for the beginning of a new cycle. The material would then be ejected back into space and would form a new star.

Black Holes

Black holes are regions where not even light can escape. But it absorbs all light. They are the evolutionary end points of stars that are at least 10 to 15 times as massive as the sun. Black holes occur when stars die. When Stars die there is no nuclear fusion as the fuel for these reactions get burnt. But at the same time the star's gravity pulls material inward and compresses the core. As the core compresses it heats up and eventually creates a Supernova explosion in which the material and radiation blasts out into space. What remains is highly compressed and extremely massive core. The core's gravity is so strong that even light cannot escape. The core sinks because of its gravity and creates a hole in space. Due to the pull of their own gravity they collapse inward. Since it has very high gravity it pulls inside any object that comes near it (The term *Adithi* found in the Rigvedic hymn refers to Black holes. *Adithi* means the one that eats up) Recently Astronomers have found sky ablaze with supermassive black holes throughout the Universe called Blazers as per data collected by NASA. Blazers are supposed to be among the most energetic objects in the Universe consisting of supermassive black holes pulling matter on to them at the cores of giant galaxies. As the matter is dragged toward the supermassive hole some of the energy is released in the form of jets travelling at nearly the speed of light.

Nebulae and Star Clusters

It is an interstellar cloud of dust inside a galaxy containing Hydrogen, Helium and so on. These are the star forming regions that form into stars later. In these regions gas dust and other materials clump together to form large masses and they attract further matter and then become massive enough to form stars. They become visible when light shines off it, when the cloud reflects starlight as in the case of reflection Nebulae or obscures light from more distant objects as in the case of dark Nebulae or the gas inside it glows in the case of Emission Nebulae. New stars are created inside Nebulae when the gases contract and the gravity start pulling the Nebula in.

Stars are often found in groups known as clusters. The open clusters contain loose groups of a few thousand young stars that were born in the same clouds and are drifting apart. Globular clusters are densely packed and are roughly spherical groups of hundreds of thousands of older stars. Based on experiments the scientists say that the star clusters are around 12 to 15 billion years old.

The Milky Way

The Milky Way is a faint band of light that stretches across the night sky.(*Rig Veda* mentions about *Prsni* , meaning 'spotted' This perhaps refers to star clusters) This light comes from stars and Nebulae in to our galaxy known as the Milky Way Galaxy or simply Galaxy. This galaxy is spiral shaped with a dense central bulge that is encircled by four arms spiralling outwards and is surrounded by a less dense halo. However we cannot see the spiral shape because the solar system is in one of the spiral arms called the Orion Arm or Local Arm. From our position, the centre of the galaxy is comparatively covered by dust clouds. The central bulge of the galaxy is relatively small and dense containing mainly older red and yellow stars.. (In *Rig Veda*, 'The Milky way' is represented by a cow) Some of these stars may be as old as the galaxy itself that is, around 15 billion years. The spiral arm contains mainly of hot, young, blue stars and Nebulae that are clouds of dust and gas inside which stars are born. This Galaxy is vast about 100,000 light years across (one light year is roughly equals 9,460 billion Kms. or 5,680,368,000,000 miles). The entire Galaxy rotates in space although the inner stars travel faster than those farther away. It is found that the Milky Way Galaxy has hundreds of billions of stars, enough gas and dust to make billion more stars and huge dark matter that are all held together by gravity. It is also found that at the centre of the Spiral there is huge energy and occasionally vivid flares are generated.

The Milky Way belongs to a group of galaxies that is known as the 'Local Group', The Local Group contains about 30 galaxies and it is 6 million light years in diameter. The local Group belongs to a much larger group of galaxies known as the Virgo Super Cluster. Our Milky Way lies on the outer edge of the Super Cluster. It began to form around 10 billion years ago. The Milky Way is 100,000 light years in diameter. The galaxy of the Milky Way is a spiral galaxy because it looks like a giant pin wheel. It was formed with more than 100 billion stars spiralling around its centre, with a diameter of 100,000 light years and the Sun is one among them. The Milky Way takes approximately 240 million years to rotate clock wise. The nearest large galaxy from the Milky Way is the Andromeda Galaxy that is also spiral like the Milky Way. Scientists believe that there is a 'Black hole' in the centre of our 'Milky Way'.

Scientists say that there are not only100 billion stars in our galaxy but beyond them are one trillion galaxies each with 100 billion stars, planets and other flying objects. There are also many star clusters in the Universe. Each one is a circular ball consisting of billions upon billions of stars and each star has its own orbit. In each star cluster planets and stars spin and orbit in a balanced manner. The normal shape of the galaxies is that of a saucer with a central sphere. The clusters rotate separately and even pass through the plane without colliding with any other stars. Stars also never get closer than a certain distance from one another (3.5 light years apart)

Sun

Sun is the star at the centre in the solar system. It is a main yellow sequence star about 1.4 million kms. in diameter. About 5.5 million years ago, a passing star or galaxy disturbed a calm and placid cloud of gas and dust known as a Nebula and caused the cloud to swirl around and gather mass. The swirl and gravity accumulated more and more gas and dust on these masses known as Proto stars. The gravity also condensed the lumps resulting in increase in gravity and of pressure in their core and the internal heat increased. When the heat reached a temperature 18,000,000 degree Fahrenheit, nuclear fusion (the process by which atomic nuclei join together to form a single heavier nucleus that is accompanied by absorption or release of energy) started and the Sun was born. The Sun exhibits sudden releases of energy. The Sun is expected to shine for about another five billion years.

The visible star atmosphere consists of three regions namely, the Photosphere, the Chromosphere, and the solar corona. Most of the visible light comes from the Photosphere. This is the part of the Sun that we actually see. The Sun has hydrogen mainly and helium. In the sun's core hydrogen is converted in to helium by nuclear fusion that releases energy in the process. The energy travels from the core, reaches the Photosphere that is the visible surface, where it leaves the sun in the form of heat and light. On the Photosphere there are dark, relatively cool areas called sun spots that usually appear in pairs or groups and are said to be caused by magnetic fields. Other types of solar activities are flares associated with sun spots and Prominences. Flares are sudden discharge of high energy radiation and atomic particles. Prominences are huge loops or filament of gas extending in to the solar atmosphere. Some last for hours and others for months. Beyond the Photosphere is the chromosphere that is the inner atmosphere and the outer atmosphere, the Corona that extends millions of kms. into space. The Chromosphere and Corona also emit white light and can be seen when the light from the atmosphere is blocked in solar eclipse. The Sun also emits electromagnetic radiation at many other wave lengths.

The interior of the Sun is made up of different layers one inside the other. The innermost layer, the solar core, is the region where the Sun's energy is produced. The solar core is made up of an extremely hot and dense gas in the plasma state where nuclear fusion reactions can take place. The Sun's core is a very dark place in spite of the reactions. Tiny particles that escape from the corona give rise to the solar wind that streams through space at hundreds of kms. per second.

The Solar Eclipse

Solar eclipse occurs when the Earth passes through the Moon's shadow. During Solar eclipse the Moon goes in front of the sun blocking most of the sun's light from the earth. A total eclipse of the sun takes place on the New Moon day when the New moon is positioned directly between the sun and Earth and casts shadow on Earth. When the Sun is totally eclipsed by Moon, the chromosphere and corona can be seen from the Earth.

Solar System

The solar system consists of a central star, the Sun, and other celestial bodies revolving around it. They are the nine planets including Pluto and their 61 known moons, a large number of small bodies like namely, asteroids, comets and meteoroids, and at least five dwarf planets namely, Ceres, Pluto, (Pluto is considered as a dwarf Planet by scientists) Haumea, Makemake and Eris and around 240 known satellites, and interplanetary medium in the form of gas and dust. It is suspected that at least 50 known objects in the solar system are dwarf planets but the number can go up to 200 or even 2000.The inner solar circle contains four small rocky planets namely, Mercury, Venus, Earth and Mars. These are known as terrestrial planets because they have a compact rocky surface like the Earth. The four planets of the outer solar system, the gas giants are Jupiter, Saturn, Uranus and Neptune that are also known as Jovian or Jupiter like planets because they are all gigantic compared to Earth and they have a gaseous nature like that of Jupiter. The solar system is mostly empty space. This vacuum of space consists of the interplanetary medium. It includes various forms of energy and contains at least inter planetary dust consisting of microscopic solid particles and inter planetary gas that is the flow of gas and charged particles mostly protons and plasma, the stream from the Sun called the solar wind. The planets are very small compared to the space between them. They orbit around the Sun in an elliptical manner. Pluto the ninth planet is the outermost planet except when it passes briefly inside Neptune's orbit. Between the rocky planets and the gas giants is the asteroid belt that contains thousands of chunks of rocks orbiting the Sun. Most of the bodies in the solar system move around the Sun in elliptical orbits located in a thin disc around the sun's equator. All planets orbit the Sun in an anti-clock wise direction as observed from above except Venus, Uranus and Pluto. Moons also spin as they orbit their galaxy, the Milky Way. We do not know yet whether there are some more planets and other celestial objects in the Cosmos that are yet to be discovered and understood.

As time passed the thick cloud of gas and debris that formed matter around the Sun formed the planets including the Earth around 4.5 Billion years ago. These planets circled around the Sun. The nine planets found so far in the solar system possess different characteristic features. They are at different distances from the Sun and they circle around the Sun in distinct orbits. These planets are Earth, Jupiter, Mars, Mercury, Neptune, Saturn, Uranus, Venus and Pluto. Pluto was considered as the ninth planet that is the farthest along with Neptune in the solar system. Pluto the smallest planet in the solar system now is considered as a dwarf planet although it has all the three features of a planet (the features are that, that it has to orbit a star, it must be small enough and cannot undergo internal nuclear fusion like stars and it must be large enough that its gravity gives it the shape of a sphere). Pluto also has a Moon as well as an atmosphere.

The Sun contains 99.85% of all matter in the solar system. The planets that condensed out of the same disc of material that formed the Sun contain only 0.135% of the mass of the solar system. Jupiter contains more than twice the matter of all the other planets combined. Satellites of the planets, comets, asteroids, meteoroids, and the interplanetary medium constitute the remaining 0.015%.

In recent years conclusive evidence has accumulated for planets orbiting other stars. Recent studies show that stars, possibly another solar system appear to be forming. It is understood that four verified solar type stars have Jupiter size planets around them. It shows that there is possibility of multiple star systems but no single stars like the Sun in the Solar system in our Universe. (This is also stated in ancient Indian scriptures)

The Planets

Earth

The Earth was formed around 4600 million years ago from a cloud of dust and gas drifting through space. Dense materials sank to the centre while lighter ones formed a thin rocky crust. The Earth is believed to contain a solid inner core made mostly of iron and nickel. This is surrounded by a liquid outer core also mostly iron and nickel. The diameter of the core is estimated to be 7000 kms. compared to 12,700 kms. diameter for the entire planet. The crust is only a few tens of kms. thick. The region between the core and crust is called the mantle. The upper part of the mantle and the crust together are called the Lithosphere. Just below this is the region of plastic consistency- the Aestheno sphere. In the beginning of its formation the earth did not contain such interior structure. Within about one million years of its formation the earth was melted by heat arising from a combination of gravitational energy left from the formation of the planet, meteor bombardment and decay of radioactive material trapped in the earth's body. While the earth was molten, gravity acted to concentrate more dense material near the centre and less dense material nearer the surface. When the Earth solidified again, except for the outer liquid core, it was left with a structure with more dense material like iron and nickel near the centre and less dense rocks nearer the surface. As the outer layers cooled, and solidified, large cracks developed because of the thermal stress leaving Lithosphere breaking up into large blocks or plates. The horizontal movement of the crusted plates of earth came to be known as the Continental drift or as Plate Tectonics in technical terms. The time scale for substantial continent drift is 10 to 100 million years. It means that the surface of the Earth looked quite differently in the distant past and the continents have changed now due to this factor. Through such an effect the present continents separated from two super continents called Laurasia, the northern continent and Gondwanaland, the southern continent. These two super continents might have been a single continent before that was known as Pangaea. When the early Earth was very hot like a molten block like rock that later melted, there was no life on earth then.

The Sun has an average distance of 149.6 million kms. from the earth. The light that is currently reaching the earth was generated in the Sun approximately 1000,000 years ago because the Sun's surface is very dense. As per estimates it takes 8 minutes and 26 seconds for the light from the Sun to reach the earth. The light from the sun is made up of many colours called Visible Spectrum and also many shorter and longer wave lengths of light that are not visible to the naked eye of humans.

Earth is the third closest planet from the Sun at 93 million miles. It is the 5th largest and most dense of all the planets of the Solar system. It rotates around the sun in slightly more than 365 days and rotates every 23.9 hours. 70% of it is water that is either in liquid form or ice. I t is not found in liquid form on the surface of any other planet. It is composed of 78% of nitrogen, 21% of oxygen, 0.9% of argon, 0.03% of carbon-di-oxide and a little of other gases. The atmosphere is thick, extending upward around 300 miles. But above 20,000 feet it becomes less dense rapidly and the layers of gases become thinner and thinner until it merges into space. 80% of the atmosphere is within 10 miles from the surface of the earth. The atmosphere is able to protect life by reducing the incoming ultra violet radiation from the Sun and the escape of the re radiated heat in to space. Earth is the only planet that supports life. The very small amount of carbon-di-oxide that is in the Earth's atmosphere produces just enough greenhouse effect (the phenomenon in which the Earth's atmosphere traps solar radiation, caused by the presence of carbon-di-oxide, water vapour and methane that allow the incoming sun light to pass through but also absorb heat radiated back from the earth's surface) to raise the Earth's temperature from -6 degrees F. to an average of 57 degrees F. Without the greenhouse effect, water would freeze and Earth would have become another lifeless planet. Now it is the only planet with liquid water to sustain life. Earth has four main layers; the inner core, the outer core, the mantle and the crust. At the heart of this planet the solid inner core has a temperature of about 4000 degree C. The heat from this inner core causes material in the molten outer core and mantle to circulate in convection currents (it is the flow of heat through a bulk macroscopic movement of matter from a hot region to a cool region). It is thought that these convection currents generate the Earth's magnetic field that extends in to space as the Magnetosphere. The Earth's atmosphere help to screen out some of the harmful radiation from the Sun, stops meteorites from reaching this planet's surface and traps enough heat to prevent extremes of cold. Exosphere is the outermost layer of

Earth's atmosphere. It extends from about 400 miles high to about 800 miles. In its lower levels, the atmospheric pressure is very low and temperature is also very low. The Ionosphere starts at about 43-50 miles high and continues for hundreds of miles. The Ionosphere is responsible for absorbing the most energetic photons from the sun and for reflecting radio waves. The Thermosphere is includes Exosphere and part of Ionosphere. In this the temperature increases with altitude. The Mesosphere is characterised by temperatures that rapidly declines as the height increases. It extends from 31 to 50 miles above the Earth's surface. The earth has got one natural satellite, the Moon. Earth has a strong magnetic field.

Life on Earth

According to scientists for almost a thousand million years after its formation there was no known life on Earth. According to scientists the earliest life appeared on Earth around 3 ½ billion years ago. The first known life forms the Bacteria and the Algae appeared on earth around 5400 million years ago. More complex plants and animals began to appear around 700 million years ago. Since then innumerable species of beings are being evolved and some life forms like the Dinosaurs survived for many million years, while others got extinct quickly. After more than 2 billion years of the formation of Earth, the primitive single celled microbial organisms became multi nuclear and then advanced life began to appear rapidly. But in the beginning the Earth's atmosphere contained volcanic gases with little oxygen that made life impossible on Earth. Constant movement of Earth's crusted plates carried continents across the Earth's surface. The scientists point out that the Earth is changing continuously. The continents are drifting slowly over the planet's surface and mountain ranges such as Himalayas that began to form around 40 million years ago are continuously being built up and worn away. Earth's climate is also changing continuously.

The first primitive, simple, sea dwelling organic structure appeared on Earth about 5, 400 million years ago. The single celled micro-organisms like the blue green Algae were able to photosynthesize and there by produce oxygen. A thousand million years later, sufficient oxygen was built up in the Earth's atmosphere and it allowed multi cellular organisms to appear on Earth. Soft bodied Jelly fish, Corals and sea worms flourished about 700 million years ago. The first animals with a hard body frames developed around 570-170 million years ago. The first vertebrates appeared around 470 million years ago and the first land animals about 50 million years after. The first land plants appeared around 400 million years ago. About 363 million years ago the first Amphibians crawled on to the land. Evolving from Amphibians, reptiles first appeared around 363- 290 million years ago. Then came the Dinosaurs, a large group of reptiles that were the dominant land vertebrates around 248-208 million years ago. They survived for nearly 165 million years until their extinction 65 million years ago. Other animals appeared about 208-146 million years ago. The bipedal, the two footed Theropods (The beast feet) emerged 230 million years ago. Theropods ranged from animals not larger than a chicken to huge creatures. This group also included Omnivorous and Herbivorous with toothless beaks. About 165 million years ago, the heaviest and the longest land animals appeared on Earth. Since the extinction of the Dinosaurs about 65 million years ago mammals have been the dominant vertebrates on Earth that included the terrestrial, aerial and aquatic forms. Plants and trees came up and animal species became more varied; new mammals were evolved and the other water borne beings came up around 146 – 65 million years ago. . This period witnessed a huge expansion of mammal life. Humans evolved around 1.6 million- 10,000 years before, first in Africa and migrated to other continents. But modern humans called the Homo sapiens lived around 30,000 years ago and hunted the animals. (The ancient Indian scriptures have a different view of the evolution of life on Earth). The Homosapiens, the species in to which humans belong to, became well developed and according to scientists they were able to communicate around 40,000 years ago or even earlier. The first written records were dated back 5000 years ago.

Earth is supposed to continue supporting life for about 0.5 to 2.3 billion years. After this period, according to Scientists, the rising luminosity and expansion of the Sun due to the gravitational depletion of its hydrogen fuel would eventually eliminate Earth's biosphere.

According to scientists life is known to exist only on Earth.

Moon

It is the Earth's only natural satellite. It is the fifth in diameter among the planetary satellites. It is more than ¼ of the size of earth with a diameter of 5470 kms. It is the poorest reflector in the solar system. It reflects only 7% of the Sunlight that falls on it. It goes around the Earth on an average in 27 days 7 hours and 43 minutes. Moon is perhaps the nearest object to us in the solar system. The Moon is dry and barren with no atmosphere or water. It mainly consists of solid rock, although its core may contain molten rock or iron. Its surface is dusty with plains that are covered in craters caused by meteorite impacts. The large craters are filled by solidified lava to form dark areas. Many of the craters are bounded by mountain ranges that form the crater walls and that are thousands of meters high. The Moon is large enough for both the Earth and its Moon to be considered a double planet system.

The Moon appears to move completely around the celestial sphere once in about 27.3 days except for small fluctuations as observed from Earth. The temperature changes are very rapid here. The temperature during lunar night (a fortnight) is around -113 degrees Celsius whereas during lunar day the temperature reaches 100 degrees as there is no atmosphere or surface water to store heat. The Moon might have formed around 4.6 billion years ago. The oldest material from the surface of the Moon is almost as old as we believe the solar system to be. It is more than a billion years older than the oldest earth rocks.

The Lunar Eclipse

When the Moon passes through the shadow cast by Earth, lunar eclipse is caused. Lunar eclipses can also be partial or total depending on whether the light of the Sun is partially or totally is blocked from reaching the Moon. During a total lunar eclipse the Moon takes on a dark red colour because it is lighted slightly by Sun light passing through the Earth's atmosphere and this light has the blue component scattered out leaving faint reddish light to illumine the Moon during eclipse.

Tide happens due to the effects of Moon on the earth's oceans.

Jupiter

Jupiter is the fifth planet from the Sun and the first of the four gas giants.

It is the largest and most massive planet in the solar system and is the king of all planets, having the most majestic appearance. It has the most dynamic atmospheric motion. The atmosphere is completely gas and liquid. Its composition is more like that of stars. It has a diameter that is about 11.2 times that of the Earth and a mass about 2.5 times the combined mass of the eight other planets. Its density is ¼ that of Earth. The atmosphere of Jupiter is only a narrow surface layer compared to its vast interior. It has a small rocky core surrounded by an inner mantle of metallic hydrogen, that is, liquid hydrogen that acts like a metal. Outside the inner mantle is an outer mantle with liquid hydrogen and helium that merges into the gaseous atmosphere. Jupiter's rapid rate of rotation results in belts that are dark, low lying, relatively warm cloud layers and zones that are bright, high altitude, cooler cloud layers that is caused by the clouds in its atmosphere. This encircles the planet parallel to the equator. Within the belts and zones turbulence causes the formation of cloud features such as white ovals and red spots that are huge storm systems. The most prominent of such cloud feature is known as the 'great red spot' that consists of a spiralling column of clouds three times wider than the earth. It rises about 8 kms. above the upper cloud layer. This planet has one thin, faint, main ring. This planet has 16 known Moons out of which four are very large. The four largest Galilean Moons are between 3000 to 5000 kms. in diameter and they differ significantly in structure. It is believed that many of the smaller Moons are Asteroids. Jupiter has large, complex, and very intense and large magnetic field that is 10 times stronger than that of Earth's. Jupiter's magnetosphere is not only big but also unique in the solar system and is also very powerful. It emits more radiation than it receives. It has a faint ring. Its atmosphere is quite complex and has a 'great red spot', a great anti cyclonic that is high pressure storm akin to a hurricane on earth and is enormous. It has persisted for about 400 years. Most of its interior is liquid.

Mars

Mars is known as the red planet and is the fourth planet from the Sun and also the outermost rocky planet and is much like Venus. It rotates around the Sun in 687 days and has a diameter of 6800 kms., that is about half that of Earth. It is very bright and so can be easily spotted in the night sky. It is reddish in colour. It is reddish in colour due to iron oxide or rust in the soil. The atmosphere of Mars is much thinner than that of earth. Oxygen makes up only 0.13% of Mar's atmosphere and one fourth of Earth's water vapour in the atmosphere. There are dark patches on the surface of Mars. These are areas where the red dust that cover most of the planet has been blown away. The wind blows away the fine dust particles and result in dust storm that obscures the surface of Mars. The dust storms create surface erosion due to the high velocity seasonal winds. The residual dust in the planet's atmosphere gives a pinkish column to its sky. The atmosphere and interior of Mars differ substantially from that of Earth. The northern hemisphere of Mars has many large plains formed of solidified volcanic lava and the southern hemisphere has many craters formed by movements on the surface crust and the branching channels, probably formed by flowing water that got dried up. There are channels on Mars as much as 1500 kms. long and 200 kms. wide. There are also several extinct huge volcanoes that include the Olympus Moons, that is 600 kms. across and 25 kms. high, that is supposed to be the largest known volcano in the entire solar system. The Martian atmosphere is much thinner than that of Earth's. There are only a few clouds and morning mists. Mars has two tiny irregularly shaped Moons called Phobos and Deimos.

Mercury

This planet is closest to the Sun at 36 million miles. It is the second smallest planet. It is much like the Earth on the inside and much like the Moon on the outside. It orbits at an average distance of about 58 million kms. Since it is the closest planet to the Sun, it moves faster than any other planet and travels at an average speed of nearly 48 kms. per second and completes an orbit in less than 88 days. It is a small planet bigger only than Pluto and is rocky. Its surface is heavily cratered by the impact of meteorites although there are smooth sparsely cratered plains. The Caloris Basin is the largest crater measuring about 1500 kms. across. This planet rotates about its axis very slowly taking nearly 59 earth days to complete one rotation. As a result a solar day from Sunrise to Sunset on Mercury is about 176 earth days. It has extreme surface temperatures ranging from a maximum of 450 degree C to -170 degree C between the sunlit side and the dark side. At night the temperature drops very quickly because the planet has an extremely thin atmosphere that is almost non-existent. The atmosphere contains only of minute amounts of helium and hydrogen received from the solar wind and traces of other gases. This planet has a significant magnetic field like Earth.

Neptune

Neptune along with Pluto, are the two planets that are the farthest planets from the Sun at an average distance of about 4500 million kms. Neptune is a gas giant and known to consist of a small rocky core surrounded by a mixture of liquids and gases. It is the eigth planet in the Solar system. Its diameter is four times that of Earth and hence the fourth largest planet and the third most massive planet. There is a large concentration of hydrogen and helium and larger concentration of heavier elements than found in Jupiter and Saturn. The atmosphere has several prominent cloud features, the largest of them being the great dark spot that is as wide as Earth, the small dark spot and the scooter. The great and small dark spots are huge storms that hit the planet by winds of about 2000 kms. per hour that are the fastest in the Solar system. The temperature at the cloud tops are around -216 degrees Celsius that is slightly warmer than for Uranus. Its internal heat produces 2.7 times more heat than it absorbs. Its period of rotation is around 16 hours. Neptune has four rings and eight known Moons out of which two are large Moons that can be seen from Earth. Triton is the largest Neptunian Moon and the coldest object in the solar system with a temperature of -235 degrees C. Triton unlike the other Moons in the Solar system orbits its mother planet, the Neptune, in opposite direction to the planet's rotation. Neptune has a dynamic atmosphere. Its average temperature is 373 degrees F. Like Jupiter and Saturn it radiates more than that it receives. Its blue colour is largely due to its absorption of red light by methane in the atmosphere.

Saturn

It is nearly 900 miles from the Sun. It is the second largest in size. It is the sixth planet and its size is almost the size of Jupiter with an equatorial diameter of about 120,500 kms. It is a gas giant. It has a spectacular ring system although all gas giants have rings. It has only a small density and hence floats on a body of water. Its composition is similar to that of Jupiter and is composed of mostly hydrogen and helium. Like Jupiter it is mostly liquid. Its interior is also similar to that of Jupiter and has metallic hydrogen that is responsible for its strong magnetic field. However its magnetic field is weaker when compared to that of Jupiter's. It is the second most massive and the most distant planet. Hydrogen makes up nearly the entire atmosphere with lesser amounts of helium, methane and ammonia. It is colder than Jupiter as it is farther from the sun with an average temperature of about -285 degrees F. The wind speed in Saturn is also extremely high and is around 1800 kms. per hour that is four times the highest speed in the atmosphere of Jupiter. However its interior is similar to that of Jupiter. Its interior is hot and it radiates more energy into space than it receives from the sun. It does not twinkle in the night like the other stars. Like Jupiter, Saturn is about 75% hydrogen and 25% helium with traces of water, methane and ammonia. As of now it is understood that Saturn consists of a small core of rock and ice surrounded by an inner mantle of metallic hydrogen. Outside the inner mantle is the outer mantle that contains liquid hydrogen that merges into a gaseous atmosphere. Saturn's clouds also form belts and zones similar to those on Jupiter but are obscured. Saturn has an extremely thin but wide system of rings that is less than one km thick. But it extends outwards to about 420,000 kms. from the planet's surface. Some of these rings are faint; others are bright enough to be seen from the earth with binoculars. Saturn has 19 known moons. Some of them orbit inside the rings. Seven of the Moons share an orbit with another Moon- that is believed to have originated from a single satellite that broke up. Titan is the second largest Moon the Solar system. Ganymede is the largest Moon.

Uranus

It is the seventh planet in our solar system and is located at a distance of 1.8 billion miles from the sun. It is the third of the gas giant planets with a diameter of about 51,000 kms. It is understood as of now that it consists of a dense mixture of different types of ice and gas around a solid core. It has traces of methane that absorbs red and orange light strongly scattering blue light. This gives a blue green colour to this planet. It does not radiate more heat than it receives. The temperature at the cloud top is about -210 degree C. Its mass is 15 times that of Earth and hence is the fourth massive planet. Its radius is about four times that of the Earth. It is unique among planets as its axis of rotation is close to its orbital plane and because of this Uranus rolls on its sides along its orbit path around the sun and its average rotational period is slightly over 17 hours. The other planets spin more or less upright. This planet is encircled by 11 rings. The rings contain some of the darkest matter in the solar system and are extremely narrow and are therefore are difficult to detect. Nine of the rings are less than 10 kms. wide. It is further away from the Sun than Jupiter and Saturn and hence its low temperature.

There are 15 known Moons for this planet. All of them are icy and most of them are further out than the rings. The ten Inner Moons are small and dark with a diameter of less than 160 kms. and the five outer Moons are between around 470 and 1600 kms. in diameter. The outer Moons have a wide variety of surface features.

Venus

It is a rocky planet and the second closest planet to our Sun at 67 million miles with a circular orbit. It is the nearest planet to Earth. Earth and Venus seem to share many features in common like size, density and composition. Hence the Earth and the Venus are considered as the twin sisters. But Venus has extremely a weak magnetic field. It rotates clockwise. Venus spins slowly backwards as it orbits the Sun causing its rotational period the largest in the solar system and is about 245 earth days. It is slightly smaller than Earth and probably has a similar internal structure, consisting of semi-solid metal core, surrounded by a rocky mantle and crust. Venus is the brightest object in the sky after Sun and Moon because its atmosphere reflects sunlight strongly. The atmosphere contains mainly of carbon-di-oxide that traps heat in a greenhouse effect far stronger than that of Earth. Hence Venus is the hottest planet with a maximum surface temperature of about 480 degree C that is extremely hot. The clouds here contain very little water vapour. There are winds in the upper part of its atmosphere with velocities as large as 300 kms. per hour. They are comparable to jet stream in the Earth's atmosphere. The surface temperature is around 500 degree Celsius. The thick cloud layers contain droplets of sulphuric acid and are scattered around the planet by wind at speed up to 560 kms. per hour. The high temperature, acidic clouds, and enormous atmospheric pressure that is about 90 times greater than that at the surface on Earth, make the environment extremely unfavourable.

Pluto (considered as a dwarf Planet by scientists recently)

Pluto considered as the ninth Planet from the Sun, is the smallest and a rocky planet composed mostly of rock and ice and is the farthest from the Sun at an average distance of 5900 kms. It is seen only as a dot of light. It is 2/3 the size of Earth's Moon but 1200 times farther away. It has a highly elliptical orbit. Its elliptical orbit causes it to pass inside the orbit of Neptune for 20 years of its 248 year orbit. Periodically it comes closer to the Sun than Neptune. Its period of rotation appears to be almost 6 ½ days. It is supposed to contain a thin atmosphere with mostly nitrogen with some methane. Very little is known about this planet as of now. Pluto is supposed to have four known Moons. Chiron that is considered to be a Moon of Pluto is large for a Moon and is half the size of its parental planet. Because of this sometimes Pluto and Chiron are considered to be a double planet system.

From its discovery in 1930 until 2006 Pluto was classified as a planet. In the late 1970s following the discovery of Chiron in the outer solar system and the recognition of Pluto's relatively low mass, its status as a major planet began to be questioned. In the late 20th and early 21st century many objects similar to Pluto were discovered in the outer Solar system. The definition adopted in the 2006, about what it means to be a planet in the solar system excluded Pluto as a planet and included it in the new category of dwarf planets along with Eris and Ceres. Pluto is the second most massive known dwarf planet in the Solar system after Eris and it is the 10th most massive body orbiting the Sun. After reclassification, Pluto came to be considered as a minor planet. However, a number of scientists continue to consider that Pluto should be classified as a planet.

Asteroids, Comets and Meteoroids, Meteors and Meteorites

Asteroids, Comets and Meteoroids Meteors and Meteorites are all debris remains from the Nebula in which the solar system formed around 4.6 billion years ago. These are small Solar system bodies in orbit around the Sun especially in the inner Solar system. They are also known as minor planets or planetoids.

The Asteroids are rocky bodies up to about 1000 kms. in diameter. But most of them are much smaller and orbit the Sun in the Asteroid belt that lies between the orbits of Mars and Jupiter. These are sometimes called minor planets. But they are rocky and metallic, objects too small to be considered as planets. They range in size from Ceres with a diameter of about 1000 kms. down to a few centimetres or even less. When Asteroids collide with Earth they are called as Meteoroids. The highest concentration of Asteroids is in the region lying between the orbits of Mars and Jupiter. It is called the 'Asteroid belt'. So far 7000 Asteroids are identified by scientists. It is believed that Asteroids come across violent collisions giving rise to complex rotations. But the internal friction cause simple rotation in relatively brief periods of time.

Comets are small bodies made up of rocky ice, including frozen water, carbon-di-oxide, methane and ammonia and dust and are a few kilometres long. They are like dirty snow balls. These may originate in a huge cloud called the Oort cloud that is known to surround the Solar system. Sometimes a Comet is deflected from the Oort cloud to orbit the Sun in a long, elliptical path. As the Comet approaches the Sun, the Comet's surface starts to vaporize in the heat, producing a brightly shining Coma that is a huge sphere of gas and dust around the nucleus, a gas tail and a dust tail. Sometimes the tail can be very long making them the largest objects in the Solar system. Many comets have two tails, a gas tail and a dust tail with different compositions and they differ in appearance with one tail long and the other curved. Comets are well beyond the Earth's atmosphere. A dozen or so comets pass through the inner Solar system each year. But those that can be seen with the naked eye occur only once in a decade or so. Comets are usually looked as omens. There is a strong evidence to prove that the Earth was struck by a Comet or small Asteroid early in this century with devastating results. The argument that the Earth is being constantly bombarded by some comet like objects the size of small houses and containing mostly water has received support from scientists. Observations indicate that these objects are vaporizing leaving behind clouds in the atmosphere that are 10 to 100 kms. across with high concentration of water vapour. Perhaps such small comets might have been responsible for all the water in the oceans and in the Earth's atmosphere.

Meteoroids are particles of debris in the Solar system ranging from sand to the size of a boulder. These contain small chunks of stone or stone and iron. Some of these are fragments of Asteroids and Comets. These range from tiny dust particles to objects tens of meters across.

If a Meteoroid enters the Earth's atmosphere, and is heated by friction and appears as a glowing streak of light then it is called a Meteor, or a shooting star. Meteors enter the Earth's atmosphere on a regular basis. But at certain times the rate of observable Meteors is higher. These periods are called Meteor showers that usually last for a few days. The majority of them appear to come from a particular point in the sky called the Radiant of the shower. Most Meteors are tiny specks of dust and rapidly burn up in the atmosphere. Some are larger and produce spectacular fireballs that are very bright and explode in some cases, with sound heard on the ground. But fire balls are rare.

If the Meteoroid does not burn up completely and strikes the Earth then we call it a Meteorite. They are only a few because most of them burn up in the atmosphere due to frictional heating when they strike the Earth's atmosphere. Meteor showers occur when the earth passes through the trail of dust particles left by a Comet.

Modern Scientific Views on Cosmology

Over the past three decades many Cosmologists including Andrei Linde invented new models and these have led to the development of cosmological thinking since the Big Bang theory. Andrei Linde's theory is titled as the 'Self Reproducing inflationary universe'. His theory is that the Universe is constantly producing new Universes. He predicts a self-reproducing eternally existing Universe. According to him there has always been a yesterday and there will always be a tomorrow. (This notion is in agreement with the age old view of Universe by the ancient Indian *Rishis*) Several NASA experiments also have confirmed the predictions of the inflationary cosmology and this model is hailed as the most important development in the modern cosmological thinking. Andrei Linde says, "If my colleagues and I are right, we may soon be saying good bye to the idea that our Universe was a single fire ball created in the Big Bang". The inflationary model postulates a 'Multiverse' (Aswas stated by the ancient *Rishis* of India) and that our Universe may collapse in a big crunch after many billion years from now. He also points out that during the early stages of life of each of the Universe there were no particles. There was only an inflation field, a region of space charged with energy. (This is in accordance with the ancient Indian view) This energy drove the expansion of Space and it decreased gradually as the Universe expanded. Once the energy of the inflation field drops below a certain level, the expansion of Space also stops and the remaining energy would form the basic particles that make up the Universe that we see today. He also points out that each particular part of the Universe including our Universe began from a singularity somewhere in the past but that singularity was just one of an endless series that had a past and that will have a future (The ancient sages of India stated that the Absolute Principle had willed the creation of the Universe and this process of creation and annihilation is an endless process each following the other like day and night)

According to a new theory our Universe crashed in to another three dimensional world hidden in higher dimensions. Cosmologists Paul Steinhardt and Nail Turok say that the Cosmos was never compacted into a single point and did not spring forth in a violent instant. They state that the Big Bang was the result of a collision between our three dimensional world and another three dimensional world less than the width of a Proton and the Universe that we know today is a small cross section of a much grander Universe whose magnitude we cannot fathom. According to them the Big Bang is only the blast in a cycle of cosmic collisions stretching infinitely into the past and future. Each collision creates a new Universe. (This view coincides with the notion of the ancient seers about the cyclical process of creation and recreation of the Universe).

The term 'Multi verse' suggest that the Universe in which the Earth where we live is just one bubble in space time foam, that contain a multitude of Universes and the Universe in which we live is only one among several disconnected Universes. (The ancient sages of India held this view even in the remote past) The great Scientist Stephen Hawking believed that alien life existed in other planets as well and also within stars or even floating in outer space. (The *Puranas* elaborates this view) He warned that a few of these species might be intelligent and threaten Earth. Contact with such species might be devastating for humanity. He advocated that man should try to avoid contact with alien life forms. New scientific research raises the possibility of monstrous creatures with the intelligence and cunningness of humans-probably the life forms that evolved in other planets in the Universe. (The ancient Indian scriptures reveal these facts clearly)

Future of the Universe

As far as the future of the universe is concerned, the scientists are of the opinion that the Universe can either expand or contract and eventually collapse or the expansion will slow down but it will not collapse. However no one is sure about this.

According to a few scientists the expansion of the Universe started many billions of years ago from a very hot and very small state. From that it evolved in to the present size.

While the Big Bang theory explains a finite Universe with a beginning and end, a new theory of the Universe suggests that Space and Time may not have begun with Big Bang but might have existed in an endless cycles of expansion and rebirth. (This view also coincides with the ancient Indian view of Cosmogony). Scientists say that even after billions of years the Universe is still expanding. The theory says that after 14 billion years the expansion of the Universe would accelerate and after trillions of years the matter and radiation would get completely dissipated and expansion would stop. An energy field that is likely to pervade the Universe would then create new matter and radiation that would restart the cycle. (This is in agreement with the ancient Indian view)

According to some the galaxies and stars are engulfed by an invisible 'dark matter'. It is not seen and it does not emit light or reflect light. Scientists believe that 90 % of the matter in the Universe is Dark Matter. The dark matter gravitates as ordinary matter and it slows down the expansion of the universe.

Cosmologist Robert Caldwell of Dartmouth University gave his view in the late 1990s according to which a mysterious force that can be called 'dark energy', is responsible for the expansion of the Universe. According to him, the expansion of the Universe would become so fast in future that it would tear apart all objects, all matter- the galaxies, the stars, the planets, and the Solar system. It is said that the atoms would be torn apart in the last 10- to 19 seconds before the end of time. In 1998 in a 10 year study of 'Supernovae', Dark energy was detected by the cosmologists. The scientists also discovered that the light from several Supernovae, some of which are very distant from the Earth had started to travel towards the Earth even when the Universe was in its very early stage of formation. The Scientists confirmed that the expansion of the Universe instead of slowing down actually is gaining momentum most probably due to the anti-gravitational properties of the Dark energy. In 2003 the NASA WMAP satellite weighed the cosmos and confirmed that 73% of it is in a form called Dark Energy and 23% is in the form of Dark Matter and the remaining 4% is the matter that makes up Stars, galaxies, and interstellar gas (The matter that exists between the star systems within a galaxy. It is the gas and dust that pervade the interstellar space) in the luminous objects of the Universe. It is also pointed out that even the distant galaxies are moving away from us so that the Universe is expanding. Edwin Hubble discovered that farther galaxies that are away from us are moving faster away from us. That means the Universe is expanding. Even in the beginning of the 20th century, Einstein had postulated an anti-gravitational force. The U S Spy telescopes are set to help the N ASA probe the Dark energy. According to scientists the fate of the Universe depends upon this Dark energy. It is found that the observation on the exploding stars known as Supernovae also indicate that the expansion of the universe is speeding up.

According to the Open Universe theory, with Dark energy, the expansion not only continues but also accelerates. In future the Open Universe will have to face 'heat death' or 'Big Freeze' or Big Rip' where the acceleration caused by Dark energy eventually becomes so strong that it completely overwhelms the effects of gravitational, electromagnetic and weak forces of the Universe.

As per the Closed universe theory, gravity would stop the expansion of the Universe due to lack of the repulsive effect of Dark energy and after which the Universe would start contracting until all matter of the Universe collapses to a point, a singularity called the 'Big Crunch'. According to Scientists 5 billion years from now the Sun would have used up its fuel and die that is around 20 billion years after the Big Bang. Once the Sun dies there will not be any life on Earth and the Solar system would become desolate. Then the Universe also would die down slowly by becoming cold and empty as it expands.

Scientific analysis also suggest that the expansion would ultimately drive our Milky way galaxy to merge with a neighbouring galaxy, Andromeda or cause the two galaxies to rip each other apart and after trillion and trillions of years in the future the Universal energy would be thoroughly exhausted and the Universe will come to an end.

All these differing claims point out that the Scientists have no unanimity of opinion regarding the question whether the Universe would stop expanding and will begin to contract or whether it will continue to expand for ever. According to the ancient Indian notion, the Universe goes through repeated process of creation, existence and destruction or Pralaya.

In Dec 20, 2011 Kepler Space Telescope team reported the discovery of a five planet system containing three small gas giant planets and two Earth sized planets. All these five planets orbit close around Kepler-20 that is supposed to be a Sun like star that is 950 light years from Earth and is smaller and slightly cooler than the Sun. It is estimated that it would take the space shuttle 36 million years to travel to Kepler-20. The scientists point out that this discovery is a stepping stone in the hunt for alien worlds. (The existence of the celestial worlds and the inhabitants there are described in the ancient Indian scriptures thousands of years ago) These five planets are known as 20b, 20c, 20 d, 20e, and 20f planets. The two Earth sized planets discovered are supposed to have a diameter of 6900 miles and 8200 miles and the three Neptune sized planets have diameters of 15,000, 24,600 and 22000 miles. The small earth sized planets or worlds are expected to have rocky compositions. The scientists say that all the five planets have closer orbits that are closer than Mercury in our Solar system. However, they point out that in our Solar system small, rocky worlds orbit close to our Sun and the large gas giants orbit farther out. But in contrast, the planets of Kepler-20 are organized in alternating pattern, big, small, big, small that look very different from our solar system.

The 'God particle' that is formally known as Higgs Boson was discovered by the scientists at the European organisation for Nuclear Research centre known as CERN at Geneva, Switzerland on the 4th July 2012. Boson is named in honour of the Calcutta based Indian scientist Prof Satyendra Dad Bose's work and whose brilliance was recognised by Albert Einstein. This is a sub atomic particle that apparently weighs about 130 times as much as an atom of hydrogen the lightest gas the Scientists say is the key to the formation of stars, planets and also after the Big Bang. It interacts with other subatomic particles that are the building blocks of atoms that slow them down. It is the reason why matter has mass. Mass gives the particles inertia or resistance from moving faster. It is compared to celebrities (the other particles) who are mobbed by groups of autograph seekers (the other subatomic particles) who slow down the movement of the celebrities. It is called 'God particle' because according to scientists its existence is fundamental to the creation of the Universe. The scientists say that they have captured the elusive God particle that gives matter mass and holds the physical fabric of the Universe together. By probing into this particle Scientists hope to understand 96% of the Universe that remains hidden from our view. They also are sure that this would result in the discovery of new particles and even hitherto unknown forces of nature.

On the 26th of Dec 2012, a former official from the British defence ministry's UFO project revealed that it will be possible for humans to contact alien life in the Universe within the next 12 years. (The ancient Indian scriptures had already repeatedly stated about the celestial beings and their relationships with the humans on earth).The development of a supersized Radio telescope called the Square Kilometre Array (SKA), he stated, will bring to light new and exciting possibilities on whether there is life out there in the Universe as this telescope can find out whether there is civilization within 100 light years.

7

Greatness of Ancient Indian Wisdom

For the questions who created this Universe? How was it created? Who created the animate beings and inanimate things in the world? Are there other regions in the world? If so who inhibit them? What are its features? Are there more than one Universe? What are the objects or bodies in the Universe? What is the relationship between creation and the creator? Do the celestial objects influence man on earth? If so how? What is the geography of earth? Is there life in other planets? What is the future of the Universe and why was the Universe ever created and so on, there are no full proof answers.

Although the statements made by the Rishis regarding the Universe cannot be modified as in the case of many scientific discoveries still the fact remains that we do find many different revelations about the Universe in the ancient Indian scriptures. However it is not certain whether these are only different interpretations made by people of later times due to the fact that the hymns were not properly understood or whether it is because they were revealed to disciples at different levels of consciousness or whether the changes actually took place over a period of very long time or whether , it is because even the Rishis could not categorically state anything for certain as the subject of Universe itself is such that it cannot be fully revealed or understood by the human mind that has its own limitation, we do not know. It may also be due to the fact that after a certain stage one can only experience the Truth but not express it in words. It is also possible that if one has to understand the Vedic hymns totally and in the sense that the Rishis of Yore wanted them to be understood, then one should go beyond the limited material, physical or gross dimensions so that he will be able to understand the unlimited, non-material, subtle, spiritual meanings of the hymns in which there are no contradictions and which reveal only the single Truth because Truth can be only one. All the paradoxes and contradictions that we see in the Truth revealed by our sages through their hymns are because of our ignorance, because our understanding is limited to the gross or limited or material and is therefore partial but not subtle or unlimited or spiritual or total. For example, if there is an assembly of people sitting in a room and if one says that the people sitting there are all in one place then it is very much true. If some other person says that all are not actually there, then that also is true. Both are correct because one is talking about their physical presence and the other is telling about their mental presence. The single truth then is, although they are all physically present in the same place at least some of them sitting there are not present there mentally. It is also like people telling that the Sun has risen or set and some other people telling that the Sun does not rise or set. Both are correct. But the single Truth that is not partial but total is that as far as the Sun is concerned it neither rises nor sets but people say the Sun has either risen or has set because when the Sun comes to their view they say it is Sun rise and when the Sun goes out of their view they say that the Sun Has set. Probably this is also the case with our understanding of the ancient hymns of the Rishis. Whatever it might be the revelations made by the Indian seers of the past have been proved to be correct and accurate even by modern scientific standards.

Although the Rishis could obtain the answers for several of these questions, and imparted them through scriptures the modern man seems to be suspicious about these revelations as they are not proved through objective experiments although the really great people with advanced level of knowledge and intelligence not only are in agreement with the revelations of ancient Rishis but are also spell bound and admit the fact that many of their revelations are scientifically true today in spite of the fact that many of the hymns as well as the scriptures themselves are lost to mankind to day either due to the ravages of time or due to manmade factors. Not only that. The hymns particularly of those in the *Vedas* that are the original basis for all other scriptures are full of hidden meanings and also contain multiple meanings that are to be understood according to the context in which they were revealed. The poetic expressions found in the hymns of the poet saints of ancient times is also very figurative containing highly subtle meanings that even a great scholar finds them very difficult to understand. When that is the case then there is no wonder if those who are at a lower level of knowledge condemning the ancient ideas and ridiculing them. These people fail to understand that the ancient *Rishis* revealed all knowledge both in abstract or spiritual terms that could be understood only by spiritually elevated persons and those who have reached a certain level of understanding and also in concrete terms by creating Deities and Super humans whom they projected mightier than humans both in their form as well as in their qualities to suit the level of understanding of those who are endowed with lesser level of intelligence and spiritual knowledge. These representations they made use of in order to teach the truth to the majority of human beings who are at a lower level of intelligence. Further, the sacred knowledge was revealed by the ancient *Rishis* mostly in the form of verses. So the *Rishis* of yore who were also poets might have made use of their poetical imaginations in bringing forth the truth in poetical language and thereby might have resorted to or made use of exaggerations. More than everything one should understand that the ancient Rishis could find answers to many of the questions about the Universe through a continuous and prolonged deep meditation. They discovered many things about the Universe with so much of mathematical precision that even the modern scientists cannot but marvel their keen intelligence and depth of knowledge that too at a time when there were no scientifically advanced and sophisticated equipments to conduct experiments.

The findings of the *Rishis* belong to the past and as such there cannot be any further changes or modifications to their revelations and therefore are final. With increasing scientific knowledge and techniques the scientists have also discovered many things about the Universe that are highly remarkable. But one major difference that we have to note here is that there can be changes, modifications and contradictions in future for all the scientific discoveries that are made today. There is every possibility that at least some of the findings of today's scientists may be condemned or may be proved wrong by another set of scientists tomorrow, and as such no scientific discovery can be taken as full proof or final even though they are the results of concrete objective experiments conducted by the scientists with the help of advanced and sophisticated technology. This is because science with its increasing levels of research and development is still progressing and will continue to progress. However the poet saints who came later did not contradict the revelations of those saints who preceded them. They also did not condemn or modify the earlier discoveries. On the other hand they were totally in agreement with the earlier revelations of the poet- saints of the earlier times.

Cosmology

The ancient sages of India could fathom the secrets of the Universe through their mystic powers. With their fertile, questioning, intuitive and inventive mind they realized the truths about each and everything, about creation, beings, Universe and their Creator and this knowledge was passed one from one generation to the other orally for a very long time before they were written down that formed the *Sruthis* and *Smrithis* of ancient India. Einstein towards the end of his life in an interview with the Life magazine said "the mind can proceed only so far upon what it knows and can prove. There comes a point –where the mind takes a higher plane of knowledge, but can never prove how it got there. All great discoveries have involved such a leap".

The sages of pre historic India through their intense and prolonged meditation came to the conclusion that spiritual knowledge alone will end in supreme and permanent happiness in this world for man. But they also knew that while living in the world man also desires material knowledge that gives him material happiness. So the *Rishis* imparted all knowledge to posterity that met the four goals of human life namely, *Dharma, Artha, Kaama* and *Moksha*. In all the ancient Indian scriptures therefore, we find knowledge about both material as well as non-material that is spiritual going hand in hand. They explained about the Universe both in concrete material terms, for the benefit of those who cannot understand the abstract teachings of the sages, as well as in abstract non material or spiritual terms to benefit those who are spiritually knowledgeable. After explaining about the cosmogony of the Universe, its Astronomy and Astrology, the concept of time, the geography of Earth and so on both in concrete and abstract terms the age old *Rishis* finally concluded that actually, in reality the Universe is neither born nor does it end as it is eternal, since creation, sustenance and destruction of the Universe takes place in a periodic manner and hence it is only a cyclical process that has no beginning or end just as in the case of beings that are born, exist and die but only to be reborn again. But in the case of beings one can attain liberation or *Mukthi* and can go beyond the cycle of birth by elevating his mind and by attaining the supreme truth. For *Gnanis* of that stature there is no more birth because that individual soul or the *Jeevatma* gets merged with the Universal soul or *Paramatama* or *Parabrahman* that is the Super Soul or the Universal energy. But it is not known when such an end will come to the Cosmos. If at all such a stage comes then there will be none to impart the truth and there will be none to obtain that knowledge as there will remain only a vast expanse of void nothing but void from that nothing will be created or will be born again as before. The same process of creation, sustenance and destruction (only to be reborn again until that time when the individual soul merges with the Universal soul) that we find in the case of the individual beings is what could be there for the Universe. This is what the sages meant when they said that the Universe is also born only to die for a new cycle of creation. In fact they went a step further and pointed out that in reality there is nothing that is ever born as there is nothing that ever dies as nothing can be born from nothing.

The ancient Indian *Rishis* had the freedom of expression unlike the Philosophers and Scientists and Mystics of the western countries. Freedom of expression and the freedom to practice and preach about that on which one had the conviction were not denied in India even from the distant past. For example Bruno was burned for claiming that the Earth rotates about its axis. Many Scientists with their ideas were burnt during the dark ages of the middle age in Europe. Galileo was condemned by the Church for stating that the Earth rotated around the Sun, that is, for asserting the truth of the theory of Copernicus. Arya Bhatta had made the same discovery as that of Copernicus about the Earth rotating around the Sun even more than a thousand or more years before the time of Copernicus and it did not cause even a flutter in India. On the other hand people even during that time held him in great esteem. As Dr Radha Krishnan has put it, Religion, science, and humanism were sisters in ancient India. India even from the distant past had an open mind and attitude to everything including scientific thinking and experimentation. Aldous Huxley commented that the freedom of the mind in India that was not witnessed anywhere in the world created the wondrous world of intellect.

Actually, in India science and religion walked together to unravel the mysteries of the Universe. The *Rishis* of ancient India who were also great scientists had understood that Science without spirituality is like a body without the soul. In Hinduism understanding of the external reality went along with the understanding of Godhead that is in the core of all beings that are created. So the ancient Indian view of understanding the material Universe depended upon an understanding of Godhead or the *Paramaatman*. They understood that the Microcosm is similar to the Macrocosm. So they came to the conclusion that the creation of the Universe is similar to that of a being. The will or the desire or *Kaama* or *Ichcha* of the Universal energy, the *Purusha* by acting upon *Prakruthi* or nature that has the three modes of existence or natures namely *Sathvik, Rajasic* and *Tamasic* creates the world as per the dictates of time. Just as a full grown being takes its birth from an egg the Universe also takes birth from the *Brahmanda* or the Universal egg. It is told in the scriptures that the *Virata Purusha* that is created from the cosmic egg, with all its innumerable parts of the body covered the entire Cosmos. This is actually the concrete explanation of the Abstract Potential energy of the Absolute, the Super Soul that engulfs the entire Cosmos. They also pointed out that the Universe preceded all creations including that of creation of Gods. At the same time the sages also pointed out that the visible, external world is only a product of the creative play of Lord's *Maya* or illusion and the Universe as we know it is actually not real but a mere illusion.

The ancient Indian wisdom gave much knowledge about the origin of the Universe, about the creation of Universe and the beings in the Universe, about the planets and other celestial bodies, the short term and long term time-span, the different *Yugas*, the characteristic features of each *Yuga*, the deluge or destruction of the Universe, the geography of earth, *Jambudvipa* and *Bharata Varsha*, the concept of Multi verses, the inhabitants in other worlds or planets, the worlds that are above the Earth and below the Earth that is, the under worlds, the influence of the celestial planets on human beings and on Earth (Astrology), who really is the human being ? (that answers the question 'who am I'), the relationship of the individual consciousness, the created beings, with the collective consciousness that is the Universal consciousness and the path by which the individual consciousness can merge with the universal consciousness with no more repeated births and deaths.

All knowledge that the ancient Indian sages gave to mankind are not available today completely. Some of the reasons for this are, firstly, the knowledge was passed on from one generation to the other orally for a very long period of time that covered many centuries. The most ancient Indian knowledge that existed in a collective form previously and that was classified by the 28th *Vyasa* known as *Krishna Dwaipayana* or *Veda Vyasa* of *Dwarapara Yuga* who also composed the great Epic *Maha Bhaaratha Ithihasa* and the *Puranas* is not available in total as many of the hymns and the other supplementary scriptures were either lost to mankind today because they were perished either due to the ravages of time or because those outsiders who ruled India in succession either destroyed them or confiscated them. Secondly the Sruthis, namely the *Vedas* are very ancient and written in Sanskrit language that has several meanings for the same word and as the hymns are full of hidden mystical meanings it becomes impossible to bring out all that they revealed. The Vedic Scholar David Frawley observed that the hymns of the *Vedas* particularly *Rigveda* the first document on Earth are full of oceanic symbolism. This poses an enormous difficulty in the interpretation of the Vedas that are available to mankind today. Thirdly since the time of those scriptures the Universe itself has undergone several changes so it becomes difficult to interpret all that they have stated in modern terms. For example what the sages said about the planets, celestial beings, their visits to the earth, the different worlds and so on cannot be proved today. Some of the regions which they had mentioned in the scriptures might have disappeared altogether and some rivers and some oceans might have got dried up, or the names of the places and so on might have changed in course of time.

Cosmology according to ancient Indian seers is not merely the study of the origin and development of the Universe but is the three fold study of creation, destruction and recreation of the Universe. This shows that Indian cosmology is rooted in a timeless, ageless Universe of eternal return. The ancient scriptures categorically state that everything that happens had already happened before, though in different guises. Carl Sagan the well-known Astronomer says that the "many billion year time scale of Hindu cosmology is not the entire history of the Universe, but just the day and night of *Brahma* and there is the ideas of an infinite cycle of births and deaths and an infinite number of Universes each with its own gods". In fact the Vedic sages started with the description of the pre creation state. From their stand point creation was not a new beginning but a rearrangement or setting things in proper order as nothing can be added or subtracted. This is the conservation of Energy that is much talked about by Scientists. The seers also pointed out that whatever is created in time cannot be eternal. So the Universe created in a *Kalpa*, the cosmic era will have to necessarily end in time. However its dissolution is not actually annihilation or death but a rebirth. During *Pralaya* or dissolution of the Universe the five basic elements that are part of the Absolute, the *Purusha*, the Supersoul are withdrawn in to the Absolute by a centripetal force, only to be recreated again. When they are projected creation results. The *Vedas* also point out that all objects whether they are animate or inanimate, similar or dissimilar share a common origin- the *Purusha*. The term '*Purusha*' stands for the pure, Absolute Spirit or energy and *Prakruthi* is nature or matter. *Purusha* is the efficient cause and *Prakruthi* is the material cause of matter or Universe. *Purusha* is neither produced nor created nor does it actually create. *Prakruthi* has the inherent tendency to create. It creates the Universe due to the presence of the inherent *Purusha* that is the Transcendental Self or the Supreme Soul, the non-attributive consciousness or *Para Brahman*. Nature or *Prakruthi* has three material modes or *Gunas* namely *the Sathva, Rajas and Thamas* and all objects that *Prakruthi* creates have these qualities. These three *Gunas* or qualities or modes of nature or *Prakruthi* cannot be separated from each other. When there is radical interaction among these *Gunas* or modes that disturb its state of balance or equilibrium, then creation results. When they are in perfect equilibrium there is no creation. *Purusha* however is not affected by this disturbance. The relation between *Purusha* and *Prakruthi* is similar to that of a magnet and a piece of iron. *Purusha* like the magnet is totally independent of the iron piece, the *Prakruthi*. But it prompts *Prakruthi* that is inherent in *Purusha* to act. When the balance among the *Gunas* get upset more and more, the *Gunas* or the modes of nature undergo a variety of changes and at that time *Prakruthi* or Nature becomes more and more determinate resulting in the creation of the Universe with varied objects and beings with varied names and forms. This, according to Vedic seers is the process of evolution that in course of time will be followed by involution or dissolution when all the objects or the material Universe merge back in to the source culminating in a state of equilibrium and becoming the undifferentiated primordial substance as before. In this manner creation and recreation or *Sarga* and *Prathi Sarga* follow each other in an endless manner. This is how creation becomes a cyclical process according to the ancient *Sankhya* philosophy of sage *Kapila*. The sages made it very clear that *Prakruthi* or *Prahiti* is the *Vivartha* or transformation of *Brahman* and creation or *Srishti* is the vibration within the root cause that results in the creation of the Universe. This is similar to the sprouting of seed into a seedling. Creation is not spontaneous but is an evolution- though the effect is spontaneous the process is evolutionary. The sprouting of a seed into a seedling that is visible to the naked eye may look spontaneous but before that the seed undergoes several process of transformation under the soil that is not visible outside. Creation is only a change in form, a manifestation of that which was unmanifest before. If that is so, then it must have been contained already within something. Desire the motive force of the Universal principle is actually the cause of creation. According to the ancient sacred texts, the cosmic egg contains everything. The entire Universe is within that egg. The egg that is spiral in shape, hollow and moist inside that resembles a womb with hard shell could carry and protect the germs or the seeds of the Universe of the previous *Kalpa* after its dissolution for subsequent creation in the succeeding *Kalpa*. The Universe represented by a Cosmic egg that expanded from a concentrated unmanifested form of the Absolute undergoes expansion and total collapse in each *Kalpa* or cycles of creation. On this basis the *Rishis* declared that creation is the result of the instrumental cause *Purusha,* the Universal or the Absolute Soul acting upon the material cause or *Prakruthi* and that these are the two forces or factors or partners in the process of creation. So from the point of view of the ancient seers of India, Big Bang could not have been the beginning of the Universe but just the starting of a new cycle of creation that must have been preceded by an infinite number of cycles of creations in the endless process of creation, dissolution and recreation of the Universe.

Huston smith the great Philosopher, scholar and writer says "Where as in western religions a creator God precedes man and the Universe, the Hindu gods are preceded by creation; the origin of the world is envisaged not so much as an act of creation, but as one organization, the making of order out of chaos. The Universe is often said to be born from the sacred syllable *'AUM'* or from an inert void in which "there was neither being nor being—- death nor non death" a single principle from which emerged the diversity of life. From this void desire was born and from desire came humans, gods and creation". Einstein observed, "Cosmic expansion may be simply a temporary condition which will be followed at some future epoch of cosmic time by a period of contraction. The Universe in this picture is a pulsating balloon in which cycles of expansion and contraction succeed each other through eternity". Stephen Hawking, the well-known Astro physicist seems to agree with the ancient seers of India when he said that "Thus when we see the Universe, we are seeing it as it was in the past." Several thousands of years ago the Indian sages had told us that what we see now has been there already and will be there in future as well. The *Vedas* pointed out that the Suns and Moons the Lord created like the Suns and Moons of previous cycles.

The *Shiva Thandava* or the cosmic dance of Lord *Shiva* described in the ancient sacred texts is indicative of the beginning of a new *Kalpa.* Carl Sagan in his book on "cosmos" says that 'for modern Physicists, then, *Shiva*'s dance is the dance of subatomic matter- Hundreds of years ago, Indian artists created visual images of dancing *Shivas* in a beautiful series of bronzes. The dancing *Shiva* statue is universally regarded as the quintessential image of Hindu art and culture. Today Physicists have used the most advanced technology to portray the pattern of the cosmic dance. Thus the metaphor of the cosmic dance unifies ancient religious art and modern Physics'. He further points out that *Shiva*'s dance is a symbol of the unity and rhythm of existence. The unending dynamic process of creation and destruction is expressed in the energetic posture of *Shiva*. He dances in a ring of fire that refers to the life- death process of the Universe. Everything is subject to continual change, as energy constantly assumes new forms in the *Maaya* or *Leela* of creation, except the God Himself whose dance is immutable and absolute. The pictorial allegory of *Nataraja* indicates the so called "five acts" of the deity; the creation of the Universe, its sustenance in space, its final dissolution at the end of the cycle of four world ages (*yugas)*, the concealment of nature of Godhead and the bestowal of true knowledge'. Physicist Fritjof Capra states that "modern Physics has thus revealed that every sub atomic particle not only performs an energy dance but also is an energy dance; a pulsating process of creation and destruction. The dance of *Shiva* is the dancing Universe, the ceaseless flow of energy going through an infinite variety of patterns that melt into one another". He also points out that the posture and balance of *Nataraja*'s dancing form show Lord *Shiva* in the aspect of *Thamas*, the expansive centrifugal force that creates and destroys the Universe. This is the first of the three tendencies (*gunas)* that permeates the Universe in *Samkhya* philosophy. *Thamas* (darkness) symbolized by *Shiva* is responsible for the constant birth, change and death of all living beings; the force *Satthv*a (tranquillity) represented by *Vishnu* the preserver, holds the atoms of every object together. These two "tendencies"- one holding the atoms of the Universe together and the other ripping them apart- create a "friction" (*rajas*) that "vibrates" the world's atoms and creates the gravity to hold them to the Earth. This is the third tendency, symbolized by the deity *Brahma*. It is the building stuff "both of matter and of subtle energies such as perception and thought". —-.. He points out, that '*Shiva*'s dance is of cosmic significance and represents the five principle manifestations of eternal energy; creation, destruction, preservation, salvation and illusion. Lord *Shiva* holds in His upper right hand an hour glass shaped small drum, the symbol of the primordial sound of creation; in His upper left hand is a flame representing the final destruction of the Universe. His lower right hand makes the gesture "fear not". With His lower left hand He points to His raised left foot, the place of refuge and salvation for the devotee. His right foot is planted on the back of the demon *Apasmara Purusha*, the personifying illusion of ignorance over whom *Shiva* triumphs. His matted hair symbolizes His power and the crescent Moon is the symbol of growth and birth. In *Shiva*'s hairdo sits the river Goddess Ganga, the personification of the Ganges River which is said to spring forth from *Shiva*'s head. He trods on the dwarf, that is symbolic of ignorance, which must be eliminated if a believer is to attain release from the eternal cycle of birth and death. Thus Lord *Shiva* veils the illusion through His enchanting act of dancing'. Richard Waterstone in his book 'Einstein and Shiva's cosmic dance' writes "There is a striking resemblance between the equivalence of mass and energy, symbolized by *Shiva*'s cosmic dance and the western theory, first expounded by Einstein which calculates the amount of energy contained in a sub atomic particle by multiplying its mass by the square of the speed of light; E=mc2". Carl Sagan also asserts in his book on 'Cosmos' that the cosmic dance or *Thandava* of Lord *Shiva* in the form of *Nataraja* signifies the cycle of evolution and destruction of the cosmic Universe. It is also viewed by some that the cosmic dance of Lord *Shiva* accompanied by the beating of the *Damaru* or drum probably suggests the sudden energetic impulses that could have propelled the 'Big Bang'. The statue of Lord *Shiva* as the cosmic dancer stands in the Plaza of the European organization for Nuclear Research in Geneva. Also the *Shiva Linga* that is egg shaped represents the *Brahmanda* that is universe. Worshipping the *Shiva Linga* is equivalent of worshipping the very Universe, a concept that is unique in the Hindu religion.

The ancient seers of India also pointed out that the concept of space and Time in its unlimited, subtle sense was there even prior to creation. Prior to creation the Universe did exist in an unmanifested form in the Absolute. Similar is the case with Space, Time as well as Directions. Surely they must have existed even prior to the creation of Universe. Otherwise where was the unmanifested Universe located before creation if there had been no Space? Similarly the unmanifest Cosmos got manifested with the play of Time. So Time in its absolute, subtle sense also must have been there even prior to the creation of the Universe. However Space and Time in its limited and gross sense could have manifested after the creation of Universe. The Rishis therefore could know about the subtle as well as gross Space and Time and differentiate between these two concepts because they were concerned both with the material as well as non-material. But the scientists' interest is turned towards the material or physical aspects only and they therefore talked about the gross or physical Space and time and concluded that these appeared only after the creation of the material or gross Universe. For example during the dreaming stage of sleep physical or gross space and time have no relevance since at that time only the mind that is not gross but subtle is awake or active but not the gross senses of the body. Within one second one can be in one corner of the Universe as well as in another corner of the Universe. Similarly within seconds the mind can take one to the remote past, as well as to the future.

The scriptures point out that after the Universal dissolution the Supreme Soul decides to recreate the Cosmos and at that point of time the very subtle atoms begin to combine and generate the cosmic wind that blows heavier atoms to group together and the souls depending upon their past *Karmas* or deeds in their previous lives draw to themselves the atoms to form the appropriate body.

Scientists like Carl Sagan have expressed amazement at the accuracy of space and time descriptions by the ancient *Rishis* who fathomed the secrets of the Universe through their extra sensory perception. Nancy Wilson Ross says, "This notion of sleeping and waking or contracting and expanding of the life force, so long a part of Hindu cosmology has recently been expressed in relevant term in an article written for a British scientific journal by Prof. Fred Hoyle, Briton's foremost Astronomer". She further says, "Plainly, contemporary western science's description of an astronomical Universe of such vast magnitude that distances must be measured in terms as abstract as light years is not new to Hinduism whose wise men, millennia ago, came up with the term *Kalpa* to signify the inconceivable duration of the period elapsing between the beginning and end of a world system".

The sages also pointed out that the concepts of 'space' and 'time' are only *Maaya* or illusion arising due to ignorance of the actual facts because what looks like 100 years for Brahma, the Creator could be thousands of years in other worlds, millions of years in some other worlds and 311trillion and 40 billion years for the Earth.

The *Puranas* also tell about the number of different life forms in the Universe. According to *Padma Purana* there are 8,400, 400 life form species, 900, 000 of which are aquatic ones, 2,000, 000 are trees and plants, 1,100, 000 are small living species, insects and reptiles, 1,000, 000 are birds, 3,000,000 are beasts and 400,000 are human species.

The scriptures also mention the concept of Multiverse. Accordingly, there are innumerable Universes, each covered by seven different layers of Earth, Water, Fire, Wind, Sky, the total energy and false ego. *Puranas* mention the existence of several million *Lokas* or worlds or Universes and say that our Universe with its *Brahma* and all other Gods is one among them. The ancient *Rishis* could postulate the concept of Multi Universes, and the plurality of the inhabited worlds. According to *Vishnu Purana* Earth is one of the thousands of millions of inhabited worlds found in the Universe. The 5th canto of *Bhagavatham* tells about innumerable universes. This is in agreement with Einstein's view. He says that each Universe is contained in a spherical shell surrounded by layers of elemental matter that mark the boundary between mundane space and the unlimited spiritual world and the region within this shell is *Brahmanda*. It is remarkable that the dimensions of *Bhoomandala* in *Srimad Bhagavatham* are consistent with the modern data on the size of the Sun's orbit and the Solar system as a whole. The *Rishis* point out that although there are innumerable Universes besides our own Universe and although they are unlimitedly large, they move about like atoms in the Absolute, the Supreme Soul and that the numbers of Universes are unaccountable and immeasurable. These countless Universes each enveloped in its shell, the *Rishis* declare, are compelled by the wheel of time to wander with in the Absolute, like particles of dust blowing about in the sky. It is also stated by them that the layers or elements covering the Universes are each ten times thicker than the one before and all the Universes clustered together appear like atoms in s huge combination. The *Rishis* stated further, that the innumerable Universes existing side by side, each containing its own Gods like *Brahma, Vishnu* and *Shiva* and the Demi Gods and so on appear and disappear in each succeeding *Manvantaras*. In this manner the ancient sages spoke about timeless universes of eternal return. This revelation might have prompted them to declare that everything that happens has already happened before for many a time, though in different guises. Nancy Wilson Ross says, "On the highest level, when stripped of mythological embroidery, Hinduism's conception of space, time and multiple Universes approximate in range and abstraction the most advanced Scientific thought".

The seers of the past imparted the knowledge to posterity in two ways. They made use of the aspect of '*Saguna Brahma*' to describe about everything relating to the Universe and so on. In order to explain all about the Universe the *Vedas* gave different names for the powers of nature or the energy that they considered as Gods or Demi Gods. For example the concept of '*Virata Purusha*' shows how the original Absolute energy contained within itself all that we see in the Universe to day. Accordingly, the Universe is the body of the highest, infinite spiritual being and therefore has some of His properties. Scientifically it means that the Universe is infinite in Space and Time and is infinitely heterogeneous. Konrad Rudnicki in his 'Cosmological Principle Of Ancient India' says, that "no mathematical model of the universe involving the ancient Indian cosmological principle can be constructed even now, since mathematics have not yet developed any tools to deal with the notion of infinite heterogeneity—- An Indian sage from many thousands years ago would say to the contemporary cosmologist: the universe is much too complicated to be put into those primitive mathematical formulae of yours—Perhaps, further developments in mathematics will make it possible to calculate a model of the Universe concordant with the cosmological principle of ancient India".

For centuries the cosmology contained in the scriptures seemed incomprehensible at times and extraordinary at other times. This has led either to the rejection of the revelations of the seers of the past because reality is beyond the reach of mundane mind or words, or total acceptance of what they said by those who had faith in the mystic vision of the seers of the past. It shows that only those who understand the real, hidden meaning of what are stated in the scriptures can benefit out of them. Carl Sagan pointed out, "Ages ago, the vast sub-continent of India birthed explorers and innovators who focused on the inner realm. These geniuses- spiritual sages or scientists of consciousness, depending on your perspective- gave us, through a series of modern translations and adapters, insights that have profoundly influenced religion, health care, psychology, the arts and other areas of life. The way we understand ourselves and the Universe has been shaped by India more than we can readily appreciate".

The revelation of the seers of India of the bygone days about creation was that in the beginning there was neither non-existent nor existent. The Supreme energy or the cosmogonic force by its sheer will created the Universe in the form of darkness enveloped by darkness. First there was Water but no light. From the Cosmic water, due to friction, Fire was generated. Due to the interaction of Fire and Water, Wind was created. The combination of Water, Fire and Wind produced froth that got solidified and the Earth was formed. It further affirms that the Supreme *Brahman* is the cause of this Universe. The Cosmic fluid originated due to the motion induced by the will of the Supreme. It moved the undifferentiated atoms into an undifferentiated cloud of dark fluid and heat was produced because of the friction of motion and the earth was formed in the form of cosmic egg or the Universe that was in an embryonic state. This is perhaps the Protostar concept of the modern scientists. Further motion of the cosmic fluid along with cosmic earth produced Sun.

Vedas also predicted the end of the Sun that the scientists have confirmed. The *Vedas* state that this cycle of life will end 2,333,227,018 years from now when the Sun disintegrates and dies. According to Scientists this is the estimated life span of Sun before it dies and becomes a Black hole.

Dr V V *Raman*, the Physicist in his introduction for his book on the 'Indic visions in an age of science' points out the visions of the Rig Vedic *Rishis* about how the world came to be. He says the *Nasadiya*

Suktha or the hymn of creation gives an idea about the cosmic creation. In this hymn the *Rishi* speaks of a pre creation stage when there was nothing and this is the vision of the pre Big Bang situation. He says, "This unimaginable phase is described as an eerie nothing where there was no air or human. There was neither the subtlest matter nor the loftiest thought of any kind. The Vedic poet postulates that the Universe must have come from an innate spiritual energy- which he referred as 'Tapas'. Then there was a deep desire on the part of something to manifest itself and that the first seed of creation must have germinated in a cosmic mind. Then the sage poet wonders, in all humility utters, whether these were real at all?" He says,

(The English translation of the Sanskrit hymn in Rig Veda, the first document of earth)

"Not even nothing existed then, no air yet and no heaven,
Who encased and kept it where? Was water in the darkness there?
Neither deathlessness nor decay, nor the rhythm of night and day
The self-existent, with breath sans air; that, and that alone was there
Darkness was in darkness found, like light less water all around
One emerged, with nothing on; it was from tapas that this was born
In it did desire, its way did find: the Primordial seed born of mind
The sages know deep in the heart; what exists is kin to what does not
Across the void the cord was thrown, the place of everything was known. Seed sowers and powers now came by, impulse below and force on high
Who realty knows and who can swear, how creation arose, when or where,
Even Gods came after creation's day, who really knows, who can truly say?
When and how did creation start? Did He do it? Or did He not?
Only He up there knows, may be, or perhaps, not even He".

Dr *Raman* adds, in another Vedic hymn the sage poet visualizes the world as having emerged from the cosmic womb or *Hiranya*

Garbha or the golden embryo. There after everything came from Him. He gave life and strength and Gods obey Him. Both immortality and death are only His shadows. The golden Embryo is a metaphysical view of the Universe emerging from a central core. One of the *Upanishads* says that "as the spider generates and draws in its filaments, as the herbs grow from the ground and hair from the body and head of a living man, so from the imperishable, the Universe springs". He says, "The filaments of the spider refer to the creation of something from a central source and its withdrawal from where it came from. The herbs refer to life and the hair from the body brings home the idea that the created elements are spread all over". Further Dr *Raman* also points out that the "Hindus believe in the periodic recurrence of creation, that is the circular concept of time. According to this notion, the physical Universe changes, evolves and dissolves into nothingness once again retracting to its original phase. In modern science this would be like zooming back into the initial black hole, only to re-emerge and repeat the procedure all over again. This is the oscillating Universe model.

In Epics this idea was described in the form of four *Yugas*, which are long periods of unequal duration. The present *Yuga* in which we are living is known as *Kali Yuga* which is supposed to have begun about 5000 years ago and is expected to last for 432,000 years. The total period of time forming all the four Yugas adds up to4, 32, 000 years. This is *Maha Yuga* or the great *Yuga*. A thousand such *Maha Yugas* make up half a day in the life of the cosmic creator, Brahma. A full day or *Kalpa* for the creation comes to 8.64 billion years. This cycle is supposed to go on endlessly with manifested phase and its inert counterpart. The notion of circular time is contained in this notion because of the cyclical occurrence of events in the Universe". He further adds, in the modern scientific world, only in the latter half of the 19th century that the idea of this kind is seen. "Only after the discovery of an expanding Universe and its theoretical connection with general relativity did the idea of a contracting Universe, and a possible oscillating model emerge, reminding us of the repeating cycle of ancient Hindu thinkers". He also points out, that in other traditions and in modern science the notion of time had been linear, that is, unidimensional, always advancing with no return to the initial state. No culture except the Indian had ever spoken of the huge time periods ever before. Others had spoken at the most only in terms of a few thousands of years. It was only after the discovery of radio activity in the latter half of the 19th century Lord Kelvin discovered the age of the Sun as of a few million years. He further adds, that Physics tells us that in the very distant future, when all the stars would spend away their energies the world would end. In the Hindu vision the cosmic dissolution marks the end of the world. It is the *Shiva* principle of dissolution or *Pralaya*. Everything is destined to vanish ultimately for a new beginning and this is the Omega point of the cosmos. Dr Raman finally asks, then why did all these happen at all? Science so far is unable to answer this question. Why did *Brahma* choose to manifest itself at all? He then takes the view of the ancient sages and says that as the sage poet stated long ago even the Gods may not know the answer. But according to *Vedantha*, it was nothing but the divine play of the divine itself. It is the grand mystery that can never be unravelled because some truths are beyond the scope of the human mind. He concludes with *Bhagavan Ramana Maharshis* statements that " all metaphysical discourses is profitless unless it causes us to seek within the self for the true reality—people try to find out about things which are external to them without trying to find out "who am I"? Only by the latter means can happiness be gained".

Most cultures based their study of the Universe a few hundreds or thousands of years, but the concept of time in India embraced billions and trillions of years. The notions of time span that are infinitesimally huge and also small even by modern standards we find in ancient Indian scriptures. They refer to time scales that vary from ordinary Earth or human days and nights to the day and night of the Gods that is called divine years, that are a few billion earth years long. The *Puranas* describe the time units from the infinitesimal unit 1/1, 000, 0000 of a second to a *Maha Manvanthara* of 311 trillion years. These calculations make one spell bound. Carl Sagan, the Physicist-Astronomer- teacher points out that ' a millennium before Europeans were willing to invest themselves of the Biblical idea that the world was a few thousand years old, the Mayans were thinking of millions and the Hindus billions".

According to Vedic Cosmology, the total age of the Universe is 311.04 trillion human years; its current age is around 155.521972944 trillion years *Sathya Yuga* lasted for 1. 728 million years, *Tretha Yuga* for 1.296 million years, *Dwapara Yuga* for 0.864 million years and *Kali Yuga* for 0.432 million human years. One day in the life of a Brahma is a '*Kalpa*' that is 4.32 billion years approximately. This is the approximate life span of the earth. In every *Kalpa*, that is each day of *Brahma*, the creator, he creates 14 'Manus' one after the other to regulate the world. In each *Kalpa* there are 14 generations of *Manus*. Each *Manu*'s life is a *Manvanthara* that consists of 71 *Chathuryugas* or *Mahayugas* consisting of four *Yugas* or eras each namely, *Sathya, Treta, Dwapara* and *Kali Yugas*. According to *Aryabhatta*, *Kaliyuga* or the Iron Age began in 3102 BC that is marked by the end of *Dwapara Yuga* with Lord *Krishna*'s disappearance from this earth. The present *Manu* is called *Vaivasvat* and he is the seventh *Manu*. After the life span of a *Manu* another *Manu* is created by Lord *Brahma*. This cycle continues until all the 14 *Manus* Perish and the Universe perishes at the end of one day of *Brahma*. Then *Brahma* goes to sleep for an equal period of 4.32 billion years. *Vedas* also declare that *Brahma*'s life span to be about 311trillion, 40 billion human years (1000 *Maha Yugas* or one *Maha Kalpa*). The life span of *Brahma* in terms of *Brahma* or divine years is 100. We are believed to be in the 51st year of the present *Brahma*'s life. When *Brahma* goes to sleep everything becomes unmanifested again until a new cycle begins. This cycle goes on for 100 divine years at the end of which Lord *Brahma* also perishes and is regenerated. Carl Sagan says that Hinduism is the only religion in the world in which the time scales correspond to that of modern scientific Cosmology. He says "its cycles run from our ordinary day and night to a day and night of Brahma, 18.64 billion years ago, longer than the age of Earth and the Sun".

The ancient seers of India gave the world not only the idea of the largest but also the smallest measurement of unit of time. They used units of time like *Krati* that was equivalent to 34,000th of a second. One *Truthi* is 300th of a second, 2 *Truthis* equivalent to one L*uv*, 2 *Luvs* is equal to 1 *Kshana*, 30 *Kshanas* equal to 1 *Vipal*, 60 *Vipal* equal to 1 *Pal*, 60 *Pals* equal to 1 *Gadi*, that is 24 *minutes*, 2.5 *Gadhi* equals

1 *Hora* or 1 hour, 24 *Horas* equal 1 *Divas* or I day, 7 *Divas* equals 1 week, 4 *Sapthch* equals 1 *Masa* or month, 2*Masas* equals 1 *Ritu*, 6 *Ritus*, equal to 1 *Varsh* or year, 100 *Varsh* equals 1 *Shatabda* or century, 10 *Shatabdas* equals 1 *Sahasrabda,* that is 10 centuries or 1000 years and 432 *Sahasrabdas* equals 1 *Yuga* that is 4320 centuries or 43, 20,00 years, 10 *Yugas* equals 1 *Maha Yuga* that is 43,200 centuries or 43,20,000 years, 1000 *Mahayugas* equals 1 *Kalpa,* that is 432,00,000 centuries or 4.32 billion years.

Again in *Puranas* it is stated that I *Nimisha* is the time taken to blink once. 15 *Nimishas* make one *Kashtha* and 30 *Kashthas* are 1 *Kaala*; 30 *Kaalas* make 1 *Muhoortha;* and 30 *Muhoorthas* make 1 day; 30 days are 1 month; Each month has 2 Lunar fortnights namely, *Shukla Paksha* and *Krishna Paksha*; 6 Months make one *Ayana*; there are 2 *Ayanas* in a year; 360 human years are equivalent to 1 year of the Gods.

The Puranas mention the smallest number as the Paramanu. Scientists are of the opinion that Paramanu equals one billionth part of a metre and this value tallies with the size of an organic molecule calculated by modern scientists.

The lengths of Yugas are defined in terms of years of Gods. There are four Eras namely, *Sathya Yuga* or *Krutha Yuga* that lasts for 4000 divine years, *Tretha Yuga* that lasts for 3000 years, *Dwapara Yuga* lasting for 2000 years and *Kaliyuga* lasting for 1000 divine years. The *Sandhyas* and *Sandhyamshas* are the intervening periods between the *Yugas* and these add up to 2000 divine years. Thus the four *Yugas* last for 12,000 divine years.

In a *Kalpa* each of the four *Yugas* occurs a thousand times. A *Kalpa* has 14 *Manvantharas* or Eras. In a *Manvanthara* each of the four *Yugas* occurs 71 times. One *Kalpa* corresponds to one day of *Brahma* 1000 *Kalpas* are one of *Brahma*'s years and 8000 of *Brahma*'s years make one of *Brahma*'s *Yugas.* One thousand such *Yugas* make up one *Savana* and *Brahma* lives for 3000 *Savanas.* This period is known as *Trivrita*. During each of *Vishnu*'s days, one *Brahma* is born and dies. During each of *Shiva's* days one *Vishnu* is born and dies. Each *Manvantara* is ruled by a *Manu* who is the ruler. So in each *Kalpa* there are 14 *Manus*. The *Devas* or Gods, the sages and the *Manus* change in each *Manvanthara*. Now we are in the seventh *Manvanthara*. In future there will be 7 more *Manvantharas* in the present *Kalpa* say the scriptures.

Prof Allan Watt writer of books on Eastern Philosophy of Harvard University says, "To the Hindu Philosophers of India, however, relativity is no new discovery just as the concept of light years is no matter for astonishment to people used to thinking of time in millions of *Kalpas* (A *Kalpa* is about 4, 320,000years). The fact that the wise men of India have not been concerned with technological application of this knowledge arises from the circumstance that technology is but one of innumerable ways of applying it". Philosopher Huston Smith said that "while the west was still thinking perhaps of 6000 years old Universe, India was already envisioning ages and eons and galaxies as numerous as the sands of Ganges- a Universe so vast that modern astronomy slips into its folds without a ripple". Prof Arthur Homes, a Geologist says, "Long before it became a scientific application to estimate the age of earth, many elaborate systems of the world chronology had been devised by the sages of antiquity. The most remarkable of these occult time-scales is that of the ancient Hindus whose astonishing concept of the Earth's duration has been traced to *Manu Smrithi,* a sacred book". Philosopher Huston Smith said that "India includes so much because her soul being infinite excludes nothing— it goes without saying that the Universe that India saw emerging from the infinite was stupendous". According to ancient Indian view that is Hinduism, the three activities namely, creation, sustenance and destruction of the Universe are done by the *Thrimurthis*, the three *Thattvas* or principles namely, *Brahma, Vishnu* and *Maheshwara*. The *Rishis* described time as cyclical, an endless process of creation, preservation and dissolution.

The scientists say that the sound of the Big Bang (scientists call this sound as 'Gong') that created the Universe could be reproduced using Physics and Astronomy. But this is already uttered in the *Vedas* through the sound *'AUM'*.

Dick Teresi who wrote several books on Science and Technology says, "Indian Cosmologists were the first to estimate the age of the earth at more than 4 billion years. They came closer to modern ideas of atomism, quantum Physics and other current theories. India developed very early enduring atomist theories of matter- possibly Greek atomistic thought was influenced by India via the Persian civilization". Swami *Kriyananda* (J. Donald Walters) says, "Hindu cosmography, for example born in hoary antiquity strikes one in certain ways surprisingly modern. India has never limited its conception of a few crowded millennia. Thousands of years ago India's sages computed the earth's age at a little over 4 billion years, our present era being what is called the seventh *Manvanthara*. This is a staggering claim. Consider how much scientific evidence has been needed in the west before men could even imagine so enormous a time scale".

The Indian Cosmologists were the first to estimate the age of the Earth at more than four billion years. Prof Carl Sagan says that, the Hindu Cosmology gives a time scale for the earth and the Universe- a time scale which is consonant with that of modern scientific Cosmology. We know that the earth is about 4.6 Billion years old and the Cosmos or at least its present incarnation is something like 10 or 20 Billion years old. The Hindu tradition has a day and night of *Brahma* in this range, somewhere in the region of 8.4 Billion years'. The *Puranas* also speak of the creation and destruction of the Universe in cycles of 8.64 billion years that is quite close to the currently accepted value regarding the time of Big Bang. Carl Sagan also states that Hindu religion is the only ancient religious traditions on the earth that talks about the right time scale and here is a great world culture which has always talked about billions of years. The many billion year time scale of the Hindu Cosmology is not the entire History of the Universe, but just a single day and night of *Brahma* and there is the idea of an infinite cycle of births and deaths and an infinite number of Universes each with its own Gods. He further says, the Indians whose theory of time is not linear like ours, that is, not preceding from past to present to future have always been able to accept, seemingly without anxiety, the notion of an alternatively expanding and contracting Universe, an idea recently advanced by certain western scientists. In Hindu Cosmology, immutable *Brahman* at fixed intervals draws back in to His beginningless, endless being the whole substance of the living world. There then takes place the long "sleep" of *Brahman* from which in course of countless aeons, there is an awakening and another Universe or "dream" emerges?"

Grig Sorman opines that 'cosmologically western science has understood only recently that the Universe is extremely old. In 1965 the temperature of the Universe was measured for the first time resulting in our present estimate of the age of the Universe as 15 Billion years old. In the ancient literature of India there are analogies. One such is, imagine an immortal eagle flying over the Himalayas only once every 1, 000 years; it carries a feather in its beak and each time it passes, it lightly brushes the tops of the gigantic mountain peaks. The amount of time it would take the eagle to completely erode the mighty *Himalayas* is said to be the age of the present manifestation of the Universe. Such a conception of time, which predates modern science by thousands of years is thought to be remarkable, especially when it is compared to the slow realization of western science and religion to the possibility of a less human like time scale—-- Eastern mysticism is also consistent with the results of quantum Physics. The mystics have always rejected the idea of a hidden clock like mechanism sitting out there, independent of human observation. The number one truth is that reality does not consist of separate things but is an indescribable, inter connected oneness. Each object of our normal experience is seen to be but a brief disturbance of a Universal ocean of existence.' Carl Sagan called Hinduism the only religion whose time scale for the Universe matches the billions of years documented by modern science.

Albert Einstein in his quantum theory makes it clear that matter and energy and all other things that we know do not have any real existence at the sub-atomic levels. Their existence is characterised by their relationship and inters connection with others. The same idea was expressed by the *Rishis* of Yore. The sages of ancient India declared that the Universe is a continuous cycle of creation and destruction by the Absolute or the fundamental energy which they termed as the *Para Brahman* and whatever we perceive in the Universe as independent and separate from that supreme power is nothing but an illusion created by the human mind, due to *Maaya, Avidya* or ignorance of the reality.

According to science the Universe began with an energy explosion, that is Big Bang and that all matter came into being from energy continuously expanding and changing. Some scientists point out that after a time, finally, the expansion may stop and the Universe will start contracting ending with a big crunch. What was before the Big Bang and what remains after the big crunch the scientists have no answer yet. But the *Rig Veda*, the most ancient Indian scripture, and that of the whole world, tells about a stage that was prior to the creation of the Universe. According to the Indian view *Kalpa* is the duration between the beginning and destruction of the Universe once in the endless series of *Kalpas*. One *Kalpa* refers to one day of *Brahma* that is preceded by an equal period of night of *Brahma*, the creator during which matter lies dormant in inert state when everything remains in a dormant state. Creation or *Srushti* is nothing but evolution of cosmos from that dormant state and its involution back into that state is called the dissolution or *Pralaya* of the universe. Just as days and nights come alternatively creation and dissolution of the universe also follow a cyclical pattern. The *Rishis* also pointed out that all matter or *Prakruthi* or nature has three modes or basic attributes namely, *Sathva* (goodness), *Rajas* (passion) and *Thamas* (inertia). During hibernation that is during the night of *Brahma* all these three qualities of nature are in perfect equilibrium position. When the equilibrium gets disturbed, creation begins (perhaps according to scientists the Big Bang happens) and the three forces of nature get realigned to form elementary particles called *Mahat* or *Apah* that combine further to form other basic particles like atoms and so on. It is also stated in the scriptures that at present *Kaliyuga* of the 28th *ChathurYuga*, of the 7th *Manvanthara* are in progress. Accordingly, 1,972, 949, 100 years have lapsed since the evolution of the present cosmos began and it has 2,347, 050, 900 years still to go before the end or dissolution or the Big Crunch of the present Universe. It is also stated in the scriptures that out of the 14 *Manvantharas*, the universe expands in the first seven *Manvantharas* and contracts for the next seven *Manvantharas*.

The scientists are not sure whether the Universe would continue to expand or will contract in course of time. However in the new theory 'the cyclic Model' of the Universe developed by Paul Steinhardt of Princeton University and Neil Turok of Cambridge university, the Hindu belief that the Universe has no beginning or end but has a cyclical pattern with repeated cycles of creation and dissolution can be found. Some scientists also view that the Big Bang is merely the prelude to big crunch. This view coincides with the Hindu notion of infinite cycle of expansion and contraction of the Universe. Contrary to the existing linear theory of time, the modern scientists have advanced a recent theory that confirms the expansion and contraction of the universe in a periodical manner. This modern theory also finds a place in the *Vedas* where through the concepts of *Kalpas* and *Manvantharas* it is stated that the world is created and destroyed at periodical intervals of time. The continuous cycle of creation propounded by John Whaler and the model developed by Paul Steinhardt in modern times is similar to the cyclical notion of the Universe of the ancient sages of India. In this manner the ancient view of the Indian sages is updated by the scientists in the 21st century.

Dr *Rajaram Mohan Roy*, a physical scientist regards *Rig Veda* as a book on Particle Physics and Cosmology that has much in common with the modern Physics but sometimes more subtle particularly regarding the explanation of the origin and evolution of the Universe. He points out that the terms *'Agni'* and *'Pasu'* found in the *Vedas* can be interpreted as 'Energy and 'Particle'; the term *'Vayu'* can be identified with *'Field'* the concept used in Physics; *'Surya'* stood for light; 'The seven horses yoked to Sun's Chariot found in the hymns might be referring to the seven columns of light spectrum; the word *'Gau'* (cow) also might have meant light, precisely the Particle of light of the Photon. It has been pointed out that the story of *Prajapathi/ Hiranyagarbha* as the Primal embryo egg as mentioned in the *Rig Veda* might be referring to the story of the Primal Atom and shows that it can split. The split atoms are the two offsprings or forms of *Prajapathi*, also *Hiranyagarbha*, the Primal Atom as the *Devas* and the *Asuras*. *Prajapathy* also refers to the Primal creator of all beings and is associated with *Hiranyagarbha* that might be representing the Sun, that is, the inner light or the inner Sun.

The Rigvedic Hymn 1.123 describes creation and annihilation of Particles which some compare with Lord *Shiva*'s dance of creation. It is also said that the cosmic dance of *Shiva* by the beating of the *Damaru* found in the Hindu religious texts suggest the sudden energetic impulses that could have propelled the Big Bang. *Subhash Kak* points out that the creation and destruction of the Universe in cycles of 8.64 million years as mentioned in the *Puranas* that are based on the *Vedas* is quite close to the currently accepted value regarding the time of Big Bang.

Scientists believe that when the Universe was very young due to some unknown reason, a small excess of matter was generated over antimatter. When matter and antimatter destroyed each other, the excess matter remained and this became the Universe. According to *Vedas* matter and energy are constantly created at the surface of the Universe. This is because matter and antimatter are attracted towards each other due to their opposite nature of electric charge and this electric force is also responsible for the resulting annihilation.

Rig Veda also points out that *Agni* has the wealth to give three times to mortals. In 1973 scientists discovered that about three times a day the sky flashes with a powerful burst of Gamma rays that have unimaginable intensity. Scientists say that these bursts are coming from Black holes. However they have no definite clue about its source. But *Vedas* are able to explain this.

All planets prior to their formation were part of their parent stars. So the nine planets of our solar system were also part of the Sun once upon a time. After separating from the Sun it took millions of years for the Earth to cool and become solid. It is said that the Earth is hollow inside with a tiny dwarf Sun at its centre. Most of the other planets are also hollow inside like the Earth. The scriptures therefore point out that just as there is life on Earth there is life in other planets as well. Perhaps unlike Earth that supports life both in its interior as well as on its periphery, the other planets may be supporting life only in its interior. *Puranas* give a detailed description of life in the underworld that is yet to be verified and discovered by modern scientists.

The *Vedas* declared that the Earth is spherical in shape, that it is flattened at the poles, that gravitation held the Universe together and so on. The *Rig Veda* also states that there are Suns in all directions.

In the 1920s Astronomers discovered that the Milky Way galaxy is not only one in Space. Outside it are other galaxies each containing thousands of millions of Suns. Scientists say that one of these galaxies is visible to the naked eye faintly in the constellation of Andromeda that is similar in size and shape to the Milky Way. It is the nearest neighbour of our Milky Way galaxy and is about 2 million light years away. Further away are the other galaxies that are very faint for the eye to locate. It is understood that million such galaxies are being photographed by scientists each containing 100, 000 million Suns. The *Rig Veda* had already stated thousands of years before that there are planets in all directions that are visible in the night sky.

The *Vedas* are very clear about rotation of Universe and continuous creation of matter and energy. While Vedas declare that whatever we perceive in the Universe as independent and separate is nothing but an illusion created by the human mind that can be termed as '*Maaya*' or ignorance due to *Avidya*. Albert Einstein in his quantum theory makes it clear that matter and energy and all other things that we know do not have any real existence at the sub atomic levels. Their existence is characterised by their relationship and inter connection to the others.

It is proved by scientists that the Vedic Alters represented various astronomical facts. It is also accepted that the myths described in the *Vedas* deal with astronomical events of the 4th millennium B C E. For example the *Agnicayana* alters described in the Vedas are supposed to be symbolic of the Universe. In this 'time' is represented by the metaphor of a bird; the three tiers represent the three divisions of space and the course of the sacrifice or *Yagna* represents year; and the place of sacrifice is identical with the cosmos. The term '*Skambha*' used in *Vedas* represent the world axis and the fire altar is symbolic representation of time.

Scientists have observed that the structure of the atom is similar to that of our Solar system. Electrons revolve around the nucleus of an atom just as planets revolve around the Sun in their specific orbits. The *Rishis* of ancient India had proclaimed long ago that what is found at the micro or individual level is similar to what is at the macro or cosmic level.

In the *Bhagavatha Purana* it is stated that atmosphere was created as protective skin of earth. And that the atmosphere surrounds the Earth to the height of 60 miles and clouds, lightning and the like are all phenomenon connected with it. According to modern science Ozone found on Earth's atmosphere below 48 kms. height is crucial for life on Earth. High in the atmosphere ozone acts as a shield to protect Earth's surface from the Sun's harmful ultra violet radiation. It is said that without this shield mankind would be more susceptible to skin cancer, cataracts and impaired immune system. But closer to earth ozone is harmful as it causes damage to lung tissue and plants. So an upset in the ozone balance can have serious repercussions on life on Earth. Scientists have discovered that changes are occurring in ozone levels with bad ozone increasing in the air we breathe and the good ozone decreasing in our protective ozone shield. New observations from a NASA space craft show that a layer in the earth's atmosphere acts like a heat shield by absorbing energy from space storms that reduces their ability to heat the lower atmosphere. But at the same time it imposes a heavy toll as it creates a billion degree cloud of electrified gas or plasma that is very hot and its particles act like radiation around our planet.

Even in the distant past the sages had stated that the Earth is divided into seven regions and contained seven oceans. The *Rishis* also spoke of several other worlds, hells and even Universes that are put forward by the modern scientists in their Multi verse notion. They also knew that there are beings in the other worlds that are either superior or inferior to human beings living on Earth. This view is also gaining ground among the modern Scientists today. It is also possible that there was life in other planets in the Solar system that might have disappeared in course of time due to unfavourable conditions that arose later and that could have made life there impossible.

The scriptures speak about seven regions above the earth. Scientists also state that the atmosphere consists of seven layers. These are the Troposphere, the layer closest to earth. It contains 90% of the total mass of the atmosphere. Rain, snow and wind take place in this layer. Above this is the Stratosphere. Above this is the Ozone sphere. Ozone layer here absorbs the ultra violet rays. Above this is the Mesosphere layer, then the Thermosphere layer and then comes the

Ionosphere layer. The comes the Exosphere, the outermost part of the earth's atmosphere that extends about 480 kms. to 960 kms. In *Vishnu Purana* it is stated that the three spheres, the *Bhur, Bhuvar and swar* Lokas are transitory whereas the three highest *Jana, Tapa and Sathya lokas* are durable. *Mahar loka* that is situated in between these two groups of Lokas has a mixed character. Although it is deserted at the time of *Pralaya*, it is not destroyed. The *Bhur loka* probably is the earth, the *Bhuvar loka* the geo sphere, the Swar loka the Solar system, Jana loka the Milky Way, galaxy, *Tapoloka* the world of galaxies and *Sathya Loka* the Universe itself. The fourth sphere consists of seven other lokas inside *Bhooloka.* The several thousand hells mentioned in the *Puranas* are supposed to burn with heat and hell fire and boiling with molten iron that resembles the modern description of Earth's inner core.

The *Bhoo loka* or Earth is visible with its mountains and seas. *Bhuvarloka,* may be the atmosphere that can be observed with its clouds, rains, thunders, and rainbows. *Swar loka* may be the solar and lunar orbits with the five visible planets of Mercury, Venus, Mars, Jupiter and Saturn and occasionally visible Comets and asteroids. *Mahar loka* may be the group of stars that we see in a starry night sky. The *Jana loka* may be the Milky Way galaxy that is seen as a faint band behind these bright stars of *Mahar loka.* The *Tapo loka* may be the *Andromeda* galaxy and the magnetic clouds. *Tapoloka* may be what is observable in the distant small stars. *Paatala loka* might be explored through submarine ships and underground cave expeditions and so on.

The *Vishnu Purana* gives an accurate description of tides during which water in the ocean seems to increase or decrease but actually not so as the quantum of water in the oceans remains the same at all times. These facts are proved by scientists like D. Gubbins of Leeds University. He admits that "this is amazing to find the facts proven only in the 20th century already present in Hindu holy books".

Vishnu Purana also describes what is beyond the Universe. It says that around the surface of the shell, namely Universe, Water flows, for a space equal to ten times the diameter of the Universe. The Water is encompassed by fire, fire by air, air by mind, mind by Ahamkara or false ego and false ego by intellect or *Buddhi* or *Mahat*. Each of these extends ten times the breadth of that which it encloses. The last is encircled by the chief principle that is infinite and its extent cannot be measured. It is therefore called the boundless and the cause of all existing things, the supreme nature, *Vishnu* that means that which expands, that is the expanding consciousness or expanding Universe that is the cause of all mundane things and beings that are innumerable. Within *Pradhana* resides the Soul as the inherent fire or as sesame oil in its seed.

The *Brahmanda Purana* points out that in the initial stage of creation of Universe some material of creation slipped from the hands of *Brahma* and collided with Earth resulting in the formation of *Moon*. In the international meeting in Hawaii in 1984 where the giant impact hypothesis discovered in 1983 emerged as the leading hypothesis, Dr Michael Drake, Director of the University of Arizona's Planetary Science Department openly admitted that the description given about the formation of the Moon given in the *Puranas* is amazing.

In *Rig Veda* it is stated that that the chariot of the Sun is drawn by seven horses. According to modern view also Sun light is made up of seven colours.

Swami *Vivekananda* is of opinion that there seems to be a great difference between modern science and all religions at this point that is, every religion has the idea that the Universe comes out of intelligence. The theory of God, taking it in its Psychological significance apart from all ideas of personality is that intelligence is first in the order of creation, and that out of intelligence comes what we call gross matter. Modern scientists are of the opinion that intelligence is the last to appear. They say that unintelligent things slowly evolve into animals and from animals into man. They claim that instead of everything coming out of intelligence, intelligence itself is the last to come. Both religions and scientific statements though seemingly directly opposed to each other are true. Take an infinite series a-b-a-b a- b and so on. The question is which is first 'a' or 'b'? If you take the series as a-b, you will say that 'a' is first, but if you take it as b-a, you will say that 'b' is first. It depends upon the way we look at it. Intelligence undergoes modification and becomes the gross matter this again merges into intelligence and thus the process goes on. The *Sankhyas* and other religionists put intelligence first, and the series becomes intelligence then matter. The scientific man puts his finger on matter and says matter then intelligence. They both indicate the same chain. Indian Philosophy however goes beyond both intelligence and matter and finds a *Purusha*, or Self, which is beyond intelligence of which intelligence is but a borrowed light. But it must be understood that it is the mind that is inside the gross body. But it is not the other way. So the gross forms come out as a result of mind that is there already. It is the mind that wills and that results in creation whether it is at the micro, individual level or microcosm or at the macro, universal level or Macrocosm. This is the reason why our ancient sages while explaining the origin of the Universe pointed out that due to the will or desire (of the mind) of the *Avyaktha* or the indeterminate, the Universal soul, the Universe that is determinate was born. It is the view of Hinduism that while the gross body that is the cosmic energy born out of the combination of *Purusha* the Supreme soul in combination with *Prakruthi,* the nature with its three modes, seem to perish only for the birth of a new body, the Conscious energy that directly gives rise to mind has no death even temporarily like the gross body that with death merges with the five elements of nature temporarily only to be reborn again in a new body. But the individual mind has no death like the individual physical body. After exhausting the repeated births and deaths of the gross body in accordance with its past karmas or actions it, the mind merges with the Universal soul ultimately.

Carl Sagan the famous Astrophysicist and Fritjof Capra, great writer, physicist and ecologist have pointed out similarities between the latest scientific understanding of the age of the Universe and the Hindu concept of a day and night of *Brahma*, which is much closer to the current known age of the Universe than the other myths about creation. According to Sagan, "The Hindu religion is the only one of the world's great faiths dedicated to the idea that the cosmos itself undergoes an immense, indeed an infinite number of deaths and rebirths. It is the only religion in which time scales correspond to those of modern scientific Cosmology. Its cycles run from our ordinary day and night to a day and night of *Brahma,* 8.64 billion years long, longer than the age of the Earth or the Sun". Capra wrote that "this idea of a periodically expanding and contracting Universe, which involves a scale of time and space of vast proportions, has arisen not only in modern Cosmology but also in ancient Indian Mythology. Experiencing the Universe as an organic and rhythmically moving Cosmos, the Hindus were able to develop evolutionary Cosmologies which come very close to our modern scientific models".

British Geneticist and Evolutionary Biologist J B S Haldane observed that the *Dasavatars,* the ten principal incarnations of Lord *Vishnu* are a true sequential depiction of the great unfolding of evolution. The *Avatars* of *Vishnu* show an uncanny similarity to the biological theory of evolution of life on Earth." Albert Einstein remarked "When I read the *Bhagavad gita* and reflect about how god created this universe everything seems so superfluous". Nancy Wilson Ross says that "many of India's ancient theories about the universe are startlingly modern in scope and worthy of people who are credited with the invention of zero, as well as Algebra and its application of Astronomy and Geometry, people who so carefully observed the heavens that in the opinion of Monier- Williams, they determined the Moon's revolution much more correctly than the Greeks".

Carl Sagan one of the great modern Astrophysicist while introducing some of the ideas of modern physics also acknowledged that of all the world's philosophies and religions, those originated in India are remarkably consistent with the contemporary scenarios of space, time and existence. Prof Allan Watts also admits that "to the philosophers of India, however, relativity is no new discovery, just as the concept of light years is no matter for astonishment to people used to thinking of time in millions of *Kalpas*".

Dr Karan Singh in his essays on Hinduism points out "The entire Cosmos is all pervaded by the same divine power. There is no ultimate duality in human existence or in consciousness. This is a truth which in the west is only recently being understood after Einstein and Heisenberg and Quantum Mechanics. The Newtonian, Cartesian-Marxist Paradigm of a materialistic Universe has now been finally abolished, it has collapsed in the face of the new Physics. Our ancient seers had a deeper insight in to the nature of reality than people had even until very recently".

Astronomy

The ancient Indian Astronomy is one of the very ancient Astronomical systems in the world. Along with Astronomy that is the study of celestial bodies the sages also revealed many facts about the planets that are below Bhu Mandala. The ancient Indian Astronomy was mixed with Astrology that studied how the relative positions of the nine grahas or planets determined human life, fortunes and misfortunes. Vedas contain much knowledge about both Astronomy as well as Astronomy. Astronomy was one of the six Vedangas that are the subsidiary sciences of the Vedas. In India the science of Astronomy was called *Khegola Sastra*. There was a famous astronomical observatory named *Khagola* at the *Nalanda* University in India in the past. In olden times Astronomy was linked with Astrology and was also referred to as, *'Jyothisha'* meaning the 'Science of light' and *'Nakshatra Vidya'* that means 'The science of stars'. In his 'Astronomy and its role in Vedic culture', *Subhash Kak* says that "analysis of texts reveals that much of the Vedic mythology is a symbolic telling of astronomical knowledge". He further states that "the study of Vedic ritual has shown that the Altar, *Adiyajna* was used to show the connections between the astronomical, the physiological and the spiritual symbolically". He points out that in *Rig Veda* it is said that *Nakshatras* are linked to the Moon's path. *Rig Veda* mentions 34 lights that include the Sun, Moon, five Planets and the 27 *Nakshatras.* Constellations other than *Nakshatras* were also known to the Vedic *Rishis.* These include the *Rksas* (the Bears), the two divine dogs (Canis Major and Canis Minor), the Boat (Argo Navis), and so on. He adds, the *Aitareya Brahmana* mentions *Mrga* (Orion), and *Mrgavyadha* (Sirrius). The Moon is called *Surya Rasmi* that is the one that shines by sun light. In *Satapatha Brahmana* there is a story about the *Nakshatras* being as powerful as the Sun in earlier times but have lost their power to the Sun later. The *Satapatha Brahmana* while explaining creation under *Prajapathi* referring to a star or time, mention is made of the emergence of *Asva, Rasabha, Aja* and *Kurma* before the emergence of Earth. These he says probably refer to the stars or constellations. The *Rig Veda* 1,164.2

defines *Asva* as the Sun. *Rasabha*, the twin asses suggesting Castor and Pollux in Gemini. *Aja* or goat probably refers to the constellation of Capricorn. *Kurma* mentioned there is a synonym of *Kashyapa* or Tortoise suggesting Cassiopeia.

It is understood that laying of the Altar for the performance of Vedic *Yagnas*, its shape, the number of bricks used and the pattern of laying the bricks all were in accordance with the principles of Astronomy. Even with the rudimentary measuring instruments the ancient seers of India were able to bring about accurate astronomical data. Ancient Indian seers operated with a time scale of astronomical proportions even before that was found in ancient Greece. The ancient sacred texts of India provided astonishingly exact scientific calculations even by today's latest scientific standards such as the speed of light, exact size of the smallest particles and the age of the Universe and so on. The earliest reference about Astronomy is found in the oldest *Veda* that is the *Rigveda*. In his commentary of *Rig Veda, Sayana* says (4th verse of hymn 1.50 of *Rig Veda*) "Oh, sun, bow to you, you who traverse 2,202 *Yojanas* in half a *nimisha*". The *Puranas* define one *Nimisha* to be equal to 16/ 75 seconds. 1 *Yojana* is about 9 miles. So according to *Sayana*, the Sun traverses about 186,000 miles per second. Robert C Priddy in his 'The critical mind and dissent' says, that *Sayana,* the earliest commentator of *Rig Veda* and a Sanskrit scripture "*RigVeda* of the Sun' say that the Sun covers 2202 *Yojanas* in half a nimisha that when calculated comes to 300,000 meters a second, that is exactly the speed of light. There are astronomical references of chronological significance in *Vedas.* Even in ancient India the Astronomers were able to arrive at near perfect measurement of astronomical movements and predict eclipses. Dr A L *Bhasham* says that *Rig Veda* lists a number of stars and mentions the 12 divisions of the Sun's yearly path, the *Rashis* and also the 360 divisions of the circle. The 360 days of a year is divided in to 12 months. The Sun's annual course was described as a wheel with 12 spokes that correspond to the 12 signs of the Zodiac. He further points out that the calculation of *Yugas* and *Mahayugas* are made from the hymns of *Rig Veda*. The Rig Veda also tells about the motion of Earth, the Sun's motion, *Ritus* and the colour of spectrum. *Yajnavalkya*, probably around 1800 BC, recognized that the Earth was round and believed that the Sun was the centre of the spheres as described in the *Vedas*. So even in the distant past, even before the Greek spoke about a flat Earth, the ancient sages knew that the Earth is spherical in shape and is in the form of a globe. Dick Terisi, author of books on science and technology, in his book on 'Ancient Roots of Modern Science' says 'that even several thousands of years before Aristotle, the *Vedas* had declared that the Earth was round and it revolved around the Sun". The hymns also mention that the Sun is the centre of the solar system and that the Earth is held in space by the Sun.

Even 2000 years before Pythagoras the *Vedas* had declared that the solar system was held together by the gravitational pull. The knowledge about the gravitational pull found in the *Vedas* was twenty four centuries before Newton discovered the laws of gravity. The motions of the Sun and Moon are described in the *Shatapatha Brahmana*. *Yajna valkya* said, that the Sun strings these worlds- the Earth, the planets, the atmosphere- to Himself on a thread. He also recognized that the Sun was much larger than the Earth. He accurately measured the relative distances of the Sun and Moon from the Earth as 108 times the diameter of these heavenly bodies that is almost close to the modern measurement of 107.6 for the Sun and 110.6 for the Moon that is obtained with the help of modern sophisticated instruments. The cosmological time scales explained in the *Surya Siddhata* on the basis of earlier scriptures, gives the average length of the Earth's revolution around the Sun, the sidereal year as 365.2563627 that is very near the modern value of 365.2563635 days. This has remained the most accurate estimate for the length of the sidereal year anywhere in the world for over a thousand years. The ancient Indian astronomy did deal with the calculation of occurrence of eclipses, determined the Earth's circumference, described the theory of gravitation, showed that the Sun was also a star and they also determined the number of planets under the Solar system.

In *Rig Veda* it is said that the Sun is the centre of the small system with planets and the Sun holds nearly the entire mass of this small system in this giant Universe that contains millions of Suns. According to *Vedas* there are also shadowy planets like *Rahu, Kethu, Gulika* and

Mandi although the famous ones are *Rahu* and *Kethu*. Science is yet to prove this.

In the *Aitareya Brahmana* it is said, that the Sun never sets nor rises. When people think that the Sun is setting it is not so; they are mistaken, indicating that the Sun is stationary and the earth is moving around the Sun. The same idea is found in *Vishnu Purana*. There it is said that the Sun is stationed for all time in the middle of the day—-of the Sun, which is neither always in one and the same place there is neither setting nor rising. Nancy Wilson Ross a great writer pointed out "Many of India's ancient theories about the Universe are startlingly modern in scope and worthy of a people who are credited with the invention of zero as well as Algebra and its application of Astronomy and geometry; a people who so carefully observed the heavens, that in the opinion of Monier Williams, they determined the Moon's synodical revolution much more correctly than Greeks—-- Many hundreds of years before those great European pioneers, Galileo and Copernicus had to pay heavy prices in ridicule and excommunication for their daring theories, a section of the *Vedas* known as the *Brahmanas* contains the astounding statement that "the Sun never sets nor rises; when people think that the Sun is setting, he only changes about after reaching the end of the day and makes night below and day to what is on the other side. Then, when people think he rises in the morning, he only shifts himself about after reaching the end of the day, night and makes day below and night to what is on the other side. In truth he does not see at all". Thus much before the time of Galileo and Copernicus, the Vedic Rishis had pointed out that there is no real Sun rise or Sunset but indications of the beginning and the end of a day. The old Sanskrit couplet '*Sarva Darshanam Sooryaha, Sooryaha, Sooryaha*' means that there are Suns in all directions. It shows that the ancient Indian astronomers, the sages, made the important discovery that the stars are visible at night are similar to the Sun that is visible during day. That means that they had understood that the Sun was also a Star although it is the nearest Star. Another *Sloka* says that 'When one Sun sinks below the horizon a thousand Suns take its place'. In *Vedas*, *Soorya* or the Sun was considered as one of the chief deities that was the source of light *(Dinakara)* as well as the source of warmth

(*Bhaskara*); the source of all life, and also the centre of the sphere. That means even in ancient times it was recognized in India that the Sun was the centre of the Universe, the solar system. Thus the concept of heliocentrism and the heliocentric theory of gravitation were referred to by many ancient sages of India. The seven horses tied by the snakes that drew the chariot of *Surya* or the Sun mentioned in the *Rig Veda* probably represent the seven columns of light and the movement of Sun's rays. The snakes with which the seven horses are tied represent the curved movement of the rays of the Sun that is proved by modern Physics. The *Vishnu Purana* states that the Equinoxes occur when the Sun enters Aries and Libra and that when the Sun enters Capricorn His northern course, from winter to summer commences and the southern course when he enters Cancer.

Sage *Kanada* in 600 BC classified all objects of creation into nine elements namely, Earth, Water, Light or Fire, Wind or Air, Ether, Time, Space, Mind and Soul. He stated that each object in creation is made of atoms that in turn connect with each other to form molecules nearly 2500 years before John Dalton. Sage *Kanada* also described the dimension and motion of atoms and the chemical reaction with one another. The *Soorya Siddhantha* written by an unknown Indian sage of the ancient past analyses all that are stated in the ancient scriptures of India about Universe namely, the kinds of time, length of year of Gods, day and night of Lord *Brahma,* the period since creation, how planets moved eastward, the Sidereal revolution, the length of the Earth's diameter and circumference, the basis for the sequence of days of the week named after the Sun, Moon and so on. There it is said that 'the Sun denominated the golden wombed *Hiranyagarbha*, the blessed, as being the generator'. He, the Sun is also referred to as 'the supreme source of light upon the borders of darkness, he revolves, bringing beings in to beings, the creator of creatures'. The *Surya Siddhanta* also says, 'Bestowing upon Him the scriptures (*Vedas)* as gifts, and establishing Him within the egg as grandfather of all the worlds, He himself then revolves causing existence'. It gives detailed methods for making eclipse calculations. Around this period *Rahu* and *Ketu* were astronomically defined as the ascending and descending nodes of the lunar orbit, intersecting the plane of Earth's orbit. The accuracy with which the eclipses are predicted is quite incredible. The *Surya Siddhanta* also computed the Earth's diameter to be around 7840 miles and the distance between the Earth and Moon as 253,000 miles. These facts are mentioned *Bhagavatha Purana*. These are close to modern measurements of 7926.7 miles and 252,710 miles respectively for the maximum distance between Moon and Earth. The ancient Astronomers *Varahamihira*, *Garga* and the scripture *Vedanga Jyothisha* refer to the constellation *Dhanishta* and point to an ancient calendar that would have been used in 1280 BCE. The *Kaushataki Brahmana* and *Atharva Veda* also refer to a similar calendar. The main work of *Varahamihira* (499-587 CE), an eminent Astronomer and Astrologer the '*Pancha Siddhantha*' that is a treatise on the five Astronomical canons written in 575 CE summarises the five earlier astronomical treatises namely *Surya Siddhantha, Romaka Siddhantha, Paulisa Siddhanta , Vasishta Siddhantha* and *Partamaha Siddhantha* tells that '*Ayanamsa*' or the shifting of equinox is 50.32 seconds. His *Brihat Samhitha* also contains Astrology, planetary movements, eclipses and so on. *Varahamihira* showed that the Moon and planets are lustrous not because of their own light but due to the Sunlight. The French astronomer Jean- Claude Bailly admires the accuracy and antiquity of Vedic astronomical measurements.

David Frawley says, that "Mathematical secrets of the Universe are mentioned in the *Vedas* like a time cycle of 4, 320, 000, 000 years and names for numbers from one to ten followed by twelve zeroes". He adds "the zodiac number 360 and its divisions and derivatives are common in Vedic texts. Vedic *Manthras* are said to be inherent in the rays of the Sun. Noted Vedic scholar *Subhash Kak* has found a planetary code in the numbering of the books of Rig Veda".

The 14 planetary systems in the Universe mentioned in the ancient scriptures of India are supposed to be horizontal planes parallel to the orbit of the Sun around the Earth as seen from the Earth and are placed vertically under each other. Each planet has its own orbit around *Sumeru,* the axis of the Universe. These extend to the inner layer of the spherically shaped Universe. The scriptures also state that there are 14 planetary systems 7 of which are above the Earth or *Bhoomandala* and seven planetary systems below the Earth.

The scriptures point out that *Bhu Mandala* is lotus shaped. The different *Dveepas* or islands and the area between two Dvipas are like the petals of a lotus flower. The *Lokaloka Mountain* forms the outermost and the highest ring of the lotus petals. The top of *Meru* Mountain, the central axis, has a diameter of 32,000 *Yojanas* and is 84, 000 *Yojanas* above *Bhoomandala* Planetary system and its base is 16,000 *Yojanas* in diameter and it is 16,000 *Yojanas* below the plane of *Bhoo Mandala*. 130, 000 *Yojanas* beneath *Bhoomanandala*, the great Earth, is the *Garbha* Ocean. This ocean covers nearly half of the Universe that is 249,800,000 *Yojanas*. Just above this ocean are the innumerable hellish planets or *Naraka Lokas* that has a thickness of 60, 000 *Yojanas* and a diameter of 500 million *Yojanas*. This area begins 70, 000 *Yojanas* below the *Bhoo Mandala* and extends to 130, 000 *Yojanas* below the Bhoo Mandala. There are nearly 550 million hellish planets in that region each having its own special features. Above the hellish planets and below the *Bhoo Mandala* are the 7 planetary systems called *Bila-Svarga* (*Bila* means dark) or underground heavenly planets which is always dark because the Sun does not enter there. As such there are no days or nights and hence time. These inhabitants also do not become old, get wrinkles, disability or grey hair. On the other hand they are always full of energy and enthusiasm. This region is lit by the shining jewels on the heads of serpents. These are like cubic cellars with 10, 000 *Yojanas* on each side. The demons who reside here enjoy heavenly sensual gratification due to their past deeds. These are more luxurious than those in which the Demi Gods live namely, the heavenly planets. *Daityas, Daanavas* and *Nagas* live here. They also possess *Vimanas* in which they travel in the Universe. The *Bhoo Mandala* has planets that are placed in ring form. In between each ring there are ring shaped oceans of salt water *(Lavanoda)*, sugar cane juice (*Ikshura*), Strong drinks (*Suroda*), Ghee (*Ghrtoda*), milk (*Kshiroda),* Yoghurt (*Dadyod*a) and sweet water (*Swadudaka*) oceans. These oceans have all the properties of water except for different tastes. Each ring of land has millions of planets.

According to *Hare Krishna* views on sciences discoveries, the farthest point of the orbit of planet Uranus measured from *Bharatha Varsha* is the same as *Aloka Varsha*, the uninhibited area. The farthest point of the orbit of Saturn is in *Adarsatalpama*, the land with a surface like a mirror that lies before the *Lokaloka* Mountain. The farthest point of the orbit of Mercury is the ring inside *Pushkara Dveepa* and its nearest point is in the ocean of milk. It is also pointed out that "the perigee, (the point located nearest earth in the orbit of a celestial body around the earth) of the orbit of Venus coincides with the outer coast of the ocean of ghee or clarified butter. The perigee of Mars is the inner coast of the ocean of milk. The perigee of Mercury is the outer coast of the ocean of milk. The perigee of Venus is the inner coast of the ocean of sweet water. The Apogee, (the point of the orbit of the Moon, or a planet or a satellite that lies farthest from earth) of the planet Mars is the outer coast of the ocean of sweet water. The Apogee of Mercury is *Manasottara*. The perigee of Jupiter is the inner edge of *Kanchana Bhumi*; that of Saturn is the *Adrsyadrsyakagiri*, the *Lokaloka Parvatha*. Behind this Mountain that is higher than *Dhruva Loka*, no sunlight penetrates and nothing is visible. Saturn is the most distant planet of our solar system visible to the naked eye.

The scriptures say that above *Bhoomandala* is the *Antariksha*, then the *Bhuvar Loka* or the middle heaven in which the *Lokas* or Planets belong to different entities. These entities sometimes come to *Bhoo Mandala* in chariots or *Vimanas* as unidentified flying objects. They visit the *Bhoo Mandala* from other planets like *Raakshasa Loka* or *Preta Loka*, or *Bhootha Loka* or *Pishacha Loka* or *Yaksha Loka* or from *Siddha Loka*. Beyond *Siddha Loka* where its inhabitants have mystical powers is the *Carana Loka*, the place of angels and heavenly musicians like *Ghandarvas*. Then there is *Vidyadhara Loka* where the inhabitants have great material knowledge. Sometimes the un-identified flying objects also come from *Bila Swargas*.

According to the ancient scriptures, the Sun is above 100, 000 *Yojanas* above the *Bhoo Mandala*. From the Sun the heavenly planetary system starts. It is known as *Deva Lokas or Bhoga Lokas* of the Demi Gods. The distance from the Sun to *Bharatha Varsha* in *Bhoo Mandala* is 150 million kms. at the physical level. The orbit of the Sun around the *Sumeru* Mountain is *Sakadveepa*. It divides the island into two. One of the heavenly planetary systems is *Indra Loka*, the kingdom of *Indra* who rules this cosmos. The inhabitants of this

Planet have a longevity of 3, 600, 000 Solar years. Above the heavenly planetary systems or *Divya Swargas* are the *Mahar Loka, Jana Loka, Tapa Loka* and *Sathya Loka* where *Yogis* or ascetics and mystics get absorbed in meditation.

The scriptures also point out that the first layer around the Universe is ten times that of the diameter of the Universe. The second layer is again ten times the thickness of the first layer. Likewise there are ten layers in total. Each succeeding covering layer around the Universe is composed of different substance as stated in *Bhagavad Gita*. These layers change from solid matter (Earth) to fluid (Water), then to luminous element (Fire), then to gaseous (Wind or Air), then to ethereal (Sky or Space), the Mind (Manas), *Bhuddhi* (intelligence), False ego or *Ahamkara* (false ego), the *Mahat- Thattva,* (the visible Primeval source of matter) and then *Pradhana*, (the unmanifested).

The ancient *Rishis* also observed that the distance from the Sun to Earth is 108 times the diameter of the Sun. The distance from Moon to earth is 108 times the diameter of the Moon, The distance from the Sun to earth is10, 800 *Yojanas*, *Sathya Yuga* lasts for 16*108==1,728, 000 years; *Tretha Yuga* lasts for 12*108=1, 296, 000 years, *Dwapara Yuga* lasts for 8*108=864,000 years and *Kali Yuga* lasts for 4*108=432,000 years. Probably this is the significance of number 108.

It is understood that five Altars with astronomical basis are found in the third millennium cities of India. Although the texts that describe their designs are dated to the first millennium B C, their contents appear to be much older.

The text on Vedic Astronomy namely, '*Vedanga Jyothisha*' written by *Logada* in 1350 BC describes the rules for tracking the motions of the Sun and Moon and also develops the use of Geometry and Trigonometry for Astronomical calculations. *Aryabhatta* (born in Kerala) in his book *Aryabhatiya*, a mathematical treatise and a text on Astronomy, written in 499 CE when he was only 23 years old, presented a mathematical heliocentric model in which the Earth was taken to be spinning on its axis and the periods of the planets were given with respect to the stationary Sun. He was the first one to challenge the western notion that the Earth was the centre of the Universe. He stated that the Earth is round and it rotates on its axis, orbits the Sun and is suspended in space and that the Sun is the centre of the whole system and the binding force that keeps all planets together. This was 1000 years before Copernicus published his Heliocentric theory. He also wrote that 1,582,237,500 rotations of the Earth equal 57,753,336 lunar orbits. This is perhaps the oldest astronomical calculated to such accuracy. He made an accurate approximation for the Earth's circumference and diameter and discovered how the lunar eclipse and solar eclipse happen. He formulated the process of calculating the motion of planets and the time of eclipses. It is pointed out that ' the earliest known precise calculation regarding the values of Earth's constant like rotation per Solar orbit, days per solar orbit, days per lunar orbit and so on were revealed by *Aryabhatta*. His computation of 'Pi' (the ratio of the circumference and the diameter of a circle) when rounded up comes to 3.1416 and the length of the Solar year as 365.358 days were extremely accurate even by modern scientific standards'. It is said that one of the subtle hymns in Rigveda gives the value of 'Pi' up to 28 digits accurately whereas with computers the value could be known only up to 16 digits. Aryabhatta also stated that eclipses were caused by the Earth's shadow over the Moon and the Moon covering the Sun. The ancient explanation that eclipses are caused by *Raahu* and *Ketu* might be the symbolic expression of the ancient seers in explaining about the eclipses. He gave the radius of the planetary orbits in terms of the radius of the Earth/Sun orbit. He also proved the ancient statement of the *Rishis* that the orbits of the planets around the Sun are elliptical and that the Earth was sphere and that the light from the Moon and the Planets were reflected from the Sun. His book '*Aryabhattiya*' published in 498 AD, described numerical and geometrical rules for calculation of eclipses. He also propounded the heliocentric theory of gravitation thus predating Copernicus by almost one thousand years. He stated that 1,582,237,500 rotations of the Earth equal 57,753,336 lunar orbits. This is an extremely accurate ratio of a fundamental astronomical ratio 1,582,237, 500/57,753,336 that is equal to 27.3964693572 and is perhaps the oldest Astronomical constant calculated to such accuracy. Through the translation of *Aryabhatta*'s 'The *Aryabhattiya*', in the 13th century the European mathematicians came to know the methods for calculating the areas of triangle, volumes of spheres, Squares and cube root. The *Brahmaphuta Siddanta*, a text on Astronomy was written by *Brahma Gupta* in 628. In the 7th century *Brahmagupta* estimated that the circumference of the Earth was 500 *Yojanas* (a *Yojana* roughly equals 7.2 kms.). As calculated on this basis, the Earth's circumference comes close to the modern known figure of the circumference of the Earth. *Brahma gupta* also stated that 'bodies fall towards the Earth as it is in the nature of the Earth to attract bodies just as it is in the nature of water to flow'. *Varahamihira* even a hundred years before *Brahmagupta* confirmed that there should be a force that might be keeping bodies stuck to the Earth and also keeping heavenly bodies in their predetermined places. The Sanskrit term for gravity is '*Gurutvakarshan*' (*Akarshan* means attraction; *Guru* means master). Similarly, the function of attracting heavenly bodies was attributed to the Sun. *Brahma Gupta* was the earliest to use Algebra to solve Astronomical problems. In his '*Brahma Sphuta Siddanta* that he wrote in 628 he developed methods for calculating the motions and places of various planets, their rising and setting, Conjunctions and the calculation of eclipses of the Sun and Moon. *Bhaskaracharya* (1114-1183) wrote the '*Siddhanta Siromani*' that contained two parts namely *Goladhyaya* meaning Sphere, and *Grahaganita* that is Mathematics of the planets. In his book he wrote on planetary positions, eclipses, cosmography, about mathematical techniques and astronomical equipments. He also expanded on *Aryabhatta*'s heliocentric model in his treatise *Siddhanta Siromani* where he mentioned the law of gravity. He pointed out that objects fall on the ground due to the force of Earth's attraction and that the Earth, the planets, constellations, the Moon and the Sun are held in orbit due to this attraction. This was rediscovered by Isaac Newton later in 1687 that is after more than 1200 years. He also discovered that planets do not orbit the Sun at a uniform velocity and accurately calculated many astronomical constants based on this model such as solar and lunar eclipses and the velocities and instantaneous motions of the planets. He calculated the time taken by the Earth to orbit the Sun up to nine decimal places. The astronomers *Madhava* and *Nilakanta Somayaji* and *Jyeshtadeva* who were members of the Kerala school of Astronomy and Mathematics from the 14th to 16th century were responsible for founding calculus and modern mathematical analysis and so on. John

Sylvain Bailly, the French Astronomer observes that "the motion of the stars calculated by the Hindus before some 4500 years vary not even a single minute from the tables of Cassine and Mayor. The Indian table gives the same annual variation of the Moon as is discovered by Tycho Breke". The *Brihata Sathaka* tells about the divisions of one day into 60 Kalas or *Ghatika*.- " of 24 minutes each subdivided into 60 *Vikala* that is 24 seconds each. The duration of time 60 *Para* is divided into *Tatpara*, then into *Vitatapara*, then in to *Ima*, then into *Kasha*— the smallest unit equal to approximately 0.000 00003 of a second (one 300 millionth)". The eminent historian T. N. Cole Brook said "compared to scientists of Europe, *Kanad* and other Indian scientists were the global masters of this field".

It is seen that the constellations other than the *Nakshatras* were also known to the Indian *Rishis* of the past. The Bears, the two divine dogs that may be Caris Major and Caris Minor, the Boat that is Argo Navis, Mrga that is Orion, *Mrgavyadha* that is Sirius are all mentioned in *Rig Veda* in 1.24.10, 10.14.11, and 10.63.10.

Srimad Bhagavatham (10.44.2) speaks of the number of stars in the sky being equal to the number of *Muhoorthas* in 1000 years or 1000*360*30=10,800, 000. This *Purana* also tells about (16.8.6 and 21.1.9) the distance of the Sun from the Earth.

Astrology

The ancient Indian Astrology known as *Jyothisha* is regarded the oldest system of Astrology known to mankind. It was there even before 5000BC. *Jyothisha* literally means 'the study of light'. *Jyothisha* is considered as the eyes of the *Vedas*. The origin of *Jyothisha* is from *Vedas*. It studies the subtle influence of celestial bodies on man and on earth. The *Rishis* of the past had understood that all that there exists in the Universe are not independent of each other but are interdependent. Perhaps this understanding had made them to study about the influence of celestial bodies on man. Originally, it was a part of *Vedangas* that are affiliates to the *Vedas*. These are considered as the explanatory limbs or *Angas* of the *Vedas*. These were originally mentioned in *Mundaka Upanishad*. *Vedangas* help in understanding the secret meanings contained in the Vedas. There are six *Vedangas* or aspects of Vedic knowledge. The first group of *Vedangas* is connected with the texts of the *Vedas* and the second group deals with the meaning of the *Vedas*. Jyothisha or Astrology that was mixed with Astronomy is in the second group of *Vedangas*. The Vedic Astrology in the past had three parts. The first one was *Siddhantha* or Astronomy with its application to Astrology; the second, the *Samhita* or Mundane Astrology that contained predictions, *Vaastu Sastra* and Omens, and the third was *Hora* or Predictive Astrology that contained several branches. Sage *Parasara* father of *Veda Vyasa* authored *Brihat Parasara Hora Satra* that is Vedic Astrology encyclopaedia around 3102 B C, that is before the starting of the present *Kali Yuga*. The various branches of *Hora Jyothisha* touched almost all aspects of life of man on earth. They are, *Jatak Sastra*, that is, predictions based on the birth chart or horoscope of the individual, *Muhoortha*, the Astrology for selecting the most auspicious time for getting the maximum advantage or return, *Swar Shastra*, predictions based on name and sounds, *Prashna*, the predictions based on the time of the celestial bodies, *Ank Jyothisha*, numerology that is based on numbers, *Nadi Jyothisha*, the ancient treatise on palm leaves dealing with detailed individual predictions, *Tajik Shastra* or *Varsh Phal*, the annual horoscope based on Sun, *Jaimini Sutras*, timing of events as per *Jaimini*, *Nasht Jatakam*, tracing or rewriting the lost horoscope, *Sree Jatak*, the female Astrology and so on. The other related branches of *Jyothisha* are *Griha Samudrika* or Astro palmistry, *Hasta Rekha* or *Samudrika Shastra* or Palmistry, *Padatal Shastra* based on the lines and signs of the sole, *Shakun Shastra*, predictions based on omens, *Swapna Vidya*, the interpretation of dreams, *Kapal Vidya*, the characteristics of a person based on the shape of his skull, and *Akriti Vidya*, judging a person on the basis of structure and moles on the body. The ancient sages like *Vasishta, Bhrugu* and *Garga* were masters of Astrology in ancient times.

According to ancient Indian Astrology the destiny or fate of a person is associated with the position of the Planets on the date, time and place of his birth. It views the individual, the Earth and its environment as a single organism where all parts are connected with each other. The sages noted that the nine planets or the *Nava Grahas* release energy waves to influence lives on Earth. The ancient Indian

Astrology that is the oldest system of Astrology in the world makes use of the actual constellation of stars, positions of planets, and Sun as seen in the sky at the time of birth of an individual. As per Indian Astrology every event in our life is influenced by the position of the celestial bodies at time, date and place of birth. Vedic Astrology tells about the understanding of life, the journey of the soul from past to present life on the basis of effects of past actions or *Karmas*, sins, remedies and so on.

According to David Frawley, (Pandit Vamadeva Sastri) an eminent practitioner of Ayurvedic medicines, Vedic Astrology teacher and writer, "Vedic Astrology contains an extensive knowledge not only of the planets, signs and houses but of the 27 Nakshatras or lunar constellations.

Geography of the Earth

The Earth or *BhooMandala*, according to the scriptures is divided into seven islands or *Dweepas*. In the middle of *Bhoo Mandala* is the *Jambu Dveepa* with a diameter of 100, 000 *Yojanas*. Mount *Meru* that is at the centre of *Jambu Dveepa* is made of gold. The shining of this mountain is so bright that it resembled fire. Around this *Meru Parvatha* or Mountain are four mountains each 10, 000 *Yojanas* high and 10, 000 *Yojanas* broad. On the top of each Mountain there is a tree each of which is 1,100 *Yojanas* high and 100 *Yojanas* broad. They spread over 1, 100 *Yojanas* across. On the first Mountain there is a mango tree the mangoes of which are the source of a river of heavenly mango juice. On top of the second mountain there is a *Jambu* tree (Rose apple) full of heavenly flowers of fruits of different colours. The fruits of this tree are the source of the river of Rose apple fruit juice. The third Mountain has the *Maha Kadamba* tree on its top that forms the source of the five rivers of heavenly liquid honey each twelve meters broad. The last mountain has a Banyan tree the roots of which are the source of the river of heavenly water. In between these four mountains there are the lakes of honey, sugar, candy juice and pure heavenly water. The waters of these lakes have mystical powers as to fulfil all desires. The *Plaksadvipa* is 200, 000 *Yojanas* broad. It has a *Plaksha* tree, a heavenly fig tree that is 1, 100 *Yojanas* high and 100 *Yojanas* broad. It shines like gold. *Salmalidvipa* is 400, 000 *Yojanas* broad. It has a *Salmali* tree, a heavenly silk cotton tree. It is also 1, 100 *Yojanas* high and 100 *Yojanas* broad. This tree is supposed to be the home of *Garuda*, the vehicle of Lord *Vishnu*. *Kusa dvipa* is 800, 000 *Yojanas* broad with *Kusa* grass that look like fire, radiating light from all sides with mild and attractive flames. The *Krauchadveepa* is 1, 600, 000 *Yojanas*. It has the Mountain *Krouncha*. The *Sakadveepa* is 3, 200, 000 *Yojanas* and has a *Saka* tree. The *Pushkaradveepa* is 6, 400, 000 *Yojanas*. It has a lotus flower that has 100,000, 000 flower petals of pure gold.

After it falls on mount *Meru* the *Ganges* divides into four branches. One of these descends via *Himalayas* to the planet of Earth. There are many other innumerable rivers with many branches on Mount *Meru*. Mount *Kesara* that is located near Mt. *Meru* is as high as Mt *Meru*. Beyond *Mandara, Merumandara, Suparsva* and *Kumuda* are eight Mountain ridges that lay in four directions. Each is 18, 000 *Yojanas* long and 2000 *Yojanas* broad and high. Towards the south of Meru is *Kailasa*. There are also many other Mountains around the foot of Mount *Meru* that resemble the stamens around the heart of the lotus flower.

There are nine *varshas* that may be islands or land regions in *Jambudvipa* that is surrounded by salt water. Each of these is 9,000 *Yojanas* long. Each *Varsha* is divided from its neighbouring *Varsha* by eight big Mountain ridges. Each of these Mountains is 2000 *Yojanas* broad and 10, 000 *Yojanas* high. The central part of *Jambu Dveepa* is *Ilavrta Varsha*. All the other *Varshas* except *Bharatha Varsha* are *Bhauma Swarga* or heavenly places in *Bhoomandala*. The inhabitants of all other eight *Varshas* except *Bharatha Varsha* live according to our earthly calculations for 10, 000 years. In other Dvipas outside *Jambudveepa* the inhabitants live for nearly 1000 years. The inhabitants there have the power of 10, 000 elephants and they are as effulgent as lightning. They always remain youthful. However the *Bauma Swarga* and the oceans in between are not visible for the naked eye.

Jambudveepa where *Bharata Varsha* is located can be understood as a part of South Central Asia. In *Puranas* it is stated that the Earth is divided into seven Dvipas or islands or regions surrounded by seven seas. The continental drift might have changed the structure and geography of earth today and therefore it becomes difficult to interpret the ancient geography of earth in modern terms. Again it is also possible that many new land regions might have appeared and many land masses, oceans, seas and rivers would have disappeared in course of time. The ancient Geography of India however shows that India was much more extended to the North West and west. Very recently, in February 2013, as per reports the Archaeologists have found a 5000 year old ruined Temple with a hearth (where Vedic Yagnas were performed) in it in Peru located in South America. There were also many rivers besides it some of which might have disappeared. For example the river *Saraswathi* that is mentioned in various scriptures is said to have dried up. It is understood that *Jambudveepa* (also known as *Sudarshanadveepa*) was the innermost concentric island that is depressed on its south and north, elevated and broad in the middle. The elevated region was known as *Ilavrata* or *Meru Varsh, and Bharatha Varsha* was towards its South.

A Few of the other important Inventions and Discoveries of Ancient India

Sir John Woodroffe, the great scholar points out that 'ages before Lamark and Darwin, it was held in India that man has passed through 84 lakhs of births as plants, animals or as inferior species of man and then took birth as the ancestor of the developed type existing today".

It is pointed out that cosmology and other scientific and art and fine arts of ancient India spread to other countries along with mercantile and cultural exchange.

Bharata Varsha was also the name for the oldest civilization in the world. One of the archaeological findings off the coast of Gujarat in India confirms a submerged city that is the oldest city that dates back to 8000 to 9000 B C.

Patanjali's (200 BCE) *Ashtanga Yoga* or eight limbed *Yoga* is considered as a unique contribution to the world. He described 84 yogic postures that would enhance the efficiency of the respiratory, circulatory, nervous, digestive and endocrine system and many other organs of the body. Through his eight limbs of *Yoga* like *Yama, Niyama* and so on, he proved that one is able to attain ultimate Bliss.

India contributed *Ayurveda* or the science of living to the world (*Ayu* means life; *Veda* means knowledge). It cures the disease by mainly removing the cause of illness.

Chanakya's *Artha Sastra* describes post mortems. *Bhoja Prabhanda* describes about brain surgery successfully performed in 927 AD, on King *Bhoja*. The usage of Anaesthesia was also known to ancient Indians. *Maharshi Charaka's* Charaka *Samhita* or the Physician's handbook, written around 600 BC is an encyclopaedia on *Ayurveda*. When the science of Anatomy was in its infancy in Europe, Sage *Charak* of India revealed facts on human anatomy, physiology, embryology, pharmacology, blood circulation and diseases like Diabetes, Tuberculosis, and heart diseases and so on. He discussed treatment for thousands of diseases for which the modern medical science is yet to find an answer. Along with diet, herbs and life style, *Maharshi Charaka* showed a correlation between mind, body and spirit and moral code of conduct. Around this period *Rishi Dhanvanthari* developed the school of surgery. *Rishi Kashyap* developed paediatrics and gynaecology. The Indians were the first to perform surgery, amputation and caesarean. The *Sushrut Samhitha* of *Sushrut* (600 BCE), is considered as an encyclopaedia of surgery. *Sushrut* is considered as the father of Plastic surgery and the science of Anaesthesia. When surgery was only in its early stages in Europe, it is understood that *Sushrut* performed Rhinoplasty, the restoration of damaged nose and other operations. He used cheek skin to perform plastic surgery to restore and reshape nose, ears and lips and so on. He also performed other surgeries like cataract, artificial limbs, fractures, urinary stones and brain surgeries, amputation, caesarean and cranial surgeries and so on. Operations were conducted with 42 surgical processes. The *Shushrut Samhitha* prescribes treatment for 12 types of fractures and six types of dislocations. *Sushrut* also analysed human embryology in great detail. He seems to have used 125 types of surgical instruments mostly designed from the jaws of animals and birds. He also seems to have described a number of stitching methods by using horses' hair, fine thread, fibres of bark, goats' guts and so on. He detailed 300 types of operations. In the fields of amputations, caesareans and cranial surgeries Indians are found to be the pioneers.

In the field of chemistry the alchemical metals were developed for medical purposes by *Nagarjuna* who wrote many books including *Ras Ratnakara* in which he explained the use of metals for quick and best healing of most grave diseases by burning metals like iron, tin, copper, etc. into ash and removing the toxic elements.

The snake and ladder game that was called as the *Moksha Padam* or *Parama Padam* or *Mokshapat* had its origin in India.

The *Mahabharata* is the largest Epic ever written so far in this world. Its 100,000 verses encompass all facets of human life.

The Martial art *Kalari Payittu* of Kerala in India is considered as the most complete and scientific martial art and is also considered as the mother of all martial arts. *Bodhidharma*, a Buddhist monk of India introduced *Kalarippayittu* in China and Japan in the 5th century and he taught that art in the temples there. (Toda's Shaolin temple) This was later evolved into Karate and Kung-Fu and Judo.

India was the world leader in Metallurgy. Extraction of zinc from ore by distillation was practised in India even in ancient times. Copper statues that are found even today date back to 500 CE. Extraction of zinc from its ore by distillation was known in India even as early as 400 BCE. The 22 foot iron pillar in Delhi cast approximately in the 400 CE with a weight around 6 ½ tones stands as the mute testimony to the highly advanced scientific knowledge of metallurgy that India possessed in those days. It has no signs of rust or decay even today. It is said that modern metallurgists are not been able to produce iron ore comparable to that quality of the pillar so far.

Gold jewellery was available in India even from 3000 BCE.

Even from the distant past Indians had exceptional skills in spinning, weaving and so on and it is believed that the primitive spinning wheels originated in India. It is said that the Indians had the capacity to make the thinnest cloth in the world.

The art of navigation was born in the river *Sindhu* some 6000 years ago. The word navigation itself is derived from the Sanskrit word *Navgatih*.

The Vedic musical science is one of the most sophisticated and complex in the world in which the meter and tunes (*ragas*) are linked to specific moods and times of a day.

The so called Pythagoras theorem that the square of the hypotenuse of a right angled triangle equals the sum of the square of the other two sides was documented by *Bandhayana* even in 6th B C. Voltaire, the famous French writer and philosopher states that "Pythagoras went to the Ganges to learn geometry". Voltaire and Seidenberg confirm that many highly significant mathematical concepts have come from Vedic culture, namely, the theorem bearing the name of the Greek Mathematician Pythagoras is found in the *Shatapatha Brahmana* as well as the *Sulabha Sastra*, the Indian Mathematical treatises written centuries before Pythagoras was even born.

The Decimal system based on the powers of ten, where the remainder is carried over to the next column, it is seen has been first mentioned in the *Taittareeya Samhita* of the Black or *Krishna Yajur Veda*. Similarly, the introduction of Zero as the nominal value and a place marker, the concept of infinity, the Binary number system that is essential for the computers, the *Kathapayadi* system by which, from the name of the *Raga* one can know the notes of the *Raga*, that is similar to the modern Algorithms are all the inventions made by the *Rishis* of the pre historic India.

It is also found that the concept of one and its mathematical properties, the arithmetic progression and arithmetic series are found in the *Vedas*. *Atharva Veda* states that 1*1 and 1/1 =1

The concept of *Shunya* or zero or void was conceived in the *Vedas* as the symbol of *Brahman* that is the sum of all distinct forms. The concept of *Shunya* is both mathematical and also is found to be rooted in Metaphysics as well as Cosmology. The symbol of zero and the decimal system of notation are described in the *Atharva Veda* showing how the number increases by ten by putting zero in front of it.

Indians were the first to calculate the velocity of light. It is pointed out that in *Sayana*'s commentary of Rig Veda it is stated that one *Yojana* equals 15788.8 meters; half of a *Nimisha* equals 8/ 75 fraction of a second. As per this the approximate value of the velocity of light is 325940 kms.

The Vedic Astrology known as *Jyothisha* is the oldest on Earth. According to this the birth chart that is the snapshot of the sky at the time of one's birth contains all information about the future of the individual where the timings of events in the life of an individual is interlinked with the transit of the planets.

The ancient weapons and missiles that are mentioned in the *Ithihasas* and *Puranas* particularly that are used by chanting *Manthras* resemble the modern day nuclear weapons. The pollution free missiles used by the ancients clearly reveal that our sages who were great scientists even in ancient times knew of the environment friendly and unlimited resources of energy. It has been proved scientifically that the regular chanting of *Mantras* reduce depression and help in overcoming bad habits and evil thoughts and ways and even addictions. It has also been proved to give inner peace and tranquillity and a strong communion with our inner realm where the Supreme energy resides.

The Indians knew the technique of making Gunpowder even in the remote past. The *Sukraneethi Sastra* contains many formulae for making Gun powder.

The technology for making Radars and Laser weapons was also known to Indians long ago. The ancient Sanskrit manuscript '*Samaranganasuthradhara*' explains this technology.

It is also understood from ancient scriptures that the sages, kings of the Earth and celestial beings possessed sophisticated chariots that resembled the modern day space ships. The chariots were made use of for astral travel by the ancients. It is also understood from the scriptures that the humans of the Earth and the beings in the other worlds, planets and so on travelled from earth to the other worlds, to farthest stars and solar systems and vice versa and they had also physical relationship between them. It is also understood from the scriptures that the ancient Indians had mastered the art of anti-gravity and had contacts and relationships with other advanced civilizations of the Universe.

Sanskrit is recognized by scholars as the world's oldest systematic language.

The Indians were the first to express numbers in decimal system. The largest number for the Indians was as big as 1053 even in 5000 BC, where as it was only 106 for the Romans.

The ancient Indian chronologies are the oldest in the world.

Even in the ancient past the Vedic sages knew the importance of environmental protection. For example they did not cut the trees indiscriminately for any purpose. To conduct *Yagas* they made use of the dried twigs of the trees that fell on the ground.

It has been found that the Vedic rituals are capable of reducing atmospheric pollution by controlling the pollutants, the evil energy. The Vedic rituals like Homas and circumambulation of holy trees and plants spread positive energy. It has been found that they also cleanse the harmful elements like bacteria and virus that live as parasites in the human body. The sacred flowers, plants and trees also are found to emit aura and increase the positive energy in man.

Geometry, Trigonometry, Calculus, and Algebra originated in India. The word Geometry has the Sanskrit root *Gyaa-Miti* meaning measuring Earth and Trigonometry, *Tri- kona mit,* meaning measuring triangular forms. The concept of Geometry emerged in India in 1000 BCE from the practice of making fire Altars in square and rectangular shapes for the performance of *Yagas,* and making of *Yantras* with complex forms of geometrical shapes, even though Euclid is credited with the invention of Geometry in 300 BCE. The treatise of *Surya Siddhantha* also describes amazing details of Trigonometry. Lin Yutang, a Chinese scholar and author wrote that "India was China's teacher in Trigonometry, Quadratic equations, grammar, phonetics" and so on. Geometry was introduced in Europe 1200 years later in the 16th century by Briggs. The *Siddhanta Siromani* written by *Bhaskara* even in the year 1150 AD contains four parts namely, *Lilavati* (Arithmetic), *Bijaganitha* (a treatise on Algebra), *Goladhyays* (celestial globe) and *Graha Ganitha* (mathematics of planets). The Arab world borrowed much from India in the field of Mathematics that even the subject of Mathematics in Arabic came to be known as 'Hindsa' that means 'from India'.

The ancient Indian scriptures describe several sophisticated weapons and missiles and complicated chariots that resemble the modern space ships, and missiles and so on. The *Mahabharatha* describes Arjuna traveling in flying chariot and encountering the *Nivata Kavachas*, probably men in space suits. *Mahabharata* describes many missiles when hurled produced a shaft of light. When focused on a target it consumed the target immediately. There are references about a 'single projectile charged with all the power of the Universe', again 'an incandescent column of smoke and fire, as brilliant as ten thousand suns rose in all its splendour', 'the unknown weapon, the iron thunder bolt, a gigantic messenger of death which reduced to ashes the entire race of the *Vrisnis* and *Andhakas*', 'The corpses of those killed by it were unidentifiable and the survivors lost their hair and their nails fell'— 'the birds turned white—- after a few hours all food stuffs were infected' are some of the effects of missiles that are mentioned in the scriptures. The epic of *Mahabharata* also mentions about *Salva*'s attack of the city of *Dwaraka* in an invisible flying *Vimana* named *Saubha*. The scriptures also mention the triple space cities of *Asuras* that revolved around Earth in three circular orbits that was destroyed by Lord *Shiva* using a single weapon, the *Pushpaka* Vimana of *Kubera*, *Raavana* and *Vibhishana* and *Raama*, *Nala* building a bridge across the ocean to Lanka, narration of the birth of the *Kauravas* from the cells of the embryo outside the womb of a woman, narration of celestial weapons presided over by Gods and divine beings that can be hurled by invoking *Mantras* and that unleash high energy in the form of fire or explosions, water or rain, air or storm that are ascribed to *Visvakarma* and *Maaya* the celestial architects and the after effects of such weapons like nails falling down, regions turning into deserts, death of embryo in the womb of the mother and so on. All these prove the technological brilliance of ancient Indians. In *Mahabharata* it is said that the *Kauravas* were born from the cells divided from an embryonic cell of flesh in artificial environment. In *Vedas* the seven *Maruts* are said to be the seven parts of the foetus cut by *Indra*.

It is seen that the ancient Indian texts like *Vimana Chandrika,Yantrasarvasva of Maharshi* or sage *Bharadwaja*, *Vyoma Yaana Tantra* of sage *Sanaka* and so on describe about Aeronautics and explain about navigation and control of speed during flight, the alloys used for various parts of aircraft, and production and use of various fuels for the aircrafts and so on. *Bharadwaja's* (800 BCE) *Yantra Sarvasva* gives great discoveries in Aviation Science, Space Science and flying machines, those that can fly from one place to another on Earth, those that can travel from one Planet to another and those that travel from one Universe to another. He also described the techniques to make flying machines invisible through the application of Solar Energy and wind, the technique of making invisible space machines visible through the application of electricity, the technique to listen to conversations in another aeroplane and the technique to see what is happening inside another aeroplane. *Parasabdagrahakata* is a subject in ancient India for monitoring the flight tracks of aircrafts, navigatory communication system and monitoring the conversation of pilots in the aircraft. Sage *Gautama* mentions 32 models of air crafts used in *Tretha Yuga*. One of the models namely the Pushpaka Vimana of the demon king Ravana is described in the Ramayana. The *Vaimanika Satra* describes *Tripura Vimana* that uses a solar powered engine to travel at three levels- on land, under water and in the air. *Sakuna Vimana* is a cross between an aircraft and a rocket- a space shuttle. The *Vaimanika Prakaranam* in *Vimana Vignana* deals with instruments like *Guha Garbha Darsha Yantra* that can locate objects hidden underground from an air craft. Dr Roberto Pinothi, an Italian scientist says that these aircrafts are similar to modern jet propelled aeroplanes and that they represent the most complex and sophisticated designs that used Radars. Julius Robert Oppenheimer, the principal developer of the atom bomb admitted that "the Vedas are the greatest privilege of this century". During the first explosion of the first atomic Bomb when he was asked if this was the first nuclear explosion he replied "yes, in modern times" indicating the happenings of nuclear explosions in the past.

The scriptures also mention about the beings in other worlds and their relationship with humans and their astral travel. These beings are the *Devas, Asuras, Gandharvas, Yakshas, Rakshasas, Pisachas, Kinnaras, Kimpurushas, Vanaras, Nagas, Suparnas, Vidhyadharas, Valkhilyas, Siuddhas*, and *Charanas* and so on. A former official from British defence ministry's UFO project recently revealed about the possibility of alien life in the Universe.

Even as early as in 700 BCE there was a giant University at *Takshashila* in India. Students not only from India but also from outside India like Babylonia, Greece, Syria, Arabia and China and so on came to study here. There were 68 different disciplines of knowledge with 10,500 students and the masters there were the great ones like *Kautilya, Panini, Jivah* and *Vishnu Sharma* and the others.

William Macintosh asserts that all History points to India as the mother of Science and Art. Sir William Jones a Sanskrit scholar who was also a judge goes to the extent of saying that human life would not be sufficient to make oneself acquainted with any considerable part of Hindu Literature. Louis Francois Jacolliott is categorical in stating "Name any modern discovery and we venture to say that Indian History need not long be searched before the prototype will be found on records". J. Donald Walters (*Swami Kriyananda*), founder of Ananda village says, "Ancient *Rishis* made claims so cosmic that even modern Physics seems only to be catching up with them and realizing after every scientific breakthrough that the ancients were there long before them". Alexander Duff, a British Christian Missionary points out that many inventions and discoveries of modern science that are considered to have emerged from Europe were actually made in India several centuries ago. All these prove that even several thousands of years before the Greeks, in India, the Hindus knew well not only cosmological, astronomical, astrological principles and the geographical aspects but also of Universal higher philosophical and spiritual truths that only later westerners such as Rutherford could compare with.

Jeffrey Armstrong who along with his wife had founded the 'Vedic Academy of Science And Arts' (VASA) says, "Indians of pre modern History calculated the age of the Universe in trillions of years———-". He further points out "This is also the culture that gave us zero, the numerals that we use- so called Arabic have their roots in India- as do Trigonometry and Calculus, astronomical calculation and a view that says that the Universe is not only billions, but trillions of years in age and that we are eternal beings who are simply visiting the material world to have the experience of being here". He again points out, "there is a lot of evidence that ancient Indian civilization was global. Many were seafaring and using extremely accurate astronomical, heliocentric calculations for both Earth and celestial motions, indicating an understanding that the Sun is at the centre of the solar system and that the Earth is round. Elliptical orbits were also calculated for all the moving celestial bodies. The findings are remarkable what India calculated thousands of years ago, for example, the wobble of the Earth's axis, which creates the movement called precession of the equinoxes- the slowly changing motion that completes one cycle every 25, 920 years-has only recently been validated by modern science".—- "The cosmology of India also describes our Universe as having fourteen parallel realities on multiple levels, all existing and intersecting within the material realm in which we are currently living". He wonders "Was this knowledge given to them by divine beings as they claim? Was there inter-galactic travel? Did the peple of India have contact with beings or knowledge from other Planets? We don't know, but what is certain is that they had mathematical/ astronomical understanding that is extremely precise and agrees with many of the results of astronomy today. There is no other way to explain why India and these ancient cultures would have such precise knowledge other than the fact that they were in a period of impressive technology and culture beyond our present understanding". It looks that in ancient times people travelled to farthest stars and solar systems in sophisticated space crafts and by astral traveling. Although one cannot prove these things through physical evidences, still we can know them through the symbolic hymns of the scriptures. It is also understood that the Vedic *Rishis* possessed complete knowledge about the science of perpetual motion that still remains a mystery today. The description of the symbol of *Swasthika* and perpetual motion wheels for example are found in the *Vedas*. Sage *Drighatama*'s description of perpetual motion wheels in his hymns found in the Vedas run parallel to the description of the Sun and solar system that suggests that the picture of the world that he conceived was based on perpetual motion incorporating cyclical process running in the universe.

In the ancient Indian approach, understanding of the external reality of the universe depended also upon the understanding of the inner realm and its relationship with the Absolute supreme energy. It is necessary that one knows all about the physical and material aspects of the Universe, but more importantly one should understand who he actually is and what is his relationship with the creator or source as this only can broaden his outlook and knowledge that ultimately will end in maximum human welfare with lasting peace and happiness to mankind as a whole. Once an individual realizes that although he is different from another individual in his gross or physical body and mind fundamentally he is not different from the other as the seed or origin of all beings is the same and after all, all the beings are just like the waves of the ocean that cannot claim any individuality and say that it is different from another wave of the ocean. Just as the waves emerge and merge with the ocean in a short span of time similarly the creations, the individual souls are also bound to merge with the supersoul in course of time. This knowledge can make one to lead his life in full wisdom and happiness. Such a person though lives in the material world with the required material knowledge that makes him wealthy, prosperous and happy still he lives with the conviction that all material knowledge and the resultant material pleasures are only temporary so he will not hanker after the material wealth. Until and unless all the people in the world get such supreme knowledge the world is bound to face war, crimes, subjugation, jealousy, hatred and so on. Once the people in the world not only become aware of this supreme knowledge but also experience the taste of this knowledge then the whole world is bound to become paradise on earth. To achieve such a goal spirituality and science should walk together hand in hand as was the case in ancient India. Apollonius Tyanaeus, the Greek thinker and traveller belonging to the first AD said, "In India I found a race of mortals living upon the earth, but not adhering to it, inhabiting cities, but not being fixed to them, possessing everything but possessed by nothing".

The French scholar Romain Rolland said "If there is one place on the face of Earth where all dreams of living men have found a home from the very earliest days, when man began the dream of existence it is India." Swami Vivekanda says that the debt which the world owes to India is immense. India gave the earliest physicians and medical science in the form of *Ayurveda*. Even plastic surgery in the some other name and method was known and practiced in ancient India; Vedic mathematics that includes algebra, geometry, astronomy, mixed mathematics of today was invented in India. In philosophy and spirituality India was even ahead of all other nations in the world. Sanskrit literature is universally acknowledged as the foundation of all European languages. In literature our Epics, poems and dramas were ranked as one of the best in the world. It was India that gave the 'Fables of Aesop' and other stories to the world originally. India was the first to make cotton and dyes. It was highly proficient in the making of jewellery and sugar was originally a product from India. It was India that invented the game of Chess, the Cards and Dice- Her material wealth and knowledge attracted the Europeans first and this was indirectly responsible for the discovery of America. Along with all these that are material, she was also rich and remarkable in Her spirituality and spiritual giants, the *Rishis*. Her influence has always fallen upon the world—- "like that of the gentle dew, unheard and scarcely marked yet bringing into bloom the fairest flowers of the Earth". He further adds "Touch him on spirituality, or religion, on God, on the soul, on the infinite, on spiritual freedom, I assure you, the lowest peasant in India is better informed on these subjects than many so called philosophers in other lands—." Scott Sandford a Space Scientist in NASA admits that it looks as though the writers of *Vedas* and *Puranas* came from the future to deliver knowledge. The works of ancient Indian sages is mind blowing. There is no doubt that *Puranas* and *Vedas* are the words of God. Dr Kevin Hurley of California university wonders, how the Hindus could have possibly known all this (the latest scientific findings) thousands of years ago, when scientists have only recently discovered this using of advanced equipment which did not exist at that time? Such concepts were found only recently.

Ian Vatson in his 'Hindu cosmology and modern science-some remarks' says that the Hindu cosmology "employs different techniques in its effort to articulate and to teach an adequate understanding of the supposed largely observable cosmos. Moreover, it admits different, indeed more areas to count as authentically, the subject matter to be accommodated by any such "understanding". He adds "Generally speaking the intentions of the Indian cosmology and of modern science in the west are roughly identical- both seek an explanation, descriptive where possible of the basics of the more or less observable cosmos. But because there are differences elsewhere in the general metaphysics, how these general intentions are carried through differs in kind from one approach to the other'. He also points out "Indeed, I believe a largely ignored vast importance of Hindu Vedantha is that, properly interpreted, it can offer a viable alternative to modern science, as an explanatory-system of the ultimate nature of the cosmos".

According to Paolo Giubellllino, the spokesperson of the European centre for Research in Particle Physics in Geneva (CERN), the search for the Absolute Truth had a wiser ancestor in ancient India. He says "India is like a historic father of the Higgs Boson Project as the inquiry into the Truth has been the pet subject for the Truth-seekers in India since very ancient times. One must remember that the revelations of the ancient seers of India about the Universe were only the result of their long, continuous and persistent meditation". The modern scientists however had to spend nearly $5 million on a Collider inside a 27 km tunnel for discovering Higg's Boson. While the Scientists state that they discovered the elusive God particle the ancient Indians had experienced in their supra conscious state the 'GOD PRINCIPLE' or PHENOMENON. That is THE difference. The modern popular Physicists like Fritfof Capra and Garz Zukay maintain that the mystics of ancient India had experienced the Truth that matches with what the scientists are discovering today. Sri Sri Ravi Shankar in one of his discourses points out that the entire Universe is a field of energy. The *Rishis* had made it very clear even in the remote past that the entire Universe is made up of consciousness only. The concept of *Brahman* they pointed out is nothing but *Tattva* or principle. This is the ultimate as we go from the gross to the subtler, starting from the *Panchabhoothas*(the five elements) then the mind, intellect, ego then the *Mahat Tattva* and even beyond it is the Primordial energy and even beyond this is the *Brahman* that is the substance of everything. It is infinite without birth and death and beyond which there is nothing. References about the Dark matter and Dark energy we find in the most ancient *Veda* namely *Rig Veda* in the *Nasadeeya Strotra* or hymn.

The hymn states that beyond everything there was nothing except energy. The hymn also states that in the beginning there was only darkness- darkness enveloping darkness all around. The ancients also described about the three types of space. the space where matter exists, then the intermediate or inner space or the space of Chitta where the thoughts float and then the *Chidakasa* that is the space of pure energy- that is *Brahman*. So *Brahman* or God is a principle, a field, the basis of everything but not him, or her. Everything including the Universe itself is nothing but the reflection of that *Brahman*. This is the God principle but not God particle experienced by the sages of ancient India. But even they, who could unravel so many mysteries of the Universe, said that the mystery of the universe is such that it cannot be known or understood totally in spite of knowing certain things.

Swami Vivekananda rightly pointed out "Give and take is the law and if India wants to raise herself once more it is absolutely necessary that she brings out her treasures and throws them broadcast among the nations of the Earth and in return be ready to receive what others have to give her. Expansion is life, contraction is death. Love is life and hatred is death—- we must mix therefore with all the races of the Earth". He added, India should welcome the latest scientific and technological knowledge from other nations. In turn she should open up her wealth of both material as well as spiritual knowledge to the others as India has plenty to offer to the world for centuries to come as the union of the two phases of the humanity namely conquest of material nature of the outside world with the conquest of the inner realm of the human mind is what is required for the world today.

W.J. Grant said that "India indeed has a preciousness which a materialistic age is in danger of missing. Someday the fragrance of her thought will win the hearts of men". Mark Twain remarked, "So far as I am able to judge nothing has been left undone, either by man or nature to make India the most extraordinary country that the Sun visits on his rounds". About India he also said that it is "the land that all men desire to see and having seen once even by a glimpse, would not give that glimpse for the shows of the rest of the globe combined".

Dr Arnold Toynbee, the great British Historian predicted that "It is already becoming clear that a chapter which had a western beginning will have to have an Indian ending if it is not to end in self-destruction of the human race". He further added, "At this supremely dangerous moment in human history, the only way of salvation is the ancient Hindu way. In the year1952 he observed that in the 21st century "it is possible that India, the conquered, will conquer its conquerors". Let the extraordinary rich culture and tradition of India that is given by the ancient sages get widespread throughout the world so that the people of this world can understand what the real India is. Let them all know that India is not a mere country with landscapes, mountains and rivers, rituals, superstitions, innumerable Gods, with the divisions of caste and creed that cropped up due to the misinterpretation of the fundamental ideas of the *Rishis* due to the selfish interests of some, but the sacred land or *Punya Bhoomi* that contains the vibrations of the positive energy emitted by the constant tapas or meditation of the sages of the past who gave all knowledge even in the remotest past that made the children of this soil to know all about the Universe, including the Earth and themselves and their relationship with that original source , the Absolute , the *Para Brahman* from where they originated. Let us strive to bring back to light the lost glory of India and after achieving this goal let us all in one voice declare it to the world saying that "We are proud to be Indians."

Index

B

D

E

F

G

Q

R

T

U

V

T

W

Y

Z